LOVE
IS THE
CURE

LOVE
IS THE
CURE

ELTON JOHN

ON LIFE, LOSS, AND THE END OF AIDS

HODDER &
STOUGHTON

First published in Great Britain in 2012 by Hodder & Stoughton
An Hachette UK company

1

A CIP catalogue record for this title is available from the British Library

ISBN 978 1 444 75700 2
Trade paperback ISBN 978 1 444 75701 9
Ebook ISBN 978 1 444 75702 6

Typeset by Palimpsest Book Production Limited,
Falkirk, Stirlingshire

Printed and bound by Clays Ltd, St Ives plc

Hodder & Stoughton policy is to use papers that
are natural, renewable and recyclable products and made from
wood grown in sustainable forests. The logging and manufacturing
processes are expected to conform to the environmental
regulations of the country of origin.

Hodder & Stoughton Ltd
338 Euston Road
London NW1 3BH

www.hodder.co.uk

*In memory of Robert Key, a dear friend
and tireless advocate for those living with
HIV/AIDS around the world*

CONTENTS

I

Ryan

I've thought about this book for a while now, though it never occurred to me how to start off.

I suppose one could begin with statistics, with numbers and charts and facts that paint the perfect picture of horror that is the global AIDS epidemic: more than 25 million lives lost in thirty years, 34 million people living with HIV/AIDS around the globe, 1.8 million deaths per year, nearly 5,000 lives taken each and every day, the sixth leading cause of death world-wide.

But I've always found it impossible to comprehend these statistics. The tragedy is so immense, the figures are so enormous, there's simply no way to wrap your mind around it all.

Let's leave the numbers for later, and begin with a story instead.

After all, I'm not a statistician; I'm a musician. I've made my living telling stories through songs. It gives me incredible joy the way people connect with my music. That is all I hope to do in this book – to tell stories that connect people with this epidemic, so we can work together to end it.

The first story I'd like to tell you is an amazing one. To understand the AIDS epidemic, to understand my passion for ending it, you need to know about Ryan White. It all goes back to my friend Ryan.

Ryan came into this world with a rare and terrible genetic disease, haemophilia, which prevents the blood from clotting and leads to uncontrollable bleeding. Haemophilia is a manageable condition today, but in the early 1970s, when Ryan was born, it was a dangerous and often fatal disease. As an infant, and then as a child, Ryan was in the hospital again and again.

Then, as if the hand he'd been dealt wasn't difficult enough, the poor boy contracted HIV, the virus that causes AIDS, through a treatment for his haemophilia. At age thirteen, the doctors gave Ryan a grim prognosis: less than six months to live. He held on for more than five years. And in that short span, Ryan accomplished what most could not hope to achieve in a thousand lifetimes. He inspired a nation, changed the course of a deadly epidemic, and helped save millions of lives. Imagine, a child doing all of that, a sick boy from a small town in Middle America. It sounds like a movie script, like a bedtime story, like a miracle. And it was a miracle. Ryan's life was an absolute miracle.

It must have been 1985 when I first learned about Ryan. I was at a doctor's appointment in New York. I forget why I was there. I picked up a magazine from a stack in the waiting room. I was mindlessly flipping through the pages when I came across an article that would change my life. I couldn't believe what I was reading, that a boy was being kept out of school, and his family was being shunned and tormented, because he had AIDS.

Ryan lived with his mother, Jeanne, and his younger sister, Andrea, in the small town of Kokomo, Indiana. Jeanne worked at the local General Motors car factory for twenty-three years. The Whites were a blue-collar family through and through, much like my own family growing up, which is perhaps why I instantly connected with them when we finally got to know one another.

In 1984, around Christmastime, Ryan was in particularly bad shape with a rare form of pneumonia. But tests at the hospital revealed a far worse diagnosis: he had full-blown AIDS. The pneumonia was an opportunistic infection attacking his badly weakened immune system.

As it turned out, Ryan had contracted HIV from a

treatment for his haemophilia called factor VIII, a clotting agent derived from donated blood. A single dose
of factor VIII could include plasma pooled from thousands of people, and some of them had HIV. Because
the HIV virus itself wasn't identified until the mid-
1980s, there was no way to screen for the disease. That's
how HIV-contaminated factor VIII was administered to
patients in the United States and throughout the world
in the early '80s, including Ryan. Thousands of haemophiliacs became HIV-positive in this way before pharmaceutical companies and the government put measures
in place to test and purify factor VIII.

Jeanne waited until after Christmas to tell Ryan that
he had AIDS. When he found out, Ryan knew exactly
what it meant: he was going to die.

Everyone was aware of AIDS by 1984, especially
haemophiliacs. While it was still a very new and frightening disease, the medical community had already
figured out the basics. They had identified the HIV
virus itself that year, and they knew that it was spread
only by sex or by direct blood exposure. More to the
point, they knew it couldn't be transmitted through
casual contact, such as sharing water fountains or toilet
seats, drinking from the same glass, eating with the
same utensils, or even kissing. There was simply no risk
of infection from being around someone with AIDS.

But there was fear. There was so much fear. It was everywhere, a ghost that shadowed Ryan's every move and haunted him throughout his life.

When Ryan was told about his condition, that he might not have very long to live, he made an extraordinary decision: to live out the rest of his days, however many there might be, as ordinarily as he could. He wanted to go to school, to play with his friends, and to spend time with his mom, Andrea, and his grandparents. He just wanted to be like any other child, even if his disease meant that he wasn't. When he first learned of his prognosis, Ryan asked Jeanne to pretend that he didn't have AIDS. He didn't want special treatment; all he wanted was a sense, however brief, of normality.

But that would not be his fate. Ryan was never allowed to live a normal life, let alone die a normal death. Shortly after he was diagnosed, a local paper discovered that Ryan had AIDS. They ran a story about it, and suddenly the whole town – and then the whole nation – knew about his condition. After that, everything changed for Ryan and his family. As a child with haemophilia, Ryan had been treated with compassion. As a child with AIDS, many treated him with contempt.

Ryan missed the majority of seventh grade, thanks to his bout with pneumonia. He was too weak to return to school that year, in the spring of 1985. By the summer, however, he was much better. He even had a paper round. He was eager to be back in school, to play with his friends, to have a semblance of a normal life. But in late July, a month before the beginning of the new school year, the superintendent of Ryan's school district announced that Ryan would not be allowed to attend classes in person, due to the widespread fear that he posed a health risk to his schoolmates – that by being near them, he might somehow infect them. It was decided that Ryan would attend school by phone instead.

The fear, I suppose, was understandable. AIDS was a fatal illness at the time, without exception. But it was well known that Ryan couldn't transmit the virus to others just by being around them. After all, Jeanne and Andrea lived with Ryan. They drank out of the same glasses, ate off the same dishes, hugged him, kissed him. They were with him constantly, especially when he was most sick. Yet even their intimate proximity to Ryan hadn't resulted in their contracting HIV. Besides, the U.S. Centers for Disease Control and Prevention (CDC) and the Indiana State Board of Health had assured the school district that Ryan posed no threat to teachers, students, or staff, and they offered guidelines for him to safely return.

Logic and science couldn't contain the fear, however.

Ryan was effectively quarantined. But he wasn't a quitter; he never, ever gave up. Not being allowed to attend school was unacceptable to him. He decided to fight to return.

Ryan and Jeanne sued the school. They had the national medical community and the State Board of Health on their side. But the judge dismissed Ryan's lawsuit. He said that the boy's lawyers had to appeal the school superintendent's decision to the Indiana Department of Education first. Ryan's days were numbered as it was, and here was a technical decision that would further delay his going back to school. In the meantime, a special phone link was set up, and Ryan dialled into school every day.

The appeals process that ensued was long, nasty, and public, with Ryan, now fourteen years old, at the centre of it all. The local school board and many parents of Ryan's schoolmates were vehemently opposed to him attending school. More than a hundred parents threatened to file a lawsuit if Ryan was allowed to return. In late November, the Indiana Department of Education ruled in Ryan's favour and ordered the school to open its doors to him, except when he was very sick. The local school board appealed, prolonging Ryan's absence from the classroom. Months later, a state board again ruled that Ryan should be allowed to attend school with the approval of a county health official.

With more than half the school year gone, Ryan was officially cleared to return to classes on 21 February, 1986. The thrill of victory, though, was short-lived. On his first day back, he was pulled from the classroom and brought to court. A group of parents had filed an injunction to block his return, and the judge issued a restraining order against him. When the judge handed down his verdict, the room packed with parents began to cheer, while Ryan and Jeanne looked on, shocked and scared. It seemed like a modern-day witch hunt, and Ryan was to be burned at the stake.

Ryan's lawyers fought the restraining order, and he *again* won the right to go back to school. This time the decision was final. On 10 April, 1986, with hordes of press on his heels and some students picketing nearby, Ryan returned to classes. He was not allowed to participate in gym class, and he was made to use a separate bathroom and water fountain, and dispos-able utensils in the cafeteria. These were needless precautions, but Ryan agreed to them in order to assuage the fears about his misunderstood disease. Still, twenty-seven children were withdrawn from school that day. Two weeks later, parents opened an alternative school, and twenty-one of Ryan's schoolmates were enrolled so as not to be in the same building as Ryan daily.

Back at school, and nearly everywhere he went in his hometown, Ryan was teased and tormented. He was called a 'fag' and other homophobic obscenities in public. His school locker and possessions were vandalised, and terrible rumours were spread about him. One anonymous teenager wrote a letter to the local paper accusing Ryan of threatening to bite and scratch other children, spitting on food at a grocery store, even urinating on bathroom walls. These were lies, of course, but it didn't matter. Having AIDS made Ryan a freak, and regardless of what he did or didn't do, he was considered as such.

If you can believe it, adults treated him even worse than children did. People on Ryan's paper round cancelled their subscriptions. When he and his family went out to eat, local restaurants would throw away the dishes they used. The parents of Ryan's girlfriend forbade her from seeing him. At one point during the Whites' legal battle with the school district, a group of school parents demanded that the county declare Jeanne an unfit guardian in order to have Ryan taken away from her, and thus taken out of school.

It wasn't just Ryan who was subjected to ill treatment and ostracism – his entire family suffered. The tyres were slashed on Jeanne's car. A bullet was shot through a window of the White family's home. Ryan's extended family was harassed, too, and even non-relatives who defended Ryan were subjected to abuse. When the local paper supported Ryan's right to attend school, the publisher's house was egged. A reporter at the paper even received death threats.

Somehow, Ryan's disease brought out the very worst in people, and there was little refuge for him and his family. Not even at church. The Whites were people of deep faith and Christian conviction. Each night, Ryan and Jeanne prayed together before bed. But after Ryan's illness became public, the community at their Methodist church began to shun them. The parishioners were so afraid of catching AIDS from Ryan that he and his family were asked to sit in either the first pew or the last. People wouldn't use the church bathroom after Ryan. Parents told their children to avoid him.

In his autobiography, Ryan tells the story of his family going to church on Easter Sunday in 1985, shortly after his diagnosis. At the end of the service, people turned to those sitting around them to shake hands and say, 'Peace be with you,' an Easter tradition at Ryan's church. No one would shake his hand this time. Not a single person would offer this sick child a blessing of peace on Easter. As they left the church that morning, Jeanne's car broke down. She tried to stop members of the congregation leaving the church car park, but no one would help her.[1]

Despite the ostracism he suffered from his church and his community, and despite the terrible pain and physical distress he experienced his entire life, Ryan was full of faith and Christian love until the end. Only a year before he died, Ryan told the *Saturday Evening Post* that he wasn't afraid of dying because of his faith in God. Even after he had endured so much abuse from fraudulent zealots, and as he was growing sicker, Ryan's faith was stronger than ever. 'There's always hope with the Lord,' Ryan told the *Post*. 'I have a lot of trust in God.'[2]

As a boy, I loved Sunday school. I loved hearing stories from the Bible, stories full of hope. To this day, while I do not practise any religion, I do take the compassionate teachings of Jesus to heart, and I have great respect for all people of faith. I am inspired by Jesus the man because he loved unconditionally, because he forgave unconditionally, and because he died for the sake of others. The same can be said of Ryan White. He was a true Christian, a modern-day Jesus Christ. That's a bold statement, I know; some might even take offence to it. But to know Ryan's story, and to have witnessed his extraordinary qualities as I did, is to come to no other conclusion.

The White family put their Christian faith to practice. They were upset at being treated so terribly by their community, of course, but they understood the fear. They knew it was caused by ignorance and misunderstanding. And so they responded with the compassion that they themselves never received. They worked hard to educate their community, to teach others about AIDS. In the end, Ryan wound up reaching far more than those in Kokomo, Indiana. He reached the entire nation.

The story of an ill young man who was kept out of school and shunned by his community wouldn't stay hidden in a small Midwestern town for long. Ryan's plight quickly became national news, and soon he was a household name. Ryan was on national talk shows and nightly news broadcasts. He was on the cover of *People* magazine. He was actually quite a shy boy, and Jeanne, a wonderfully unpretentious woman, certainly wanted no attention for herself. But the Whites felt it was their duty to speak out, to tell the world what they were experiencing. They wanted to make life better for thousands of others who were suffering in the same way – and not just other haemophiliacs who had contracted HIV but *everyone* living with the disease.

While bigots such as the famous preacher Jerry Falwell and the American politician Jesse Helms were spreading the hateful message that AIDS was a curse from God against gays, here was a dying teenager and his mother, thrust into the spotlight, standing shoulder-to-shoulder with *all* people living with HIV/AIDS. It was the height of bravery, the height of compassion. I love them for it to this day. By speaking out, Ryan and Jeanne helped to normalise the epidemic and relieve some of the terrible stigma and fear surrounding it. In doing so, they also hastened the government response and increased the urgency of medical research. What's more, they demonstrated what we now know to be the truth – that we must love all those living with HIV/AIDS if we are ever going to eradicate the disease itself.

Like millions of people, when I read about Ryan in that magazine, sitting in the doctor's waiting room, I was incensed. More than that, I was overcome with the desire to do something for him and his family. 'This situation is outrageous,' I thought. 'I've got to help these people.'

As angry and motivated as I was, I hadn't a clue what I could do for them. I suppose I was thinking that I would help raise awareness about what the White family was going through, or perhaps raise money to fight AIDS. But how could I help others when I couldn't help myself?

The truth is, I was a huge cocaine addict at the time. My life was up and down like a fucking yo-yo. My sense of values was buried under my self-destruction. I was still a good person, a kind person, underneath – otherwise I would have never reached out to the Whites in the first place. All I hoped was that somehow I could bring this boy and his family some comfort and support.

It turned out, in the end, the Whites would do far more for me than I ever did for them.

In the spring of 1986, after Ryan won his right to return to school, he and Jeanne came to New York to attend a fund-raiser for AIDS research and to appear on *Good Morning America*. I saw their interview, and I called Jeanne the next morning. I wanted to meet Ryan. I wanted to help. I invited Ryan and his family to one of my concerts.

Ryan was too sick to attend the first concert I planned to bring him to, but eventually I was able to fly the Whites to Los Angeles. They came to two of my shows, and then I took the family to Disneyland, where I had arranged a private tour and a party for Ryan. I wanted to give him an adventure – limos, planes, fancy hotels – a carefree time to take his mind off his pain and his difficult circumstances. But what I remember most about that visit is that I had at least as much fun as Ryan, if not more.

I felt instantly comfortable with the Whites, instantly

connected to Ryan. While we came from different countries, we really were cut from the same cloth. The Whites were commonsense, straight-shooting people. They were caring and humble and always grateful. What I did for them on that trip, and subsequently, was out of the pure love I had for this family. And that's really what it was: love. I fell in love with the Whites right away.

Getting to know the family put into stark relief what a terrible mess I was. You can't imagine how selfish I was at the time, what an asshole I had become. It was partly the drugs, partly the lifestyle I had created, partly the people around me, who indulged my worst instincts. I had everything in the world – wealth, fame, *everything* – but I'd throw a fit if I didn't like the curtains in my hotel room. That's how upside down I was. That's how pathetic I had become.

Ryan, on the other hand, was dying. His family had been tormented. And yet, during his trip to L.A. and every time I was with him from then on, he was relentlessly upbeat. At Disneyland, Ryan was so weak that I had to push him around in a wheelchair for part of the time. For a child, being wheelchair-bound at Disneyland must be incredibly frustrating, not to be able to run around and play at one of the world's largest playgrounds. But Ryan loved every minute of it. He loved life. Ryan wasn't thinking about dying; he was thinking about living, and he was getting on with it. His time was too precious to feel sorry for himself. I was with Ryan quite a lot over the years, and I can't remember a single time when he complained about anything. I know he wasn't a perfect child; there's no such thing. But Ryan was special.

So are his mum and sister. Jeanne was going through the most torturous episode any parent could imagine: watching her child die a slow and painful death, and not being able to do anything about it. But she never asked, 'Why me?' She embodied forgiveness and acceptance and perseverance at every turn, even though she must have suffered greatly in her most private moments.

Andrea was just like Jeanne; you couldn't get her down, and you never heard her complain. The youngest in the family often gets all the attention, especially someone like Andrea, a beautiful teenage girl, an athlete, a wonderful student. But Andrea's life took a backseat to Ryan's illness. She had to give up competitive roller-skating, her passion, for financial reasons. Like Ryan, she lost friends and was teased. She had it very rough. I was amazed by how she dealt with the reality of her family's situation with maturity and wisdom well beyond her years.

This family inspired me in a way that I cannot fully

explain. Being around the Whites touched me at my very core. I guess you could put it this way: I wanted to be like them. I wanted to be part of their family. They made me want to change, to be a better person, to be the person I knew I was on the inside. But this wasn't an easy thing to do, because of my addictions, because of my lifestyle. I was beginning to open my eyes to reality, but it took Ryan's death to open them completely. When his eyes closed, mine opened. They've been open ever since.

After the Whites came to L.A., from then on, I did whatever I could for them. Little things, mostly. Ryan came to more concerts. I sent gifts and flowers and cards. I called to check in. In 1987 Jeanne decided to move the family to Cicero, Indiana, a small town outside Indianapolis. She knew it was the right thing to do after Ryan confided in her that he didn't want to be buried in Kokomo. They needed to escape the place that had caused them such grief – that much was clear. One day, Jeanne called. With a great deal of hesitation in her voice, she asked if I might loan her part of the down payment she needed for her new home in Cicero.

To that point, Jeanne had never asked for a single thing. That she was now coming to me for help meant she badly needed it. I knew how desperate she was to give Ryan and Andrea a better life, so I told her to forget about a loan, I would simply send her the money. But Jeanne absolutely *insisted* on a loan. In fact, she made both of us sign a home-made contract stating that she would pay me back! Sure enough, years later, I received a cheque from Jeanne. I put the money straight into a college savings account for Andrea. Jeanne resisted, of course, but I told her that I *wanted* to help, that it meant something to me to support her family in this way. Looking back on it, I think she was being more charitable in continuing to accept my assistance than I was being supportive in giving it.

The Whites had a completely different life in their new home in Cicero. They were welcomed with open arms. Ryan did have a few friends in Kokomo, but in Cicero he became something of a local hero. The Whites were not only accepted but embraced, and Ryan thrived in his new school, making the honour roll as well as making many good friends.

It's not the case that the residents of Cicero were better or kinder human beings than the residents of Kokomo. My own opinion is that people are more or less the same all around the world; and besides, these two towns are only thirty miles apart. In fact, people in Cicero had many of the same questions, and shared many of the same fears, as people in Kokomo. Was it safe for the other children to be around Ryan? Did he pose a health risk to the community? The difference was that Cicero knew more about HIV/AIDS by the time Ryan arrived.

For one thing, Ryan had done much to educate the entire nation. Everyone knew his story, and in learning about Ryan's plight, America learned about AIDS as well. In addition, Ryan's new school held extensive AIDS education classes for the entire student body as well as the staff. The school board even sponsored conferences for parents and other members of the community to learn about AIDS, all before Ryan ever set foot in the classroom. He also had a champion and a wonderful friend in Jill Stewart, the president of the school student body, who happened to live down the street from the Whites.

Thanks to Jill's efforts, and the community's, Ryan's classmates were compassionate toward him, not fearful. Parents understood that their children weren't at risk, and they were able to ease any concerns among Ryan's classmates. Some children even taught their nervous parents about the disease. In the end, people weren't afraid; they were supportive. Cicero was able to see beyond Ryan's illness and focus on the amazing person he was.

Ryan found a bit of peace in Cicero, though not from his disease. He never wanted to give up – that goes without saying – but his fragile body had endured too much. In the spring of 1990, toward the end of his junior year of high school, Ryan was hospitalized with a severe respiratory infection. Jeanne called to tell me that Ryan was on life support. I immediately flew to Indiana. NFL star Howie Long and actresses Judith Light and Jessica Hahn were on the same US Airways flight. They had befriended Ryan and taken up his cause as well.

I spent the last week of Ryan's life by his hospital bedside, supporting Jeanne and Andrea in any way I could. Mostly that meant playing the family receptionist, and I was honoured to do it. Many people were trying to reach Ryan by phone and by mail – friends, celebrities, politicians, everyone wanted to express their support. Ryan was in and out of consciousness, but he was awake when Michael Jackson called. Michael was the biggest star in the world at the time, perhaps the most famous man on the planet. Years earlier, he had befriended Ryan as well, and one of Ryan's prized possessions was a red Ford Mustang that was a generous gift from him. As Ryan lay dying, he was so weak that he couldn't speak to Michael. I held the phone to his ear as Michael offered him kind words of comfort and love.

I grew very close to Jeanne during the final week of

Ryan's life. She described me then as her guardian angel, since I was able to help the family during this terrible moment by handling logistical details, and by simply being there for them. But it was the other way around. Jeanne and her family were guardian angels to me. And the message they were sent to deliver was very clear: it might be my deathbed next.

I had all the money in the world, but it didn't matter, because I didn't have my health. I wasn't well. But unlike Ryan, a cure existed for my substance abuse, for my self-destructiveness. As I stood next to Ryan's hospital bed, holding Jeanne's hand, seeing his bloated and disfigured body, the message was received. I didn't want to die.

As it happened, on the evening of 7 April, I was scheduled to play a massive concert in Indianapolis, not far from Riley Hospital for Children, where Ryan was being treated. The show was called Farm Aid IV, the fourth in a series of concerts meant to raise awareness and donations for family farmers in America. Months earlier, I had happily agreed to join Garth Brooks, Guns N' Roses, Neil Young, Jackson Browne, Willie Nelson, John Mellencamp, and many other amazing performers to put on this show. But at that moment, with Ryan near death, I didn't want to leave his side.

I rushed to the Hoosier Dome and hurried onstage. Other performers were in their usual stage dress, but I was wearing a baseball cap and a Windbreaker. I was so upset that I didn't care what I looked like, and it showed. Even 60,000 screaming fans couldn't chase away the grief I felt then. Since there were many musicians, each of us performed only a few songs. I started with 'Daniel' and then played 'I'm Still Standing.' Before my third song, I told the crowd, 'This one's for Ryan.' They burst into applause. The news of Ryan's hospitalization was a national story, and everyone knew he didn't have long to live. I played 'Candle in the Wind,' and the response was overwhelming. I looked out into the crowd, and people were holding up their lighters, thousands of little vigils flickering in the darkness for my dying friend.

When I finished the song, I ran offstage and rushed back to the hospital, back to Ryan's bedside. That's where I was, hours later, when Ryan died on the morning of 8 April 1990.

I'll never forget the funeral. I'll never forget the numbness of tragedy. I'll never forget what he looked like in the open casket, or the drive from the service to the cemetery. It was raining. We drove very slowly, in both grief and caution. I'll never forget Jeanne thanking me, in the middle of the greatest loss of her life, taking the time to acknowledge my being there with her. How surreal it all felt, like an awful dream.

It was the end of a very long week. It was the end of a very long fight.

Jeanne had asked me to be a pallbearer and to sing a song at Ryan's funeral. I wasn't sure that I would be able to keep my composure, but I agreed to do the song. I couldn't say no to her, but I didn't know what to sing. I didn't know what would be appropriate for such a tragic and painful occasion.

I ended up going back to my very first album, *Empty Sky*, and to the song 'Skyline Pigeon,' which Bernie Taupin and I wrote together. It's always been one of my favorites, and I thought it was the best track on that first album, maybe even the best track we had written to that point. It's a song about freedom and release, and it seemed fitting for Ryan's funeral. Now that he had passed away, I figured that Ryan was free to go wherever he wanted, his soul was free to travel, his spirit was free to inspire people around the world. I decided I couldn't be alone on that stage, though, so I taught the choir from Ryan's high school to sing along with me.

There was a picture of Ryan on the piano in front of me, his casket behind me. I hardly ever sing that song any more. My godson died several years ago, when he was only four years old. I played 'Skyline Pigeon' at his funeral, too.

There were more than 1,500 people in attendance at Ryan's funeral – not only his family and friends but celebrities he had touched and dignitaries of the highest order. Michael Jackson was there. Judith was there. Howie and Phil Donahue were among my fellow pall-bearers. First Lady Barbara Bush was there, too. Everyone was overcome with grief, even those who barely knew Ryan.

Some people from Kokomo attended the funeral as well, including the lawyer for the parents' group that had tried to block Ryan from attending school. He offered his condolences to Jeanne and asked her to forgive the way their town had treated Ryan. She did, without a moment's hesitation.

Over the course of the year following his death, Ryan's gravesite was vandalized four times. The poor child couldn't even rest in peace. Still, Ryan's message lived on. On the base of his tombstone, seven words are inscribed: patience, tolerance, faith, love, forgiveness, wisdom, and spirit.

I loved my friend Ryan more than I can express. I loved that he didn't have an ounce of quit in his heart. I loved that he didn't have a speck of self-pity in his soul. It wasn't just the way he held his head high as he struggled with not one but two terrible diseases. It wasn't just the way he bravely confronted death at an age when most children have no clue how precious life really is. No, Ryan was a true hero, a true Christian, because he unconditionally forgave those who made him suffer.

It's easy to think that Ryan's time on earth was hell. But he never saw it that way. He loved being alive. He loved the simple pleasures of friends and family. He lived his short and painful life with total grace and, above all, total forgiveness. In living the way he did, and in dying the way he did, Ryan changed the world. And he changed *my* world.

There's a scene in *The Lion King* where Rafiki, a wise and trusted elder, tells Simba, the hero of the movie, that he can bring Simba to see his deceased father. Rafiki leads Simba to a pool of water. At first, Simba sees only his own reflection. But then, the image of Simba's father appears in the pool. Rafiki tells Simba, 'He lives in you.' When I was writing and recording songs for *The Lion King*, that scene always reminded me of Ryan, and it still does, all these years later.

Ryan lives in me. Ryan and his family helped me to see the meaning of dignity, the importance of self-respect, the power of compassion. I'm here today because of Ryan. He inspired me to fix my life and to start my AIDS foundation. He continues to inspire me each and every day. I know that he looked up to me, and the thought of disappointing him now, even though he is long gone, makes me shudder. I try to honour his memory by living the way he would want me to live, by being the person he thought that I was.

Our friendship was the catalyst that helped to change my life. Indeed, Ryan *saved* my life. But mine is only one of countless lives that were saved by Ryan White.

Two years before he died, Ryan testified before the President's Commission on AIDS, which was a committee formed by the Reagan administration to investigate the epidemic and provide policy recommendations to the White House. Ryan and Jeanne travelled to Washington, and Ryan, only sixteen years old at the time, bravely told his story and greatly impressed the commission. Just weeks after Ryan died, Jeanne travelled back to Washington and exhibited extraordinary bravery of her own. Still reeling from the loss of her son, she personally lobbied members of Congress to dramatically increase funding for AIDS research, treatment, and education.

In August 1990, only four months after Ryan's death, Congress passed the Ryan White Comprehensive AIDS Resources Emergency (CARE) Act in his honour. The bill, which was approved with overwhelming and bi-partisan support, more than doubled government spending to combat the AIDS epidemic. Today, over twenty years later, Ryan's law provides more than $2 billion in AIDS treatment and prevention services each year to half a million Americans. The vast majority of those who receive assistance through the Ryan White CARE Act are low-income, uninsured people living with HIV/AIDS. In other words, the law embodies what Ryan taught me, and what he taught us all – that we must show compassion for everyone. Only then will we win the fight against this terrible disease.

In casual conversation with HIV/AIDS professionals, you often hear, 'This program is funded by Ryan White.' Of course, they are referring to the law. But the law exists because of the person, my friend. That Ryan's name is spoken by hundreds, maybe thousands, of people each day is an incredible testament to the impact of his life and legacy.

Ryan White's candle burned out long ago, but his legend never will.

2

A Decade of Loss

Ryan was not the first friend I lost to AIDS, and he was not the last. So many have been taken from me by this disease – sixty, seventy, eighty, I honestly don't know how many. I'd rather not count. But I never want to forget them.

That's why I have a chapel in my home in Windsor, in an old orangery on the property. It's where I go to remember the people in my life who touched me, who made me the person I am today. When I go inside it's like stepping back in time. I'm flooded with sadness and warmth.

Pictures adorn the walls. My grandmother. Princess Diana. Gianni Versace. Guy Babylon, the amazing keyboard player I lost to a heart attack in 2009. Then there's another wall, full of plaques that list name after name after name. People who, in my memory, are frozen in time as young, vibrant, and full of life. None of them are here any more. They all died of AIDS.

These were close friends, lovers, and people who worked for me. Many of them died in the 1980s, wiped out by a cruel and relentless plague. The first person I knew who died of AIDS was my manager's assistant, Neil Carter. He was a lovely young man, and I was distraught when I learned he had the disease. Three weeks later, he was dead. His was the first plaque I placed in my chapel.

Today, AIDS in the West is increasingly thought of as just another chronic condition that can be controlled with medication. We see people like Magic Johnson living long and healthy lives, and we wouldn't know they had such a terrible disease unless they told us. Thank heaven for that.

But when you got AIDS in the '80s, you died – quickly and horribly.

Imagine your mouth filling up with so many sores that you cannot eat. Your lungs filling up with so much fluid that you cannot breathe. A fatigue so crushing that you cannot lift your head off the pillow. Losing control of your bladder, your bowels, your mind. This is how my friends died in the '80s. It's how millions continue to die around the world.

I will never, ever forget being in those hospital rooms, seeing the hollow, devastated look in the eyes of friends who were racked by pain and by the knowledge that only death would end their suffering.

The physical depredations of AIDS were bad enough. Then there was the terrible indignity that AIDS visited on the infected: the shame and the stigma.

In the West, we often recall the madness and the misinformation, the suffering and the hopelessness of AIDS in the '80s as a sad but thankfully closed chapter in history. For much of the world, however, this chapter continues. In many parts of Africa, Asia, Latin America, and the Caribbean, AIDS is every bit the death sentence, every bit the scarlet letter, that it was for a New Yorker or San Franciscan who contracted the disease in 1982. It's a similar story among poor and low-income people in Western countries – more so than we like to admit. When I think back on the '80s and recoil at the horror of that time, it infuriates me that history is repeating itself right now, all over the world.

Today, even though AIDS is a top killer worldwide, it's often an afterthought among the public and in the press. Back in the '80s, though, as Ryan's story vividly illustrates, the outbreak of AIDS was greeted by a level of public hysteria that was unprecedented in modern history. And because the earliest reported infections were among gay people, intravenous drug users, and Haitian immigrants in the United States, it was all too easy for society to scapegoat and scorn them. Of course, there were plenty of heroic advocates for people living with HIV/AIDS back then. But very early on, there were far too many in the media, religious institutions, governments, and the general public who sent an unmistakable message to people with AIDS: We do not care about you.

I can't imagine any worse treatment for a human being. To have people believe they are completely on their own, that they must struggle without a loving touch or a kind word, is one of the cruellest things you can subject another to, no matter the illness or the situation. That's precisely what happened to thousands of people with AIDS in the '80s. They were rejected by their families and ostracised by their communities. They were made to feel that they had somehow brought the disease upon themselves through their own sinfulness or lack of virtue.

I'm deeply ashamed that I didn't do more about AIDS back then. My friends were dying all around me, and with few exceptions I failed to act. I gave some money to foundations. I performed at AIDS benefits. I helped the Whites. I recorded a song called 'That's What Friends Are For' with Gladys Knight, Stevie Wonder, and Dionne Warwick; the proceeds from that single went to the American Foundation for AIDS Research, or amfAR. But the fact is that I was a gay man in the '80s who didn't march. I didn't give the time or effort that I easily could have, and should have, to fight AIDS and support those who had it.

Instead, I was consumed by cocaine, booze, and who knows what else. I apparently never got the memo that the 'Me' Decade ended in 1979. The Elton ego train kept rolling right through the '80s. I spent most of that time as a passive bystander to this human calamity that was unfolding all around me. I was very conscious of AIDS. I knew what it was. I knew it was killing my friends. I just didn't have the strength or sobriety to do anything about it.

I don't remember the first time I heard the word 'AIDS.' Perhaps that's because the disease began its rampage across the globe a few years before it even had a formal name. But I do remember hearing about gays falling ill of some strange disease as early as 1982. There were hushed whispers at parties and rumours in the air. A palpable fear took root in the gay community long before it consumed the general public. I also remember that my earliest understanding of and inter-action with AIDS occurred in America. America is where I often lived and worked. It's where the disease first emerged as an epidemic. And it's where the fate and future of AIDS would be decided by America's powerful government, media, and research institutions.

Although no one knew its significance at the time,

the first official reporting of the AIDS epidemic was on 5 June 1981, when a weekly CDC bulletin noted a strange outbreak of a rare pneumonia in five gay men in Los Angeles.[1] A month later, reports surfaced of a rare cancer called Kaposi's sarcoma appearing in forty-one homosexuals in New York and California. These were initially presumed to be isolated outbreaks, and no one knew exactly what was causing them.

It was only later that researchers realized these rare pneumonias and cancers were connected.

A select few cancer doctors and epidemiologists realised something serious was afoot from the word go. But among the public, the media, and most policy makers, few were paying attention to these outbreaks that seemed to affect only urban gays on the coasts.

When you go back and read the news stories from 1981, however, it is absolutely eerie. In hindsight, there was clearly a gathering storm of the epidemic to come. In a 3 July 1981 *New York Times* story on the Kaposi's sarcoma outbreak, reporter Lawrence Altman described most cases involving 'homosexual men who have had multiple and frequent sexual encounters with different partners.' Most had also used drugs. Altman said researchers allowed for the possibility that a virus could have caused the outbreak, but they thought it seemed unlikely. After all, cancer isn't contagious. Altman noted toward the end of the article, however, that the patients seemed to have severely compromised immune systems, as evidenced by 'serious malfunctions' of 'T and B cell lymphocytes.'[2]

What Altman described – the sex, the drug use, and most important the compromised immune systems and T-cell damage – would soon be recognized as the defining risk factors and characteristics of AIDS. But until then, these strange outbreaks would be known as peculiar afflictions of the gay community. In fact, as outbreaks popped up in new cities, they were often described as 'gay cancer' or 'gay pneumonia.' Once researchers realised that these diseases and other strange opportunistic infections that were emerging in otherwise healthy gay men were connected, they began calling it Gay-Related Immune Deficiency, or GRID.

But that didn't last long. By 1982, heterosexual injection drug users were getting sick. Soon, the disease showed up in the infant children of infected mothers. And there was a notable cluster of the disease among people of Haitian descent in Miami and New York. Some medical professionals were calling it the '4H disease,' named for the four groups thought to be at highest risk of infection: homosexuals, haemophiliacs, heroin users, and Haitians. Then, in August 1982, the CDC coined the name that would stick, a name that would soon cause panic around America and the world: Acquired Immune Deficiency Syndrome.

For a while, to the extent the epidemic was considered at all, it was considered an affliction of 'them' – the queers, the junkies, the immigrants, those people we don't like to think about or talk about. But AIDS became a disease of 'us' the moment rumours hit that it was in the general blood supply. First, AIDS began showing up in people with haemophilia, like Ryan. The real panic took off when patients started contracting the disease from blood transfusions during surgery, and although the numbers would ultimately turn out to be relatively small, the public began to feel as if anyone could get the disease. 'Fear of AIDS Infects the Nation,' blared a *U.S. News & World Report* headline at the time.[3]

Fear of AIDS in the blood supply was completely understandable; it was based on facts. But the worst public fear about AIDS was that you could contract it just from casual contact with an infected person. This was, of course, utter nonsense. You can't get HIV from a toilet seat or a swimming pool, from mosquitoes, by hugging someone with AIDS, or by breathing the same air in a room with someone who is HIV-positive. Blood and sexual fluids are, and have always been, the *only* transmission routes for HIV. Period.

As I've said, this was well understood very shortly

after the epidemic was discovered. By early 1983, scientists had not identified precisely what virus was causing AIDS, but they knew for certain that casual contact did not transmit it. Some public health organisations, including the CDC, did what they could to get the facts out, but they were overwhelmed by a tide of misinformation, often from people and organisations that should have known better. On 6 May 1983, the *Journal of the American Medical Association* published a news release with the headline 'Evidence Suggests Household Contact May Transmit AIDS.'[4] As late as 1985, a White House lawyer who is now the chief justice of the U.S. Supreme Court, John Roberts, sent a memo to President Reagan saying, 'There is much to commend the view that we should assume AIDS can be transmitted through casual or routine contact.'[5]

With these mixed signals coming from high-ranking government officials and the medical establishment, it's no wonder that people indulged in irrational fears. In New York, the state Funeral Directors Association recommended that its members refuse to embalm people who had died of AIDS.[6] In Louisiana, the state house of representatives overwhelmingly passed a measure permitting the arrest and quarantine of any person with AIDS (the law was thankfully revoked soon thereafter).[7] In San Francisco, when a local TV station tried to tape a special to increase public understanding of AIDS, the studio technicians refused to let people living with HIV/AIDS onto the set.[8]

Across the country, reports began to emerge of targeted persecution and violence against people with HIV/AIDS, particularly gays. In Seattle, one group of young men rampaged through a local gay district, beating people with baseball bats and raping two men with a crowbar. When one of the attackers was arrested, he told police, 'If we don't kill these fags, they'll kill us with their fucking AIDS disease.'[9]

Calming this rampant hysteria required a forceful response from the American government, the only institution big enough, powerful enough, and knowledgeable enough about AIDS to make a difference. But the sad truth about AIDS in the '80s is that President Ronald Reagan, his administration, and many leaders in Congress refused to engage in the fight. They exhibited neither the urgency nor the focus that the crisis required. We needed a plan to kill this monster. We needed real money to fund research, treatment, and education. Most of all, we needed leaders who cared.

The AIDS epidemic flared and raged in the '90s because no one put it out when it was smouldering in the '80s.

The indifference started at the very top. President

Reagan did not publicly utter the word 'AIDS' until 1985, four years and some 13,000 cases into the epidemic. He did not give a speech on AIDS until 1987. Perhaps no one better catalogued the pattern of official indifference and apathy than the journalist Randy Shilts, whose 1987 book, *And the Band Played On*, remains the definitive investigation of what did and – more important – what did not happen during the early years of the AIDS epidemic. His book is full of stories, some of which I've recounted here, of frantic researchers and doctors on the front lines of the AIDS fight, begging their superiors, the Reagan administration, and Congress for more resources and attention to combat the disease. They were repeatedly ignored. Shilts himself died of AIDS in 1994.

In public, many administration leaders were sounding the right notes, as Shilts documents in his book. Margaret Heckler, for example, the secretary of Health and Human Services (HHS), spoke before the U.S. Conference of Mayors in June 1983. She pointedly told the crowd, 'Nothing I will say is more important than this: that the Department of Health and Human Services considers AIDS its number-one health priority.'[10] But behind the scenes, Heckler's very own people were contradicting what she said in public. A month after she told Congress the AIDS fight was fully funded,

Dr Edward Brandt, the assistant secretary for health at HHS, wrote in an internal memo that 'it has now reached the point where important AIDS work cannot be undertaken because of the lack of available resources.' He said that critical prevention programmes had been 'postponed, delayed or severely curtailed.'[11]

Over at the CDC, Don Francis, an epidemiologist leading the organisation's AIDS research, was far more blunt. In a letter to the director of the Center for Infectious Diseases, he wrote, 'The number of people already killed [by AIDS] is large and all indications are that this disease will not stop until thousands of Americans have died . . . Our government's response to this disaster has been far too little.'[12] At the time, for a government scientist to say as much was extraordinarily brave. Dr Francis and others like him were true heroes in their efforts to get their superiors, and the country, to wake up.

It's not as if the Reagan administration and Congress were incapable of responding forcefully to public health crises. As Shilts noted, in October 1982, when seven people in Chicago were killed by cyanide-laced Tylenol, federal, state, and local officials mobilized all the manpower and money necessary to figure out what had happened and to develop procedures to ensure it didn't happen again.[13] There was a similar all-hands-on-deck attitude years earlier when a rare pneumonia, later named Legionnaires' disease, struck and killed thirty-four people at a July 1976 American Legion convention in Philadelphia.[14] And yet AIDS – an epidemic that was killing thousands of Americans and people around the world by the mid-'80s – didn't even warrant enough attention for the president of the United States to utter its name in public.

The charitable explanation for the official inaction on AIDS is that decision makers just didn't know how bad it really was. If you were a doctor seeing AIDS patients every day, a CDC epidemiologist tracking the geometric spread of the disease, or a gay man living in New York's Greenwich Village or the Castro neighbourhood in San Francisco, you could see that this was something new and terrible. You knew the only chance to beat the disease was to channel the same urgency and attention you'd give to something your life depended on. Because it very much did. We needed what one prominent AIDS researcher called 'a minor moon shot.'[15] But for many in government, perhaps AIDS felt like a distant, vague threat. Everyone knew someone with cancer or diabetes. In the early 1980s, however, most people didn't know anyone with AIDS.

I think that people are fundamentally good, which is why I *want* to believe the primary reason that AIDS did not receive the attention it deserved was due to ignorance – that people just didn't know. But, in my heart, I know this isn't true. I've lived too long and seen too much to accept that AIDS was ignored because we didn't understand the danger of the disease. AIDS was ignored because too few people in power cared about those who had it.

At a congressional hearing in 1982, California congressman Henry Waxman, one of the earliest champions for people with HIV/AIDS, described what I still believe to be the core truth about the epidemic:

> This horrible disease afflicts members of one of the nation's most stigmatized and discriminated-against minorities. The victims are not typical, Main Street Americans. They are gays, mainly from New York, Los Angeles and San Francisco. There is no doubt in my mind that, if the same disease had appeared among Americans of Norwegian descent, or among tennis players, rather than gay males, the responses of both the government and the medical community would've been different.[16]

Of course, we'd soon discover that AIDS was not a gay disease at all. It was a disease that could cut down anyone, anywhere. But AIDS would continue to carry that early gay stigma throughout the 1980s, and for many religious and governmental leaders, that was all the excuse they needed to turn their backs and blame it all on a community they already loathed. Even to this day, AIDS remains a disease closely associated with the gay community.

It still stings to recall the pure, unadulterated hatred that was spewed at gays and AIDS sufferers. Jerry Falwell, the founder of the Moral Majority and a key ally of President Reagan, said that 'homosexuals are violating the laws of nature. God establishes all of nature's laws. When a person ignores these laws there is a price to pay.'[17] Pat Buchanan, the former Nixon speechwriter and future presidential candidate, echoed that sentiment when he was quoted as saying, 'The poor homosexuals – they have declared war upon nature, and now nature is exacting an awful retribution.'[18]

You couldn't help but detect a touch of glee in these statements. People such as Falwell had been preaching for years that the Lord would condemn America for its sinful ways. And here, finally, was a righteous God inflicting a plague on those faggots who had been flouting His divine laws. It was truly sickening. And if you think this hatred was purely the domain of funda-mentalist preachers and combative commentators, consider what happened in Texas in 1985. That's where the state health commissioner, Dr Robert Bernstein, proposed that AIDS patients be quarantined from the general public.[19] It's where the former mayor of Houston, Louie Welch, said one way to curb the AIDS epidemic would be to 'shoot the queers.'[20]

I know that these awful bigots weren't representative of their constituencies, or everyone in the church or in government. Not even close. And didn't we all stop paying attention to the fire-breathing preachers when they blamed the gays for 9/11 and Hurricane Katrina? Good grief. But in the 1980s, these people had real power. Jerry Falwell's Moral Majority helped put President Reagan in the White House in 1980. He delivered the benediction at Reagan's renomination at the Republican convention in 1984. The man had *major* influence. He could have used it to heal. If he'd managed a more thorough reading of the Bible, perhaps he would have noted the part where Jesus heals the leper who had been shunned by everyone else.

But Falwell and his ilk used their power to incite hatred. Their horrifying words and inaction gave people license to ignore the suffering of those with HIV/AIDS. They contributed to the general sense that AIDS was not a national or a global problem but a gay problem, a drug-addict problem, an urban problem. And by doing so, they helped guarantee the AIDS epidemic would get far worse.

In 1985, as the situation was indeed worsening, two things happened that significantly changed the perception and trajectory of the AIDS epidemic.

French and American researchers had finally identified the virus that caused AIDS by 1984, and although there was a dispute over the credit for discovering the virus and what it should be called, it would eventually become known as the human immunodeficiency virus, or HIV. But it wasn't until March 1985 that the U.S. Food and Drug Administration (FDA) approved the first-ever blood test to screen for HIV. The test was relatively crude, and it was initially used only to screen donated blood. But it was something. Scientists finally knew what was causing AIDS, which gave desperate patients some small hope that this would eventually lead to a treatment.

That wouldn't come until 1987. Until then, doctors couldn't do much for AIDS patients other than help manage the symptoms. This forced many of those living with HIV/AIDS to turn to a variety of strange, experimental, and mostly useless treatments. I remember friends flying to Mexico to get amino acid injections. Adopting radical nutritional regimens. Taking all kinds of off-label drugs used to treat illnesses such as cancer or metal poisoning, with the hope that these would somehow, someway have an effect on their disease. These people, every single one of them, would be disappointed. There would be no miracle cure coming. But that first HIV test laid the groundwork for a revolution in the way scientists and doctors treated and researched AIDS.

Then, later in 1985, a second announcement revolutionized the way the American public saw the disease: Rock Hudson, one of the most famous leading men in the history of Hollywood, announced that he was dying of AIDS. When the news first hit over the summer, the public wasn't told exactly how Hudson had become HIV-positive. People close to Hudson speculated he might have got the virus from a blood transfusion during heart surgery.[21] But everyone in Hollywood, and in the circles I ran in, knew that Rock was gay and that he had in all probability contracted the disease sexually.

The media attention was absolutely insane. People simply could not believe that this strapping, six-foot-five-inch movie star, this paragon of the alpha American male, had AIDS. By the time Hudson died on 2 October 1985, the secret of his sexuality was out, but somewhat to my surprise, this didn't seem to turn the public against him. Instead, I remember hearing a lot about Rock Hudson being the new 'face of AIDS' and comments like 'If Rock Hudson can get it, anyone can get it.'

I've always found it deeply ironic that after four years of gay men dying of AIDS, a turning point in Americans' perception of the disease was . . . a gay man dying of AIDS. But Rock Hudson didn't fit prevailing stereotypes of homosexuality. He was the ladies' man who starred in *Pillow Talk* with Doris Day. He was a close friend of Ronald and Nancy Reagan. Rock became the 'respectable' face of AIDS, and perhaps AIDS itself became a bit more respectable, a bit less vile, because he had it.

Hudson's death didn't miraculously end the apathy and the bigotry surrounding the disease, of course. Far from it. But it did help to change the way the public perceived people with AIDS, and it compelled the government to get more serious about the disease. Less than three weeks after Hudson died, the U.S. Senate appropriated $221 million for AIDS research, nearly twice the amount approved the year before. After Rock Hudson's death, ignoring AIDS was no longer an option. The perception of AIDS was changing. So was the reach of the disease itself. By 1985, AIDS had been discovered throughout the globe. It was a true pandemic.

Although powerful institutions such as the U.S. government and the media had finally begun to recognise AIDS for the public health crisis that it was, fear and ignorance would continue to cloud the response. Many of the people who had been indifferent to the disease early on became pure hysterics in the late 1980s, peddling hare-brained ideas to tame the epidemic. Conservative icon William F. Buckley suggested tattooing everyone with AIDS. He wanted to brand the forearm of IV drug users and the buttocks of homosexuals.[22] The more 'respectable' version of Buckley's scarlet lettering called for mandatory HIV testing of all gays and other 'high risk' individuals. Never mind that HIV tests in the '80s often gave false positives. Or that mandatory testing would drive the very people who needed to be in the medical system away from it. Or that virtually every major public health official considered the idea idiotic. Mandatory testing was the type of simple, straightforward idea you could sell to a public that was justifiably frightened of a disease they still didn't quite understand, because their government was doing little to educate them about it, let alone fight it.

The idea of mandatory testing was surprisingly discredited by, of all people, C. Everett Koop, Ronald Reagan's arch-conservative surgeon general. Known mostly to the public for his anti-abortion views, Koop's 1986 report on AIDS was a revelation. The report didn't just dismiss mandatory testing as impractical and counter-productive. It called for AIDS education at 'the earliest grade possible' and for the widespread distribution of condoms.[23] This was heady stuff. Five years into the epidemic, the surgeon general's report represented the first major governmental effort to educate the public about AIDS. The fundamentalists were furious at Koop's frank discussion of the disease and the sexual behaviour that spread it, but to his credit, he stood by his findings. (It's interesting to note as a point of comparison that, a year earlier, the British government had distributed information about HIV/AIDS to every single household in the UK)

In 1987, President Reagan finally gave a speech on AIDS. It was, in many ways, an underwhelming speech, filled with platitudes and too few commitments to action. But finally the president said what the nation needed to hear: 'It's also important that America not reject those who have the disease, but care for them with dignity and kindness . . . This is a battle against disease, not against our fellow Americans.'[24] We could have used those words in 1982, but they were better late than never.

As the Reagan administration was waking up from its long AIDS slumber, the scientific fight against the disease was moving forward as well. In March 1987, the first treatment to slow the progression of AIDS was approved by the FDA. The drug, AZT, was an anti-retroviral that had proven in clinical trials to delay the onset of AIDS in HIV-positive patients. Patients who received AZT treatment remained HIV-positive – the drug wasn't a cure – but it allowed them to live a bit longer with the virus. The drug was adding a few months or years to patients' lives. And it often had awful side-effects. In fact, the symptoms caused by AZT were sometimes worse than those of the disease itself. The anaemia was crippling; it caused haemophiliac-like symptoms. Some people were taken off the drug because it was too toxic, but often, doing so would cause a spike in AIDS symptoms. It was a horrible way to survive. I remember some of my friends taking AZT and suffering terrible nausea and vomiting. A few developed anaemia. But after years of utter despair, this drug was a ray of hope. It was something to slow the disease down, and it promised more treatments to come.

For many, however, AZT would come too late to make a difference. That was tragically the case for Ryan White, as it was for one of my very closest friends, a man whom I loved dearly, and a man who was loved by millions of people around the world: Freddie Mercury.

Freddie didn't announce publicly that he had AIDS until the day before he died in 1991. Although he was flamboyant onstage – an electric front man on a par with Bowie and Jagger – he was an intensely private man offstage. But Freddie told me he had AIDS soon after he was diagnosed in 1987. I was devastated. I'd seen what the disease had done to so many of my other friends. I knew exactly what it was going to do to Freddie. As did he. He knew death, agonizing death, was coming. But Freddie was incredibly courageous. He kept up appearances, he kept performing with Queen, and he kept being the funny, outrageous, and profoundly generous person he had always been.

As Freddie deteriorated in the late 1980s and early '90s, it was almost too much to bear. It broke my heart to see this absolute light unto the world ravaged by AIDS. By the end, his body was covered with Kaposi's sarcoma lesions. He was almost blind. He was too weak to even stand.

By all rights, Freddie should have spent those final days concerned only with his own comfort. But that wasn't who he was. He truly lived for others. Freddie had passed on 24 November 1991, and weeks after the funeral, I was still grieving. On Christmas Day, I learned that Freddie had left me one final testament to his selflessness. I was moping about when a friend unexpectedly showed up at my door and handed me something wrapped in a pillowcase. I opened it up, and inside was a painting by one of my favorite artists, the British painter Henry Scott Tuke. And there was a note from Freddie. Years before, Freddie and I had developed pet names for each other, our drag-queen alter egos. I was Sharon, and he was Melina. Freddie's note read, 'Dear Sharon, thought you'd like this. Love, Melina. Happy Christmas.'

I was overcome, forty-four years old at the time, crying like a child. Here was this beautiful man, dying from AIDS, and in his final days, he had somehow managed to find me a lovely Christmas present. As sad as that moment was, it's often the one I think about when I remember Freddie, because it captures the character of the man. In death, he reminded me of what made him so special in life.

Freddie touched me in a way few people ever have, and his brave, private struggle with AIDS is something that inspires me to this day. But his illness, I'm ashamed to admit, wasn't enough to spur me to greater action. I've railed against government and religious leaders who were indifferent to or who actively undermined the fight against AIDS. They deserve every bit of criticism I'm throwing their way. They could have done so much more.

I could have done so much more, too.

As I said, I was appallingly absent from the early

fight against AIDS. With large swathes of the government asleep at the switch, grassroots activists led the way. Everyday Americans such as Larry Kramer, who simply would not go away, who would not shut up about the crisis in their communities. People like Elizabeth Glaser, the great advocate for paediatric AIDS research, whose determination forced people in power to pay attention to AIDS. But the most famous, and one of the very first to stand up for those living with HIV/AIDS, was my dear friend Elizabeth Taylor.

Elizabeth was the brightest star in Hollywood, one of the biggest celebrities in the world. Everyone knew her as beautiful and classy and elegant, and she was most certainly all those things. But she was also willing to get her hands dirty. She was willing to stand up for gay people when few others would. She was willing to get into the nitty-gritty of AIDS policy and to fight for the cause, without a moment's hesitation or thought for her own reputation.

When Rock Hudson announced he had AIDS, Elizabeth stood by his side and stood up for him in public. As early as 1986, she was testifying before Congress, urging more funding for emergency AIDS research. And Elizabeth helped to take the AIDS fight global, speaking in 1989 at an AIDS benefit in Thailand, the first event of its kind in South-east Asia. Many people even credit Elizabeth for personally convincing President Reagan to speak publicly about AIDS in 1987. Perhaps most important, she lent her support to Dr Mathilde Krim, who, with Elizabeth's assistance, built amfAR into a world-class organisation focused on HIV/AIDS biomedical research. To this day, it is one of the foremost AIDS organisations in the world.

Another wonderful friend who helped change the public perception of AIDS was Princess Diana. Diana and I were very close, not only in our friendship but in our world-views. Indeed, our relationship stemmed from the fact that we shared the same values, the same sense of humour, the same love of people and connecting with them. Diana was one of the most compassionate people I've ever known, and she used her tremendous pulpit to communicate the power of love and understanding.

When it came to the AIDS epidemic, like Elizabeth, Diana was among the first global figures to speak out. She did more than that, in fact. She reached out, quite literally, to those living with HIV/AIDS. In 1987, Diana opened the first hospital AIDS ward in Britain. Reports of her shaking hands with AIDS patients raced around the globe, and a big deal was made of the fact that she was not wearing gloves. At the time, many were still frightened to have any contact whatsoever with someone living with HIV/AIDS. Diana, with a simple yet profoundly human gesture, helped to ease the hysteria and correct the harmful misinformation surrounding the disease.

In the years that followed, Diana continued to raise awareness about the AIDS crisis, and pictures of her touching and interacting with HIV-positive people went a long way to calm irrational fears that continued to persist. In fact, she never stopped championing those living with HIV/AIDS. In 1997, just before her tragic death, Diana and I had been in discussions about her taking on an active role with my foundation as global ambassador for our work. She met with my staff, and we were all thrilled at the prospect of working together. Had she not been taken from us so soon, I know she would have continued to greatly impact the fight against AIDS.

Princess Diana, Elizabeth Taylor, Elizabeth Glaser, Mathilde Krim, Larry Kramer – these are my heroes, among many others. They worked hard and they accomplished much when it mattered most. I should have been by their side, following their example. Today, all I can do is follow in their footsteps. But back then, in the '80s, I could have made an impact early in the fight, just like them. I was a huge star. I had lots of money. I had powerful friends. And I was gay.

I sometimes like to joke that I'm the acceptable face of homosexuality, a blokey, non-threatening type, someone your mother wouldn't mind having over for dinner. If I had been a more committed advocate for people living with HIV/AIDS in the '80s, maybe I could have diminished, just a bit, the stigma or the suffering of some poor gay man in San Francisco or Dallas or Dublin. Maybe not. But at least I could have tried.

Instead, I spent the '80s sinking ever deeper into a drug addiction that began in 1974, when I was recording my album *Caribou* in Colorado. Even though I'd been a fully fledged rock star for years by then, I still hardly even knew what cocaine was. I was unbelievably naive. I remember walking to the back of the studio one day, seeing a line of white powder on the table, and asking my manager, 'What on earth is that?' He told me it was cocaine. I figured I'd take a little sniff.

I knew some people who could casually do cocaine once a month. I was not one of those people. By the 1980s, I was completely hooked on coke, booze, and eventually food. Then I became bulimic, too. I was guilty of every single one of the seven deadly sins, except sloth. No matter how bad it got, I never lost my work ethic or my love of music.

But I had become numb to everything else. I had friends dying left and right of AIDS. I would go to the funerals. I would cry. I would mourn, sometimes for weeks on end. None of this changed my behaviour. In fact, it just got worse. I was doing more drugs to block out the horror of it all. I was sleeping around without protection, drastically increasing the chances I would contract the very same disease that was killing the people closest to me. It's no small miracle that I never contracted HIV myself.

I was extremely selfish and self-destructive. I could barely hold myself together, let alone be out there with the Elizabeth Taylors of the world as an AIDS advocate.

It took Ryan's death to wake me up, to transform my life.

3

Starting Over

I returned to London after Ryan's funeral and locked myself away at home, as had become customary, even before his death. I had reached the point where I didn't know how to speak to someone unless I had a nose full of cocaine and a stomach full of liquor. And increasingly even that wasn't enough.

I remember watching television a few days after the funeral; they were running a tribute to Ryan, playing a recap of the funeral service. There I sat, watching myself on-screen at one of the lowest points of my life. I looked horrible. My hair was white, my skin pale. I was bloated and gorged. I looked tired and sick and beaten down. Seeing myself that way, at Ryan's funeral, was almost too much to take. I had been overcome by addiction; I was completely out of control. I looked, quite frankly, like a piano-playing Elvis Presley. As messed up as I've ever been. There was no question: I was going to change, or I was going to die. Even while spiralling, I knew that much was true.

And I desperately *wanted* to change. I remember many days when I would just sit there, alone in my room, drinking, using, bingeing, listening to Peter Gabriel and Kate Bush sing 'Don't Give Up' on repeat.

In this proud land we grew up strong
We were wanted all along
I was taught to fight, taught to win
I never thought I could fail
No fight left or so it seems
I am a man whose dreams have all deserted
I've changed my face, I've changed my name
But no one wants you when you lose.

'No one wants you when you lose.' That line always got me. I would listen to those lyrics, and then it would get to the chorus – 'Don't give up,' they would sing, and I would weep at the thought. I didn't want to give up, but I was falling farther down the rabbit hole with every gram of cocaine. I would think, 'I'll get well one day. I will. I will. I hate this life. I hate me. I hate what I've become.' But I couldn't – or, I should say, wouldn't – ask for help.

Everybody tried to get me to stop. And I appreciate

that enormously now, I really do. But at the time it infuriated me. Many people in my life back then had to suffer through my rage, my denial, my refusal to listen. I knew I was an asshole. I knew I had a problem. But I believed, wrongly, very wrongly, that I was intelligent enough and wealthy enough and famous enough that I could get control all by myself. Of course, the more I thought that, the worse I got.

Some people call it a 'high bottom.' It's what happens when you hit rock bottom, but you aren't actually in the gutter. That's where I was. I was successful. I was rich. I had a boyfriend at the time, Hugh Williams, who loved me dearly, and I loved him. I had the respect and admiration of strangers. It was the life I had always wanted – or, at least, something approximating it. 'How could I have hit rock bottom,' a voice in the back of my head would say, 'when I'm on top of the world?'

But I had. The drugs had taken over my life. So had the alcohol. And the food. My self-obsession had morphed into an incredibly low self-image. I could no longer control anything. Not how I acted, or what I took, or what I ate. About the only thing I could control was whether I kept it down. So in addition to bingeing on coke and booze and food, I was purging. Then I'd rinse and repeat. I was an addict. I was bulimic. And everything was getting worse. Each day, I would think about how much I wanted to change. But each day, the disappointment that I hadn't changed drove me to use more. It was a bitter, bitter cycle.

I was reminded of Ryan constantly, of how disappointed he would be in me, alive and capable of doing plenty of good in the world but instead choosing to satisfy my worst urges at every opportunity. To this day, I am relieved beyond words that he never knew that side of me. I don't want to imagine what the weight of his disappointment would feel like. Better to think of how proud I know he would be if he could see how much I've changed. And how much he changed me.

Weeks passed, and things didn't get any better. Then one day – I remember it like it was yesterday – Hugh told me he was going to rehab. He didn't want to be a drug addict any more, he said. He didn't want to live this life any more. He needed help and he couldn't do it himself. Looking back, I should have been proud of him for the sheer bravery of that decision. I should have supported him. Of course, I didn't. I was furious.

I should say that I had, and on occasion still have, a terrible temper. It was made worse by the fact that I was in a very bad place, that Hugh calling himself a drug addict might as well have been him calling me one. And though I *was* one, how dare he say so! I said some horrible things to Hugh – things I would forget saying if I could, things that no one should have to hear. It wasn't enough, thank goodness, to stop him. Hugh left for rehab that day. I, on the other hand, retreated further into my addictions.

I withdrew to my house in London and used solidly for a week. Locked in a room with my cocaine and my own stubbornness. The truth was, as much as I tried to convince myself that Hugh had betrayed *me* – that he had left *me* alone, that it was *his* fault, that *he* was wrong – I knew how ridiculous that was. I was the true culprit. Besides, I loved Hugh very much, and I missed him terribly. I was alone with my addictions, my self-pity, my self-loathing. You really can't be more alone than that.

One day, somehow, I worked up the courage to try to find Hugh. I got in touch with his ex-boyfriend Barron Segar, who is now on the board of the Elton John AIDS Foundation (funny how things work out), and he was able to track Hugh down at a halfway house in Prescott, Arizona.

I still remember how nervous I was when I called him. I thought he might hate me for the things I had said, the way I had acted. He should have. I wouldn't have blamed him for it. What made matters worse is that I knew he was in recovery, and he probably wouldn't want to associate with someone who was still using.

That's one of the things they tell you. You can't be around that sort of thing. And 'that sort of thing' was me. Still, I had to give it a try.

My fingers trembled as I dialled the phone number. And then, there he was, finally, on the other end of the line. I told him I wanted to come see him, that I needed to. 'Listen,' he said, 'you can come to see me, but you need to speak to my counsellor on the phone first. There are some things I want to say to you that need to be said. I'll have a counsellor and you'll have a counsellor and we'll sit and we'll talk.'

I agreed. 'Whatever it takes,' I thought. I called up Hugh's counsellor, who told me that it was fine for me to visit, but before I did, I needed to write down the three things I disliked most about Hugh. And he would be doing the same. We would sit down face-to-face and discuss our lists.

I knew what was about to happen. It was going to be some kind of intervention. There was a time, not long before that phone call, when I would have simply hung up. But this time was different. I knew this needed to happen, whatever it would be, however it would unfold.

Later that week, I flew to Arizona. I arrived at the hotel in Prescott and went up to the room. I knocked on the door and waited with intense anxiety for someone to answer. The door opened, and there he was. There was Hugh. He looked absolutely terrified to see me. The two counsellors were there, too. Hugh invited me in and introduced me to them. One of them asked me to sit directly across from Hugh and told me that through all of it we needed to look each other in the eye. I was told to go first; I was to read my list of three things I didn't like about Hugh.

'You're untidy,' I said. 'You don't put the CD back in the case when you're done with it. And you leave the lights on when you leave a room.' That was my list. That was all I could come up with.

Then it was Hugh's turn. He pulled his paper out of his pocket, and I could see that he had written a full page. I can't remember everything he said, but I'll never forget this part: 'You're a drug addict. You're an alcoholic. You're a food addict. You're bulimic. You're a sex addict. And you're codependent.' His voice was quivering while he said it. He must have been terrified of how I would react. Knowing my temper, he must have thought I was going to tell him to fuck off. 'How dare you talk to me like that!' he must have thought I would say.

But I stayed silent. I sat there and I took it. I was scared, too. I was shaking as much as he was. But I kept saying to myself, 'You've got to stay here and you've got to hear this. You've got to hear the truth.'

'You need to get help,' Hugh said. That was the last thing on his page, and then there was silence. It was my turn to respond. It was the pivot point of my entire existence, right there in that hotel room in Prescott. I had a choice, and what came next honestly changed my life forever.

'You're right,' I said through tears. 'You're right. I'll go somewhere. I'll get help.'

In that moment, my soul came alive again. I could feel it. It's a strange thing to say, but it was as if my pilot light came back on. Instead of fear, I felt relief. Instead of anxiety, I felt calm. It was as if Ryan were sending me a message, letting me know it was going to be okay. I've learned that you have to listen to those messages when they're being sent, just like the message I received standing by Ryan's deathbed just two months prior. This time, I was ready. I was ready to change.

Immediately, I was on the phone with my doctor. If I was going to go to treatment, it was going to happen right away, and on my terms. But that would be its own challenge. It turned out that, at the time, there weren't many places that treated men for eating disorders. Back then, men were thought to account for about 10 per cent of people with such disorders. It just wasn't considered a real problem. What made matters harder was that there were even fewer rehab facilities that were willing to treat multiple problems at once. Dual diagnosis was discouraged, for reasons I still do not agree with. Most treatment centres expected you to go to one facility to be treated for your eating disorder before you went to another for your drug addiction, and then yet another for alcoholism. That wasn't acceptable to me. I felt very strongly at the time (and I still do) that all of my problems had the same root cause, and that I couldn't treat one without treating them all. Luckily, we found a place in Chicago that would take me in and treat all my addictions at once: Parkside Lutheran Hospital.

Less than three months after Ryan died, I was on a plane to Chicago, determined to change my life. I entered rehab in July of 1990, and I am incredibly proud to say that I have been sober ever since.

My time at Parkside Lutheran was as challenging as it was transformative. The first days were especially difficult. When you deprive your body of cocaine after having used very much and very frequently, as I had, the craving for it is inconceivably enormous. I went through bouts of extreme anxiety and irritability. I couldn't sleep. I couldn't think about anything but my own misery. This was compounded by the fact that I had stopped using not just cocaine but everything I had self-medicated with: the booze, the food, the sex.

I was depressed and alone. I felt sick and weak and foggy. Needless to say, the first stages of rehab were among the most trying periods of my life.

The most important part of my time in rehab was that, to all with whom I interacted, I was not Elton John the rock star. I was just Elton. Elton the addict. For years I had thought that my station in life provided me with the tools I would need to help myself. I thought I was somehow uniquely situated to overcome what other people could not. How wrong I was.

From the moment I walked into that hospital, the playing field was levelled. We were all the same. Suffering, struggling addicts who wanted to get better but didn't know if we could. We were all people who had made bad choices and seen the consequences, but then made the same choices despite ourselves. And we had done so again, and again, and again. The truth of it all was that simple: no matter where we had come from, what we had accomplished or failed to accomplish, what our life experiences had been up to that point, we were all the same. And none of us would get better without asking others for help.

The path to recovery wasn't a straight one, by any means. I remember quite clearly, on many occasions, wanting desperately to run away. Two separate times, I came awfully close to doing just that. It didn't merely seem like the easier path; it categorically was. I could have left, been on a plane back to London, and been back in my room, with the relief that would come with the buzz of cocaine and a drink. If not for Ryan and Hugh, I would indeed have run away.

Thank God I stayed. Over time it did get easier. I could feel a genuine transformation happening inside me. I was working hard at it, and I could feel myself changing. Every day of staying sober was a challenge, but it was invigorating to feel that I was regaining control over my life, my direction, my choices. And I'd say the biggest driver of my progress was the overwhelming kindness of the strangers I met in rehab.

People were remarkably helpful. They seemed willing to do anything for me, even though they didn't know me. They talked to me, they encouraged me, they listened to me. I still get emotional when I think of all the friends I met there, people who would come up and spend time with me during a meeting, after a meeting. They would phone me to check in. I was surrounded by innumerable acts of human kindness. It brought me back to life, I really believe it did. Enormous empathy. Enormous compassion. And because it was coming from people who had gone through what I had, who were just like me, it was easy to accept their embrace. Before rehab, I would say to those who tried to help me, 'What do you know? You don't understand.' But these people, they understood. They really understood. It didn't matter what their religion was or their political party or their background. That never, ever came into it. They were just helping their fellow man. And I was lucky that man was me.

There was an incredible dignity in the process, an extraordinary amount of humanity, and to feel that way when I was most vulnerable was unexpected and welcome. I talked a lot. But mostly I listened. And I spent a long time on my recovery, sometimes kicking and screaming along the way. But I did as I was told. I took the help and direction of others. And it worked. No one can alter his or her behaviour instantaneously. You can't change overnight. And yet you *can* change. It is possible. But it requires learning to become a human being again first.

Six weeks after I entered the programme, I was released. It was September 1990. I returned to London. There were a lot of people who wanted to see me take the stage immediately, to get on with the life I had left behind while in rehab. I chose, instead, to take an entire year off. Recovery, I was told, and have since learned, is a long process. It doesn't end after six weeks. It doesn't end when you leave the hospital. It never ends. It takes constant, hard work. For the first time in my life, I would dedicate myself to my own betterment. When I returned to my career, I wanted to return truly transformed. This was, after all, a second chance I hadn't deserved. In Ryan's memory, I could not afford to squander it.

4

Starting Up

Several months after returning to London, I decided to relocate to Atlanta. I wanted to be back in America, a country that had been very good to me, but I felt I ought to avoid Los Angeles and New York, where temptation might well get the better of me. During this time, the first thing I wanted was to continue to get well. And the second thing I wanted – just as badly as the first, really – was to give back.

In sobriety, I was constantly reminded of the good I could have been doing to help those with HIV/AIDS – my friends, people like them, people like me – but how little I had actually done. There were many potential acts of selflessness that I chose to forgo in exchange for another line or another drink. I had been lucky to emerge from the '80s without having contracted HIV myself. And I was even luckier to have emerged from treatment healthy, able to do something meaningful with my life. I owed a lot to many people – Ryan,

Jeanne, Andrea, Hugh – but to that point, I simply had not delivered. It was time to do something about that.

The first step was, literally, a small one, but it was inspirational. Hugh was in Atlanta with me, and he and I participated in AIDS Walk Atlanta. This was the city's first AIDS walk, I believe, and there were thousands of people who came out to participate. I was very glad to be one of them. Raising awareness is a critical aspect of the fight against AIDS today, and it was even more so in 1990. The mass of people taking to the street made quite an impression – on me and on the public – and I was thrilled to stand up and to be counted that day. I was also incredibly moved. There I was, in the street, surrounded by people who had been directly impacted by the AIDS epidemic. Some of those I walked with were HIV-positive. Or, like me, they had friends or family members who had died of AIDS. For the outside world, the AIDS Walk put a human face to the epidemic. For me, it crystallized the need to get more personally involved.

Soon after, I started volunteering for a wonderful organisation in Atlanta called Project Open Hand, a charity that arranged the delivery of home-cooked meals to AIDS patients all over Atlanta. My dear friend John Scott and I would drive around the city and deliver meals to home-bound people who were very sick. I'll never forget the tragedy we witnessed doing this work. The stigma at the time was punishing. If you had AIDS, you were ostracised by most of society, period, just as Ryan had been shunned by his community in Kokomo. In Atlanta, and all over America, people were contracting HIV and then losing their jobs, their insurance, their friends; even their own families would turn away. People with HIV/AIDS were on their own in every sense. And the sicker they got, the more difficult it was for them to leave the house. The stigma associated with the disease was so intense that if someone with full-blown AIDS had a medical emergency and needed to go to the hospital – as people invariably did in the early 1990s before effective treatment was available – some emergency personnel refused to assist AIDS patients. The people to whom we were delivering meals were literally shut out of the world, and as a result far too many became shut up in their homes – a retreat not of choice but of unjust circumstance.

There was something about volunteering that reminded me of the strangers I had met while in treatment. To the people we were visiting, I wasn't a celebrity. Some must have recognized me, and I do remember a few startled looks as I walked through the door with a hot meal. But to most, I was just a rare friendly face, coming for a brief social interaction, offering a meal and what little comfort came with it. It was also a reminder of just how hard things were for people dying of AIDS – a recognition that it wasn't just the disease but society's response to the disease that had taken a toll. There were some people John and I delivered meals to who opened their doors and were happy to greet us. There were others who cracked their doors just wide enough to take what we were offering, give a quick thanks, and shut themselves back in. And, sadly, there were still more who had completely closed themselves off to the world that had betrayed them. For these poor souls, we just left the meal on the front porch. We would ring the doorbell, but no one would answer.

I imagine that everyone I ever delivered a meal to is dead. I am still haunted by the thought of how many good, innocent people suffered horrible deaths completely alone in those years.

In volunteering for Project Open Hand, John and I were making a small difference. But I wanted to do more. I *had* to do more. People were dying. People like *me* – gay men, addicts or those in recovery, my friends, and my friends' friends. It was an atrocity, and I wasn't going to sit idle any longer.

John and I soon got involved with other organisations in the city. We learned of the Grady Ponce De Leon HIV Center in Atlanta, a facility that aimed to identify all of the existing opportunities for someone who was suffering from HIV, whether it was indigent care, critical care, or other social services. The programme helped people with everything from finding a doctor to applying for unemployment insurance after losing a job. I was honoured to cut the ribbon to open the Center and raise awareness that this amazing resource was available to the Atlanta AIDS community.

And then, in October of 1992, Elizabeth Taylor asked me to join her for a benefit concert at Madison Square Garden to raise money for HIV/AIDS research. As I said, Elizabeth had been a trail-blazer in the fight against AIDS, and she was one of my closest friends. I immediately agreed. It turned out to be a beautiful event, and we raised a lot of money for the cause. It was also the final catalyst for one of the most important decisions I have ever made in my life – the decision to start a foundation devoted to fighting AIDS.

Several things in the lead-up to the benefit concert and then in its aftermath had struck me. First, it was clear that you could leverage fame and celebrity not only to raise a considerable amount of money but to raise awareness, too, something that was critical to breaking down the stigma that had grown up viciously around the AIDS epidemic. But second, as effective and important as individual benefit concerts were, the process felt piecemeal to me. When someone like Elizabeth Taylor mobilised the troops, we were, of course, happy to answer the call. And the money raised at such events went directly to fighting the disease. But there was something missing: a general lack of co-ordination. A single place where the money could be pooled and spent strategically would be more efficient and more effective. That way, I thought, we could maximise the bang for our proverbial buck.

It also struck me that the majority of the money being raised and spent in the fight against AIDS was getting directed toward a search for treatment and hopefully a cure. There's no question that, given the U.S. government's initial denial and then modest funding for research, this should have been the priority – and amfAR was doing an amazing job of filling the void. Especially then, in the early 1990s, we were convinced that the greatest hope for a cure lay in the minds of research scientists in labs around the world.

But there were other aspects of the disease that seemed, to a large degree, underfunded and overlooked: helping people protect themselves from HIV in the first place and helping HIV-positive people live better and die with dignity. That meant more than new drugs, which, again, were essential. It also meant transportation to the hospital or the pharmacy to get medicine. It meant access to doctors and nutrition and counselling. It meant education and programmes for prevention. It meant teaching people the importance of condoms, about how the disease is transmitted and, most important, how it isn't. It meant efforts to eliminate stigma and discrimination, and it meant medical, legal, and housing support for highly marginalised populations, those who were suffering the most but who had been pushed aside by a society that preferred to ignore reality rather than confront it. It meant, ultimately, recognising that people were forced to suffer as much emotionally as they were physically. All of this had to change.

As I had these epiphanies, a few days after Elizabeth's concert, the idea took shape in my mind. I called John. 'I'm starting an AIDS foundation,' I said, 'and I want you to run it.' John agreed, and two months later the Elton John AIDS Foundation – EJAF – opened its doors.

Or, I should say, 'door.' The door to John's home, that is. You might think that a celebrity foundation would have fancy offices and chauffeurs and a cappuccino maker. But we didn't have anything like that, and we still don't. Besides, celebrity foundations in 1992 were rare and, apart from Elizabeth Taylor's foundation, did not focus on AIDS. No one was really doing anything like that back then. So we improvised. John ran the organisation for two years from his breakfast table in

Atlanta. Virginia Banks, who worked on my team in Los Angeles, became the foundation's secretary and John's right hand. I asked Sarah McMullen, my publicist, to do double duty, working both as my PR guru and also as the foundation's fund-raiser. Thankfully, she agreed. And that was it. Just the four of us and an amazing board of directors. To this day, we continue to run the foundation with a skeleton crew.

When we started out, we didn't have any experience or infrastructure at all, only the feeling of absolute urgency, the sense that no amount of effort was sufficient. And it wasn't just our sense; it was the reality of the epidemic in those days. You cannot quantify the magnitude of human suffering – physical and psychological – the disease caused back then. So there was no time to lose. EJAF was created as an emergency response. And I had no inkling that the foundation would still be needed two decades later. As bad as things were in 1992, many of us thought that a cure was on the horizon, that some brilliant scientist would master the virus's code so that we could destroy it, that we would be able to close up shop and declare victory within a few years. Twenty years have now passed, and those hopes seem heart-wrenchingly naive. The barriers to a cure were far greater than any of us could have known at the time.

In formulating our response strategy, we asked two important questions: How would we define the foundation's mission? And how would we turn our ideas into action as swiftly as possible?

Strange as it may sound, the solutions were largely driven by the lessons I had learned in rehab. To get well, I had to confront the reality of my own life and change it. That required self-reflection. It required a willingness to be honest with myself. I felt that this confrontation with reality, this embrace of honesty, had to be part of how my foundation took on the epidemic. We had to face facts.

Of course, the realities of AIDS were – and are – very uncomfortable for many people. The disease exists in every population, but it is heavily concentrated in marginalised populations, in people society finds awfully easy to turn its back on: the gay community, sex workers, drug users, the impoverished and uneducated. If we were going to be honest about the disease, we needed to target populations that were suffering from it, regardless of how uncomfortable it might make people feel.

I wasn't going to shy away from that. Because, guess what? People do survive on the streets selling sex. People do use drugs. That won't change by our turning a blind eye to them. And I knew, from personal experience, that everyone deserves the same level of dignity and humanity.

After all, I was a recovering addict. Who was I to feel superior to anyone else? I didn't, and I still don't. The bottom line is, we're all human, and we all deserve to be helped and to be loved. I was determined to infuse my foundation with that set of values. To this day, what drives our work more than anything else is the idea that all people with HIV/AIDS deserve dignity and compassion.

I was also determined to have a hands-on relationship with our work. I wasn't interested in just lending my name to the cause, or performing a few songs on stage now and again. I had more to give than that. I wanted to give my ideas and my energy. I wanted to give my time. This was going to be a major priority in my life, I felt, just as important as my career.

To start off, we wanted to focus on the tremendous need for the basics – the real basics – food, lodging, transportation, medical attention, education, legal support, and counselling. These were the things that John and I had seen firsthand were lacking, the kinds of things we knew we could improve. The mission I decided on was to provide funding for such basic programmes, with the ultimate goal of reducing the incidence of HIV/AIDS, eliminating the stigma and discrimination associated with the disease, and providing direct treatment and care services to HIV-positive people, to allow them to live with dignity.

Within the first year, all of the critical elements had come together for the organisation. I covered the operating costs initially, so that every dollar we raised would go into services. But there was such an overwhelming need, we felt as if we could never – and would never – get the money out the door fast enough. Everything we did, every fund-raiser we held, every cheque we wrote, it all felt like one act of genuine desperation. We never even considered putting together a savings account. All we thought about was how to raise money, more and more money, and then get it into the right hands immediately. I know, looking back, that we were doing good work. But we were also witnessing such immense and wrenching suffering that I don't think any of us believed we were succeeding. I don't think you can ever really feel that way when so many people are dying.

Raising money, it turned out, was not the hardest part, thanks to the hard work of John, Virginia, Sarah, and our amazing board of directors. I had convinced many great friends from the music and entertainment industry to join our board to help get EJAF up and running: Robert Earl, the founder and CEO of Planet Hollywood and later the CEO of Hard Rock Cafe, and Art Levitt, the CEO of Hard Rock Cafe International; Howard Rose, my long-time agent; Al Teller and his right-hand man, Glen Lajeski, of MCA; Johnny Barbis, the music executive and my manager of many years; and Michele Burns, the former CEO of Mercer Consulting who, at the time, was a senior partner at Arthur Andersen. All of our original board members were serious businesspeople and also wonderfully caring friends of mine. They made the right connections for us and taught us how to run EJAF with the efficiency of a successful commercial enterprise like the ones they had built. They raised an extraordinary amount of money, and I'm so proud that several of them remain on our board to this day.

Many of these early board members helped us establish innovative ways of fund-raising, by using our celebrity and commercial connections to develop and market products that would be sold for the benefit of EJAF. It was amazing that heavy-hitting companies and people were willing to spend money for us this way. Barron Segar, a banking expert, helped devise a credit card that directed a percentage of expenditures to support the foundation's work. Billie Jean King and Ilana Kloss had the idea for 'Smash Hits,' an event that would bring tennis stars together for a fund-raising event built around exhibition matches. We've held Smash Hits every year since 1993, and it's grown to be one of our most important and successful fund-raisers each year. Eddi Barbis was instrumental in engaging and sustaining a long-term, cause-related marketing project. The photographer Herb Ritts, who sadly died of complications from AIDS himself, auctioned his amazing work to support EJAF. Whoopi Goldberg developed a T-shirt for us that was sold at Planet Hollywood, and Jane Fonda and Ted Turner lent their celebrity and efforts to our cause as well, giving the foundation a tremendous boost in both resources and credibility.

Over the years, we've partnered with many companies on a range of fund-raising products and activities, and it's been fantastic for all of us – the companies elevate their profiles while raising a ton of money for an important cause, and the foundation directs the proceeds to critical efforts. It's exciting to see that, today, so many other organisations have adopted this model.

So raising money was, in some ways, the easy part. The challenging part was, how do we distribute funds with lightning speed and in a strategic way at the same time? John and I didn't have the expertise to know which organisations in which cities or states needed our funding the most. But we knew that we had to figure it out, and we weren't going to waste a dime. One possibility was to create our own in-house grants process, whereby organisations around the country could apply for funding, and we could assess their relative merit. But there were problems with that model. The first, and most immediate, was that it would become quite expensive and labour-intensive to develop. We felt we didn't have time to do it, and we didn't want to sink funding into our own operations rather than pushing the money out the door to the people it was intended for. Beyond that, there was a sense that building our own grant-giving structure would be duplicative. There were other organisations that already had these structures in place. They could handle the distribution better than we could; we didn't need or want to re-invent the wheel. So, very early on, we made a key decision: our job would be to raise the money, and we would build partnerships to get it into the right hands. With the help of experts on our board, including Dr Charles Farthing and the incredible activist Eli Saleeby, this is how we would proceed.

We did an extensive search and were lucky – extraordinarily lucky – to find the National Community AIDS Partnership. The partnership was the brainchild of the Ford Foundation. To run their partnership, Ford hired an executive director, Paula Van Ness, who to this day is one of the most brilliant women I have ever met. What she understood in those early years was essential: with so many separate organisations providing their own services to their own regions, we needed some kind of nationwide model, something that would help us respond to the crisis in a truly co-ordinated and strategic way. We needed, for example, to get funding to places that had become epicentres of the disease – Los Angeles, New York, Atlanta. But we also needed to distribute funds in places like Tulsa, Oklahoma, where the number of AIDS patients was far fewer but where the suffering was just as great.

The goal of the partnership wasn't just to collect money and distribute it; it was to mobilise social service organisations that already existed, that already had infrastructure, and to turn their attention to HIV/AIDS. The National Community AIDS Partnership offered challenge grants to these organisations, and EJAF provided the funding. Organisations would get a grant, say, $10,000, with the requirement that they raise an additional $10,000 from their local communities. In this way, Paula worked with each organisation to develop independent, local fund-raising mechanisms. Thus, the partnership created AIDS treatment, care, and prevention start-ups all over the nation.

It was a terrific win-win situation for us and for the communities involved. There was no cost to EJAF in using the National Community AIDS Partnership's challenge grant distribution model. Nearly every single dollar we sent through the partnership was distributed to communities. And we weren't responsible for determining the most efficient use of that money. The local organisations knew their own critical needs; they got to decide where and how those funds would be distributed. EJAF's board would assess and approve each project we funded. On top of that, each dollar we spent through that process was matched at least two to one, if not three to one or more. The model was an extraordinary success, and it drove home an important early lesson that has stayed with us to this day: partnerships really do work, and replicating what others are doing is an absolute waste of money.

I will never forget the exhilaration and anxiety of those early days. I had the duelling senses that we were accomplishing great things but at the same time not accomplishing nearly enough. All we cared about was that people were dying, and we wanted to get them the care they needed and, at the very least, to enable them to live and die with dignity. It wasn't until a few years into the process that we really began to understand the kind of impact we were having. I clearly remember the day we received a report from the National Community AIDS Partnership that quantified our efforts. We had raised $1.5 million, and thanks to the challenge grant distribution model, we had generated $7 million in matching funds. Our model was working better than we could have ever imagined. We were moving the needle in a very real way.

With Ryan White, a young boy who contracted HIV through treatment for hemophilia, at Disneyland in October 1986. Upon first hearing Ryan's story, I reached out to the White family to offer my help. It turned out, in the end, the Whites would do far more for me than I ever did for them. *(Jeanne White-Ginder)*

Ryan White and I first met back-stage at a concert held in Oakland, California, on October 3, 1986. *(Jeanne White-Ginder)*

With Ryan's mother, Jeanne White, at Ryan's bedside at James Whitcomb Riley Hospital in Indianapolis in 1990. *(Taro Yamasaki / Time & Life Pictures / Getty Images)*

Embracing Jeanne as we grieve at Ryan's funeral.
Ryan passed away on April 8, 1990.
(Taro Yamasaki / Time & Life Pictures / Getty Images)

With my friend and fellow AIDS activist Princess Diana, backstage at a concert in 1993. Diana opened the first hospital AIDS ward in Britain in 1987. She was one of the most compassionate people I've ever known.
(Richard Young)

With Freddie Mercury, front man of the band Queen and one of my closest friends, at the Live Aid concert in London in July 1985. Freddie was diagnosed with AIDS two years later. He passed away on November 24, 1991.
(Rex USA)

With my dear friend Billie Jean King in 1975. Billie Jean and her partner, Ilana Kloss, had the idea for "Smash Hits," an event that would bring tennis stars together for an EJAF fund-raising event built around exhibition matches. We've held Smash Hits every year since 1993, and it's grown to be one of our most important and successful fund-raisers each year.
(James Fortune / Rex / Rex USA)

With my partner and EJAF chairman David Furnish, Larry Kramer, and David Webster at "amfAR and ACRIA Honor Herb Ritts" in New York City. Larry Kramer, who cofounded the Gay Men's Health Crisis in 1982, is one of my heroes in the fight against AIDS. *(Dimitrios Kambouris / WireImage / Getty Images)*

David, Elizabeth Taylor, and I attend EJAF's thirteenth annual Academy Awards Viewing Party. A longtime AIDS activist, Elizabeth was the founding international chairman of amfAR, the American Foundation for AIDS Research. She was willing to stand up for gay people when few others would. *(KMazur / WireImage / Getty Images)*

Stevie Wonder, Gladys Knight, Dionne Warwick, and I reunite backstage after singing "That's What Friends Are For" at the amfAR New York Gala on February 9, 2011. We originally recorded the song in 1985, with proceeds of more than $3 million going to support amfAR. *(Larry Busacca / Getty Images)*

With David and Dr. Mathilde Krim at amfAR's Cinema Against AIDS 2002 benefit gala in France. Mathilde Krim is the founding chairman of amfAR. *(Evan Agostini / ImageDirect / Getty Images)*

ELTON JOHN AIDS FOUND*A*

Presenting a special award to John Scott at the "An Enduring Vision" gala in New York, November 2, 2005. John was EJAF's first executive director. In the organisation's early days, his kitchen served as our makeshift office.

EJAF-UK executive director Robert Key at his MBE investiture for services to charity. Robert ran the foundation in the UK until he passed away in 2009.

(© Gerry Lane)

With David, current EJAF-UK executive director Anne Aslett, Desmond Tutu, and Robert Key at EJAF's fund-raising ball in Cape Town, South Africa, on January 8, 2005. *(Marc Hoberman)*

With David and EJAF executive director Scott Campbell at the National Association of Broadcasters Education Foundation gala on June 11, 2007. I was honoured to receive the Service to America Leadership Award. *(© Oscar Einzig)*

With David and EJAF trustees Johnny and Eddi Barbis at EJAF's seventh annual "An Enduring Vision" benefit, held in New York on November 11, 2008. EJAF honoured the couple that night with an Enduring Vision Award. *(Theo Wargo / WireImage / Getty Images)*

By 1993, we had created a sister organisation in London dedicated to the same mission. As in the United States, we benefited immeasurably from a number of great friends who joined the board of directors of our fledgling UK foundation. Johnny Bergius was a prolific fund-raiser whose commitment to our cause led him to literally climb several mountains and journey to the North Pole in support of EJAF. Marguerite Littman, founder of the AIDS Crisis Trust, one of the first AIDS charities in the UK, lent us her expertise and ultimately integrated her charity into ours. James Locke, who has been living with HIV for almost thirty years, was an inspiration when we were starting out. Frank Presland, an old friend and legal genius, made fantastic contributions to our early efforts. Rafi Manoukian, the wonderful philanthropist, consistently helped us raise our sights in our global work.

Another UK board member was my dear friend Robert Key. Early on, I asked Robert to take on the job of running EJAF-UK I had known him since the 1970s, when he started handling my record releases. I was thrilled that he agreed to take on the new role, and I knew he would be the perfect person to get our UK organisation off the ground. He was so personally committed to the cause that he initially refused a salary, though eventually the board forced him to accept one because of the amazing work he was doing. He ran the foundation until his untimely death in 2009.

The mission of EJAF-UK was the same as that of EJAF-U.S., but the mechanism was different. There was no UK equivalent of the National Community AIDS Partnership, and so Robert went out on his own and met with the various organisations that were working on HIV/AIDS treatment and prevention. He learned about the kinds of services they were providing for people living with HIV in London, but he also learned something else. It appeared that there was a burgeoning AIDS epidemic in Africa. The disease wasn't just a Western crisis. And so the UK arm of EJAF adopted a global focus. Robert, together with Anne Aslett, who now heads up the foundation, made EJAF-UK one of the first private foundations to have an explicit strategy in support of people living with HIV/AIDS in Africa and beyond. To this day, the UK office makes major investments to fund programmes in Europe, Africa, and Asia, while the U.S. office directs its grants to the Americas and the Caribbean.

None of this would have been possible without Robert. He was a force of nature. He made it his personal mission to learn everything about HIV/AIDS and what it was like to live with the disease. He wanted to understand what it felt like to experience the stigma and isolation, the opportunistic infections that would crop up, and the stress of knowing you could die at any moment. He spent time visiting hospitals, shelters, prisons, anywhere and everywhere, to meet and even nurse HIV-positive people of all ages and walks of life. Like Ryan, he bravely battled the stigma around AIDS with his own kindness, compassion, and love.

For the sixteen years that he ran my UK foundation, Robert saw firsthand what people living with the disease needed, and he used his experience to do some ground-breaking things such as ensuring the creation of a national HIV/AIDS Hardship Fund for people in poverty and pushing for higher standards of nutrition for AIDS patients. Thanks to him, EJAF was on the front lines of the UK's response to the African epidemic.

Robert's death was a blow to the AIDS community and a personal tragedy for me. He wasn't just a wonderful friend – he was one of the greatest crusaders against AIDS I have ever met.

There were many others who inspired me tremendously during those early years of my foundation. First and foremost among them is my partner of nearly twenty years, David Furnish, who is also chairman of the board of EJAF in both the United States and the United Kingdom.

David and I met in 1993, when I was still in the process of transforming my life and focusing on my recovery and my health. At the time, in addition to conquering the addictions that had imprisoned me for so long, I had purged many of the people around me who were enabling my destructive lifestyle in the first place. After completing my rehab and returning to London, I was looking for some new friends, and I was introduced to David at a dinner party I held one night.

But David would become so much more than a friend. We shared the same passions, the same sense of humour. We instantly connected, and we quickly fell in love. It's impossible to overstate David's impact on my life at that time, and ever since. He is there for me in every way imaginable. He focuses my energies in positive and productive ways. I would not be the man I am today if not for David. He was, is, and always will be the most important person in my life, alongside our son. We are partners in everything, including the work of EJAF. Together we were able to keep the foundation going, and growing, during its formative years.

Princess Diana was another source of inspiration to me, and as I mentioned, she had hoped to be a source of support to EJAF as well had her life not come to an end so tragically. Diana was always wonderfully encouraging, and not only about my AIDS work. Like David, she helped me keep my life on track during the first years of my recovery. I was sober and taking care of myself, but it wasn't always easy, and having the support of true friends like her was simply priceless.

One of my favourite memories of Diana was in 1993, when I went to battle with the *Sunday Mirror*, a British tabloid that had published a ludicrous story alleging I had lapsed back into bulimia and was seen eating and then spitting out my food at a party. Never mind that I was thousands of miles away when the party had taken place. I sued the paper for libel and eventually won. But one day, when the lawsuit was still under way, I received a letter in the mail. It was a handwritten note from Diana that read, 'Thank you on behalf of bulimics everywhere!' What a wit that woman had. She and I had bonded years before over our eating disorders, and she wasn't above poking a little fun at the seriousness of our struggles with food and with the press.

Like Diana, Elizabeth Taylor also kept us going with her example and her incredible sense of humour, and she supported my foundation in every way she could. Even as I grieved her recent passing, I was moved to learn that she had left a generous contribution to EJAF in her will, which speaks volumes about the tremendously caring woman she was.

But one story really says it all about Elizabeth. Ever

since EJAF was founded, we've put on a massive Academy Awards viewing party that serves as the biggest annual fund-raiser for EJAF-U.S. One year, despite being in horrible pain and very poor health, and on her birthday, no less, Elizabeth attended the event to help us raise awareness about HIV/AIDS, as she had done many times previously. There were dozens of photographers and reporters – perhaps more than a hundred, in fact – cramming the very long red carpet at the entrance to the fund-raiser. Elizabeth had a terrible time getting around at that point. But, with David on one arm and two of her grandsons on the other, Elizabeth walked the entire stretch. And not only that, she spoke to every single journalist and posed for every single camera that was aimed her way. More to the point, Elizabeth spent the whole time talking about the importance of EJAF's work and the urgency of the AIDS epidemic. She never once strayed from that topic. Elizabeth must have been on her feet for an hour, and the whole time she was as energetic and graceful as ever. Finally, when she reached the end of the red carpet and finished her last interview, Elizabeth turned her beautiful smile to David and whispered into his ear, 'Get me my fucking wheelchair!'

I miss my friends Elizabeth, Diana, and Robert more than you can imagine, and every single day. I think about them constantly, and EJAF would not be here but for their herculean efforts, inspiration, and support. With their help and David's – and thanks to John, our small but dedicated staff, and our wonderful board of directors – within only a few years, we were becoming a major player in the fight to rid the world of AIDS. There was much work to be done, huge mountains to climb. But, wherever he was, I hoped with all my heart that another dear and departed friend, Ryan, was proud. Indeed, I felt a sense of pride in myself as well. I was sober. I was giving back. I was alive. For the first time in years, I was really, truly, alive.

5

A Crisis of Caring

From this vantage point, looking back on it all, it's amazing to think how much has changed in the twenty years since I started the foundation. It's also amazing to reflect on how much remains the same.

For one thing, given the scope of the AIDS crisis today, we still operate with a sense of urgency, with the attitude that no matter what programmes we've put in place or how much money we've raised, it's simply not enough. And it isn't. In 1992, some 1.5 million people had HIV/AIDS. Today, it's 34 million. If that isn't an absolute emergency, I don't know what is.

Another thing that hasn't changed is the way we do business. The lessons we learned in those early days are important still; they remain the basis of our work and the key to our success. We still operate with a stream-lined staff of only three people in New York and nine in London. We still leverage partnerships in order to have as big an impact as possible. And our fidelity to these lessons has been the reason for EJAF's longevity and impact. It's how we've raised and distributed $275 million in twenty years – an astonishing sum that I'm very proud of. It's how we've touched millions of lives by funding hundreds of organisations and projects in fifty-five countries.

But something else hasn't changed very much in the past two decades. Even after all these years, HIV/AIDS remains a disease of the marginalised, of the poor, of the dispossessed.

Consider the AIDS epidemic in a populous city in the Americas, one of the worst outbreaks anywhere. This city is, in many ways, just like any other. It has wealthy neighbourhoods and poor ones, suburbs and a vibrant downtown. It has grand buildings, nice restaurants, and world-class museums. It's a dense city, the capital of a large nation, and it's home to people from all walks of life. But what makes this city unique, among other things, is its horrifying AIDS crisis. The CDC and UNAIDS define an epidemic as 'generalised and severe' when rates of infection are higher than 1 per cent of the population. In this city, more than 3 per cent are HIV-positive. Thus, the city's AIDS epidemic is worse than that of many nations in West Africa, and it has roughly the same rate of infection as countries such as Uganda, Nigeria, and Congo.[1]

You might think the city in question is a large metropolis in a developing country – perhaps São Paulo, or Mexico City, or Port-au-Prince. But it isn't. The city I'm describing is *Washington, DC*. That's not a typo. It is the sad and horrible truth: one of the worst AIDS crises in the Western Hemisphere happens to be in the capital of the richest and most powerful nation on earth.

In Washington, the trend lines of the AIDS epidemic trace the contours of long-standing economic and racial inequities in America. The vast majority of HIV-positive people in Washington are black, and many are poor. Half of Washington's population is African American, but they represent nearly 80 per cent of the city's AIDS epidemic. A staggering 7 per cent of black men in the District are HIV-positive, and black women are fourteen times more likely to be infected than white women. Ward 8, a political district of Washington east of the Anacostia River, has the city's highest HIV/AIDS prevalence rate. It is also 94 per cent black and has the city's highest poverty rate. In recent years, Washington's AIDS mortality rate has declined among whites while it has increased among blacks.

No one in their right mind would say that they do not care about impoverished black people in Washington. But these statistics suggest otherwise. And the anecdotal evidence, too, is overwhelming.

Over the years, the *Washington Post* has published a series of exposés detailing the failures of the city's Administration for HIV Policy and Programs. The stories they uncovered tie my stomach in knots. A city worker discovered boxes with thousands of records of people with AIDS that had never been entered into databases that the CDC and community-based organisations rely on to fight the disease.[2] Washington's underfunded AIDS surveillance team went for years without critical staff members, and thus couldn't even tell how bad the epidemic was in order to plan an appropriate response.[3] According to the *Post*, the city health department awarded $25 million 'to nonprofit agencies marked by questionable spending, a lack of clients, or lapses in record-keeping and care.'[4] Meanwhile, so many wonderful and deserving nonprofit groups that provide essential services in Washington are under-funded and short-staffed. I know this personally, because EJAF supports many amazing community organisations in the District of Columbia.

I could go on listing instances of despicable neglect when it comes to the AIDS epidemic in Washington. The more important point, however, is that countless people have died as a result.

The *Post* told the shocking story of one such victim, a fifty-year-old woman named Renee Paige. Renee had once been a vibrant presence in her neighbourhood, but she became terribly sick from AIDS. She was thrust into extreme poverty and, eventually, homelessness. After spending a freezing night on a park bench, unprotected from the pouring rain, Renee went to a community meeting, told her story, and begged for help. But none came. The *Post* reported that she died soon after, 'alone, on the bench, one mile from the HIV/AIDS Administration and within two miles of a dozen nonprofit groups that help people with AIDS.'[5]

How can this be? How can the capital of the United States of America have one of the most severe AIDS epidemics in the world? How can a woman with AIDS, like Renee, die practically around the corner from the bloody White House? It doesn't make any sense.

And yet, when you come to understand the nature of the AIDS epidemic, it makes *perfect* sense. The truth is as sad as it is simple. People like Renee will continue to die, and this epidemic will continue to spread, until we treat everybody suffering from HIV/AIDS with the very same level of dignity and compassion, no matter who they are or where they live.

Nowhere is this more apparent than in the United States, a country whose AIDS epidemic tells us so much about the AIDS epidemic everywhere. AIDS in America is not anywhere near the national emergency it is in countries such as South Africa, which has the highest number of people living with HIV/AIDS in the world. But the AIDS epidemic in the United States is serious. Roughly 1.2 million Americans are HIV-positive, and the CDC estimates 50,000 new infections each year. The rate of new infections has been steady at this level for several years, though the number of people who die of AIDS in America has greatly declined since 1995.

With that in mind, we should consider the following statistics:

As in Washington, DC, the majority of HIV-positive people in America are black, or gay, or both. African Americans make up only 14 per cent of the U.S. population, yet they represent 44 per cent of new infections. In 2009, black Americans had HIV infection rates seven times higher than whites. More to the point, AIDS was the third leading cause of death for middle-aged African American men and women in 2008. Rates of infection have sky-rocketed among gay men, especially among young gay and bisexual men who are black. In fact, 60 per cent of new infections are among gay or bisexual men overall. According to one CDC study involving twenty-one major U.S. cities, one in five gay men is HIV-positive.[6] Another study estimated that some 16.9 per cent of HIV-positive Americans spent time in federal or state correctional systems in 2006.[7] And 9 per cent of new infections are among injection drug users.

Let me be perfectly blunt, and unapologetically so: if we demonstrated the same compassion for gay men, poor people, minorities, sex workers, prisoners, and drug users that we do for other, less marginalised people, there would be no more AIDS in America. The reality is that until we give everybody the same access to treatment and prevention, AIDS will never, ever go away. It's that simple.

I don't mean to pick on America here. I adore and admire the United States. I'm a British citizen, of course, but I fell in love with America when I first visited back in 1970. I've lived part-time there for twenty years, and I spend much of the year in Atlanta and Los Angeles when I'm not on tour. America has given me a great deal, and it's my home as much as anywhere else in the world. And I should emphasise that America has done far more than any other nation to fight the AIDS epidemic. We would be absolutely nowhere without the life-saving research and actions taken by the U.S. government, the medical research community, and ultimately the American taxpayers.

However, my point is this:

AIDS, like every contagion, has evolved to take advantage of human weakness. A retrovirus, HIV is able to infiltrate our DNA, and it sabotages our immune system to the point that even ordinary infections become deadly. But what makes AIDS so frightening, so very lethal, is that it takes advantage of more than our biological weaknesses. It takes advantage of our *social* weaknesses. Indeed, what is truly killing tens of thousands of people in America and millions of people around the world is not just a virulent contagion but a lack of human compassion – a lack of love – for those who are living with HIV/AIDS.

AIDS might as well stand for 'Appalling Indifference to the Disenfranchised in Society.' The disease thrives, more than anything else, on our prejudice against those who are HIV-positive and most at risk of becoming infected. It thrives on bigotry and indifference toward the most vulnerable. Today, the 'deficiency' that kills almost 2 million people each year is not a microscopic virus called HIV; it is a macroscopic force called stigma. The 'syndrome' that has allowed AIDS to evolve into a global plague is not immunological; it is, quite simply, an absence of empathy for our fellow human beings.

It's a difficult thing to comprehend, but even if there *were* a cure for AIDS, it would not end the epidemic. Even if there *were* a vaccine to prevent HIV infection, inoculation alone would not stop the spread of the disease. This is not a pessimistic assessment; it is a realistic one, based on what is happening right now in the world.

We already have the tools and tactics that have been proven by research and science to halt the spread of the virus: condoms, health education, and needle exchange programmes. Yet conservative religious and political leaders continue to stand in the way of implementing what we know for a hard fact will save millions upon millions of lives.

We already have advanced treatments that not only allow those with HIV to live long and healthy lives but also prevent the spread of the disease – a miraculous discovery announced in 2011. Yet, right now, millions of people around the world – including in the richest nations – are at risk of dying in the near term, and transmitting the virus to their partners, because they don't have access to these life-saving medicines.

Of course, we must continue our search for a vaccine. We must pursue new research. But we must also summon the compassion needed to build a more equitable and just world.

The story of AIDS in Washington demonstrates what happens when we do not show compassion to those living with HIV/AIDS. But let me tell you another story, a story about the difference we can make when compassion drives our response to the AIDS epidemic.

In 1981, a woman named Elizabeth Glaser was nine months pregnant with her first child when she went into labour and began to hemorrhage badly. She lost so much blood that she had to be given multiple transfusions. Thankfully, her baby was delivered safely – a beautiful little girl whom Elizabeth and her husband, Paul, named Ariel.

Elizabeth, Paul, and Ariel were no ordinary family. Paul Michael Glaser was a famous actor, screenwriter, and director. At the time Ariel was born, he was known to millions as 'Starsky,' a star of the immensely popular 1970s television show *Starsky and Hutch*. Elizabeth, an accomplished woman in her own right, was a director at the Los Angeles Children's Museum. They were what you might call a power couple: well connected and well-to-do. Despite Elizabeth's life-threatening delivery, with the birth of Ariel, the Glasers had everything in the world going for them, and then some.

In 1985, when Ariel was four years old, she became very sick, and the doctors couldn't understand why. As a precaution, she was tested for HIV and, to the horror of her parents, was positive. The Glasers learned that Elizabeth had contracted HIV during the blood transfusion she received. Elizabeth had passed the virus to her daughter while breast-feeding. Paul and Elizabeth had since had a baby boy, Jake; he had the virus as well, having contracted it from Elizabeth while in her womb.

The entire family, except for Paul, was HIV-positive.

Facing the toxic stigma that surrounded AIDS at the time, Elizabeth and Paul withdrew Ariel from nursery school. They withdrew socially as well. Despite their fame and status within Hollywood, the Glasers were forced to suffer privately with those closest to them, while their doctors did the best they could to care for what was then an entirely untreatable disease.

In 1987, however, the FDA had approved the first AIDS treatment, AZT, which was demonstrated to delay, if only by a short while, the onset of full-blown AIDS in those with HIV. But Elizabeth and Paul quickly discovered that the government had not approved AZT for use in children like Ariel and Jake. The reason, they learned, was that paediatric AIDS had barely registered on the radar of the medical community, pharmaceutical companies, and policy makers. At the time, there were roughly a thousand cases of paediatric AIDS, and they represented only 2 per cent of the epidemic in the United States.

The bottom line was that the medical community wasn't responding quickly enough, and Elizabeth and Paul's little girl was dying.

In 1988, Ariel succumbed to AIDS. She was seven

years old. Elizabeth was distraught not only at the death of her young daughter but also at the thought – the seeming certainty – of losing her baby boy, Jake, as well.

Ariel's death transformed Elizabeth. She became a woman on a mission, and her single-minded focus was to bring attention and resources to bear on behalf of all HIV-positive children, including her son. Before Ariel died, and then months after burying her first child, Elizabeth travelled to Washington to share her painful story with members of Congress. While Elizabeth and her family's HIV-positive status was still unknown to the public and the press, she bravely confided in policy makers on Capitol Hill and implored them to help.

It worked. Congress soon voted to increase funding for paediatric AIDS research by $5 million. Elizabeth had made a real difference. But she didn't stop there. Through a family connection, she arranged a meeting with President Ronald Reagan and First Lady Nancy Reagan to share her story. They were moved, but little came of her White House visit; the research dollars just weren't flowing fast enough or to the extent necessary. And so Elizabeth decided to take matters into her own hands. She started a paediatric AIDS foundation to raise the money herself. Elizabeth was soon directing millions of dollars from her foundation to critical research that would have a tremendous impact.

In the meantime, the *National Enquirer* had seized on the Glasers' story. The tabloid published the details of their family tragedy for all of America to read, and they even went so far as to print photographs of little Ariel's grave. Elizabeth was understandably furious. She was suddenly thrust into the national spotlight.

Yet, with extraordinary poise, Elizabeth used the media attention, unwanted as it had been, to raise awareness about AIDS and its impact on children and adults alike. Her public advocacy culminated in her impassioned speech at the Democratic National Convention in 1992. She delivered sharp words to a national audience about presidents Reagan and Bush, criticising them for talking about their concern for those with HIV/AIDS while doing far too little to actually fight the epidemic.

Thankfully, Elizabeth succeeded where those two presidents failed. In the early 1990s, due primarily to her lobbying, Congress dedicated tens of millions of dollars to paediatric AIDS research. Eventually, scientists discovered how to prevent the transmission of HIV from mother to child. By the mid-2000s, only around 100 children in the United States were born with HIV each year, down from a peak of some 900 cases in 1992.

Today, the battle against the epidemic of paediatric

AIDS in America, and in much of the West, has largely been won. Very few American children contract HIV in utero, and practically none die of the disease.

Elizabeth didn't live to see this victory come to pass; she died of AIDS in 1994. But her impact and legacy live on through the Elizabeth Glaser Pediatric AIDS Foundation, which, over the years, has had a profound global impact. Today, the foundation carries on with the help of Elizabeth's son, Jake, now a young man who leads a vibrant, healthy life. Indeed, her work helped save his life.

But this work is far from over. While paediatric AIDS has been almost entirely extinguished in the United States and other developed countries, there are 3.4 *million* children infected globally and more than 1,000 new paediatric infections *each day*. Elizabeth's tragedy continues to unfold for countless mothers and their children.

Today, the worldwide epidemic of paediatric AIDS is so much worse than Elizabeth could have ever imagined. And yet, thanks to her, we know exactly how to end it. Indeed, we know how to end the disease not only among children but among all people, all over the world: with relentless compassion.

At the Democratic convention in 1992 – which she described as the most important week of her life

– Elizabeth told an audience of thousands at Madison Square Garden, and millions watching on television, how her AIDS-stricken daughter, Ariel, was the inspiration for her work:

> She taught me to love, when all I wanted to do was hate. She taught me to help others, when all I wanted to do was help myself. She taught me to be brave, when all I felt was fear.[8]

In her speech, Elizabeth called AIDS a 'crisis of caring.' She said that she was motivated not only by her own personal suffering, not only by her compassion for children, but also by her empathy for gay people, poor people, people of colour, and all who lived with the disease, and died from it, around the world.

Elizabeth's story shows us the way forward. It also begs the question, if we can end AIDS for children in America, why can't we end AIDS for everyone, everywhere?

The answer is that we *can* end AIDS. We simply haven't. Not yet.

6

Confronting Reality

South Africa is one of my very favourite places to visit. It's a magical country, and the people of that nation, having suffered through terrible hardship, are extraordinarily resilient. I have great love for them. I wish they had greater love for one another.

South Africa has one of the worst AIDS epidemics in the world, spread mainly by heterosexual sex. It also has one of the worst rape crises anywhere. This is no coincidence. The two are intertwined. By itself, rape is horrific. But for many women who are raped, the nightmare has just begun. According to one study, the rate of HIV infection is so high in South Africa that if a woman is raped by a man between twenty-five and forty-five years of age, there is at least a one-in-four chance that he is HIV-positive.[1]

In South Africa, a woman is raped every twenty-six seconds. But women aren't the only victims. Women and men, girls and boys, and horrifically even babies are victims of sexual assault. As the father of a young child, I have trouble contemplating such a thing. But it is terribly real, thanks in part to a poisonous superstition that having sex with a virgin is a cure for HIV/AIDS. Rape is so widespread in South Africa that some believe very young children and babies are the only sure virgins.

The situation is now out of control. In 2009, South Africa's Medical Research Council conducted a study surveying the extent of the rape crisis. Researchers found that one-quarter of the men interviewed admitted to raping someone.[2] Another study found that more than 60 per cent of boys over the age of eleven believed that 'sex is a male's natural entitlement and forcing a girl to have sex does not constitute a rape nor an act of violence.'[3]

If a society doesn't think there's anything wrong with rape, then anybody who speaks out against it will be stigmatised. One rape survivor in South Africa told the international relief organisation Médecins Sans Frontières, 'People laugh at me and say, "Oh, you will get HIV/AIDS now." These are my neighbours and people who live around me. They don't seem to think the men that raped me did anything wrong.'[4] When then vice president Jacob Zuma was on trial for rape, a charge of which he was acquitted, his supporters rallied to his cause, lobbing insults at his accuser and shouting, 'Burn the bitch,' outside the courthouse.[5]

In cases where rape victims are stigmatised, there are horrific consequences for the AIDS epidemic. Rapes are massively under-reported in South Africa, because of the shame associated with such violence and with being HIV-positive. Women who are raped fear they will be blamed or ostracised if they seek help or report the crime – they are shamed out of coming forward.

These fears are very well founded. Even if a woman goes to the authorities, it's unlikely she will get the help she needs. Rape survivors might wait by the roadside until police collect them, take them to the station to make a statement, and, many hours later, transport them to a hospital for examination and treatment. Police often dismiss these statements entirely. This highly demeaning and ineffective process seldom results in arrests of the perpetrators or help for rape survivors. So most women who are sexually assaulted face it alone. They wipe their own tears and find a way to move on.

But if rape survivors don't come forward, if they don't seek medical attention, they can't get access to emergency post-exposure prophylaxis (PEP) medicine, a type of anti-retroviral treatment that can prevent HIV infection within a short time after exposure. Thus, the rape and AIDS epidemics intertwine to form a vicious downward spiral.

My foundation decided to do something about the stigma surrounding rape and AIDS in South Africa, and the lack of care available for women and children who are sexually assaulted. Our intent was to offer the highest quality services to those for whom so little existed. To that end, in 2002 we joined with Médecins Sans Frontières and a network of more than fifteen local organisations to establish a twenty-four-hour, seven-day-a-week acute care centre that provides services to survivors of rape in Khayelitsha, a large township outside Cape Town. The centre, called Simelela, is the first of its kind in South Africa. In Xhosa, the local language, 'Simelela' means 'to lean on.'

Simelela provides medical services, and it also tries to combat the stigma of rape and violence against women by empowering them to gain more control over their sexual lives. Women can walk in off the street, day or night, and receive treatment. Workers at the clinic bring women in need of help to the centre. Shockingly, girls under the age of fourteen make up one-third of Simelela's clients. But the good news is that Simelela can help them. Staff members give all clients post-rape medical care, PEP treatment to prevent HIV for those who need it, and a forensic examination, and they work with clients to make a detailed police report as well. Women and children who visit Simelela are treated with dignity, care, and love.

Before Simelela, this level of support for rape victims was sadly lacking. But today, thanks to the dedication and hard work of the centre's caregivers, Cape Town's rape and HIV epidemics are being tackled head-on, and with real results. Not a single client of the centre who has been given PEP treatment has contracted HIV. And, not long after Simelela was founded, the clinic was seeing more rape clients in a month than the only previous available service – some fifteen kilometres away – saw in a year. Today, the staff at Simelela also work with local police, other clinics, and courts to ensure that every woman's confidentiality is protected and that she is supported every step of the way.

Simelela has grown and started to extend its reach. It is now recognised as a model of post-rape care for South Africa. Indeed, Simelela's model is even being incorporated at a new district hospital in the middle of Khayelitsha to provide a flagship service for women and children who have been raped.

We still have a very long way to go. Changing people's attitudes about women, about HIV, and about sexual violence won't happen overnight. But the very fact that rape survivors in Khayelitsha now have a place to seek help is a tremendous victory. Building a rape crisis centre, acknowledging that rape is in fact a crisis and that survivors need services – these are monumental steps. Simelela is beginning to break the stigma surrounding sexual violence.

When I visited the Simelela centre in 2007, I met an extraordinary young woman named Fumana. She was raped by her cousin when she was only eight years old. She didn't tell anyone. Later she tested positive for HIV. But she told me the most remarkable thing. Today she says that she is *proud* to know her HIV status. She is proud because most people are afraid to talk about the disease, afraid to talk about rape, so they don't get tested, they don't know their status. But this beautiful, healthy woman knows about her disease, she is getting treatment for it, and she is *empowered* as a survivor of sexual violence. Fumana speaks out about what she endured, and in doing so she is helping to break the stigma surrounding the disease. In fact, Fumana is now studying forensics, so she too can support victims of rape.

I was deeply moved to meet her. I told her that in sharing her story and in talking about her status, she is a real hero. The more voices that are heard, the more heroes who come forward, the less society can ignore the reality of rape and AIDS in South Africa. I should note that Fumana's story and EJAF's work with Simelela have inspired our support of services at clinics in Uganda and Kenya, serving thousands of women. Fumana, through her bravery, has helped them all.

I'm very proud of the work that Simelela does. I know it makes a difference. But how many South African women have been raped since you started reading this chapter? How many children have had their innocence torn from them? How many people will be infected with HIV because stigma keeps them from getting the education, the services, and the treatment they need to prevent it? How many will die as a result?

AIDS will never end until we confront the reality of the epidemic and how it spreads. That means directly addressing the most difficult issues facing society, including poverty, drug use, sexual identity, and, yes, sexual violence. And the only way to do that, the only way to face these truths, is to overcome our own prejudices, to overcome stigma.

It is stigma that keeps us from doing what is necessary to end this epidemic. It is stigma that keeps us from confronting reality. To end AIDS, we must end stigma. It's the single biggest obstacle to stopping the global epidemic. I've seen how people's lives can be ruined because of it. I've seen how society's response to the AIDS epidemic can be warped by it. But I've also seen how, with time and effort, stigma can be alleviated.

John Scott once told me about how, in 1993, he and our very close friend Eli Saleeby, one of the founding board members of EJAF, went to visit a friend of theirs who was suffering from full-blown AIDS. When John and Eli arrived at their friend's apartment in Atlanta, he was so sick that he had to be taken to the hospital right away. Their friend was transported in a special ambulance for AIDS patients, because, as I said, during the early years of the epidemic, even health-care workers were needlessly frightened of people with HIV/AIDS.

The ambulance took John and Eli's friend to an indigent care facility in downtown Atlanta, but John and Eli wanted to make sure he received the best medical treatment possible, so they arranged for their friend to be moved to Grady Hospital, the city's major medical centre. At this point, John and Eli's friend was incredibly sick with vomiting and diarrhoea, and he was in terrible pain. But once he arrived at Grady Hospital, he sat on a gurney in a hallway for almost twenty-four hours. For an entire day, he just lay there, wasting away in his own suffering, his own humiliation, like he didn't matter at all. No one wanted to deal with him, to be near him, to treat him. Such was the stigma surrounding AIDS in a major American hospital in 1993.

Fast-forward to 2010, when Eli himself had been living with HIV for nineteen years. Eventually, he developed severe complications, including lymphoma. It happened so quickly that by the time Eli's doctors began treating the cancer it had already spread like wildfire. John got a call one day. Eli had fallen in a pharmacy parking lot and didn't know who or where he was. John got on the first flight he could and arrived at the exact same hospital he and Eli had taken their friend to nearly twenty years earlier, Grady Hospital in Atlanta. John couldn't help but think of the experience they'd had there before.

But this time, it was a completely different story. John didn't find Eli abandoned as an untouchable in some hallway. To the contrary, Eli had a six-person medical team. They immediately briefed John. They walked him through his friend's condition. They treated Eli, and John for that matter, with total respect and compassion. They didn't care about Eli's disease – they cared about Eli. And they did everything they could for him. Sadly, Eli passed away, but he did so in peace and with the dignity that he deserved.

Fighting stigma is difficult work. Over time, it can – and will – be overcome, but only when we acknowledge what stigma is, how it works, and why it is so deadly when it comes to HIV/AIDS. There has been plenty of research done on stigma, studies conducted and published by people far more knowledgeable than myself. I'm no expert, but anyone can understand the basics. We've all seen it and experienced it.

Consider how we often stigmatise the way people look – someone's height, weight, or a physical feature or deformity that strays from what we think is 'normal.' Another kind of stigma is rooted in moral or religious judgements. We impose our own values on others, and condemn them for falling outside what we think is the 'right' way to live. We see addicts as 'weak-willed,' for example, or homosexuals as 'sinful', and we marginalise them accordingly. And then there's the age-old stigma based on various differences among people – for instance, their race, class, faith, gender, ethnicity, nationality, or sexual identity.[6]

AIDS touches on many of these stigmas at once. The illness can be visible and debilitating. It's spread through sex and shared needles. It disproportionately impacts gays, minorities, and the poor. Very quickly, we've built up several layers of stigma. The more layers there are, the more difficult they are to peel back and to remove.[7]

This is the heart of the AIDS crisis and why it is so very difficult to beat. Thanks to stigma, instead of directing our animosity and fear at someone's disease, we direct it at the person who is sick. Ultimately, this makes the epidemic even worse. HIV-positive people are pushed into the shadows. They often do not receive treatment or care, because they are afraid to make public their HIV status. They are afraid to tell their families and their doctors. They are afraid to seek treatment. They are ashamed. And this shame is deadly.

Recently, someone I've known for a very long time confided in me that he had tested HIV-positive. He was so scared to tell me that he could hardly look me in the eye. He thought that I would be angry with him, that I would reject him. He thought that I would tell him he'd been irresponsible and that I would no longer want to be his friend. He said, 'Elton, will you forgive me?' I was stunned. I replied, 'What do you mean, forgive you? There's nothing to forgive. You haven't done anything wrong. You're my friend and I love you.' Here he was, feeling scared about the disease, ashamed to tell an old friend, and upset with himself for contracting HIV all at once. This is the danger of stigma. You can't overestimate what a powerful force it is.

And it's a very old force, at that. AIDS is not the first disease to be stigmatised, of course. Not by a long shot. Venereal diseases such as syphilis, for example, have long been stigmatised as an indication of a person's sexual and moral life. Throughout history, people with syphilis were shunned and scorned. In the United States, for instance, immigrant populations were singled out as particularly prone to the disease and likely to spread it. People who already hated immigrants had one more reason to loathe them.

Even non-venereal diseases have long been stigmatised. In 1832 a cholera epidemic broke out in New York neighbourhoods where poor, ethnic minorities and immigrants were concentrated. It was thought that the disease was spread by 'immoral' sexual behaviour and alcohol use. And the cramped, dirty, and unhygienic quarters in which these impoverished communities resided – and which certainly contributed to the spread of disease – became the subject of society's contempt, instead of its concern. Rich people thought of cholera as something that only impacted the poor. Thus, it went untreated. This lack of compassion, rooted in stigma, allowed cholera to eventually spread unchecked to the general population. Of course, it wasn't until the disease went mainstream that society started to do something about it.[8]

A century and a half later, the AIDS epidemic followed a similar course. It began in the 1980s as a 'gay disease.' At the time, homophobia kept the U.S. government from allowing funding for any educational programmes or materials that included instructions on how to have safe homosexual sex. Thanks to people such as Senator Jesse Helms, federal funding was banned for any AIDS education materials that seemed to support or encourage, even indirectly, 'homosexual activities.'[9] In other words, you couldn't teach gay men how to have safe sex. Of course, this allowed HIV to spread, and spread, and spread. Had the government cared about gay people, had homosexuals not been so stigmatised, the epidemic could have been, to some extent, contained. But the government didn't care about gays, HIV spread uncontrollably, and we are suffering the impact of that indifference to this day.

Sadly, governments haven't yet learned the fundamental lesson that to beat an infectious disease you must treat everyone equally, with compassion, and with dignity. I was reminded of this while on the European leg of my concert tour in 2010. Reading the paper over breakfast one morning, I came across a horrible story. In Malawi, Tiwonge Chimbalanga, a transgender woman, and Steven Monjeza, a man, had each been sentenced to fourteen years of hard labour in prison. They had been prosecuted for committing 'indecent acts.' Their crime had been nothing more than being in love.

I was stunned and disgusted. Malawi has a terrible AIDS epidemic, one of the worst anywhere. Almost 12 per cent of the population between the ages of fifteen and forty-nine is HIV-positive. More than 50,000 people die of AIDS each year. That's why EJAF has worked in Malawi since 1998, assisting with treatment and prevention efforts. In 2006, we co-funded an effort by Médecins Sans Frontières in the district of Thyolo to help the government provide universal access to treatment for all HIV-positive Malawians. It has been a great success, in no small part because of the government's own policy of non-discrimination when it comes to access to care. Everyone should theoretically be able to get treatment, including gays.

When I learned of the persecution and prosecution of Chimbalanga and Monjeza, my first thought was of the terrible injustice of their situation. I then thought of the destructive impact the government's actions would have on our HIV treatment and prevention work in Malawi. With the threat of prosecution looming, gay people would be far less likely to seek treatment through a government programme. By stigmatising a subgroup, by making a legal example of them, the Malawian government was driving AIDS further into the shadows, perpetuating the epidemic they were hoping to end. This sort of state-sanctioned discrimination costs lives, and it was counter to the work EJAF was funding in Malawi. I didn't keep these thoughts to myself, of course; I wrote an open letter to the Malawian president, Bingu wa Mutharika, that was published by *The Guardian*. Luckily, Chimbalanga and Monjeza were pardoned, and they were spared their unjust sentences.

Reading about Chimbalanga and Monjeza, I also couldn't help but think back to the day I was legally bound to the man I love. David and I had been together at that point for twelve years. It was important to both of us to obtain our civil partnership on the very first day it became legal in Britain: 21 December 2005. We went to the town hall in Windsor, and honestly we weren't sure what to expect. We thought some hateful people might react negatively to the idea of same-sex partnerships. We worried they might take out their bigotry on us. And we were happy, and very relieved, when we received nothing but warm wishes on that special day. Not one hateful or bigoted sentiment was expressed. And it's been that way ever since.

David and I are an openly gay couple, very much in love, very much in the public eye, and people treat us wonderfully everywhere in the world, from Africa to Asia to the Middle East. Of course, we aren't your ordinary gay couple. We are celebrities, and I know we're treated differently because of it. And yet, the acceptance David and I are very fortunate to experience makes me hopeful that, one day, gay people everywhere will be embraced for who they are and treated just the same as we are treated, and just the same as straight couples are treated. All people, including Chimbalanga and Monjeza, should be allowed to love each other openly and in peace the way David and I do. Unfortunately, the vast majority of gay people around the world suffer some degree of homophobia. In fact, homosexuality is banned in too many places to name. Gay sex is a crime in more than seventy-six countries.[10]

Discrimination against gays is wrong, but it's so much more than that. Homophobia harms everyone in the societies in which it is prevalent, because it hinders health education, it frustrates activities that could help prevent the spread of HIV, and it discourages people from seeking treatment. In Uganda, for instance, a radio station was fined when one of its programmes discussed the need for HIV/AIDS services for gay men.[11] In India, people have been arrested, beaten, and charged under anti-sodomy laws for giving out information on safe sex.[12] Gay people in many African countries are at greater risk of contracting the disease because they are less likely to receive information and treatment.

Fighting homophobia is central to fighting AIDS, because the stigma associated with being gay prevents the response we need to beat the disease.

To understand this, consider the AIDS epidemic in Thailand, as detailed in a recent report by amfAR.[13]

Many Asian countries, including Thailand, have been waging war against AIDS for decades, and some have made some real progress. But almost all of them have failed to make a dent in the spread of AIDS among gay men because homosexuality in many Asian communities is terribly stigmatised. This has certainly been the case in Thailand.

In the mid-'80s, Thailand's Ministry of Public Health knew of only forty-three reported AIDS cases. There were almost no prevention efforts in place, as the government didn't think of AIDS as a real problem. In 1987, the official rate of AIDS was almost zero. But by 1989, it had risen to between 18 and 52 per cent among different groups of injection drug users. In just one year, from June 1988 to late 1989, the rate went from zero to 43 per cent among female sex workers in Chiang Mai.

Naturally, the government took notice. They smartly instituted a range of prevention efforts, including a condom campaign that was estimated to prevent 8 million new infections. They were aggressive and successful. Rates of extramarital sex went down. Brothel visits decreased. Condom use increased. The results were meaningful and led to a dramatic decline in new HIV infections, from 143,000 new infections in 1991 to 19,000 in 2003. In 2004, the global AIDS community convened in Bangkok at the XV International AIDS Conference, in part to mark Thailand's successful response and tout it as an example to be replicated elsewhere.

But here's the problem: the government's anti-AIDS campaigns never targeted men who have sex with men. That was too uncomfortable, too taboo. And so this community in Thailand was ignored. It's no surprise, then, that things kept getting worse. Men continued to have unprotected sex with each other. They continued to contract HIV at alarming rates. They continued to die. While HIV infection rates among other groups in Thailand were going down, the infection rate for men who had sex with men in Bangkok was sky-rocketing. In 2003, it was over 17 per cent. By 2005, 28 per cent were HIV-positive.

To me, Thailand is a perfect example of what's wrong with today's AIDS response. It's a perfect example of how stigma spreads AIDS. The government of Thailand saw a problem. They saw their people getting sick and dying. To their great credit, they reached out to marginalised populations and the general public alike. They provided critical prevention information and programmes to drug users, prostitutes, and the poor. It's amazing, really, how much of an effort the government made to reach traditionally stigmatised populations.

But the stigma against homosexuality ran so deep that it could not be overcome. And for that reason, among others, Thailand still has a very serious AIDS epidemic on its hands.

When it comes to homophobia, what's true in the developing world is true of Western countries as well. According to the CDC, the only group in the United States with HIV rates that significantly increased between 2006 and 2009 were gay and bisexual men, and particularly black gay and bisexual men under the age of thirty.[14] And it's no surprise. Homosexuality is still incredibly stigmatised in America, and particularly in the African American community.

There are so many stigmas to confront, so many that must be peeled back to expose the reality of the AIDS epidemic. Many of them relate to sex or sexual identity. After all, sex is how HIV is most commonly spread. But it's also spread through injection drug use, which is responsible for some 9 per cent of new HIV infections in the United States. Sharing needles is common among addicts. Needles cost money, after all, and when you're hooked on heroin, your only thought is being able to afford the drug itself. Why buy a needle when you can borrow one? Tragically, this is how so many people have contracted HIV, by sharing a needle with someone who has the virus.

Fortunately, there's a very easy way to prevent the spread of HIV among those who use injection drugs. Needle exchange programmes provide clean needles to active drug users. It's a straightforward and inexpensive means of preventing new cases of HIV. It's also effective in fighting addiction, because most needle exchange programmes serve as a bridge for people to enter drug treatment. That's exactly what we need to get people off drugs and to curb the spread of HIV all at once. The world's first needle exchange programme was set up as early as 1984 in Amsterdam. Thanks to a robust effort of needle exchange and widespread HIV testing, counselling, and drug treatment programmes in Amsterdam, over time there have been significant reductions not only in HIV but also in diseases such as hepatitis B.[15] Needle exchange programmes have had amazing success in that city and many others.

Needle exchange clearly works. But in the United States, it's against the law for the federal government to spend money on needle exchange programmes. And there is only one reason for such a ridiculous policy: stigma.

Many American politicians are opposed to such programmes on moral or political grounds. They don't like the idea of using tax dollars for a service that helps rather than punishes drug users, even if doing so prevents the spread of a deadly disease and helps transition active users off drugs. Conservative members of Congress have successfully blocked federal funding for needle exchange programmes for two decades, despite the fact that studies by government health agencies, including the National Institutes of Health, have found that these programmes really work.[16] In 2009, Congress finally voted to allow federal support for needle exchange. Unfortunately, in 2012, Congress reinstated its ban for political reasons.

A national, federally funded needle exchange programme in America could prevent 4,000 new HIV infections per year. It could drastically reduce the incidence of AIDS. It could also drastically curb drug use. For heaven's sake, it could even save money spent on law enforcement, hospitalisation for the uninsured, and treatment programmes for those living with HIV. It would pay for itself. But thanks to the stigma surrounding drug use, the U.S. government willfully ignores the health and well-being of vulnerable addicts. It ignores the reality of drugs and AIDS in America. This costs lives in a very real, and very tragic, way.

Even in America, even after thirty years of the AIDS epidemic, even after the tremendous progress we've made in understanding and treating HIV/AIDS, the stigma surrounding the disease is significant. Today, thirty-four

American states have criminal laws that punish HIV-positive people for exposing another person to the virus – even if there's no actual risk, no actual transmission. Too many HIV-positive people are now in prison, serving absurdly long sentences, for alleged 'crimes' such as biting and spitting. It doesn't matter that there's no way to transmit HIV through saliva. The stigma is so bad that it has warped the nation's laws and ruined countless lives.

In 2011, I saw an incredible short film, 'HIV Is Not a Crime,' which was produced and directed by Sean Strub, a longtime AIDS activist and a real hero of the movement. It tells heartbreaking stories of Americans whose lives have been destroyed thanks to legal prosecution based on their HIV status.[17]

Nick Rhoades, for example, had an undetectable viral load, used a condom, and did not transmit HIV to his partner. However, he and his partner later broke up, they became estranged, and his ex-partner pressed charges against Nick on grounds of his HIV status alone. Nick was charged with a class B felony, which is on par with manslaughter and kidnapping. He was convicted, sentenced to twenty-five years in prison, and deemed a lifetime sex offender. Of his trial and sentencing, Nick said, 'HIV. Gay. Sex. It's like a gift, wrapped up on a platter [for prosecutors]. It doesn't matter what the facts are or the science.'

Ultimately, Nick was spared the twenty-five-year sentence and instead put on five years of probation. He had to register as a sex offender every three months, he couldn't visit social networking websites, and he had to wear a GPS ankle bracelet to be monitored twenty-four hours a day. For being HIV-positive, he was treated like a fully fledged criminal.

Sean's film also tells the story of a woman, Monique, who had been prosecuted under a similar law. While she insisted on safe sex, she hadn't disclosed her HIV status to her partner. Monique was afraid of the stigma surrounding HIV in her community. She was later prosecuted for not telling her partner that she was HIV-positive. Monique's prosecution only validated her worst fears about how society would respond to her disease.

The stigma surrounding AIDS creates a vicious and deadly cycle. It encourages those with HIV to hide their status because they are afraid of being not only ostracised but also criminalised. It encourages society to blame those with HIV. It rationalises pre-existing prejudices. It stymies the response we need to curb the epidemic. Indeed, it causes the epidemic to spread. In fact, stigma is a major reason why the epidemic is worsening among certain populations, even while we're making progress among others.

Is it any wonder there is a high incidence of AIDS among injection drug users in countries where injection drug use is stigmatised? Is it any wonder rape is a major cause of HIV transmission in South Africa, where rape itself is a cause of shame for women and a reality that society long refused to acknowledge, let alone confront?

In one article I read, the head of the Northeast Florida AIDS Network in Jacksonville said that she had trouble finding office space for the organisation. Landlords refused to rent to them because they didn't want people with AIDS in their buildings.[18] Is it any wonder, then, that Jacksonville, Florida, has the third highest rate of new AIDS cases among American cities? Is it any wonder that some 240,000 Americans have HIV but don't know it, when HIV has been criminalised in the majority of American states? Who would want to know their HIV status when testing positive could land them behind bars?

In a twisted way, it all makes sense. The places where stigma is the worst have the worst AIDS epidemics. That's because stigma itself prevents an appropriate response to the disease. It not only perpetuates the epidemic; stigma makes the epidemic impossible to beat.

But here's the thing: If the entire world, every government, every charity, every individual, decided tomorrow that needle exchange wasn't a bad thing, that we should, in fact, start needle exchange programmes all over the world, programmes that would reach every last injection drug user, we would eliminate the disease from that population. And yet AIDS would still exist in Uganda, where homosexuality is illegal and punishable by death. AIDS would still exist in Bangladesh, where female sex workers are denied their rights, are frequently victims of violence, and are almost totally unable to protect themselves from the disease because they are stigmatised. AIDS would still exist in South Africa, where HIV is spread largely through heterosexual sex and where the stigma around sexual violence complicates society's response.

Unless we eradicate stigma everywhere, we will never eradicate AIDS everywhere.

7

The Heart of the Matter

I'm far from the first person to preach the importance of compassion, indeed the *need* for compassion, when it comes to combating AIDS. Long before I ever got into this work, many brilliant, dedicated professionals from all around the world were orchestrating a compassionate response to the epidemic. I'm simply, and humbly, following in their footsteps. And while I would never suggest that I'm an AIDS expert, I have seen quite a lot through the work of my foundation.

Over the years, I've had the opportunity to meet some of the greatest heroes in the global fight against AIDS. They include my many extraordinary colleagues around the world who are in the trenches, day after day. I've been lucky enough to travel the world and visit dozens of projects that EJAF has funded. I've seen the difference these heroes are making. Compassion is a nice sentiment, but it's so much more than that. I've seen with my own eyes what's possible when compassion is put into practice. The organisations that my foundation supports have made incredible progress in fighting stigma and AIDS through their compassionate policies and programmes.

I try to spread this message everywhere I go, and it's not always well received. In 2007, my foundation organised a free concert in Ukraine to raise awareness about the terrible AIDS crisis in that country. Sadly, religious groups encouraged people to boycott us. They believed that gay people were responsible for the spread of AIDS and that I was promoting homosexual propaganda. Nevertheless, on the day of the concert, from behind my piano that June evening, I was stunned and overjoyed to see hundreds of thousands of people, including many religious leaders, packed into Independence Square in Kiev. They were undeterred by the bigotry and the stigma surrounding homosexuality and AIDS. I told the crowd that I was there to support their country's fight against HIV/AIDS, and I asked them to find the courage to show love and support to all those living with the disease. The crowd roared, and it filled me with hope. It made me think of how far we'd come since EJAF had first started working in Ukraine, five years earlier, in 2002.

Ukraine has the worst epidemic of HIV/AIDS in Eastern Europe, with more than 400,000 people infected and the fastest-growing rate of new infections in the world. The epidemic there is a classic example of how stigma and fear work hand in hand with the disease, spreading it further, killing people faster.

Sixty per cent of infected Ukrainians are tragically young, between the ages of twenty and thirty-four. At the greatest risk are 100,000 homeless young people in major cities such as Kiev, Odessa, and Donetsk. You'll find them sprawled on crumbling streets or in abandoned buildings, relics of the Soviet era. Many of them turn to prostitution to survive; 35 per cent of those who do have HIV/AIDS. Others numb their painful lives by injecting cheaply concocted drugs, like a cocktail called 'screw' made of surgical liquid, cough syrup, and the phosphorous tips of matches. More than 40 per cent of these drug-addicted, homeless youths are HIV-positive.[1]

These young people, and many other HIV-positive Ukrainians around the country, have often been treated with contempt by religious groups, by their communities, by people who think AIDS is brought on by sin. They are shunned. Spat upon. Ostracised. Made to feel worthless. Having your humanity wholly rejected because of whatever you're going through is the worst thing that can happen to you. As I've said, not to be cared for or cared about, not to even be thought about, is the most painful feeling a human being can ever experience. To make people feel as though they are completely on their own in their struggles, that they are invisible to everybody else, regardless of their circumstances, is utterly inhumane. For far too long, this was exactly the plight of those who were sick and dying of AIDS in Ukraine.

The Ukrainian government was not entirely indifferent to the problem. In 2000, the authorities paid it appropriate lip service, calling the situation a national emergency. But what happened next, unfortunately, is what happens in many other countries. The government developed an unsound, incoherent, and underfunded policy framework to combat the disease. It was a plan in name only. They made fancy-sounding decrees, passed a few laws, created a few programmes. But on the ground, in the lives of real people – especially stigmatised people – nothing happened. Nothing changed.

In the meantime, the disease spread. Prostitutes, drug users, gay people, young people, all of whom had the highest rates of the disease, were afraid to seek treatment. Who would, in the face of such bigotry? Gay men in particular were terrified of what would happen if they came out of the shadows. Those who did were basically told, 'There's nothing we can do for you. Go home and die.'

When EJAF first started working in Ukraine, there were only a few clinics where people could safely get the care they needed. One such safe haven was the Lavra Clinic in Kiev, right next door to the city's historic Orthodox church, the Kiev-Pechersk Lavra, or Monastery of the Caves. People with HIV/AIDS from all over Ukraine did whatever it took – walked, bused, hitchhiked, crawled, used all their savings – to make their way to Lavra for life-saving treatment in a supportive and non-discriminatory environment.

But to address such a large and fast-growing epidemic, much more mobilisation was needed. So EJAF got involved with an amazing group called the All Ukrainian Network of People Living with HIV/AIDS, or AUKN for short. It's an organisation of HIV-positive people, some of the most marginalised in Ukraine, a group of ex-drug users, the pariahs, the hopeless. We worked with them for about three years to help build their organisation and set up a variety of programmes throughout the country. Initially, AUKN was reaching around 1,700 people each month. Today, their impact has grown more than thirtyfold, connecting some 57,000 people living with HIV/AIDS and 5,500 children affected by the disease with the services they need. As a network of people infected and affected by HIV themselves, they are also breaking down the stigma and discrimination that serve as barriers to treatment by reaching 53,000 prisoners with HIV testing.

AUKN embodies a critical tenet of EJAF's work. You have to go where the disease is. You have to look squarely at the darkest realities of our society and find those who are at the fringes, who are suffering the most. These are the people who need our help. And, as it turns out, these are also the people who can alter the course of the epidemic.

By 2007, AUKN was widely respected and hailed for its successful work. In fact, when the Ukrainian Ministry of Health was shown to be so corrupt that the Global Fund to Fight AIDS, Tuberculosis, and Malaria wouldn't finance its AIDS programmes, AUKN stepped in. The Global Fund selected AUKN as Ukraine's official recipient of a major grant to fight AIDS. This network of the dispossessed now manages the Global Fund's $51.9 million AIDS treatment and care budget for all of Ukraine! Of course, they were able to do this because, years earlier, EJAF saw them not only as people who deserve better but also as agents of change. Our compassion was empowering to them. And they became quite powerful, indeed. AUKN, working with a consortium of partners including the William J. Clinton Foundation, was able to successfully force the government to reform the notoriously corrupt drug procurement process in

Ukraine. As a result, the price of AIDS medicines dropped 90 per cent, doubling the number of people the government could afford to treat.

Working with AUKN and witnessing their incredible achievements encouraged us to get involved with other organisations in Ukraine. Today, we are also supporting training for child-care specialists to work with HIV-positive children across the country. And we're funding the establishment of six sites specifically to provide services for gay men, who will be able to get information, condoms, and referrals for testing and treatment. In a country that still deals with rampant homophobia, this is a huge breakthrough.

The head of AUKN and many of its founding members came to my 2007 concert in Kiev. It was the first chance I had to meet them in person. The founder of AUKN told Anne Aslett, the executive director of EJAF in the United Kingdom, and me, 'When no one else wanted to have anything to do with us, it was the Elton John AIDS Foundation that believed in us, that believed that our group played a central role in the solution to the problem.' Now, the Ukrainian government lauds their work. The international community acknowledges their achievements. They're making important progress on the ground.

That's the power of compassion. That's the virtuous

cycle we must replicate the world over in order to beat the AIDS epidemic.

One of the places most in need of such a virtuous cycle is Haiti, where extreme poverty and the stigma surrounding sexual identity complicate that country's vicious AIDS epidemic. One of EJAF's grantees in Haiti is an organisation called Fondation SEROvie. Since 1997, SEROvie has been the first and only institution in Haiti to provide health services to – and advocate for the rights of – lesbian, gay, bisexual, and transgender (LGBT) people. By focusing on both health care and human rights, SEROvie is trying to break the cycle of discrimination, poverty, and AIDS in a country with an extremely high HIV infection rate of 1.9 per cent.

My foundation first got involved with SEROvie in 2007, through our partnership with an amfAR initiative targeting men who have sex with men around the world. It's another example of our lessons learned at work: connect with reputable organisations that have enormous reach, like amfAR, and build partnerships on the ground with other groups, like SEROvie, that know exactly what people need and how resources should be spent.

In the Haitian capital, Port-au-Prince, SEROvie does everything from distributing condoms to sending peer educators to the homes of HIV-infected people. This is difficult work in an impoverished society with tremendous stigma against gay and transgender people. Many of SEROvie's clients are already very poor and therefore more likely to engage in risky, transactional sex to earn money. Through our partnership with amfAR, we supported SEROvie's vocational training programme to give young men the skills they need to support themselves in a healthy way instead. This was just one of the many amazing projects the organisation was running.

But everything changed at 4:53 p.m. on 12 January 2010, when a 7.0-magnitude earthquake reduced much of Port-au-Prince to rubble. SEROvie's executive director, Steeve Laguerre, has since described the horror of that moment: 'We were having our usual support group meeting on a quiet Tuesday afternoon when the worst happened. The sound is unforgettable. I can't even describe the horror as the ceiling and the wall of the conference room started to fall and the chaos started.'[2] That day, SEROvie lost fourteen of its staff members.

The earthquake exacerbated the already overwhelming AIDS crisis in Haiti. Many HIV/AIDS clinics were destroyed, many health workers were killed. Almost no one could get access to badly needed medication. It wasn't too long afterward that the executive director of EJAF in the United States, Scott Campbell, went to

Haiti to see first hand just how bad things were. What he witnessed was heart-breaking and deeply frustrating. But he also saw cause for hope. Since the earthquake flattened SEROvie's home, the staff was operating out of tents. They were relentless. No amount of tragedy or turmoil could keep them down. They had not given up.

At the same time, their work was harder than ever. When the infrastructure of the country was decimated, the LGBT community, which was already marginalised, became further isolated. They lost their support networks and safe spaces. As one lesbian in Port-au-Prince said, 'Loneliness, invisibility, and social isolation are persistent problems for us.'[3] SEROvie had always been a haven for these stigmatised populations, and now even that was gone. Family and friends who previously provided support and shelter were scattered. Try to imagine how terrifying it would be to live in a place where your only protection from violence and bigotry was the lock on the door of your home. Now try to imagine the fear when that home – with its door and its lock – came crashing down. When he visited, Scott said the fear was palpable.

The discrimination that the LGBT community faced after the earthquake is hard to stomach. Many gay men reported physical assault, rape, and even being denied aid. One young gay man named Lengemy told SEROvie that he was kicked out of an emergency food distribution line.[4] Can you imagine that, in the midst of one of the worst humanitarian crises ever experienced by a country, people were being denied the basic necessities for survival because of prejudice, because of sexual orientation?

Some of this, strangely enough, was a function of good intentions. As a matter of general disaster policy, food aid is distributed only to women because they are more likely to get it to family members. But many gay men don't have women in their families. When SEROvie sent a letter to the American Red Cross requesting an exception to that policy, the organisation was told to consult with the Haitian Red Cross, because they couldn't give targeted assistance to specific minority populations. Believing that the Haitian Red Cross wouldn't help, SEROvie didn't bother.[5]

Still, SEROvie kept serving the people who flocked to them. In the face of incredible challenges, not the least of which was being forced to operate out of tents, the organisation quickly reassembled and got to work. Steeve Laguerre says that the key to success is to listen to what people want and need – or, to put it another way, to demonstrate compassion to those who are suffering. Initially, SEROvie spent a lot of time and resources providing counselling and distributing what little rice, cornmeal, and cooking oil they had. Then they shifted their focus to other basic needs like shelter and safety. To prevent the spread of waterborne diseases brought on after the earthquake, they taught their clients about decontaminating water, keeping their living spaces clean, and using mosquito nets. They also continued their work to prevent the spread of HIV/AIDS. EJAF is now helping SEROvie to establish an HIV testing and counselling clinic in its Port-au-Prince office, the only clinic in Haiti that will address the specific needs of the LGBT community.

Like many of the successful programmes that EJAF partners with, SEROvie addresses its clients as whole people. They look at their needs and help them live their lives with self-respect and dignity. Whether that involves giving them the means to access affordable housing, the confidence and skills to find good work, or the discipline to take their medicine every day, SEROvie treats each individual as worthy of care. As a result, they are able to help address other aspects of people's lives that make them vulnerable to HIV/AIDS, as well as many other diseases.

Despite how much time has passed since the 2010 earthquake, life is still extremely challenging for LGBT Haitians, especially those living with HIV/AIDS. While he was in Port-au-Prince, Scott heard the most horrific stories. One man was reportedly raped by four other men – but when he went to the police to report the attack, they laughed at him. They said that since he was gay, he must have enjoyed it.

I can't imagine what it must be like to keep waking up every day to help another client with a dreadful situation. To fight another battle with the authorities. To do impossible work in impossible circumstances. But SEROvie keeps going – and they're making progress. They have stepped up their advocacy efforts and are training government officials, law enforcement, and others to reduce the stigma and discrimination their clients face. They are working relentlessly toward a society that protects, not persecutes, its citizens living with HIV/AIDS. They are trying to start a virtuous cycle, and EJAF will continue to help them do so.

We're also hoping to trigger such cycles in America. There, the AIDS epidemic is very different from Haiti's, but not as different as you might think. As it turns out, in developing and developed countries alike, the fight against AIDS comes down to compassion.

I love the American South, where I've spent much of my life. I am always blown away by how beautiful that part of the country is. There's something especially magical about Southwest Louisiana. Cypress trees that frame the haunting bayou. Flooded rice paddies and lonely prairies without a house or a living soul for miles. It's one of the most rural places in America. And as with much of rural America, there is a quiet but deadly AIDS crisis that has been simmering for decades. Nearly 1,000 people in this one small corner of Louisiana are HIV-positive. They are among the poorest, most marginalised people in the nation. And they are mostly African American.

The HIV/AIDS epidemic is raging in the African American community nationally, and especially in the South. As I've said, almost half of all HIV diagnoses are among African Americans. Shockingly, AIDS is a leading killer of African American women aged twenty-five to forty-four, accounting for roughly 11 per cent of all deaths in this demographic. That's why EJAF has invested heavily in projects around the United States that target African Americans as well as other communities that are still disproportionately impacted by AIDS.

Now, it's one thing to be in a major city with basic facilities. It's quite another to be sick and alone in the middle of nowhere. Frankly, I wonder if most Americans know how bad it is for some people in the rural South. Take Loretta. She was thirty-three years old and a single mother when she found out that she was HIV-positive. Her ex-husband had been incarcerated. She was already chronically depressed; with her HIV diagnosis, she was terrified of what would happen to her. Who would care for her three sons?

Loretta is like a lot of women in Southwest Louisiana. Young, African American, from a poor family. Many don't get the education they need, and many drop out of school, get married young, or have children while they're still teenagers. These women are at high risk for contracting HIV.

As recently as 2008, emergency rooms in Southwest Louisiana were clogging up with people admitted with late-stage AIDS. The scenes of emaciated people who had wasted away from the disease looked more like something you would expect to see in sub-Saharan Africa, not America. In an age when antiretrovirals are widely available in the richest country in the world, people were needlessly dying. They still are. It's no wonder that Loretta was paralysed with fear by her diagnosis.

In response to the crisis in Southwest Louisiana, Terry Estes, the executive director of the Southwest Louisiana AIDS Council (SLAC), and Dr Carlos Choucino, the medical director of the Comprehensive Care Clinic in Lake Charles, Louisiana, decided they needed to develop better ways to reach people living with HIV/ AIDS. They learned from research that 'navigator' models, where people are guided to get access to comprehensive services, are very successful with AIDS patients. So, in 2008, SLAC and the Comprehensive Care Clinic partnered to identify patients throughout the region who needed access to care, especially in nearby rural areas.

Loretta was referred to SLAC and immediately connected with Angela Hursey, the organisation's health system navigator. Angela is an amazing woman, one of the many heroes doing battle on the front lines of the AIDS epidemic. She personally connects with every client who walks through the door, and she becomes a fierce advocate for his or her health and welfare. She believes in her clients, and in turn helps her clients to believe in themselves.

It's this sort of individual attention that makes all the difference. People living with AIDS often feel like statistics – and it's no wonder, because that is how they're treated most of the time. But at SLAC, Angela insists on treating her clients like human beings, with individual needs, concerns, challenges, and circumstances. This sounds simple and obvious, yet it's all too rare in healthcare settings. I can relate to the need for individual attention and care, because that was what really helped me to get clean and to stay sober. Being treated with dignity, with compassion, like a real person with individual struggles, is what empowered me to turn my life around.

Whenever someone like Loretta walks into SLAC, Angela's first order of business is to get the person immediate access to care. She will literally take her clients to the hospital screening office so they can figure out what kind of financial assistance they might be able to get. She'll walk them to the lab to get tested. She'll go with them to their first doctor's appointment. She'll do whatever it takes to get them to take control of their health. If they stop going to their appointments or taking their medication, she'll pick them back up and walk them through the process all over again. After her clients are stable, she'll hand them over to a medical case manager to keep track of their progress.

I have to pause for a moment to point something out. EJAF is thrilled to have SLAC as our grantee. And we're grateful for the many other philanthropists who help fund their work. But SLAC and other groups like them would not be able to operate without the funding and assistance provided by the Ryan White CARE Act. I am deeply touched, and grateful, that Ryan's name is attached to this extraordinary work.

And it really is extraordinary, and very much needed, because it's still the case that in communities across America people with AIDS are sometimes treated like dirt. If they're gay, it can be even worse. They're so afraid of the judgement of their communities, even their families, that they won't get tested. Despite how far we've come, people in America today still experience the abuses that Ryan suffered. That's why some HIV-positive people travel hours from their homes to get help from SLAC. The organisation works hard to make clients whose families have ostracised them feel safe.

Thanks to SLAC and its dedicated caseworkers like Angela, Loretta started managing her disease. She went back to school to finish her GED. Today, she volunteers with SLAC, facilitating a women's support group. She even has her own office space, where she mentors other people who are struggling to come to terms with HIV/ AIDS.

Loretta is doing what Ryan did. She is taking her experience, her story, and sharing it with others. She is using it to help them get through this incredibly difficult experience. She's a living reminder that we cannot simply treat the disease; we must treat the person.

When confronted with an enormous crisis like AIDS, it's easy to feel helpless. And in the face of huge numbers – millions of people infected, billions of dollars spent – it's easy to feel, as an individual, or even as an organisation, that we can't make a difference. But SLAC is an example of how a relatively small amount of money can go a really long way when compassion is at the centre of our efforts.

This is true for all marginalised populations, everywhere. Take the formerly incarcerated, for instance. They are among the most marginalised populations in the United States. And the formerly incarcerated who are HIV-positive are even further marginalised.

In New York, after an HIV-positive prisoner finishes his sentence, he's whisked away from an upstate detention facility and dropped off at the Port Authority bus station in Manhattan. He's usually given no more than $50, three days of medication, and a list of social service organisations that might be able to help.

Imagine: You are standing all alone by the bus or the subway. You haven't been outside the walls of prison, let alone in the middle of Midtown, in years. You have nowhere to go, maybe no one to call. And the clock has started ticking – you have seventy-two hours until your medication runs out.

For Carl, after twenty-four years in prison, that experience made him feel like he was Rip van Winkle, waking up to a whole new world. Everybody around him was talking into a mobile phone. He had used a token the last time he rode the subway; what on earth was a MetroCard?

The world had changed, and so had Carl. He was infected with HIV in prison, and he left with AIDS.

Carl was luckier than many; someone he 'ran with' picked him up from the Port Authority. They spent the next three days driving around to every single organisation on the list he was given when he was released from prison. At all of these places, places that were supposed to help him, he heard the same thing: 'Where's your Medicaid card?'

Carl had been released without any documentation of his HIV status, and since he didn't have Medicaid, there were few places he could go to be tested. He waited hours at a city agency to apply for public assistance in order to get the funds he needed to buy medication, but there was a forty-five-day waiting period to determine if he was eligible for benefits.

Carl's story is all too common. The United States imprisons a higher percentage of its population than any other nation in the world: more than 2.3 million people, or 1 in every 104 adults. Almost a quarter of the world's prisoners are in America. And as of December 2008, about 1.5 per cent of all prisoners in the nation were HIV-positive. When these HIV-positive prisoners re-enter society, very few are connected with services to give them stability and support while they figure out how to handle their health and their new lives.

That was the case for Carl. He was overwhelmed, exhausted, and almost totally defeated when he showed up late in the afternoon at Bailey House, a halfway house in East Harlem for people living with HIV/AIDS. By the time he walked through the front door, he was out of medication and he was a ball of anxiety. That's when Carl met Chris Olin, a caseworker for Project FIRST at Bailey House – another real-life hero. Chris is one of those exceptional people. You know, those people who just immediately put you at ease. Chris said to Carl, 'I've got this for you.'

It can be paralysing to be in the throes of your own crisis. I remember that feeling when I walked into rehab, like I had no control over anything that was happening to me, like I didn't know where to begin. When I was told not to worry, when I was told that people were going to help me, it was like an enormous weight lifted off my chest. Suddenly I had a chance to get better, because I wasn't alone any more.

I imagine that's how Carl felt when he met Chris. It was the first moment in a long time, maybe ever, that Carl had been treated with such dignity. That his anxiety, the trauma in his life, had been acknowledged. That somebody had his back and said, 'I'm with you.' That's when everything changed for Carl.

Project FIRST stands for Formerly Incarcerated

Rental Support and Training, and it's a programme run by Bailey House to support HIV-positive ex-offenders who are homeless or in danger of becoming homeless. It helps people like Carl with whatever they need to get back on their feet, to stay healthy, and to stay out of trouble. Within the first few weeks, Project FIRST connects their clients with a rental assistance programme run by the City of New York. Because of the flexible funding that EJAF and others provide, Bailey House is able to cover necessities such as security deposits and first month's rent, so that clients can get into safe housing immediately. After all, if you don't have anywhere to lay your head at night, how are you going to get the rest of your life together?

My foundation has been supporting this project at Bailey House since 2007, and we couldn't be happier with how far they've come. Since Project FIRST got off the ground in 2003, they have successfully placed more than two hundred people in permanent housing, and they have also connected them to the care they need to ensure their health and well-being. Many are still in the same apartments.

To me, Project FIRST is a tremendously efficient weapon against the AIDS crisis in New York City. We know that ex-offenders leave prison with dispro-portionately high rates of HIV. We know that they often don't have a way to get the medical care they need, let alone a place to live. We know that their lack of job opportunities makes it all the more likely that they could slip back into risky sex, drug abuse, and other behaviour that would put them in danger of spreading the disease or land them back in detention. Common sense says, let's address all of these problems quickly – let's not be afraid to help the very people who need the most help. Let's not let stigma get in the way.

One of the things I love most about Project FIRST is that the programme does more than fight AIDS; it helps people in the most basic ways. Caseworkers like Chris walk clients through the system and show them how to do everyday things such as open a bank account and figure out where they can go grocery shopping. They help clients get back into the community, find a doctor, take their medications regularly, get vocational training, and start taking care of themselves. For instance, Chris connected Carl with a clinic where he could go for medical tests, treatment, and medications, and Chris also got the necessary documentation of Carl's AIDS status and income level to qualify him for housing assistance.

People who go through Bailey House's programme have much better health outcomes. And they are far less likely to end up back in the penal system. Typically, more than 40 per cent of U.S. prisoners wind up returning to state prison within the first three years of being released. Fewer than 10 per cent of Bailey House beneficiaries are reincarcerated.

A few months after meeting Chris, Carl walked back into Bailey House looking like he had just come off a golf course. The angry, anxious, and desperate ex-offender was now a dapper, healthy, employed man, wearing Bermuda shorts and a polo shirt, supporting himself, managing his HIV, and in a relationship with a woman he met at Bailey House. Today, Carl is mentoring fellow ex-offenders and doing peer outreach to get others living with HIV into care. He also testifies in front of the New York State Parole Board about the value of programmes such as Bailey House's. It's no wonder that he's willing to do so much for the organisation. As Carl has said many times, 'Chris and Bailey House saved my life.'

The Elton John AIDS Foundation has funded hundreds of projects. Each one operates a bit differently. Each does different work for different populations. But every project we fund has one thing in common: it is committed to a compassionate response and to fighting the stigma that spreads HIV/AIDS. The organisations target their work to the most marginalised populations, those who most need the services but are least likely to get them. They advocate against policies that promote discrimination. They shine a light on the taboo subjects that nobody wants to talk about but that have everything to do with this horrible disease. Most of all they treat each person they see in a holistic way.

That term, 'holistic,' is thrown around a lot in medical circles. You hear doctors talking about caring for the whole patient, seeing to all of his or her medical needs at once. With HIV/AIDS, as with most diseases, it's more than just the way the body itself works. So many people with the virus are also poor and vulnerable. They often need shelter, food, mental health services, employ-ment opportunities, and people to care for and support them. They need critical help at critical moments to ensure their disease doesn't come to define, or end, their lives.

It's crucial to treat every single person – regardless of background or circumstance or HIV status – as a whole person, as an individual with dreams to fulfil and goals to achieve. When we treat people as worthy of love, their worth is realised for all the world to see. Ultimately, this is the most powerful weapon we have against stigma, and indeed against AIDS.

Whether you are the richest man alive or you have absolutely nothing, you deserve to be treated with dignity and compassion. That is the insight that inspires the work of my foundation. And that, I have come to believe, is how we will end AIDS.

8

A Great Power

Every now and again, someone will ask if I get nervous on stage. Or they'll want to know about the most intimidating audience I've ever played to. At this point in my career, I've been lucky to perform at some of the world's most extraordinary venues, sometimes for audiences of half a million people. Every time I walk out on stage it's not nerves that I feel but the thrill of performing and the excitement of the crowd. I still love it after all these years. But there was one stage that made me nervous beyond belief. One audience that was more intimidating than any other. It wasn't a stadium concert with a sea of screaming fans. I can't ever recall being more nervous than on the day when I testified before the United States Senate.

It had been a decade since I created the foundation. As I said before, our intention was never to become one of the biggest AIDS organisations in the world – far from it. We were simply trying to help people in need. But, sadly, the need never ended; it grew steadily with each passing year. And so, in 2002, after ten years of doing this work, I had become – much to my surprise – a voice people listened to on the subject of fighting AIDS.

That's how I was summoned one day to Washington. I got word through EJAF that Senator Ted Kennedy intended to hold a hearing on the state of the AIDS epidemic and the international response to it, as part of his effort to increase funding for treatment programmes around the world. He planned to invite several witnesses to educate the Senate Health, Education, Labor, and Pensions Committee on the disease, and to make the case for a new appropriation of money. His office asked me to be one of them. I was deeply honoured by the invitation. And, from that moment on, I was extremely nervous as well.

I still remember our car driving up Pennsylvania Avenue toward Capitol Hill. I don't care how many times you see the U.S. Capitol Building; each and every time it is simply breath-taking. There's something about the way it was built, its very design, that exudes power and influence, and reminds you of the extraordinary history contained within.

Our car turned onto Constitution Avenue and headed up toward the Russell Senate Office Building. We got out and were greeted by a member of Ted Kennedy's staff – and a dozen reporters. We rushed quickly past them and into the grandeur of a Washington icon. The archways and columns. The marble statues. The awe-inspiring rotunda that echoed the noise of our shoes as we walked, adding a pointed sound of purpose to each step. We followed the staffer up one of two sweeping marble staircases. 'We're going to have breakfast and a small reception in the Caucus Room,' she told us. 'There are a lot of senators looking forward to meeting you.'

The Caucus Room, I was told, has an impressive history all its own. When the *Titanic* sank, this was where they held hearings to investigate what went wrong. It's where the Army–McCarthy hearings were held and where the Watergate hearings took place as well. And for reasons I swear I will never understand, it's where I was welcomed for a breakfast held in my honour. The room itself is something to behold. Pilasters from floor to ceiling in the classic Corinthian style. Imposing red curtains with gold fringe, draped across three massive windows. Century-old chandeliers and a ceiling with exceptional detail. It was enough to intimidate anyone, more than enough to intimidate me. And that was before I realised who was standing inside.

Senator Kennedy made a beeline toward me. We had never met before, but he shook my hand with both of his and embraced me as an old friend might. I've met a lot of famous people in my day, but shaking Ted Kennedy's hand was like touching history. He was a political icon from one of the most important families in America. The brother of President John F. Kennedy and of U.S. senator and attorney general Bobby Kennedy. A former presidential candidate himself and an extraordinary statesman. I wasn't sure what to say to such a man, but he instantly put me at ease.

The next thing I knew, I was shaking hands with Senator Orrin Hatch. Now, it's probably easy to imagine my not being a particularly big fan of Senator Hatch. He is an extremely conservative Republican from Utah, and we disagree on just about every issue I can imagine. But after Ryan's death, it was Senator Hatch who pushed for the Ryan White CARE Act. It was Senator Hatch who, with his friend Senator Kennedy, authored the bill. And it was the two of them together who ensured that the bill made it through Congress with bipartisan support. And so, in truth, as I stood there shaking Senator Hatch's hand, with Senator Kennedy just behind me, I was surrounded by AIDS heroes, by people who had used the power of their station to save millions of lives.

I met several other senators and members of Congress

before sitting down for breakfast, and I saw a few familiar faces, too. The International AIDS Trust was hosting the breakfast, and Sandy Thurman, my friend and its president, was there to greet me. Sandy is a legend in the AIDS advocacy community, and because she was based in Atlanta, I knew her well. In 1997, she had been named the director of the Office of National AIDS Policy at the White House by President Bill Clinton, a fitting choice for that critical job. She, too, would be testifying.

Deborah Dortzbach, the international director of the HIV/AIDS programmes for World Relief, was there as well. Our organisation had worked quite closely with hers. And there were others, also testifying, whom I knew by reputation but hadn't had a chance to meet until then. Dr Peter Mugyenyi, one of the world's most respected AIDS specialists, had come all the way from Kampala, Uganda, where he founded and directed a clinical research centre. Also present was a relentless advocate for women's health during the AIDS crisis, Dr Allan Rosenfield, the legendary dean of the Mailman School of Public Health at Columbia University.

These were, without question, some of the most respected leaders in the fight against AIDS. And there I was, a bit dumbfounded to be among them.

The outpouring of support I felt that day was

remarkable. It contrasted starkly with the early days of the disease, when fear and stigma kept AIDS deep in the shadows of American life. Here we were, many years later, in one of the most powerful places on earth, talking about what we could do to fight the disease together. I was very moved.

After breakfast, I was escorted by Ted Kennedy back to his office, where we were joined by Senator Hatch, Senator Patrick Leahy, Senator Bill Frist, and Senator Hillary Clinton for a candid conversation about how much money it would take to truly combat AIDS globally and what strategies we could employ to get it done. The perspectives in the room were amazing. These were not only U.S. senators; they were also leading experts in the fight against AIDS. In 1981, Bill Frist was a third-year surgical resident in Boston when reports of the disease started surfacing. To that point, doctors had considered blood to be mostly sterile; suddenly they knew it could be deadly. Frist had to radically alter his surgical procedures. Double gloves during surgery and eye protection. In the very early days, before there was treatment of any kind, Frist wouldn't make his assistants scrub in to work on an AIDS patient if they were afraid to; that's how little was known about the HIV virus then, how much fear persisted even in the medical community.[1]

Then there was Senator Clinton, who had travelled the globe as First Lady during the height of the AIDS crisis. She knew well that, by 2002, the AIDS epidemic abroad was very different from the one unfolding at home. She knew the stakes, because she had seen the effects herself. I was struck by how incredibly well educated all of the senators were on the crisis. Each and every one of them really knew what he or she was talking about. I was humbled by their respect for me and my work, their recognition that I wasn't just a rock star with a hobby. They were interested in my perspective, and I was honoured to share it with this group of distinguished leaders.

I had, by that point, got control of my nerves. The warmth I was shown certainly helped. And a good thing, too, because moments later, a staffer knocked on the door. 'Senator,' he said to Kennedy, 'it's time.'

The hearing room was smaller, but no less grand, than the Caucus Room. And it was absolutely packed with people. By then, I had broken off from the senators and was ushered down the aisle to a table up front, where those of us testifying would sit. As soon as I sat down in front of my name placard, I was surrounded by photo-journalists. How surreal that moment was. I'm no stranger to cameras, but there was something about the context that made it all feel very different. I was about to perform, but the stakes were higher than they'd ever been.

Above the flashing cameras I saw the senators enter the chamber and begin filling in the dais. 'The hearing will come to order,' said Ted Kennedy, who chaired the committee. The room fell quiet. 'We welcome our guests this morning, who bring to this issue the challenges that we are facing in international AIDS, a wealth of experience and an extraordinary sense of compassion, and a series of recommendations about how we as a country can be even more effective in giving this the kind of world priority that it deserves.'

Senator Kennedy then recognised his colleagues, who one by one gave their opening statements, each more poignant than the last. When they were finished, we were told that we had just about an hour for our testimony and that there would be questions from the senators after our statements. Sandy gave her statement first. It was beautiful, profoundly important, and extremely compelling.

Then it was my turn.

I thanked Senator Kennedy and the others for this honour – for asking my opinion, especially as a British man. And then I began to read from remarks I had prepared.

'I've worn many hats in my career, but the hat of

policy maker is not one of them,' I said. 'I will not take up your time to tell you facts and numbers you already know. Instead, I will tell you how I feel.'

I told them that it had been twelve years since we had lost Ryan White, how devastating it had been, but how extraordinary Congress's reaction to Ryan's death had been as well. 'The month Ryan died,' I said, 'this committee passed the Ryan White CARE Act that dramatically increased funding for care and treatment of people with AIDS. Mr Chairman, the rest of the world looks at this legislation as a sign of what America can do for its people. We are here today to explore what America can do for the world.'

I then tried to give them a sense of what my foundation had been able to accomplish internationally, the kind of projects we were funding, the kind of difference, in small ways, we were making. I told them about an AIDS hospice in Soweto, South Africa, that we'd established. 'Among people with AIDS, the greatest fear is not the fear of dying,' I told them, 'but the fear of dying alone. At our hospice, no one dies alone.

'But, Mr Chairman, our hospice in South Africa has eight beds, and the nation has more than four million people infected with HIV. We are doing everything we can with what we have, and we have comforted many people and saved many lives. But we have not done nearly enough. The people on the front lines fighting this disease need reinforcements, and they need them now.'

I called on Congress to increase funding for education and prevention, for voluntary testing and counselling, for care for those who were dying of AIDS, and for orphans.

'If the world is going to make a significant, decisive intervention to change the course of this pandemic, it's going to have to start here. And it might as well start now,' I said. 'When Ryan White was asked by a reporter if he had a message for medical researchers working on AIDS, he said, "Hurry up." We all need to hurry up. Every day we delay, we lose more lives, and we lose a little more of our humanity.'

The point I wanted to drive home was not only the urgency. It was the possibility. There really was something the United States could be doing, something profound. That is, if it chose to. This wasn't a case of wanting to solve an unsolvable problem. Millions of lives were on the line, and millions could be saved by the U.S. government.

'It's true that one nation cannot defeat AIDS in two hundred nations,' I admitted. 'But two hundred nations cannot defeat AIDS without the help of one. This one. If the U.S. does little, other nations will see in that an excuse to do little. If the United States does a lot, other nations will do a lot, because they will see in your resolve a new hope of victory. When the United States fights, it wins.'

With that, and a few more thank-yous, I concluded my remarks. I took a deep breath, inhaled the scene around me, and hoped that, just maybe, something I had said would make a difference, if only a small one.

When the hearing was over, Senator Kennedy invited us back to his office for a private gathering. The walls were lined with pictures of his famous brothers. It was a reminder that history is made by the people who stand up to make it. We walked outside on his balcony overlooking the Capitol and took it all in. I thought about what had happened that day, but more than that, I thought about what might happen tomorrow. I thought about the future, the next battle lines to be drawn in the fight against AIDS.

Senator Chris Dodd and a few others who had testified stood out there with us, and Senator Dodd thanked us for our commitment to ridding the world of the disease. During my testimony I had said that, while I wasn't a student of American government, it was my under-standing that there were two sides of Pennsylvania Avenue, and only one end – Congress – was in charge of the money. That it was up to them to take up the fight.

Senator Dodd had responded from the dais in jest, 'Tell that to the other end.' He meant that I should press my case with President George W. Bush at the White House, of course.

But as it turned out, I wouldn't need to do any such thing. Just nine months later, everything changed when, on 28 January 2003, President Bush gave his second State of the Union address.

I had never been a fan of the second President Bush. I found his worldview to be totally warped. I thought the values he claimed to uphold didn't match his policies. I thought his rhetoric against gay marriage, against civil unions, really against any expansion of gay rights at all, was deeply harmful and homophobic. Needless to say, I was not looking forward to watching the speech.

But I planned to watch it anyway. I'd lived part-time in the United States for many years at that point, and it felt to me, even though I was a British citizen, that I had an obligation to hear what the president had to say, even if I expected to disagree. And, in fact, I disagreed with almost all of it. This was the speech, you may recall, where Bush made his case for going to war in Iraq. It was the speech where he claimed that there was a grave threat of weapons of mass destruction from Saddam Hussein, and that in the name of the 'war on terror' we had to act swiftly.

Still, I remember that speech not because of what was said about Iraq or terrorism or abortion or taxes. I remember it for what President Bush said about AIDS:

> Today, on the continent of Africa, nearly 30 million people have the AIDS virus, including 3 million children under the age of 15. There are whole countries in Africa where more than one-third of the adult population carries the infection. More than 4 million require immediate drug treatment. Yet across that continent, only 50,000 AIDS victims – only 50,000 – are receiving the medicine they need.

I couldn't believe what I was hearing. The president of the United States, standing in front of a joint session of Congress, was calling attention to the crisis we had spent more than a decade fighting. I knew the statistics he cited. I'd cited them myself hundreds of times.

'AIDS can be prevented,' he implored. 'Antiretroviral drugs can extend life for many years. And the cost of those drugs has dropped from $12,000 a year to under $300 a year, which places a tremendous possibility within our grasp.'

At that point, as if I were watching a football game, my heart was racing. 'Ladies and gentlemen,' Bush continued, 'seldom has history offered a greater opportunity to do so much for so many. We have confronted, and will continue to confront, HIV/AIDS in our own country. And to meet a severe and urgent crisis abroad, tonight I propose the Emergency Plan for AIDS Relief, a work of mercy beyond all current international efforts to help the people of Africa.'

Then, he told us the numbers. I can't overstate what a big moment this was:

This comprehensive plan will prevent 7 million new AIDS infections, treat at least 2 million people with life-extending drugs, and provide humane care for millions of people suffering from AIDS and for children orphaned by AIDS. I ask the Congress to commit $15 billion over the next five years, including nearly $10 billion in new money, to turn the tide against AIDS in the most afflicted nations of Africa and the Caribbean.

This was the moment when funding the global fight against AIDS became a question of 'billions' instead of 'millions.' It's hard to put into perspective just how huge it was. But this should give you an idea: Just four years earlier, we had considered it a tremendous victory – we actually celebrated – when President Clinton had convinced Congress to increase global AIDS spending from $125 million to $225 million. This was more than sixty times that amount.

Indeed, President Bush's global AIDS initiative, which became known as the President's Emergency Plan for AIDS Relief, or PEPFAR, was the largest commitment by any nation to combat a global disease in history. The $15 billion was to be spent in just a five-year period, from 2003 to 2008. And when it was renewed in 2008, that number more than tripled to $48 billion, an extraordinary sum.

Congress responded to the president's request. Many of the same senators I had met with and testified before were instrumental in passing PEPFAR. The results, thanks to their efforts and President Bush's commitment, have been breath-taking: According to the U.S. State Department, which administers PEPFAR, the United States has given almost 4 million men, women, and children around the world access to antiretroviral treatment. It supported HIV testing and counselling for nearly 10 million pregnant women in 2011 alone. And because PEPFAR got antiretrovirals into the hands of more than 660,000 HIV-positive pregnant women, America was able to ensure that some 200,000 infants were born *without* the disease. Thirteen million people received care and support through PEPFAR in 2011, and 40 million received testing or counselling. President

Bush's decision to take aggressive action has, without question, saved *millions* of lives.

PEPFAR also meant that EJAF-UK and other non-profit organisations could look at dramatically expanding their work in Africa. Because the drugs and much of the infrastructure was to be paid for under PEPFAR, EJAF could find smart ways of scaling up programmes for women and children infected with HIV from the hundreds to now the hundreds of thousands. I have met dozens of these beneficiaries: pregnant women whose babies will live their lives HIV-free.

Of course, PEPFAR's creation and implementation was not without controversy. PEPFAR explicitly excluded certain populations, including sex workers, which is both intolerable and illogical. As I've written here many times, you cannot win a war if you refuse to fight it on certain battlefields. There was also controversy around the requirement by PEPFAR that significant funds be spent on abstinence-only educational programmes, which are a complete waste of money, since they've been proven to be marginally effective at best. It would be far better to spend those resources on treatment and also on prevention programmes that actually work. But, taken on the whole, the impact of PEPFAR is truly staggering. It was, and today continues to be, the single greatest assault on HIV/AIDS since the disease emerged.

There were lessons to be learned in watching liberal Democrats and conservative Republicans come together to make PEPFAR a reality. The first, and one of the most important, is that you cannot assume the worst in people. Instead, it may be possible, more times than you'd think, to work with someone on a shared goal. To find common ground. To achieve great things through unlikely partnerships.

It was easy for me to despise President Bush from afar, to assume, wrongly, that he would never be an ally in any fight I was involved in. The truth, it turned out, was quite different. I learned this during the creation of PEPFAR in 2003, and again in 2004, when I finally had the opportunity to meet him.

I was very surprised and flattered to be selected to receive the prestigious Kennedy Center Honors, which are given to only a few entertainers each year in recognition of their cultural contributions to American life. It is a big deal – I knew that much. But to be quite honest, at the time, David and I were torn about whether I should accept the honour. The award itself is presented by the sitting president of the United States, and I was no great fan of George W. Bush, apart from his position on AIDS. More than that, I was morally opposed to many of his policies, and I took personal offence at many of his pronouncements. Ultimately, however, David and I came to realise that the Kennedy Center Honors were bestowed not by a president but by a nation, and my love and respect for America were much more important than any political statement I could make by refusing to accept an award from George W. Bush.

David and I flew to Washington, and the first order of business was a formal dinner at the U.S. State Department, during which each Kennedy Center honoree is presented with a medallion. After a few kind words, Colin Powell, the secretary of state, hung the medallion around my neck. When I got back to my seat, David and I chuckled to ourselves, because as it turns out the medallion itself is several metal bars attached to a big, rainbow-coloured ribbon that looks identical to the gay-pride flag. And I was very proud to wear it, of course.

The next day, we went to the White House for the formal citation reading ceremony. As we walked up those grand steps, it wasn't excitement we felt but apprehension. We were entering the lion's den, we thought. David and I had no idea how we would be treated or what the experience would be like for a same-sex couple visiting a Republican White House that seemed openly hostile to gays. But we were immediately put at ease by an Air Force pilot who was assigned to be our White House escort. You've never seen a more handsome man in your life, especially in that uniform! And what's more, I instantly knew he was gay. These were the days when you weren't supposed to 'ask,' and they weren't supposed to 'tell.' But, of course, I couldn't help myself. 'You're gay, aren't you?' I said. He smiled and nodded. To this day, our Air Force escort is a great friend of ours.

The award presentation was in one of the beautifully ornate receiving rooms at the White House. President Bush read citations for each honoree. When it came to my turn, the president began to list some of my hit songs over the years, including 'Crocodile Rock,' 'Daniel,' and – in one of the president's legendary verbal miscues – 'Bernie and the Jets.' Just then, First Lady Laura Bush interrupted the president and yelled out, 'It's "*Bennie* and the Jets"!'

The president and everyone in the audience had quite a laugh. That is, except Dick Cheney. When President Bush finished reading my citation and the audience applauded, David and I were stunned to see the vice president sitting there with his arms folded and a scowl on his face. It may have been that he still had raw feelings about my quote to a British publication a few weeks prior, that 'Bush and this administration are the worst thing that has ever happened to America.' I suppose I can't blame him for being unhappy with me about that!

That evening, there was a wonderful gala concert at the Kennedy Center Opera House – a very moving event during which my friends Billy Joel and Kid Rock serenaded me with my own songs. David and I sat in a special box with my fellow awardees: Warren Beatty, Ossie Davis and Ruby Dee, Joan Sutherland, and John Williams. At intermission, our group filed into the hospitality area behind the box. Our seats were next to the president's, and little did I realise that our boxes shared this hospitality room in common. Suddenly I was standing next to a bunch you wouldn't think of as my usual concert-goers: Donald Rumsfeld, Dick Cheney, Condoleezza Rice, Colin Powell, and, yes, President Bush.

It was a surprising moment indeed, but the real surprise would come when the president and I had a chance to speak. I remember having the greatest conversation with him. He was warm, charming, and very complimentary, not only about my music but also about the work of my foundation. He knew all about what we were doing, and he was endlessly knowledgeable about HIV/AIDS as well.

President Bush and I discussed the epidemic for quite

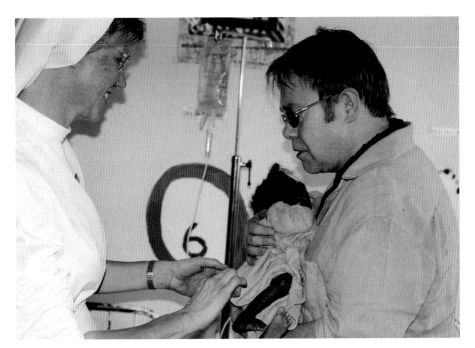

Discussing the prognosis for a baby with AIDS in rural South Africa. *(Sydney Duval)*

With Fumana and David in 2008 at the Simelela Rape Crisis Centre in Khayelit-sha, South Africa. Simelela is a twenty-four-hour, seven-day-a-week acute care centre that provides services to survivors of rape, the first of its kind in South Africa. Since being treated at the Simelela center, Fumana has devoted herself to rape survivor advocacy. *(Polly Steele)*

Senator Hillary Clinton, Senator Ted Kennedy, Director of the Office of National AIDS Policy Sandy Thurman, and I meet before testifying at a Senate hearing on the state of the AIDS epidemic on April 11, 2002. *(Vivian Ronay / Retna Ltd. / Corbis)*

At the Senate hearing on April 11, 2002, with Sandy Thurman. In my testimonial, I said, "When Ryan White was asked by a reporter if he had a message for medical researchers working on AIDS, he said, 'Hurry up.' We all need to hurry up. Every day we delay, we lose more lives, and we lose a little more of our humanity." *(Vivian Ronay / Retna Ltd. / Corbis)*

With former president Bill Clinton at EJAF's eighth annual benefit held on November 16, 2009, in New York City. EJAF honoured President Clinton that night with an Enduring Vision Award. The William J. Clinton Foundation has fought for the rights of those living with HIV/AIDS worldwide since 2002. *(Larry Busacca / WireImage / Getty Images)*

WE ALL
IF ONE OF US DOES.

In this December 2005 public service campaign, shot by Mark Seliger and spearheaded by Kenneth Cole and KNOW HIV/AIDS, David and I joined other participants in demonstrating our commitment to the global fight against HIV/AIDS. *(Photograph by Mark Seliger)*

Holding a child at a mother-baby clinic in Cape Town, South Africa. EJAF-UK has helped more than 200,000 HIV-positive pregnant women in Africa to access medicine that protects their babies from acquiring HIV. *(Polly Steele)*

Holding baby Lev during a news conference at the state orphanage for children with HIV/AIDS in Makeyevka, Ukraine, on September 12, 2009. David and I were legally unable to adopt Lev from Ukraine, but the experience changed our lives by inspiring us to have a child. *(Handout / Reuters)*

Visiting a state orphanage for children with HIV/AIDS in the town of Makeyevka, Ukraine, on September 12, 2009. EJAF first started working in Ukraine in 2002, funding an organisation that now supports more than 57,000 Ukrainians living with HIV/AIDS. *(© Gleb Garanich / Reuters)*

At EJAF's twentieth annual Academy Awards Viewing Party in West Hollywood on February 26, 2012. David and I have been together since 1993, and we are partners in everything, including the work of EJAF. Our beautiful son, Zachary, was born on Christmas Day, 2010. *(Larry Busacca / Getty Images)*

Performing at an event to celebrate the life and legacy of Ryan White in Indianapolis on April 28, 2010, marking twenty years since Ryan's death. He continues to inspire me each and every day. *(Nathaniel Edmunds Photography)*

a while, and he asked if there was anything he could do to help EJAF. I thanked him for his offer, but I said that his commitment to PEPFAR had already done a world of good, and I commended him for all he was doing to fight AIDS abroad. At that point, I felt compelled to ask if there was anything I could do to help him. 'Yeah,' he said, with a look of dead seriousness on his face. 'Tell the French they need to give more money.'

You see, at that point, France had not yet made a significant commitment to fighting the global AIDS epidemic, and President Bush was truly angry about it. The French government has since spearheaded the creation of a wonderful multi-government programme called UNITAID, which funds the purchase of HIV/AIDS medication and other global health needs for poor countries through a small tax on the purchase of airline tickets. But back in 2004, President Bush was lobbying for them to do more. This wasn't a political issue to him, or some side project. He genuinely cared about people around the world who were dying of AIDS.

I'll never forget our meeting that night. President Bush and I haven't seen each other or talked since, and like many people, I deeply regretted much of what he did in office, especially the wars he waged in Iraq and

Afghanistan. But my encounter with George W. Bush reminded me not to rush to judgement about people, especially when it comes to fighting AIDS. More than anything, we need allies in this fight, not enemies.

That was one important lesson learned from the implementation of PEPFAR. The other was one I grew to understand, not just from watching PEPFAR's creation but from my own experience testifying before Congress, and from years of EJAF's work around the world: there is no institution on earth, not one, that is as capable of making sweeping changes as government.

Governments have the power to entirely remake the societies they govern. They have the power to battle, to wage war, not just on other nations but on poverty, on injustice, on epidemics. They have the resources and influence to change the future, and the choice of whether or not to do so. And with a disease such as AIDS in particular, they have a unique ability to fund treatment and care, education and prevention. They can ensure that all their citizens have access to life-saving medicine. Governments are, without question, the single biggest factor in determining whether AIDS will be a death sentence for their people, or whether their HIV-positive citizens will survive.

Governments of the world are more than just resources for funding. They also have an unmatched ability, without spending a penny, to fight the terrible torment of stigma. Government, after all, has the ultimate megaphone. All it takes is a president or a prime minister to say, 'It doesn't matter who you are or where you come from, you deserve the dignity of having your life valued as much as the rest of us.' All it takes is for lawmakers to speak up for their marginalised constituents. All it takes is leaders to proclaim they will not let a disease ravage people living in their communities. In an age of ubiquitous communications, these statements alone can have a tremendous impact.

This is a sunny analysis of the power of government, but there is also a darker reality at work, and one I must acknowledge. Government has extraordinary power for good, but it can also be the world's greatest impediment to change. Governments can decide to make homosexuality illegal, to force people to stay, by law, in the closet. Governments can decide that needle exchange, however effective it may be, is just too loathsome a concept, that if the disease must spread through and kill drug users, then so be it. Governments can choose to act, and they can also choose not to. More often than not, the latter is the case.

In some ways, this is what foundations like mine have the hardest time overcoming. There are places around the world where we want to help, where we have the resources to help, but the obstacles of government are far too great. Too often, we aren't able to reach the people who most need our assistance. How can you get the treatment you need when coming out into the open can lead to criminal punishment? The answer, all over the world, is that you can't.

That is why perhaps the biggest stumbling block we face in our effort to eradicate AIDS is the prevalence of governmental backwardness.

Look at India, for example, the world's second-most populous country. Homosexuality was made illegal there by British colonial law in 1861. It was decriminalised, finally, in a 2009 ruling by the New Delhi high court, a ruling that is currently being appealed to India's Supreme Court. In the meantime, other courts have chosen to ignore the ruling. Men are still going to jail for having sex with other men.

This is both horrifically bigoted and hugely problematic from an institutional perspective. Gay men with HIV/AIDS in India must fear for their liberty when they seek treatment; a lot of them, as a result, choose not to get help. And so the disease spreads. The damage of homophobic laws is only compounded when political leaders choose to use their bully pulpit to spew hatred. This we saw in India in 2011, when the nation's health minister told an HIV/AIDS conference that he believed sex between men was 'unnatural.' 'Unfortunately,' he told the audience, 'there is this disease in the world and in this country where men are having sex with other men, which is completely unnatural and shouldn't happen, but it does.'[2]

This was an unspeakably inappropriate comment to make to any audience, by any person, but when you consider that this man was a national health minister, and the audience he was speaking to was a group of people trying to combat HIV in his country, it becomes all the more outrageous. There are 2.5 million people infected with HIV in India, and their government has said essentially, 'We don't care about *any* of you because *some* of you are gay.'

The irony is that as the health minister continued to speak, he illuminated one of the central points I've been making, one that people like him are largely responsible for causing. 'In our country,' he said, 'the numbers of men having sex with men are substantial, but it is very difficult to find them.' Difficult, of course, because homosexuality in India is still, for all intents and purposes, illegal.

We will never eradicate this disease when governments use their power so destructively, when they codify stigma and then spread it. Nor will we eradicate AIDS until governments understand the fundamental truth about the populations they govern: there is no 'other.' They might like to think about the groups they marginalize – drug users, gay men, people of colour, the poor – as somehow living segregated lives. But communities don't work like that. We all interact with one another, even when we don't know it. We do business with each other. We live next to one another. Oh, and by the way, yes, we have sex with each other. And so the idea that we can ignore marginalised populations – that we can let them retreat into the shadows to die and that doing so, morality aside, won't have any impact on the rest of the community – is as shamefully stupid as it is tragic.

When AIDS is ravaging drug users, it matters for those who don't use drugs. When AIDS is racing through the gay community, it matters for those who aren't gay. There is no 'other,' and if governments keep treating the disease as an 'other' problem, we will fail to end this epidemic.

One of the most heart-breaking examples of government stupidity is unfolding right now in Ukraine. As I mentioned, Ukraine is a nation where the disease is moving at a terrifying pace through the population. It is also a place where, recently, the government made a terrible choice, one that very well might result in the deaths of many Ukrainians.

Earlier, I told the story of the Lavra Clinic in Kiev, a wonderful institution that is one of the few lifelines for people living with HIV/AIDS in Ukraine. This extraordinary clinic is regarded by gay men in that country as the only safe place they can go to get treatment. And now, as I write this, it has been ordered to close by Ukraine's government.

You see, the clinic is adjacent to the historic Kiev-Pechersk Lavra monastery. The land the clinic sits on is owned by the monastery, and the monks there have apparently decided they no longer want the clinic next door. In June 2011, Ukraine's prime minister approved an order to close the clinic. Of all the land in Ukraine, they chose the location of the Lavra Clinic to make way for a luxury hotel.

The government claims that they will just relocate the facility, but no one at the clinic – not the doctors nor the patients – has been told where it will be moved. And at the time of the government's order to shutter the facility, the clinic hadn't been relocated at all. Keep in mind that even a modest delay in treatment could spell death for patients who depend on the Lavra Clinic's support. It's unclear at this point if the government has any intention of opening the clinic elsewhere. What is clear is the following: since Lavra is the most important HIV treatment centre in Ukraine, if its services are suspended or closed, people are going to get sick and die.

I've been to Ukraine many times, because EJAF funds a number of programmes there. I've seen firsthand the extraordinary life-saving services that clinics in Ukraine provide. And so, in November 2011, I returned to Kiev as part of a desperate campaign to turn things around. At a press conference, I'd had it. 'For fuck's sake, Ukraine!' I yelled for all who could hear it. 'You live in the twenty-first century, not the nineteenth century! This is a disgrace! It's a disgrace how some human beings are treated in this country!'

In the months since the order to close the clinic was handed down, EJAF has done everything it can to help raise awareness. Thanks to the protests of AUKN, Lavra's clients and supporters, EJAF, and many others, the debate is ongoing as to the ultimate fate of the Lavra Clinic. We're heartened that it seems we've been able to delay to this point the eviction of Lavra's patients.

But when it comes to the larger fight against AIDS in Ukraine, we are not naive. We are fighting a losing battle there, not because the disease is too strong but because it has the government as its accomplice.

Ukraine is one of the few countries in the region to acknowledge its AIDS crisis. Backsliding now, sending a message that people who are at risk of contracting

HIV don't matter, will disastrously inflate the epidemic. The whole country will feel the effects of that. We know this because, tragically, it has happened in every other region where there is an HIV epidemic.

Government inaction will make Ukraine's already surging AIDS crisis even worse, full stop. And that will make the problem worse for *all* Ukrainians. Already the disease is spreading, out of the shadows, out of the drug dens. Further government inaction, obstruction, and delay are intolerable.

The point here is not just to condemn the Ukrainian government, though they certainly deserve it. The point is that unless governments treat all their citizens equally, we'll never end AIDS. That's the plain truth, no matter the continent or the context. It is as true in the West as it is in the developing world. It is true in poor countries and rich countries, in North America and North Africa. And so governments must make a choice. They can choose to spread stigma or they can choose to quash it. They can choose to spread treatment or instead spread bigotry and death. They can embrace the truth of this disease or they can continue to believe the lies they are telling themselves about HIV/AIDS and the people it affects.

Unfortunately, governments have a habit of lying not only to themselves but also to their people. I have been shocked at the misinformation that governments have spread, senselessly, at the direct cost of human life. But nothing I've seen in all my years of doing this work has shocked me more than the misinformation propagated by the government of South Africa.

It was in South Africa, several years ago, that President Thabo Mbeki became a leading voice among those known as AIDS denialists. In 2000, he spoke at the XIII International AIDS Conference in Durban and rejected all of the science we had learned about the disease to that point. He said that AIDS was caused by poverty, poor nourishment, poor health. He said it was the result of a failing immune system. And he said, emphatically, that it was not caused by a virus. As such, he concluded, it could not be treated with medicine. So he rejected free medicine for his people. He rejected grants for treatment and prevention programmes. He used the power he had been granted to stand between his citizens and efforts to save their lives.[3]

These were not abstract pronouncements by a fringe member of a government. These were the policies of a president – the leader of the nation. And the result, according to a Harvard paper published in 2008, was that 330,000 people died unnecessarily from the disease, and another 35,000 babies were born with it.[4] A quiet holocaust.

Mbeki was eventually ousted. Without him, South Africa has reversed itself, aiming to get treatment into the country as swiftly as possible. But the misinformation still lives on, not just in the minds of those who trusted the words of President Mbeki but also in the words of the new president, Jacob Zuma. When he was still the country's vice president, Zuma told South Africa that he'd had sex with an HIV-positive woman, but not to worry, he had taken a shower afterward to reduce his chance of contracting the illness.[5]

How many people, I wonder, have contracted the disease because they took Zuma's inexcusable advice to shower after unprotected sex?

I'm pleased to report that, as president, Zuma has mobilised more government support for the fight against AIDS in South Africa than any of his predecessors. But therein lies the great contradiction of government, and I'm not the first to point it out. The power to heal. The power to harm. Extraordinary power, and too often it is concentrated in the hands of those who don't understand the consequences of their deeds and words. And sometimes, the power is in the hands of truly evil people who just don't give a damn about human life.

This contradiction plays out not only in the developing world, not only in Eastern Europe and sub-

Saharan Africa, but also in the West. And, yes, even in the United States. *Especially* in the United States.

It might shock you to learn that in America today, thousands of low-income people are on government waiting lists to receive lifesaving HIV/AIDS medication that they cannot afford. These people are not necessarily poor. They are often either unemployed or work in jobs without health insurance and simply don't make enough to pay for their AIDS medication.

Consider the case of Steven Dimmick, a thirty-one-year-old man from Jacksonville, Florida. As the *Chicago Tribune* reported, he was forced to sell his car and his home, and he filed for bankruptcy protection in order to raise the cash for his HIV/AIDS treatment.[6] A federal effort called the AIDS Drug Assistance Program (ADAP) was designed to prevent people like Steven from falling through the cracks. But now waiting lists are swallowing them up. And make no mistake: the people on these lists will eventually die without treatment. Tragically, some have.

In 2011, more than 12,000 low-income, uninsured HIV-positive Floridians relied on ADAP to receive their medication. But many more needed help. Because Florida's ADAP program has been so severely underfunded, another 4,000 people sat on a waiting list for the treatment they needed to survive. Steven was one of these people. ADAP is a nationwide program, and at the time Florida had the largest waiting list of any state.

In 2011, Florida's governor, Rick Scott, sought deep budget cuts, and his administration proposed cost-saving changes to the state's ADAP program. The changes would have meant some 1,600 people who were receiving ADAP assistance would lose it. In June 2011, David and I wrote a letter to Governor Scott urging him to reconsider his administration's proposed changes to ADAP. We tried to explain to him what a lack of treatment would mean, not just for those living with the disease like Steven but for Florida and for the nation at large. We pleaded with him that 'denying HIV treatment to low-income people not only harms their health and increases the incidence of drug-resistant HIV, it also makes it more likely that these people can and will spread the disease to others.' David spoke to the Florida press. We wrote op-eds. We started an online petition and sent more than 4,000 signatures to Governor Scott.

The response we received was shocking. It was a letter from the Florida surgeon general, Dr Frank Farmer, written on the governor's stationery. It said, strangely, that because the waiting list for ADAP was so high, the Department of Health was considering new eligibility standards 'in an effort to ensure that Florida is allocating the dollars appropriated for AIDS drugs to those who are most vulnerable.' The implication, I suppose, being that there were people getting ADAP support who could afford to pay their own way. It was utter nonsense.

Dr Farmer defended the actions of Governor Scott's administration by suggesting that other states had taken similar cost-cutting steps. And then he had the audacity to close with the following: 'We cordially invite you to consider an ADAP fund-raising concert series in Florida. We would love to welcome you to the Sunshine State and I am confident your concerts will be a huge hit!'

A fucking benefit concert. As if that could raise anywhere *close* to the money needed to plug the gap. It was as condescending as it was completely idiotic. The American state of Florida, with its $69.1 *billion* annual budget, was proposing to outsource its AIDS efforts to a British musician. What a ludicrous idea, that a celebrity could be a substitute for a government. That really says it all, I think.

In the end, when the U.S. federal budget for 2011–2012 was passed, it included a $48 million increase for ADAP funds. It was enough to prevent Florida from making additional cuts. But it wasn't enough to cover thousands of people around the nation who, as I write this, continue to sit in desperation on waiting lists.

It is all too easy for political leaders to think about AIDS only in the abstract. It is all too easy for them to forget that there are real people counting on them for help, people who deserve the same chance to live a long life as anyone else.

In the end, the only way we will end AIDS is with a commitment to do so not just from *one* government but from *all* governments. A commitment from governors and presidents. From premiers and prime ministers. From Asia to Africa to Europe.

Governments can be the greatest force in the fight to rid the world of AIDS. But only if they so choose.

9

A Great Responsibility

About four months after President Bush announced PEPFAR in his State of the Union address, we were all feeling incredibly optimistic. Ten years into the foundation's creation, it really seemed as if, for the first time, we were on the verge of a breakthrough. The American government had made a historic commitment to ending AIDS. There was so much hope, so much adrenaline. It made me think of Ryan a lot. I guess many things do, but during those days, when it seemed as if we were turning an important corner, I felt his presence even more. This was his legacy, after all.

It was a reminder, too, of how important all kinds of institutions are in the fight against AIDS. Not just governments but corporations, religious groups, charities. How much good they can do, how many resources they can amass, and how much influence they can impart. It was a reminder of possibility – the possibility that we *could* end AIDS forever if we tried.

Maybe that's why the *New York Times* article I read one morning that May of 2003 felt like such a punch to the gut. It opened like this:

> A division of the pharmaceutical company Bayer sold millions of dollars of blood-clotting medicine for hemo-philiacs – medicine that carried a high risk of transmit-ting AIDS – to Asia and Latin America in the mid-1980s while selling a new, safer product in the West, according to documents obtained by the *New York Times*.[1]

The medicine the article was referencing was factor VIII, the same medicine that had caused Ryan to contract HIV. In the early 1980s, the evidence was overwhelming that factor VIII was dangerous in its current form. And so Bayer, the drug's manufacturer, introduced a safer version in 1984.

According to the *Times*, the company had a large surplus of the old, HIV-tainted factor VIII, and they weren't about to throw it away. That would waste costs. So instead, they sold it. Abroad.

Bayer claimed this wasn't their fault. Customers still wanted the old stuff, as they doubted the new drug's effectiveness, so Bayer gave it to them. Some countries, they said, were slow to approve the new drug. There was also a shortage of plasma for the new medicine.

They were simply meeting demand, they claimed. When doctors in Hong Kong, who had become worried about the growing number of haemophiliac patients with HIV, asked for the new factor VIII, Bayer urged them to use up their existing stocks of the old, infected treatment first. And that's not all. The company kept manufacturing the old product as well, even *after* they knew that each batch had the potential to transmit HIV.

As the *Times* reported, the company already had a lot of fixed-price contracts in place, so they were going to get paid the same amount whether they sold the new drug or the old one. And the old one was cheaper to make.

'These are the most incriminating internal pharmaceutical industry documents I have ever seen,' Dr Sidney M. Wolfe, director of the Public Citizen Health Research Group, told the *Times*. Indeed, in February 1985, a full year after the newer, safer product had been introduced, an internal company task force asked, quite simply, 'Can we in good faith continue to ship [potentially tainted] products to Japan?' They couldn't – not in good faith, not with a clear conscience. But they did.

It's impossible to know how many people died because of Bayer's actions. What we do know is that the company exported more than 100,000 vials of potentially tainted factor VIII after they had already begun selling the safer product elsewhere. We know those transactions were worth $4 million – about $8 million in today's dollars.

While Bayer still insists on its innocence in the matter, it was only recently discovered in 2011 that the company reached a settlement – without any admission of liability – in the protracted legal battle that resulted from its reprehensible actions. The exact details of the settlement have not been disclosed, but according to one source, Bayer agreed to pay $50 million in restitution.[2]

Bayer said in the *Times* that Cutter (the division of the company that sold factor VIII) had behaved 'responsibly, ethically and humanely' in continuing to sell the original drug overseas. But as far as I am concerned, it was greed – this was business, after all, and business is about money, not lives. We all know the power of greed. But this story is a stark reminder of the terribly evil decisions people make in the name of profits. It is a story we should never, ever forget.

As I read the details in that article, I thought of Ryan and ached for the unnamed thousands who had died just like he did. Ryan, like so many of my friends, contracted the disease too soon, before we had any real treatment, before we knew what was causing it and how to prevent it. But how many people must there have been, in Hong Kong, in Taiwan, in Argentina, and elsewhere, who didn't need to contract the disease at all? Who didn't need to die?

A year earlier, I had told the congressional committee, 'The drug companies are the only organisations in the world whose resources can rival those of rich governments in battling the disease.' But, I also told Congress, 'they have broken a public trust. They can't expect to keep pulling in profits, have their research subsidised, and then go missing in the midst of a worldwide health emergency. They can't keep telling us they're in the business of saving lives, if they always put business *ahead* of saving lives. We need them – and everyone – as partners.'

What I was referencing in my testimony was not the evil actions of the pharmaceutical industry; it was the evil of *inaction*.

As I wrote earlier, there have been extraordinary advances in AIDS treatments over the last thirty years, a true testament to the incredible brilliance of researchers and scientists who dedicated themselves to ending the disease. A lot of those scientists are employed by drug companies. A lot of them aren't.

What drug companies will tell you is that pharmaceutical development doesn't just happen. It requires big investments, sometimes hundreds of millions of dollars; it requires years of testing, sometimes more than a decade, through several rigorous phases. If things don't work out, if the drug fails, the companies are on the hook for the entire investment. And if they do work, companies need to make back the money they invested – plus a reasonable profit – when their new drug is sold.

This is just how it works, they'll tell you, and it's why, as sorry as they may be about it, the AIDS drugs on the market are very expensive – prohibitively so for the vast majority of people in the world living with the disease. There is just no other way around it.

But this is only half true. Maybe less than half.

It is incredibly rare for pharmaceutical companies to be working on the kind of research they are describing as so expensive without help – a lot of help – from taxpayers. Drug companies aren't the only ones investing in research. The biggest cost they face is shared. Much of the basic, critical research is funded by public or non-profit entities. This research doesn't even make it to the drug company until a big breakthrough has been made. And even then, the drug companies get funding to turn the breakthroughs into something they can sell.

AmfAR, for example, has invested more than $340 million and issued grants to more than 2,000 research teams. The work they've funded is largely responsible for the development of all kinds of HIV treatments.

They funded the research that showed how antiretro-virals could block mother-to-infant transmission of the disease. Their grants helped improve diagnostic and monitoring capabilities, and research they've enabled has helped us to understand the virus better. Currently amfAR is funding HIV vaccine research.

And that's just one non-profit organisation. The U.S. government and the international community have spent billions of dollars on AIDS research to date. So the drug companies are not, as they claim, doing this work on their own. And yet they charge prices as though they were. No wonder they are among the most profit-able companies in the world.

It's worth remembering that it was the CDC, not a drug company, that first warned the world about the HIV virus and first identified the ways in which it was transmitted. It was a doctor working at a French non-profit institute, not a drug company, who isolated the virus. It was the government-funded U.S. National Institutes of Health, not a drug company, that spear-headed the initial research into the disease. It was amfAR that sponsored the research into the protease inhibitors that worked as second-line treatments. And in 1996, it was a researcher named David Ho, director not of a private drug lab but of the non-profit Aaron Diamond AIDS Research Center in New York City, who discovered the so-called AIDS cocktail of life-saving medicine, using those same protease inhibitors investigated by amfAR, that would revolutionise treatment for millions of people living with HIV/AIDS.

I don't write this to suggest that the drug companies have no role. They play a crucial one. But I have strong objections to the story they prefer telling and the consequences of it. The distance we have come with AIDS treatment is one of the greatest collective achievements of humankind. It is not, as they would have you believe, a product entirely of the pharmaceutical industry's own work.

The truth is, the drug companies can afford to sell AIDS medication for less – a lot less – and still make a fine profit. They have the power to act, to step up, and to become the boldest leaders of all in the fight to end the disease. I'm not saying that drug companies shouldn't earn a profit. They wouldn't exist if they couldn't make money, and we very much need them to exist. The question is, does their profit on life-saving drugs have to be so high that it prevents them from saving lives as intended?

Let me put it this way. Pretend for a moment that you are a multibillion-dollar, multinational drug company. If you found out that you could save millions of lives and make a profit while doing it but that your profit margin would be just slightly less than it is now, would you do it?

How about if I sweeten the deal? What if you had to charge a lot less for your AIDS medicine in the developing world, but in exchange for doing so, you could get access to millions of new customers? What if your per-pill profits were smaller, but in the aggregate, you could make more money than you do now because suddenly you were flush with new orders? And what if I told you that those millions of customers whose lives you were saving were going to need to take the pills you produce every single day for the rest of their lives?

In other words, what if I told you I could get you millions of lifelong customers you would otherwise have no access to, and profits for as long as AIDS exists? And all you have to do is lower the price.

Who *wouldn't* take that deal?

This isn't a hypothetical scenario. This was an actual deal offered to the major brand-name drug companies by the William J. Clinton Foundation a number of years ago. A deal they outright rejected.

In 2002, former president Bill Clinton's foundation began to take on the issue of AIDS. President Clinton has often said that he regrets not doing far more to fight AIDS when he was in the White House. I regret that he didn't do more as well. But, since he left office, the work of his foundation has been game changing.

The Clinton Foundation started in the Bahamas, where they discovered that the government was paying about $3,600 a year per person for generic AIDS drugs, instead of the list price of $500. 'How could this be?' they asked. Upon investigating, the Clinton Foundation discovered that middlemen were jacking up the prices. So they called up the generic manufacturer and made a deal that cut out these middlemen and made the drugs a whole lot cheaper for the Bahamian government to buy.[3]

That episode sparked the interest of the former president and his staff. Were AIDS drugs more expensive than they had to be? Could something be done about that?

President Clinton put together a small team of management consultants who figured out a couple of important things: First, they concluded that they could streamline the drug companies' operations, making it cheaper to produce the drugs. Then they figured out they could do the same thing for every company along the supply chain. Make everything run faster, better, more efficiently, and you make everything cheaper.

But this was just the start. Next, their plan was to get the drug companies to produce at a much greater scale, which would make each individual pill far less expensive to manufacture. It's like when you go to the grocery store: you can buy one soda for $1 or a twelve-pack for $6, which is just $0.50 per soda. Half the price. Buy a twenty-four-pack for $8, and now it's just $0.34 a soda. Imagine how cheap it would get if, instead of buying twenty-four sodas, you were buying twenty-four thousand. The price per soda would drop to pennies.

So the idea was simple enough: if the drug manufacturers produced a lot more drugs, the drugs themselves would be a whole lot cheaper to make and thus to sell. That would mean, with the same government expenditure, far more drugs could be purchased and many more lives could be saved.

The problem was that no drug company was going to make more drugs if it couldn't be sure it would have customers to buy them. At the time, the Clinton Foundation estimated there were only about 70,000 people receiving treatment in the developing world. But there were millions who needed it.[4]

That's where the foundation stepped in. First, they went to governments in Africa and the Caribbean and made a basic pitch: If we can get you cheap AIDS drugs, will you commit to buying a lot of them? Then they went to the drug companies and made the reverse pitch: If we can get you 2 million customers in the developing world, help you make your operation and supply chain a lot more efficient, and guarantee you a profit, will you sell your drugs for a lot less than you do now?

The governments said yes. But the brand-name drug companies balked. They didn't want any part of it.

I'm not sure what President Clinton said in those meetings. He's one of the most persuasive men on earth, that much is well known. And this was, after all, a great deal. The drug companies were going to make good money, and they were going to make it from selling drugs to a huge population of customers they didn't have access to. And that's just the business piece of it – countless lives would be saved as well. But the companies turned down the offer. Somehow they had found a way to reject a deal that would have made them more money and made a real impact in the fight against AIDS at the same time.

The good news is that Bill Clinton is not easily dissuaded. If the brand-name manufacturers wouldn't step up to the plate, fine, he would take his offer elsewhere. His foundation approached generic manufacturers in India, South Africa, Thailand, and other countries, and asked if they were interested in the same deal. But there was a catch: if the generic companies manufactured the drugs, they'd be at risk of violating the patents of brand-name companies. He told them to go for it anyway. They'd have his full support. 'No company will live or die because of high price premiums for AIDS drugs in middle-income countries,' Clinton said in Thailand, 'but patients may.'[5]

The Clinton Foundation held up their end of the bargain. So did the generic drug manufacturers. And in May 2007, Clinton's foundation was able to announce an incredible deal. Prices would fall, on average, 25 per cent in low-income countries. They would fall, on average, 50 per cent in middle-income countries. And one-pill-a-day treatments would be made available for less than $1 for developing countries, which represented a 45 per cent discount in Africa. The deal, in total, would impact sixty-six nations all over the world. It was just this side of a miracle, and the major drug companies played no role in the equation whatsoever.

I've talked about the critical role of governments in fighting AIDS. I said that no institution was as capable of sweeping change. But governments alone will not solve this problem. Governments aren't the only institutions in our society. They're not the only players on the field. If we are going to rid the world of AIDS, we need a commitment from governments, yes, but we also need a commitment from many others. And we badly need a commitment from the drug makers.

The generic manufacturers have been quiet heroes in all of this. In fact, they supply some 80 to 90 per cent of all AIDS medicine worldwide. But the generics are tiny compared to the big guys. Globally, the brand-name companies bring in about eight times the market share of the generic companies. We need the big pharmaceuticals on board, too. I'm not asking them to become charities instead of companies. I'm not naive enough to think that would work, nor would it be wise. I'm asking only that they keep the faith with their missions a little better. If you can make money while saving lives, then more power to you. But if you choose to make even more money at the *expense* of people's lives, then you should be ashamed. The pharmaceutical companies have an obligation not just to their shareholders but also to the global public. If they ignore that obligation, the fight against AIDS will never be won.

This is a battle that requires as many reinforcements as possible, from every institution in our global society. And I should say that while governments are essential, and while drug companies are, too, they're not the only ones. We need other corporations, as many as are able to lend a hand. You'd be amazed what an effect they can have.

I remember back in 1987 when General Motors was one of the first major businesses outside Hollywood to launch an AIDS prevention and education programme for its employees. At the time they employed 519,000 workers. That's a lot of people who learned the details of the disease because executives at the company decided that AIDS mattered. And the fact that GM was willing to take this step, I'm sure, played a big role in other companies getting on board, too.

Or take a more contemporary example: Walgreens, America's largest drugstore chain, has designated more than five hundred of its pharmacies as 'HIV Centers of Excellence' in communities heavily affected by HIV/ AIDS. These stores are staffed with specially trained pharmacists. Their shelves are fully stocked with anti-retrovirals, and many of these stores carry female condoms, which can be very hard to find. The pharmacists call their patients frequently. They work with drug companies to get medicine donated to patients who can't afford to pay. They even help those who are suffering through related crises – addiction, for example – to seek help or treatment.

This is how you make a difference. And, by the way, this is how you can make money while doing so. Walgreens is contributing to the fight against AIDS, of course, but I imagine they're also turning a profit by filling prescriptions and obtaining new customers. That's just fine by me. There's nothing wrong with doing good and doing well at the same time, as they say.

There are countless other ways corporations can have an impact. For example, our foundation partnered with the Kaiser Family Foundation and the Black AIDS Institute on Greater Than AIDS, a wonderful initiative among public and private sector partners that aims to educate and mobilise those most affected by the AIDS epidemic in America. As part of this effort, major media companies and other corporate allies are working alongside health departments and AIDS service and community-based organisations to increase the knowledge and understanding of HIV/AIDS and to confront the stigma surrounding the disease.

There are scores of corporations that have been essential to the fight, even if they aren't on the front lines themselves. Our foundation has received millions of dollars from hundreds of corporate donors over the last twenty years. There is an enormous amount of money pumping through the corporate world, and there are good-hearted people at these companies. I know this firsthand. Our goal should be to channel some of these resources and the efforts of corporate executives into the fight against AIDS.

In fact, every institution of influence, every institution with resources, must step up if we are to win this battle.

We can't do it alone. We can't do it with only some. We need everyone, from the boardrooms to the front lines. We need them all – governments, corporations, and, yes, even religious institutions. *Especially* religious institutions.

In the summer of 2010, the German journalist Peter Seewald sat down with Pope Benedict XVI over several days for an interview he planned to turn into a book. They spoke about a number of issues, but the one that caught the most public attention was the conversation they had about AIDS.

Seewald asked the pope about the church's efforts to fight AIDS, especially in light of its strict opposition to contraception. 'Critics,' Seewald said bluntly, 'object that it is madness to forbid a high-risk population to use condoms.' Pope Benedict gave a lengthy response. At the end of it, he seemed to do what AIDS advocates had demanded for as long as the disease has been known; he seemed to reverse the church's position on condoms:

> There may be a basis in the case of some individuals, as perhaps when a male prostitute uses a condom, where this can be a first step in the direction of a moralization, a first assumption of responsibility, on the way toward recovering an awareness that not everything is allowed and that one cannot do whatever one wants.[6]

Seewald was surprised by the pope's reply. 'Are you saying, then,' he asked, 'that the Catholic Church is actually not opposed in principle to the use of condoms?' Again, an astounding reversal from the pope:

> She of course does not regard it as a real or moral solution, but, in this or that case, there can be nonetheless, in the intention of reducing the risk of infection, a first step in a movement toward a different way, a more human way, of living sexuality.[7]

Now, if you're like me, you could read the pope's words a dozen times and still wonder what in God's name (literally) he is talking about. But when reports of these quotes broke, there was a sense of utter elation. It turns out that even these contorted statements were a radical departure from the church's deeply held, long-time position against condoms.

In the fight against AIDS, I'm sorry to say, there have been few institutions more destructive than the Catholic Church itself. And to a large degree this has been due to the church's stance on condoms. In the late 1960s, Pope Paul VI sent a papal letter to all the bishops of the church, laying out his – and their – official position. He outright rejected the use of contraception of any kind, in any circumstance, saying it was 'to be absolutely excluded as lawful means of regulating the number of children.'[8]

The impact of that decree was felt worldwide long before the AIDS crisis emerged. But in the '80s and '90s, when it became clear that there was a deadly sexually transmitted disease ravaging populations, that there was no cure for it, and that the only method to prevent transmission was the use of condoms, the church's position became all the more untenable. It wasn't just leading to unwanted pregnancies; it was leading to death – by the millions.

Sadly, Pope John Paul II was horrifically rigid. Just a few months after Ryan White died, the pope travelled to Africa, where he emphasised, even while talking about the need to combat AIDS, that contraception was a sin. It is not at all an exaggeration to say that his words were deadly.[9] I hold him personally responsible for all those who died as a result of heeding his advice, or who couldn't access condoms due to his ill-founded and immoral decree. I've said before that his words resulted in genocide, and I stand by that statement. For as much love and adoration as there is in the world for Pope John Paul II, I will never forgive him for this.

What's worse, if you can imagine anything worse, the church actively *misinformed* its worshippers. It's one thing, I suppose, to tell people that the use of condoms is a sin. It is entirely another to tell them that condoms do not work at all. And yet that's exactly what happened. As *The Guardian* reported in 2003, 'The Catholic Church is telling people in countries stricken with AIDS not to use condoms because they have tiny holes in them through which HIV can pass.'[10]

This, of course, is categorically untrue. The correct use of condoms reduces the risk of HIV transmission by 90 per cent. But that didn't stop the church from preaching otherwise. It didn't stop Pope Benedict XVI, in 2009, from saying in Africa that the use of condoms actually makes the problem of HIV worse.[11] Nor did it stop the church from lobbying for a law in El Salvador that required condoms to carry a false warning label that said they don't protect against HIV.[12]

It's essential to note here that not everyone in the Catholic Church agrees with this position and that countless Catholics, especially nuns and priests who minister to people living with HIV/AIDS, have chosen to reject the church's dogma. They encourage the people they work with to use condoms. They find the church position impossible to square with the death and suffering it has unleashed.

I've met a lot of these dedicated and faithful Catholics. Our foundation has worked with them in many different countries. To spend any time with these caring priests and nuns is to know that *they* are the real church. They are the people truly obeying and representing the teachings of Christ. I remember Nicholas Kristof of the *New York Times* recounting a story of a priest in Brazil, who told him, 'If I were pope, I would start a condom factory right in the Vatican. What's the point of sending food and medicine when we let people get infected with AIDS and die?'[13]

Given this sordid history, all the unnecessary suffering and death, you can understand how important it was to have Pope Benedict shift the church's position, if only slightly. I have to give him credit for that, even as I reject what he's said about condoms making the AIDS crisis worse. He hasn't gone as far as I want him to, or as far as we need him to, and his position seems contradictory at best. But this fiercely conservative pope has taken a first step toward a change in the church's position on condoms – a step few thought he would ever take, on a road that could lead, if the Vatican chooses, toward the eradication of AIDS.

If we can't do it without government on our side, or drug companies on our side, or corporations on our side, we certainly can't do it without religious institutions on our side. Their power is too great, their influence too far-reaching, for us to succeed with them as our adversaries. And so we need them to stand with us in the fight against AIDS. Yes, that means outreach and treatment and support – which, in fairness, the Catholic Church does quite a bit of. But it means more than that. It means encouraging prevention based on logic and science. It means rejecting stigma instead of reinforcing it. It means ending, once and for all, the misinformation campaign that is killing people all over the world.

This is especially true for the Catholic Church, both because of its history and because of its extraordinary reach with some 1 billion faithful. But it is crucial for all religions, all houses of worship, no matter how big or small, in all nations. There is no excuse for furthering pain and injustice in the name of any god. As I've said, I am not a religious man. But I know there is no god, not in any religion, who believes we should turn our backs on the sick. No god could possibly condone inaction and misinformation that result in death. No loving god could possibly embrace those consequences.

These, as I see it, are the major institutions that matter most and that have the most responsibility to act. Governments. Corporations. Religious organisations. They each have the power to respond to the AIDS crisis in different ways. They each have the ability to do extraordinary good and terrible harm, and they all have that choice to make for themselves.

But even if they act responsibly, even if they join together in common cause to end this disease, they still cannot do it *entirely* alone. There are roles they can't – or, at least, won't – ever take on. And that leaves holes in the strategy, gaps that can be filled only by non-profit organisations working within civil society.

Think about it. President Clinton was able to cut the price of AIDS drugs by doing something with his foundation that he never could have done from the White House: encouraging other nations to violate international patents. That's an example of a big non-profit organisation doing big things. But there are small organisations, too, foundations not run by ex-presidents, non-profits working on the front lines, doing work you won't ever see governments do.

For instance, EJAF funds a fantastic Washington, DC-based organisation called HIPS, which stands for 'Helping Individual Prostitutes Survive.' They're focused entirely on sex workers living with HIV or at risk of contracting it. That's a marginalised, stigmatised population that we have to assist if we're going to end the disease, but it's one the American government won't be supporting anytime soon, I can assure you.

Without non-profits, critical work like this would go undone. Charitable organisations have a tremendous role to play in fighting AIDS and a tremendous responsibility as well, just like every other institution I've discussed here. Because the work of non-profits is essential, the way they undergo their work is essential, too. Non-profits must act appropriately and with the same accountability that we demand of governments and corporations and religious institutions.

Whether you're operating a grant-making foundation like EJAF, or a small on-the-ground organisation like the many we fund, the strength of the operation determines the reach of its impact. And that matters a great deal. If we're going to end this disease, the impact of non-profits must reach as far as possible. Resources are so precious that we can't be wasteful; otherwise, we're harming the cause.

There are a lot of wonderful people who want to do important work. They have what they believe is a unique idea, and they decide to start a non-profit. But what some fail to do before they start, or even after, is to determine whether another organisation is already doing what they've set out to undertake. Sometimes non-profits re-invent the wheel without realising it. Other times they figure out that they're duplicating another organisation's effort, but they convince themselves that they can do it better anyway. Sometimes they're right, sometimes that works out. But too often it doesn't, and scarce funds are wasted.

If you're going to start your own organisation, more power to you. I think it's fantastic, and for me, it's been a life-changing experience. But it's essential that new organisations fill a need that isn't already being met. Otherwise it's a waste of that organisation's time and its donors' money. Non-profit organisations that work together on a particular issue need to see themselves as part of a single strategic team, not as isolated players.

This was the core of EJAF's operating philosophy in the early 1990s, and it remains so today. We figured the thing we could do better than others was raise money. But rather than trying to determine the best way to use the money we raised (which would have itself cost a lot of money), EJAF-U.S. found an organisation that had figured out how to do that already – the National Community AIDS Partnership. Instead of hiring teams of people to go out on the front lines, we identified organisations that were already on the ground doing the work, and we made sure they had funding to be successful.

Indeed, at the UK arm of my foundation alone, through strategic partnerships we've leveraged an additional $350 million on top of the funds that have been raised directly by EJAF. In the United States, we've leveraged another $127 million. Simply by working with other organisations to fight AIDS in a coordinated and united way, we've greatly increased our direct impact.

This idea of leverage must be paramount for non-profits, most of which have very limited resources. Finding opportunities to maximise those resources through programming or fund-raising partnerships is essential. It's like the old saying: 'The whole is greater than the sum of its parts.' In my experience, any achievements made in charitable work are *collective* achievements. Leveraging partnerships is not only a very good idea; it is an absolute necessity.

Ultimately, perhaps more than anything else, non-profits need credibility to succeed. And that credibility comes not just from success in the field but also from proof that the headquarters are being run as efficiently as possible. It matters to donors, who may choose to write a large cheque or withhold a large cheque, depending on how the operation is being handled. When you lose credibility on how you run your organisation, you lose donations. And when you lose donations, you lose the ability to meet your mission.

That's why I'm most proud of the fact that EJAF has operated with relentless efficiency from day one. Ever since the years when we were scraping by with a makeshift office in John Scott's kitchen, we have continued to keep our overhead costs as low as possible. As a result of the tight ship we run, EJAF has been awarded

Charity Navigator's highest four-star rating for seven years in a row. More important, our efficiency is why we've received such tremendous support from many wonderful individuals and corporate sponsors over the years. Our donors know that we take our work and their contributions seriously, and that their funds will be used wisely to achieve maximum impact.

So, you see, we all have a role to play. Governments, corporations, religious institutions, and civil society. We can't afford to have anyone on the sidelines. We are all responsible for ending AIDS, and we must all contribute to that worthy goal. But none of us can succeed alone. Beating this epidemic will require every major institution of modern life to fight together and find common cause despite vast differences. That is an incredibly daunting task, uniting the world in this way. But I believe it *can* be done.

If we work together, and with compassion at the centre of our efforts, it really is possible to end AIDS.

IO

Ending AIDS Forever

You might think that I'm naive, plain and simple. Just another celebrity with a foundation, another rock star who thinks he has the answer to the world's ills. AIDS is a deadly disease, not something we can wish away with sappy sentiments and positive thinking. This is the real world, and it's not always a nice one. There is so much fighting, so much hate. How could *love* be the cure for anything at all?

When it comes to AIDS, however, love *is* the cure. Indeed, as of this moment, and for the foreseeable future, it is the *only* cure.

AIDS isn't like other diseases. It's special, you could say. Consider the difference between AIDS and cancer. If you were able to treat everyone with cancer on the planet, if you could give everyone the best, most cutting-edge treatment possible, other people would still get cancer. And, sadly, a lot of those who received treatment would still die.

The same goes for other diseases among the top killers worldwide, such as heart disease, or stroke, or diabetes. Existing science alone can't yet abolish these afflictions. We don't yet know how to fully treat or fully prevent these epidemics. We will need further medical advances to accomplish that.

But, at this point, if all AIDS research were to suddenly stop, if we were never to make another discovery in our understanding of the HIV virus, we could still beat it. We could save the life of nearly *every* HIV-positive person and prevent *all* future infections. We could end AIDS. And that is an *amazing* fact. It's a fact that makes AIDS rather unique among the world's deadliest pandemics.

Right now, while we don't yet have a cure for AIDS, we do have the next best thing: medicine that can return dying AIDS patients to near perfect health and give them very long lives. There can sometimes be unpleasant side-effects of the medication, of course, as with many drugs. And some people, like my friend Eli, can still lose their lives to complications, despite receiving the very best medical treatment.

But today's treatments are overwhelmingly life-saving, and that's the bottom line. HIV is no longer a death sentence. With treatment, HIV morphs from a lethal virus into a chronic condition that can be managed.

With treatment, almost every single HIV-positive person can live happily, comfortably, productively, and – to echo my friend Ryan's only wish – *normally*. Today, you can be HIV-positive and lead a very normal life indeed.

What's more, if we made treatment universal, over time, we could end the AIDS epidemic *forever*.

Let me explain.

In 2011, researchers funded by the U.S. government made a miraculous discovery: people living with HIV who receive treatment are up to *96 per cent less likely* to pass on the virus to a sexual partner. In other words, current treatments are so effective that they reduce the presence of the HIV virus in an infected person's body to almost nil. The chance of infecting others plummets as a result. That means *treatment is also prevention*. And therefore if we treat everyone, we can drastically reduce the spread of HIV. By giving medication to every single person living with HIV/AIDS in the world today – or even *almost* everyone – we can prevent tens of millions of future infections. We would save millions of lives of those already infected, yes, but we would also begin to end this disease by stopping it from spreading.

At the same time, we must double-down on other highly effective and proven preventive measures. Free condoms, sex education, and needle exchange programmes are essential components of any effort to end AIDS.

Ideally, we would provide these to marginalised and high-risk populations such as sex workers, injection drug users, and men who have sex with men. Also, it turns out that heterosexual men who are circumcised are about 60 per cent less likely to pass HIV to a sexual partner, and therefore many AIDS advocates suggest voluntary male circumcision as a very important tool to stop the spread of HIV. Finally, to keep AIDS on the run, we must also ensure that all those who receive medication stay on it for the rest of their lives. That's because of the way our current treatments work. If people with HIV stop taking their medicine, the virus comes roaring back. Even worse, it can come back stronger, more virulent, and potentially resistant to today's treatments. If many HIV-positive people were to stop taking their medicine all at once, it could trigger a new AIDS epidemic, one that we might not be able to treat or prevent.

Consider, then, where we are today in the treatment and prevention of HIV/AIDS. We have amazing drugs that can hold the virus at bay indefinitely and all but stop it from spreading. We have prevention methods that can further eliminate any chance of transmitting the virus. What this means is that we don't need to wait for a vaccine for HIV, though I desperately hope we will find one soon. What we need to end AIDS *right now* is the compassion, the empathy, the commitment, and, yes, the love to make sure that everyone who is HIV-positive has access to existing treatments and established prevention methods.

You can't say that about cancer or heart disease or practically any other epidemic. But because of the efforts of scientists and doctors and researchers all over the world, you *can* say that about AIDS. If we can find the love as a global community to agree that every life has equal value, if we can summon the compassion to provide treatment and prevention for everyone living with HIV – and I mean *everyone*, no matter who they are, where they live, or how rich or poor they may be – we can end AIDS forever. We can prevent 34 million people from dying and tens of millions more from getting sick in the first place, and we can contain the virus itself among those already infected. Over time, as HIV-positive people would live normal lives and die normal deaths, new infections would plummet, and the HIV virus would simply cease to exist. The AIDS epidemic would be over.

Can you imagine that? *An AIDS-free world.* The very thought makes my heart leap. And it's entirely within our grasp. This isn't a fairy tale; it's really, truly possible. We can cure this disease without a cure. We can end AIDS with love.

That is why the reality of AIDS treatment and prevention today is so incredibly tragic. For all the progress being made in expanding HIV treatment around the world, it is still the case that not even *half* of the 14.2 million people in low- and middle-income countries in need of antiretroviral therapy received it in 2010. That means there is still a lot of work to be done. What's more, we aren't widely implementing the prevention efforts that are proven to be effective. In some places, we are not even implementing them at all.

You might think this is because it's simply too expensive to provide treatment and prevention to all who need it. After all, so much in our world comes down to dollars and cents. Surely it must cost a fortune to purchase medicine for tens of millions of people with HIV and, in so doing, begin to end the epidemic. If such a thing were possible, if such a thing were *affordable*, we would have done it already, you might reasonably conclude. Money must be why humanity has not taken the necessary steps to end AIDS.

I wish that were true. I wish it were a matter of resources alone. But it isn't. It's a matter of compassion. It all comes down to love.

In 2011, experts at UNAIDS; the Global Fund to Fight AIDS, Tuberculosis, and Malaria; PEPFAR; the Gates Foundation; the World bank; and the World

Health Organization, among others, conducted an exhaustive joint study.[1] They modelled a way to use all existing treatments and proven prevention methods to end AIDS. Then they tallied the cost and determined how resources would need to be spent over time. What they concluded is astonishing.

According to UNAIDS, in 2010 some $15 billion was available worldwide to fight AIDS in the developing world.[2] The consortium of experts determined that it would take only an additional $5 to $7 billion per year to go from treatment and prevention for *some*, to treatment and prevention for *all who need it*. This additional spending would, the experts say, prevent 12.2 million new infections and save 7.4 million lives between 2011 and 2020 alone.

Initially, funding would ramp up, but then it would steadily decline. Worldwide spending would need to rise from $16.6 billion in 2011 to $22 billion per year in 2015, and from that point it would drop to $19.8 billion in 2020. After 2020, the cost of a worldwide campaign to end AIDS would continue to decline precipitously, because far fewer people would become newly infected and the cost of treatment would drop for those already living with HIV.

And there you have it. We know how to end AIDS, and we know what it would cost: an additional $5 to

$7 billion each year from now until 2020, and not very much more than we're spending today beyond that.

At first, this sounds like quite a lot of money. In the hands of an individual, it would be an incredible windfall. If you had several billion dollars, you'd be one of the richest people on earth. But when you put several billion dollars in the context of other spending, you quickly realise that it's not very much money at all. In fact, it's a tiny, almost meaningless sum in the grand scheme of things.

Consider that in 2010, Americans alone spent $11 billion on vitamins, $16.9 billion on chocolate, and $18.7 billion on pet food. A handful of Wall Street banks paid out $20.8 billion in bonuses to employees and executives that same year. More recently Apple, Inc., made profits of $13 billion in the first quarter of 2012 alone. In fact, at the beginning of 2012, Apple had cash reserves of $96.7 billion. That's right; a single corporation has, sitting in its bank account, far more than the additional funds we would need to finance a global campaign to end the AIDS epidemic.

I'm not suggesting that Americans should starve their pets or that Apple should use iPhone profits to fight AIDS. My point is simply this: the several billion dollars in additional spending needed to end AIDS is a pittance when compared to even minute snapshots of global commerce. And for governments – especially in Western countries, developed economies, and large developing countries – several billion dollars a year is the practical equivalent of the change in your pocket.

I mean that quite literally. Take the United States, for instance, the world's richest nation, with the largest economy. The budget of the American government in 2011 was $3.7 *trillion*. This is an incomprehensibly large figure. For reference, a billion is to a trillion dollars what $1 is to $1,000. If you had $3,700 in your current account, would you not part with an extra $5 to $7 to save millions upon millions of lives?

I should say here that the U.S. government has already pledged $48 billion to PEPFAR from 2009 to 2013 to fight AIDS, tuberculosis, and malaria in the developing world. And in 2010, the Kaiser Family Foundation estimated that the United States provided 54.2 per cent of all international AIDS assistance.[3] The American people and their government are doing more than any other nation to fight this disease, and Americans should be very proud of this fact. Indeed, they should be celebrated for it. But imagine, with another $5 to $7 billion per year – a rounding error in the federal budget – the United States could *single-handedly* end AIDS. For a small fraction of what was spent on the war in Iraq, America would forever be heralded as the country that won the war against AIDS. And yet this need not be an American burden to bear. Governments of the world could easily commit the necessary funds to end AIDS. The cost would be a single drop in the vast ocean of worldwide government spending. The money would not even be missed.

I don't mean to suggest that money is the *only* thing we need to end AIDS. It is absolutely necessary, but not by any means sufficient. In addition to greater resources, we need greater understanding, and that is where you, my dear reader, come in.

HIV/AIDS is a disease that not only attacks the human immune system; it attacks the human social system. It infects our civic institutions with fear, our communities with hate, our corporations with greed, our churches and synagogues and mosques with loathing. There is no medicine, no creation of science, that will inoculate us from these social afflictions. And that is why the cure for AIDS is a matter of changing hearts and educating minds.

To end AIDS, we need countries like Uganda to change their laws so we can reach gay people in need of help. We need the Catholic Church to stop telling its members that condoms are sinful, and even worse that they do not work. We need pharmaceutical companies to give up some profits in the name of humanity. We need charitable organisations to keep up the amazing work they are doing, marching forward with a vengeance and moving the front lines of our fight against AIDS.

But these institutions aren't nameless, faceless monoliths. They start with individuals, and they are guided by individuals. Whether they do good or ill is up to individual choice. And while the disease is bigger than any one of us, the cure requires something from each of us.

It requires us to talk to our partners, to practise safe sex, and to get tested, and we must encourage friends and loved ones to do the same. It requires us to stand up for those living with HIV/AIDS and those most at risk of becoming infected. It requires us to educate ourselves about what governments and religious organisations are doing – and not doing – in our names. It requires us to embrace all those who need and deserve our compassion.

In other words, ending AIDS requires love, and lots of it. And the best way to engender love is to foster dialogue. We can only love one another if we understand one another. That is why I have written this book. And I hope that you will talk about what you have read here with others. When AIDS is an uncomfortable and untouchable subject, the disease spreads. But when we bring it to the fore, when we aren't afraid to confront it, information spreads. Compassion spreads. The cure spreads.

Please, help me spread the cure.

Ending this disease is no longer a matter of money. And it is no longer a matter of technology. It is a matter of finding the will to do what is necessary to save countless lives and beat this terrible pandemic. It's a matter of fighting stigma and politics, intolerance and indifference. The question is not whether we *can* do it, or whether we can *afford* to do it. The question is whether we *care* enough to do it.

No one is blameless in this terrible equation of apathy. Including me. I am the first to stand up and say that I did not do enough. I did not care enough. But I have changed. And so can we all. So can our institutions. So can our communities. So can our global society. I believe that with every fibre of my being. If I didn't believe it, I wouldn't have written this book. If I didn't believe it, I would have simply given up. But I won't give up, I never will, because I have seen the power of compassion. I won't give up, because I believe in love.

In 2009, David and I visited an AIDS orphanage in Donetsk, Ukraine. It was a familiar scene to me, I'm sad to say. Dozens of children, perhaps even a hundred, many of whom were HIV-positive, many of whom were only infants and toddlers, living in dorm-like conditions and being looked after by a wonderful but terribly under-resourced staff.

A boy gravitated toward me. He was eighteen months old, and his name was Lev. In an instant, he stole my heart. I held Lev, and I was in love. I had always said I was too old, too selfish, too set in my ways to have children, even though David was keen for us to have a family one day. The truth is that I love children – David and I are godparents many times over. But with our hectic schedules, with my travelling on tour constantly, it didn't seem like it would ever work out for us to have a child of our own.

All that changed the minute Lev's eyes met mine. David and I tried to adopt Lev. We were heart-broken that Ukraine's draconian laws prevented us from doing so without waiting several years, during which time Lev would have to remain in the orphanage. I couldn't stomach that, so instead Lev and his brother went to live with their grandmother.

It was then that David and I decided to have a child. Lev had sent us a message we could not ignore. Our son, Zachary, was born on Christmas Day in 2010.

Zachary is the light of our lives. Already he has taught me so much about life, and so much about love. In a very real way, the stories I've told here – the lessons they've taught me – are how I came to be blessed with my beautiful son.

I would not have Zachary but for the strangers who demonstrated such care and compassion for me at the lowest moments of my life. I would not have Zachary but for my friendship with Ryan White. I would not have Zachary but for my decision twenty years ago to make it up to Ryan and those I had let down because of my addictions and indifference. I would not have Zachary but for the creation of EJAF. I would not have Zachary but for my visit with David to the AIDS orphanage in Donetsk.

I would not have Zachary but for love.

It comes down to a simple equation, really. If you give love out, you get love back. If you take nothing else from the stories I've told here, please take that lesson to heart. It's the only thing that matters. It's why we need a global movement for love, and not just when it comes to AIDS. We need to love the poor, we need to love the sick, and we need to love those who we perceive as different. If love drives our actions, we can end AIDS. If love drives our actions, we can build a better world.

Every day, I watch Zachary learn a little more about life. Everything to him is fresh, everything is new. There is no hate in his heart, only wonder. We all came into the world that way. Our attitudes are learned from others. Our perspectives are shaped by experience. Zachary is learning from David and from me. Other children are learning from their families, from their communities, from the world around them and how they are treated by it. We can teach love as easily as we can teach hate.

Let us teach Zachary and his generation the power of love. Let us do so by ending AIDS.

Acknowledgements

First and foremost, I would like to thank my partner in all things, including this book, David Furnish. As chairman of the Elton John AIDS Foundation, David plays an instrumental role in the work you have read about here. EJAF is our joint passion, and I couldn't have written this book without his love, inspiration, guidance, and significant effort.

Scott Campbell, the executive director of EJAF-U.S., and Anne Aslett, the executive director of EJAF-UK, are, along with David, the reason my foundation has had such an incredible impact in recent years. Scott and Anne are more than trusted advisers and dedicated professionals. They are also very dear friends, and I thank them both for making this book possible and for their tireless work on behalf of EJAF.

I would also like to thank EJAF's staff in London and New York for continually achieving results far beyond their small numbers. I am grateful each and every day for their innumerable contributions to the fight against AIDS. They are the authors of this book as much as I am.

EJAF's outsize impact is due not only to its dedicated leadership and staff but also to its brilliant board of directors, which comprises many old friends who are deeply and personally dedicated to our mission and our work. EJAF is profoundly lucky to draw on their wisdom, passion, and ingenuity. In addition, we could not function – indeed we would not exist – without the extraordinary generosity of our donors and sponsors. So many supporters have been on the journey with us and shared our vision for years and years. Time and again, they came through when it was most needed. It's no exaggeration to say that their generosity has saved and transformed countless lives.

I've told many stories in this book of people from around the world – people living with AIDS; people on the front lines of the fight against the epidemic; people who are fighting for their lives, for the lives of others, and for a more just society. These people are real-life heroes. They are my heroes. Their struggles and their resilience have inspired me deeply. I wrote this book because I wanted the world to know their stories, and I thank them all for the opportunity to share something of their lives – and, I hope, to improve the lives of many others in so doing.

While I have been intimately involved in the fight against AIDS for twenty years, I am no expert on the history or science of the HIV/AIDS epidemic. That's why I have drawn on the work of many gifted researchers, journalists, academics, and AIDS advocates throughout this book. We should all be grateful that they have dedicated their professional efforts to helping the world better understand this disease and spreading information that contributes so greatly to fighting it.

I was thrilled when Michael Pietsch decided to take on this project. He believed in the message of the book from day one, and I appreciate his many insights and contributions, as well as those of his terrific staff at Little, Brown.

Finally, I would like to thank Ben Yarrow, a long-time partner of EJAF on our strategic communications, for working with me on this book and helping me bring it to fruition. Ben and his outstanding team at West Wing Writers – Ryan Clancy, David Heifetz, Dylan Loewe, Brittney Moraski, and Sarada Peri – were wonderful collaborators, and I am very grateful to have had the benefit of their many talents.

Notes

CHAPTER 1: RYAN

1 Ryan White and Marie Cunningham, *Ryan White: My Own Story* (New York: Signet, 1992), 93, 134, 135.

2 Cory SerVaas, 'The Happier Days for Ryan White,' *Saturday Evening Post*, March 1, 1988.

CHAPTER 2: A DECADE OF LOSS

1 Avert, 'History of AIDS up to 1986,' accessed February 23, 2012, http://www.avert.org/aids-history-86.htm.

2 Lawrence K. Altman, 'Rare Cancer Seen in 41 Homosexuals,' *New York Times*, July 3, 1981, accessed February 14, 2012, http://www.nytimes.com/1981/07/03/us/rare-cancer-seen-in-41-homosexuals.html.

3 'Fear of AIDS Infects the Nation,' *U.S. News & World Report*, June 27, 1983.

4 Randy Shilts, *And the Band Played On: Politics, People, and the AIDS Epidemic*, 20th anniversary ed. (New York: St Martin's Griffin, 1988), 299.

5 John G. Roberts and Deborah K. Owen, 'Presidential Briefing Memo,' *Frontline*, accessed December 23, 2011,

http://www.pbs.org/wgbh/pages/frontline/aids/docs/ robertsmemo.html.

6   Shilts, *And the Band*, 321.

7   Jack Friedman and David Van Biema, 'Breaking America's Heart,' *People* 28, no. 5 (1987), accessed December 15, 2011, http://www.people.com/people/archive/article/ 0,,20199548,00.html.

8   Shilts, *And the Band*, 321.

9   Ibid., 352–53.

10 Ibid., 324.

11 Ibid., 295.

12 Donald P. Francis, 'A Plea for More Funding,' *Frontline*, accessed December 23, 2011, http://www.pbs.org/wgbh/ pages/frontline/aids/docs/francisplea.html; Shilts, *And the Band*, 273.

13 Shilts, *And the Band*, 191.

14 Ibid., 110.

15 Philip Boffey, 'Reagan Defends Financing for AIDS,' *New York Times*, September 18, 1985, accessed December 23, 2011, http://www.nytimes.com/1985/09/18/us/reagan-defends-financing-for-aids.html.

16 Shilts, *And the Band*, 143.

17 Associated Press, 'AIDS Gets Mixed Response from Clergy,' *Ocala Star-Banner*, October 5, 1985, accessed January 4, 2012, http://news.google.com/newspapers? nid=1356&dat=19851005&id=-35RAAAAIBAJ&sjid =UAYEAAAAIBAJ&pg=2891,3418390.

18 Shilts, *And the Band*, 311.

19 Michael Hirsley, 'Aids Education Effort May Have

Backfired,' *Chicago Tribune*, November 10, 1985, accessed January 4, 2012, http://articles.chicagotribune.com/ 1985–11–10/news/8503170436_1_aids-victims-common-cup-blood-banks.

20 Abigail Trafford and Gordon Witkin, 'The Politics of AIDS – A Tale of Two States,' *U.S. News & World Report*, November 18, 1985.

21 Rock Hudson and Sara Davidson, *Rock Hudson: His Story* (New York: William Morrow, 1986), 158, accessed March 2, 2012, http://www.amazon.com/dp/0688064728/ref=rdr_ext_tmb.

22 William F. Buckley, 'Crucial Steps in Combating the Aids Epidemic; Identify All the Carriers,' *New York Times*, March 18, 1986, accessed December 23, 2011, http://www.nytimes.com/books/00/07/16/specials/ buckley-aids.html.

23 Shilts, *And the Band*, 587.

24 Ronald Reagan, 'President Reagan's amfAR Speech,' *Frontline*, accessed December 23, 2011, http://www.pbs.org/wgbh/pages/frontline/aids/docs/amfar.html.

CHAPTER 5: A CRISIS OF CARING

1 Black AIDS Institute, *Deciding Moment: The State of AIDS in Black America 2011*, accessed December 7, 2011, http://dl.dropbox.com/u/20533079/2011stateofaidsfullreport.pdf.

2 Jose A. Vargas, 'An Overwhelmed D.C. Agency Loses Count of AIDS Cases,' *Washington Post*, December 30, 2006, accessed December 7, 2011, http://www.

washingtonpost.com/wp-dyn/content/ article/2006/12/29/ AR2006122901543.html.

3   Jose A. Vargas and Darryl Fears, 'At Least 3 Percent of D.C. Residents Have HIV or AIDS, City Study Finds; Rate up 22 Percent from 2006,' *Washington Post*, March 15, 2009, accessed December 8, 2011, http://www. washingtonpost.com/wp-dyn/content/article/2009/03/14/ AR2009031402176.html.

4   Debbie Cenziper, 'Staggering Need, Striking Neglect,' *Washington Post*, October 19, 2009, accessed December 8, 2011, http://www.washingtonpost.com/wp-dyn/content/ article/2009/10/17/AR2009101701984.html.

5   Ibid.

6   Centers for Disease Control and Prevention, 'HIV and AIDS Among Gay and Bisexual Men,' accessed March 22, 2012, http://www.cdc.gov/nchhstp/newsroom/docs/ fastfacts-msm-final508comp.pdf.

7   Anne C. Spaulding, Ryan M. Seals, Matthew J. Page, Amanda K. Brzozowski, and William Rhodes, 'HIV/ AIDS Among Inmates of and Releasees from U.S. Correctional Facilities, 2006: Declining Share of Epidemic but Persistent Public Health Opportunity,' *PLoS One* (2009), accessed February 14, 2012, http:// www.plosone. org/article/info:doi/10.1371/journal.pone.0007558.

8   'Remarks by Elizabeth Glaser: July 14 Madison Square Garden, New York City,' *Washington Post*, August 25, 1992.

CHAPTER 6: CONFRONTING REALITY

1   Rachel Jewkes, Yandisa Sikweyiya, Robert Morrell, and Kristin Dunkle, 'Understanding Men's Health and Use of Violence: Interface of Rape and HIV in South Africa,' South African Medical Research Council, accessed February 12, 2012, http://www.mrc.ac.za/gender/violence_hiv.pdf.

2   Ibid.

3   Peacewomen, 'South Africa: Rape Contributes to HIV/AIDS Spread Among SADC Women and Girls,' accessed February 12, 2012, http://www.peacewomen.org/news_article.php?id=1538&type=news.

4   Médecins Sans Frontières, 'Shattered Lives: Immediate Medical Care Vital for Sexual Violence Victims,' accessed February 12, 2012, http://www.doctorswithoutborders.org/publications/article_print.cfm?id=3464.

5   David Smith, 'Quarter of Men in South Africa Admit Rape, Survey Finds,' *The Guardian*, June 17, 2009, accessed February 12, 2012, http://www.guardian.co.uk/world/2009/jun/17/south-africa-rape-survey.

6   Erving Goffman, *Stigma: Notes on the Management of Spoiled Identity* (New York: Simon & Schuster, 1963).

7   G. M. Herek, 'Illness, Stigma, and AIDS,' in *Psychological Aspects of Serious Illness* (Washington, DC: American Psychological Association, 1990), 103–50, also available online as a preprint of chapter, accessed April 24, 2012, http://psychology.ucdavis.edu/rainbow/html/AIDS_stigma_1990_pre.pdf.

8   Ibid.

9   Ibid.

10 Eddie Bruce-Jones and Lucas P. Itaborahy, 'State-Sponsored Homophobia: A World Survey of Laws Criminalising Same-Sex Sexual Acts Between Consenting Adults,' International Lesbian and Gay Association, accessed February 12, 2012, http://old.ilga.org/Statehomophobia/ ILGA_State_Sponsored_Homophobia_2011.pdf.

11 International Gay and Lesbian Human Rights Commission, 'Uganda: Persecution of Lesbians and Gay Men Intensifies,' accessed February 12, 2012, http://www. iglhrc.org/cgi-bin/iowa/article/pressroom/ pressrelease/517.html.

12 Human Rights Watch, 'Epidemic of Abuse: Police Harassment of HIV/AIDS Outreach Workers in India,' accessed February 12, 2012, http://www.unhcr.org/ refworld/docid/3d4fc51f4.html.

13 amfAR, 'MSM and HIV/AIDS Risk in Asia: What Is Fueling the Epidemic Among MSM and How Can It Be Stopped?' accessed February 12, 2012, http://www. amfar.org/uploadedFiles/In_the_Community/Publications /MSM%20and%20HIV%20AIDS%20Risk%20in%20 Asia.pdf.

14 Centers for Disease Control and Prevention, 'HIV and AIDS Among Gay and Bisexual Men,' accessed February 12, 2012, http://www.cdc.gov/nchhstp/newsroom/docs/ fastfacts-msm-final508comp.pdf.

15 Steffanie A. Strathdee and David Vlahov, 'The Effectiveness of Needle Exchange Programs: A Review of the Science and Policy,' *AIDScience* 1, no. 16 (2001),

accessed February 13, 2012, http://aidscience.org/Articles/aidscience013.asp.

16 AIDS Action, 'Syringe Exchange and HIV/AIDS,' accessed March 2, 2012, http://www.aidsaction.org/attachments/518_Syringe%20Exchange.pdf.

17 '*HIV Is Not a Crime*, 2011 Film by Sean Strub, Edit by Leo Herrera/HomoChic,' YouTube video, 8:12, posted by 'SeanStrub,' November 30, 2011, accessed April 24, 2012, http://www.youtube.com/watch?v=iB-6blJjbjc.

18 Madison Park, 'As HIV Epidemic Grows, Florida City Grapples with Fear and Denial,' CNN, November 29, 2011, accessed February 13, 2012, http://www.cnn.com/2011/11/29/health/jacksonville-hiv-florida/index.html.

CHAPTER 7: THE HEART OF THE MATTER

1 Evgeny Lebedev, 'On the Streets with Ukraine's Lost Generation,' *The Independent*, December 1, 2011, accessed December 17, 2011, http://www.independent.co.uk/lifestyle/health-and-families/features/elton-john-on-the-streets-with-ukraines-lost-generation-6270102.html.

2 Paul Smith, 'Welcome to the Occupation,' accessed December 22, 2011, http://www.welcometotheoccupation.com/2010/01/hr-carnival-to-aid-haiti-serovie.html.

3 IGLHRC/SEROvie, 'The Impact of the Earthquake and Relief and Recovery Programs on Haitian LGBT People,' accessed December 21, 2011, http://www.iglhrc.org/cgi-bin/iowa/article/publications/reportsandpublications/1369.html.

4 Ibid.

5 Ibid.

CHAPTER 8: A GREAT POWER

1 Bill Frist, *A Heart to Serve: The Passion to Bring Health, Hope, and Healing* (New York: Center Street, 2009), accessed February 13, 2012, http://books.google.com/books?id =VRg1v0jSoWUC&1pg=PT182&vq=aids&pg =PT3#v=onepage&q=1981&f=false.

2 Heather Timmons and Nikhila Gill, 'India's Health Minister Calls Homosexuality "Unnatural,"' *New York Times,* July 5, 2011, accessed February 13, 2012, http://www.nytimes.com/2011/07/06/world/asia/06india.html.

3 Sarah Boseley, 'Mbeki Aids Denial "Caused 300,000 Deaths,"' *The Guardian,* November 26, 2008, accessed February 13, 2012, http://www.guardian.co.uk/world/2008/nov/26/aids-south-africa.

4 Pride Chigwedere, George R. Seage, Sofia Gruskin, Tun-Hou Lee, and M. Essex, 'Estimating the Lost Benefits of Antiretroviral Drug Use in South Africa,' *JAIDS Journal of Acquired Immune Deficiency Syndromes* 49, no. 4 (2008): 410–15, accessed February 13, 2012, http://journals.lww.com/jaids/Fulltext/2008/12010/Estimating_the_Lost_Benefits_of_Antiretroviral.10.aspx.

5 'SA's Zuma "Showered to Avoid HIV,"' BBC News, April 5, 2006, accessed February 13, 2012, http://news.bbc.co.uk/2/hi/africa/4879822.stm.

6 Bruce Japsen, 'Budget Squeeze Could Make HIV Treatment Costlier, Rarer,' *Chicago Tribune,* February 9,

2011, accessed March 23, 2012, http://articles.chicago
tribune.com/2011-02-09/business/ct-biz-0209-aids-
treatment-delays-20110209_1_hiv-drugs-aids-patients-
aids-drug-assistance-program.

CHAPTER 9: A GREAT RESPONSIBILITY

1 Walt Bogdanich and Eric Koli, '2 Paths of Bayer Drug
in '80s: Riskier One Steered Overseas,' *New York Times*,
May 22, 2003, accessed February 14, 2012, http://www.
nytimes.com/2003/05/22/business/2-paths-of-bayer-
drug-in-80-s-riskier-one-steered-overseas
.html?pagewanted=all&src=pm.

2 Jim Edwards, 'Bayer Admits It Paid "Millions" in HIV
Infection Cases – Just Not in English,' CBS News,
January 28, 2011, accessed March 23, 2012, http://www
.cbsnews.com/8301–505123–162–42847237/bayer-
admits-it-paid-millions-in-hiv-infection-cases----just-
not-in-english/.

3 Jonathan Rauch, '"This Is Not Charity,"' *The Atlantic*,
October 2007, accessed February 14, 2012, http://www
.theatlantic.com/magazine/archive/2007/10/-ldquo-this-
is-not-charity-rdquo/6197/.

4 Ibid.

5 Celia W. Dugger, 'Clinton Foundation Announces a
Bargain on Generic AIDS Drugs,' *New York Times*, May
9, 2007, accessed February 14, 2012, http://www.nytimes.
com/2007/05/09/world/09aidsdrugs.html.

6 'Pope Benedict on the Use of Condoms: Book Excerpt,'
BBC News, November 20, 2010, accessed February 14,

2012, http://www.bbc.co.uk/news/world-europe-11804798.

7 Ibid.

8 Vatican, 'Encyclical Letter Humanae Vitae,' accessed February 14, 2012, http://www.vatican.va/holy_father/paul_vi/encyclicals/documents/hf_p-vi_enc_25071968humanae-vitae_en.html.

9 Jonathan Clayton, 'Condom Ban by John Paul Only Escalated Crisis,' *The Australian*, March 19, 2009.

10 'Vatican: Condoms Don't Stop Aids,' *The Guardian*, October 9, 2003, accessed February 14, 2012, http://www.guardian.co.uk/world/2003/oct/09/aids.

11 Riazat Butt, 'Pope Claims Condoms Could Make African Aids Crisis Worse,' *The Guardian*, March 17, 2009, accessed February 14, 2012, http://www.guardian.co.uk/world/2009/mar/17/pope-africa-condoms-aids.

12 Nicholas D. Kristof, 'The Pope and AIDS,' *New York Times*, May 8, 2005, accessed February 14, 2012, http://www.nytimes.com/2005/05/08/opinion/08kristof.html.

13 Ibid.

CHAPTER 10: ENDING AIDS FOREVER

1 Joint United Nations Programme on HIV/AIDS, 'A New Investment Framework for the Global HIV Response,' accessed March 15, 2012, http://www.unaids.org/en/media/unaids/contentassets/documents/unaidspublication/2011/JC2244_InvestmentFramework_en.pdf.

2 UNAIDS, 'World AIDS Day Report 2011,' accessed March 23, 2012, http://www.unaids.org/en/media/unaids/

contentassets/documents/unaidspublication/2011/
JC2216_WorldAIDSday_report_2011_en.pdf.

3   Jennifer Kates, Adam Wexler, Eric Lief, Carlos Avila, and
    Benjamin Gobet, 'Financing the Response to AIDS in
    Low- and Middle-Income Countries: International
    Assistance from Donor Governments in 2010,' UNAIDS
    and Kaiser Family Foundation, accessed April 18, 2012,
    http://www.kff.org/hivaids/upload/7347–07.pdf.

About the Author

The monumental career of international singer-songwriter and performer Sir Elton John has spanned more than five decades. He is one of the top-selling solo artists of all time, with thirty-five Gold and twenty-five Platinum albums and twenty-nine consecutive Top 40 hits, and he has sold more than 250 million records worldwide. Elton holds the record for the biggest-selling single of all time, 'Candle in the Wind,' which sold 37 million copies. The National Academy of Recording Arts and Sciences has awarded Elton five Grammys and the Grammy Legend Award, and honoured him with the MusiCares Person of the Year Award. Elton was inducted into the Rock and Roll Hall of Fame in 1994. Additionally, he was the first artist honoured by the Billboard Touring Conference with its Legend of Live Award, which recognises those in the concert business who have made a significant and lasting impact on the industry. He continues to tour all over the world. Elton was honoured with a commemorative banner during his sixtieth performance at Madison Square Garden for the 'Most Performances by a Single Artist' at the legendary venue. His induction into Madison Square Garden's Music Hall of Fame coincided with his sixtieth birthday. In September 2011 Elton began a three-year residency at the Colosseum at Caesars Palace in Las Vegas with an all-new show, *The Million Dollar Piano*.

His album with Leon Russell, *The Union*, produced by T-Bone Burnett, was released in October 2010 to rave reviews. The first single was nominated for a Grammy for Best Pop Collaboration with Vocals. In April 2011 the Tribeca Film Festival opened with the world premiere of Cameron Crowe's documentary *The Union*, which features the writing and recording of the Elton John and Leon Russell album.

The smash-hit stage production of *Billy Elliot*, for which Elton composed the music, originally opened in London and garnered him a top-five hit in the UK with the song 'Electricity.' *Billy Elliot* was nominated for a record nine Olivier Awards, winning Best Musical, among others. It opened on Broadway on November 13, 2008, to critical acclaim. It was nominated for a record-tying fifteen Tony Awards and won ten, including Best Musical. In March 2011 *Billy Elliot* opened in Toronto to rave reviews.

Elton received an Academy Award for *The Lion King* and Tony Awards for both *The Lion King* and *Aida*. He served as the executive producer for the hugely successful animated feature *Gnomeo & Juliet*, which opened in February 2011.

In 1992, Elton established the Elton John AIDS Foundation (EJAF), which today is one of the leading non-profit HIV/AIDS organisations. EJAF has raised $275 million to date to support hundreds of HIV/AIDS prevention and service programmes in fifty-five countries around the globe. In 1998, the queen of England knighted him Sir Elton John, CBE. In 2004, he received Kennedy Center Honors for his lifetime contributions to American culture and excellence through the performing arts.

Index

The
Russian

Why everyone loves James Patterson and Detective Michael Bennett

'Its breakneck pace leaves you gasping for breath. Packed with typical Patterson panache . . . **it won't disappoint**.'
Daily Mail

It's no mystery why James Patterson is the world's most popular thriller writer. Simply put: **Nobody does it better**.'
Jeffery Deaver

'No one gets this big without **amazing natural storytelling** talent – which is what Jim has, in spades.'
Lee Child

'James Patterson is the **gold standard** by which all others are judged.'
Steve Berry

'Patterson boils a scene down to the single, telling detail, the element that **defines a character** or moves a plot along. It's what fires off the movie projector in the reader's mind.'
Michael Connelly

'James Patterson is **The Boss**. End of.'
Ian Rankin

POLICE DEPARTMENT
One Police Plaza
New York, NY 10038

Req #: 2014-PL-10945
File #:

PERSONNEL FILE

TO BE FILLED IN BY IMMEDIATE SUPERIOR:

Detective
MICHAEL BENNETT

☑

6 FOOT 3 INCHES (191CM)   200 POUNDS (91KG)
IRISH AMERICAN

EMPLOYMENT

Bennett joined the police force to uncover the truth
at all costs. He started his career in the Bronx's
49th Precinct. He then transferred to the NYPD's
Major Case Squad and remained there until he moved
to the Manhattan North Homicide Squad.

EDUCATION

Bennett graduated from Regis High School and studied
philosophy at Manhattan College.

FAMILY HISTORY

Bennett was previously married to Maeve, who worked as a
nurse on the trauma ward at Jacobi Hospital in the Bronx.
However, Maeve died tragically young after losing a battle
with cancer in December 2007, leaving Bennett to raise
their ten adopted children: Chrissy, Shawna, Trent, Eddie,
twins Fiona and Bridget, Ricky, Brian, Jane and Juliana.

Following Maeve's death, over time Bennett grew closer to
the children's nanny, Mary Catherine. After years of on-
off romance, Bennett and Mary Catherine decided to commit
to one another, and now happily raise the family together.
Also in the Bennett household is his Irish grandfather,
Seamus, who is a Catholic priest.

PROFILE:

☐ AMENDED REPORT

BENNETT IS AN EXPERT IN HOSTAGE NEGOTIATION,
TERRORISM, HOMICIDE AND ORGANIZED CRIME. HE WILL STOP
AT NOTHING TO GET THE JOB DONE AND PROTECT THE CITY
AND THE PEOPLE HE LOVES, EVEN IF THIS MEANS DISOBEYING
ORDERS AND IGNORING PROTOCOL. DESPITE THESE UNORTHODOX
METHODS, HE IS A RELENTLESS, DETERMINED AND IN MANY
WAYS INCOMPARABLE DETECTIVE.

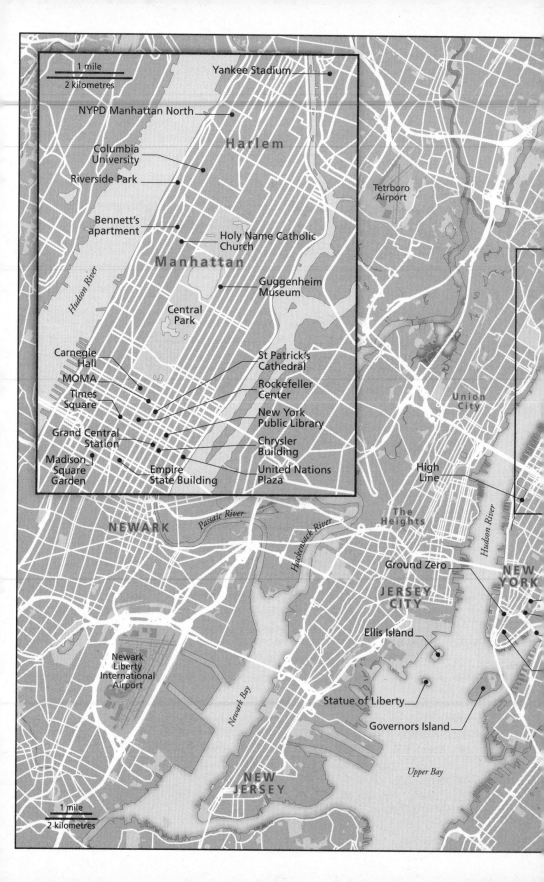

1 mile
2 kilometres

Yankee Stadium

NYPD Manhattan North

Harlem

Columbia
University

Riverside Park

Tetrboro
Airport

Bennett's
apartment

Holy Name Catholic
Church

Manhattan

Guggenheim
Museum

Central
Park

Hudson River

Carnegie
Hall

MOMA

Times
Square

St Patrick's
Cathedral

Rockefeller
Center

New York
Public Library

Grand Central
Station

Chrysler
Building

Madison
Square
Garden

Empire
State Building

United Nations
Plaza

Union
City

High
Line

NEWARK

Passaic River

Hackensack River

The
Heights

Ground Zero

NEW
YORK

JERSEY
CITY

Ellis Island

Newark
Liberty
International
Airport

Newark Bay

Statue of Liberty

Governors Island

NEW
JERSEY

Upper Bay

1 mile
2 kilometres

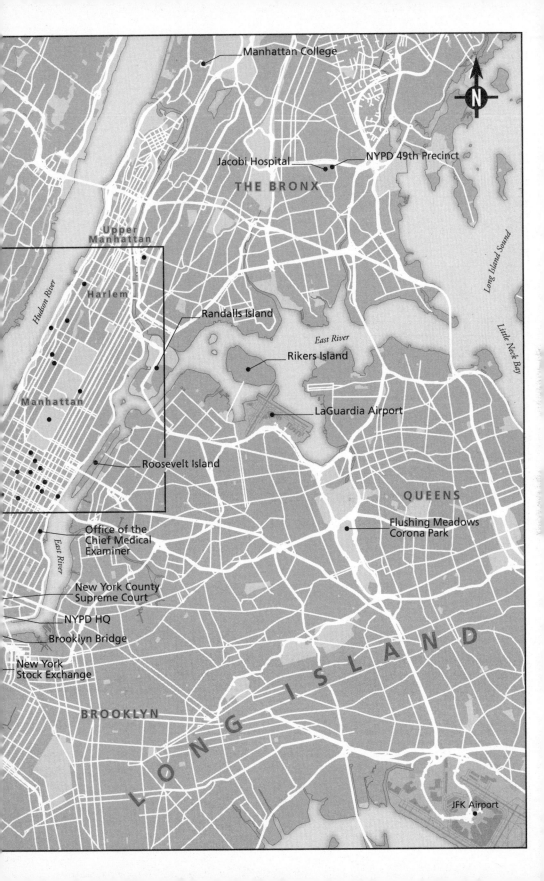

Manhattan College

Jacobi Hospital

NYPD 49th Precinct

THE BRONX

Upper
Manhattan

Harlem

Hudson River

Randalls Island

East River

Rikers Island

Long Island Sound

Little Neck Bay

Manhattan

LaGuardia Airport

Roosevelt Island

QUEENS

East River

Office of the
Chief Medical
Examiner

Flushing Meadows
Corona Park

New York County
Supreme Court

NYPD HQ

Brooklyn Bridge

New York
Stock Exchange

BROOKLYN

LONG ISLAND

JFK Airport

N

A list of titles by James Patterson appears at
the back of this book

The
Russian

JAMES
PATTERSON
& JAMES O. BORN

CENTURY

Cen   mpanies
wh   use.com

Penguin
Random House
UK

First published in Great Britain by Century in 2021

www.penguin.co.uk

A CIP catalogue record for this book is available from the British Library

ISBN 9781780899466
ISBN 9781780899473 (trade paperback edition)

Printed and bound in Great Britain by Clays Ltd, Elcograf S.p.A.

The authorised representative in the EEA is Penguin Random House Ireland,
Morrison Chambers, 32 Nassau Street, Dublin D02 YH68

Penguin Random House is committed to a sustainable future for
our business, our readers and our planet. This book is made from
Forest Stewardship Council® certified paper

MIX
Paper from
responsible sources
FSC® C018179

The
Russian

CHAPTER 1

I CHECKED THE street in both directions in front of an upscale coffee house called Flat Bread and Butter on Amsterdam Avenue near 140th Street. The street was about as quiet as New York City gets.

There's never a good time to be breaking in a new detective on the squad, but this moment was one of the worst. The new detective's name was Brett Hollis. He was a sharp up-and-comer. He may not have been experienced, but he looked good. Full suit and tie. Not a hair out of place. He almost looked like he could be one of my kids dressed for church.

Occasionally I have a hard time trusting a well-put-together cop. I figure cops who take the job seriously have a permanent disheveled look. Like mine.

Hollis was also young. Maybe too young.

My lieutenant, Harry Grissom, hadn't used the word *babysit,* but he'd said to make sure this kid didn't get into any trouble. Sort of what a babysitter does. Normally I wouldn't mind, but we were in the middle of a major murder investigation.

Chloe Tumber, a first-year student at Columbia Law, had been found stabbed to death with some kind of sharp tool. One Police Plaza was keeping recent developments quiet, but Chloe was the third victim—after one in the Bronx and another in Brooklyn—to die by similar means. The stab wounds had been made by blades with slightly different markers. We suspected the killer had a toolbox full of sharp implements.

I turned to the rookie and said, "Remember, this guy Van Fleet is a person of interest. Not necessarily a suspect. Follow my lead."

Hollis nodded his head nervously, saying, "We need to call in our location."

"Why?"

"Policy says we have to check in on the radio for safety reasons."

I smiled at the young detective. "I appreciate your knowledge of the NYPD policy manual, but in real life, if we called in every location we stopped at, we'd do nothing but use the radio all day." I stepped into the coffee house without another word, trusting Hollis would follow.

The coffee house was narrow, with about ten tables and a bar with ten stools. A good-looking young man wearing the name tag JESSE stood behind the counter and welcomed us.

I said, "Is Billy around?"

"You guys cops?"

Hollis stepped forward and said, "What about it?"

Jesse shrugged. "You got the look. Listen, Billy doesn't steal from me and he shows up for his shifts—that's all I care about."

Jesse set down his rag and jerked his thumb toward the rear of the narrow coffee house. "He's in the back."

I followed Hollis through the constricted hallway, boxes of paper towels and toilet paper stacked along the walls. Hollis walked past the bathrooms and storage room into the kitchen. That's where we found Billy Van Fleet. The tall, slim, pale twenty-eight-year-old was busy washing dishes. He looked up and smiled, clearly making us for police officers. Guess we did have the look.

I saw Hollis take a step forward, and I placed a gentle hand on his shoulder, saying, "Be cool."

"What can I do for you, Officers?" the dishwasher asked, drying his hands and straightening his shirt.

I held up my shield. "Billy Van Fleet?"

He nodded.

"When was the last time you saw Chloe Tumber?"

"Why?"

Hollis's demeanor changed in an instant. "We're asking the questions," he snarled.

Van Fleet held up his hands and said, "Okay, okay, just asking."

Hollis kept going. "How about you tell us where you were last night between 8 and 11 p.m."

Van Fleet kept his eyes on Hollis, which I figured I'd use to my advantage. Maybe I'd let my new partner lead the interview. That way I could watch Van Fleet and see what made him nervous.

Right now he seemed very calm. Until suddenly he wasn't. Without warning, he spun and sprinted away from the sink, blasting through the rear exit. He was fast.

Hollis broke into a run, calling over his shoulder almost cheerfully, "He's our man!" just as Van Fleet hit the safety bar on the door, letting sunshine flood into the dark kitchen.

CHAPTER 2

I COULD'VE BROKEN into a run with Brett Hollis. But that would've been counterproductive. Hollis was trying to keep the suspect in sight. I was sure he'd give this guy a good run for his money. But veteran cops don't engage in foot chases. Experience is supposed to teach you something. It taught me to either find a car or use my head.

I knew this neighborhood. Every block of it. Traffic had picked up on Amsterdam Avenue, and no one runs toward a busy street. This guy had a plan. I figured he'd take the alley a block down and move away from any pedestrian traffic. If I were him, I'd head toward St. Nicholas Park. It wasn't that far away.

I broke into a light jog. We needed this guy—make no mistake. Van Fleet was the first lead we'd had in Chloe Tumber's homicide. Which, despite the different blades used, looked to be connected to those two other cases. All three victims were young women who'd suffered gruesome injuries moments before their deaths. And the three crime scenes looked similar. *Messy.* Though I couldn't shake the feeling that the mess was deliberate, almost designed for effect. We were still developing a theory as to why.

I found the garbage alley I was looking for between two buildings, with its gates, as usual, left wide open. Then I saw an abandoned dog leash. A long one. Maybe twelve feet, and already hooked to a pole behind a pizza place. I took the leash in my hand and stepped to the other side of the alley.

Ten seconds later, as if on cue, Van Fleet slid around the corner, ducked a drainage pipe that stuck out into the alley, and picked up the pace again. He never even saw me. As he neared the dog leash, I jerked the line. His feet tangled and he tumbled down onto the alley's nasty asphalt, slipping in some pizza grease congealed in the middle of the alley and knocking over an empty forty-ounce beer bottle like it was the last bowling pin in the lane.

Before I could even reach Van Fleet, Hollis barreled around the corner. He didn't notice the drainage pipe, and ran full speed into it, headfirst. The impact made the pipe reverberate like a gong and knocked him completely off his feet. I could only imagine what the collision sounded like inside his brain.

I cuffed the suspect, then looked over at Hollis. His nose was flattened, blood spraying from it like a busted sprinkler attached to his face. "You okay, Brett?"

He mumbled, "I'm good," as he struggled to his feet. Blood poured onto his clean white shirt and made dark stains on his power tie.

With Van Fleet's hands cuffed behind his back, I helped him

up and started to lead him back to the coffee house. I didn't want to embarrass Hollis, so I walked slowly as he tried to keep up.

Hollis's wound was so spectacular, a corner bodega owner abandoned the outdoor displays she was stocking and rushed inside for a handful of crumpled paper towels. She forced them on Hollis, who held them to his nose.

Hollis wasn't complaining. I had to admit, I liked his toughness.

CHAPTER 3

AS SOON AS we got back to Flat Bread and Butter, we slipped in the same back door we'd all burst out of. I don't think Jesse even realized we'd left the building.

I sat Van Fleet down on a stool next to an oven. "Why'd you run when we asked you about Chloe, jerk-off?"

"She's always complaining that I'm too clingy, that she's too busy with law school and her part-time job to have time for me. She said if I didn't give her some space, she'd call the cops on me." He sighed.

"What'd you do when she said that?"

"Nothing. I haven't called her in a week." He paused and cut his eyes to Hollis and me. "Okay, maybe I *tried* to call her a couple of times."

Hollis plopped down on a chair next to a metal desk built into the wall. He didn't look good. I said, "Why don't you go get that checked out, Brett?"

"I'm fine." He'd added some paper towels from the kitchen to the ones from the bodega. It was a giant ball of paper, slowly turning dark red.

I turned back to Billy Van Fleet. "Three days ago Chloe Tumber made an official complaint against you, said that you'd been stalking her. I don't suppose you can tell me where you were last night, can you?"

"Here." He shrugged. "I was here from 6 p.m. until one o'clock. Never left. Jesse was here with me the whole time."

I shot a quick look at Hollis, who jumped off his chair and headed to the front of the restaurant to talk to Van Fleet's boss. A minute later, he came back and nodded. "It checks out."

"Someone slipped into Chloe's apartment last night and murdered her. Your history of harassment, plus the running, makes you look like a good suspect. Convince us otherwise."

For his part, Van Fleet looked legitimately stunned. "Chloe's dead?"

I quickly filled him in, leaving out the details of the bloody scene at her apartment.

It had been gruesome. I could tell Hollis had been trying hard to hold it together back at Chloe Tumber's apartment. He'd choked up. "He stabbed her in the eye?" he'd said, his voice breaking.

He'd picked right up on the most distinct detail, the kind that could never be revealed to the media for fear of giving ideas to budding criminal minds.

I'd held his arm for a moment and said, "Everyone gets a little shaky in the aftermath of a violent murder, Brett. This is bad. Really bad. I wanted you to see how bad things can get."

All cops are human. Any one of us who tells you crime scenes don't affect them is lying. Yes, we're professionals. Yes, we've seen it before. It's especially hard for those of us with children. Every time I view a messy crime scene, it's hard not to think of the victim as someone's kid, and I always say a silent prayer for them and their families.

But Billy Van Fleet was taking the news remarkably well.

"If you didn't kill her, who did?" I asked.

Total silence from Van Fleet.

I looked at him and said, "We need to find out what happened to Chloe, if there was anyone who wanted to hurt her. I don't understand why you wouldn't talk to us."

"Never talk to the cops. Never snitch. It's bad for the reputation," he said, like it was a mantra.

"What reputation? Aside from a lot of petty arrests, you live with your parents and work at a coffee house that makes Starbucks look like a hellhole," Hollis scoffed.

The skinny white guy had a smile on his face as he said, "I'm a gangsta—that's what we do. I learned a long time ago that nothing happens to me if I run from the cops. I figured it out on my second arrest. I'm up to sixteen arrests and haven't been proven wrong. I've never gotten one extra day in jail for running from the cops. I even have a blog about it."

Gangsta? Give me a break. Van Fleet had none of my young partner's toughness. And I was less than impressed at how quickly he seemed to have already moved on from the news we'd just delivered—that the woman he'd been obsessed with had been murdered. Then I made a connection. "Has this got something to do with your half-ass acting persona?"

"There's nothing half-assed about staying in character. It will serve me well when my one-act play opens Off-Broadway next month. I'm playing a convicted felon who doesn't put up with any shit."

I said, "Well, I'm playing a cop who's tired of putting up with shit."

I was pissed off. And we were no closer to finding Chloe Tumber's killer.

CHAPTER 4

DANIEL OTT, TECH consultant, gazed at the New York *Daily News* sitting on his desk in the Manhattan Family Insurance office. He smiled. The headline, in bold letters, said, THREE'S NO CHARM IN BIG APPLE MURDERS.

Numbers were logical. People were not. Besides, he loved the thought that all of New York City was reading about the murders he had committed.

When Ott looked up, he noticed the heavyset office administrator, Warren Talbout, heading his way. Ott quickly resumed his work, installing the desktop computer software his company had created to facilitate communications integration between phones and computers.

Talbout, who wore a graying walrus mustache, stopped by and said, "How's the upgrade going, David?"

Ott looked up. "It's Daniel. And the upgrades are coming along fine. I should be finished later today."

The office administrator nodded and waddled away. Ott wasn't upset the man had gotten his name wrong. Few people in any of the offices where he worked bothered to learn his name. He was only ever anywhere for about two weeks at a time. Just a reasonably friendly, totally nondescript guy who made it easier for them to move data between their phones and their computers.

In fact, he liked to think that no matter where he went no one ever noticed him, like a forgettable piece of furniture. He was about five foot ten and one hundred sixty-five pounds, slim for adult males in the US. With no distinctive features whatsoever.

Young Ott had been taunted for being thin and sickly. But as he learned and grew, he found he could do things no one else could. He understood math and numbers like most people did language, though he was also good with languages. He'd easily landed this job with Computelex. He made plenty of money and got to fly across the entire country—business class.

Mostly, Ott blended in and traveled with hardly anyone even speaking to him. He was happy he'd found uses for his super-power. Now he was the one doing the taunting.

Ott read some of the article. No comment from the NYPD spokeswoman about details connecting the murders. Ott knew TV news wasn't as careful as print. News shows would play up an angle to increase ratings; before too long, they'd create special graphics and theme music for these murders.

He didn't want to be too obvious, but he couldn't keep his eyes off the page. He'd stop every couple of seconds to look up and nod hello to someone walking past. Everyone who worked at the insurance company stayed busy and avoided idle chitchat. That focus gave him room to indulge himself in this big comfortable office, with its north-facing view of the park and abundant takeout options—all the trappings of a secure, safe haven.

His cell phone chimed with a short, low, professional tone. He smiled and snatched the phone from his belt. Technically it was his lunchtime. His mouth stretched into a wide grin as he said, "Hello, sweetheart."

He was surprised by giggles and his two daughters singsonging together, "Hello, Papa!"

"Hello, my little dumplings. I thought it was your mother calling."

"She's right here. We wanted to surprise you."

"And what a great surprise it is." Ott's three-year-old, Tatyana, and five-year-old, Lilly, were his absolute prizes. He worked hard so that they would never know hard times. And he was raising them to be polite and respectful. Thankfully their mother, Lena, had few of the arrogant habits most American women did.

Lena was Polish and had proven to be a good wife and a great mother. She was simple and sweet, very meek. They'd met online, and Ott quickly knew she was the woman for him. He even spoke a fair amount of Polish. They used it as a code to talk privately around the girls.

He chatted with his daughters, who told him about their homeschool lessons, the books they were reading (or pretending to read), and how they'd raced their mother and won.

Ott never would've imagined he could feel as much love as he did for these girls. He wondered if either of his parents had felt anything for him approaching the love he had for his daughters.

He doubted it—his father had barely acknowledged him, except to make mean jokes, and his mother had just seemed exhausted all the time. When she died, Ott had felt relief for her, that she could finally rest. Since then, he'd probably spoken no more than thirty words total to his father.

Lena got on the line, and his mood shifted. His wife tended to bring up less enjoyable topics, problems that needed solutions. She said, "We need to enroll the girls in a dance class. And the dog has a cough again."

Ott hid a groan as he hurried his wife off the phone. "I'm sorry, dear, I have to get back to work."

She said she understood and told him she couldn't wait to see him. He smiled after hanging up, thinking about his two separate—and very different—lives. Over the past year, it had become clear that he needed both to survive, though it was a daily challenge to keep them from crashing into each other.

Ott loved his wife and girls, but he couldn't deny himself the pleasure he got from killing. The feeling could make his head spin, and he had an increasingly difficult time containing his urges. He felt the sensation in his entire body, like wave after wave of excitement. A release. A renewal. He wouldn't describe it as sexual in nature—it was more primal and satisfying.

Usually the victims were obvious to him. It had to do with their attitudes. That was his catalyst, his reason to act: he could not abide women with insolent, demeaning attitudes. He no longer put up with arrogance and ridicule from women. Nor could he understand why American women thought they were smarter, prettier, and more important than anyone else in the world. There was something about their egotistical speech patterns that shocked his nervous system.

His work dictated the pace he kept in his avocation. Since he only took victims outside his home area, occasionally choosing his next victim from an office where he had done contract work, the length of his business trips determined how patient he could be.

He did his best to be patient, let some time lapse. Usually. But sometimes the urge hit him so strongly that he couldn't wait.

He'd been in New York for only about a month now and had already succumbed to the temptation of three perfect victims. It was more than he usually allowed himself, but then again, in a city as big as New York, he was almost surprised the media had even connected them. Not that he was concerned. At each crime scene, he'd been careful not to leave any evidence that could be linked to him, and careful about security cameras.

Today would be his last day in this office. He'd figured out a way to reroute the company's computer network to integrate more easily with the software he was installing. He never bothered to explain his work to the clients, just to his boss back at Computelex headquarters in Omaha. HQ was the only one he needed to impress.

Ott moved from his desk to work at a control box in a tiny room at one end of the floor. He had been in there before and realized that from that vantage, he could hear everything in the manager's office, the copy room, and the break room, which all surrounded the control box.

As he worked, he overheard two women talking. It took him a moment to realize they were standing in the break room. He recognized one of the voices as belonging to an intern, a smart girl from somewhere north of the city.

He was about to go back to his desk when he heard the

intern say, "How much longer is that telephone tech going to be here?"

The other woman said, "I think he's supposed to finish up today."

"I'm so glad I'm studying communications in college. I'd hate to do such lonely, anonymous work. It doesn't suit me."

Ott stood still for a moment. Silent. Furious. *Who the hell is this arrogant bitch to think she is better than me?* In fact, he was widely recognized in the industry as one of only six or seven techs in the whole country who could do what he did. And he got paid well for it too. More than this bitch intern would ever make in communications or whatever useless degree she was getting.

His hand started to tremble with anger. Then he smiled with a new sense of purpose.

He always felt energized the moment he found a new victim.

CHAPTER 5

IT WASN'T QUITE nightfall by the time I got home to my family. I've spent my career trying to keep my family life as separate from my work life as possible. If I'm thinking about some gruesome crime I'm investigating, I'm not focusing on the kids the way I need to be, and it's important to focus exclusively on the children for a fair amount of time each day.

But today was one of those days that wore me down. The unidentified killer who'd violently murdered these women had gotten into my head. It was hard to stop thinking about the case, even as I was welcomed home by three beautiful, happy young girls.

Though frankly I'd expected more than 30 percent of my kids to greet me at the door.

That's right, I have ten children. Six girls and four boys. All adopted. Each with his or her own unique personality and challenges. And I wouldn't trade a single one of them for anything in the world, though as anyone with a lot of kids will tell you, it takes an enormous amount of energy.

My twins, Bridget and Fiona, were always good for a double hug, and my youngest, Chrissy, still insisted on a giant hug and a quick lift and whirl around the room. It's possible she didn't insist as much as she used to. But I still did it anyway, every day.

I wandered farther into the apartment and found my fiancée, Mary Catherine, sitting at a small writing desk in our bedroom, working on some wedding details. We were getting married in a matter of weeks, and the quick look she gave me revealed that she was feeling rather overwhelmed.

"I need some fresh air," Mary Catherine said. "Get changed, real quick. You promised we'd ride our new bikes at least three times a week. Let's go."

I knew not to argue. Also, it's bad policy to ignore commitments. And I never break a promise. It took me only a minute to slip out of my work clothes and into sweatpants and a Manhattan College T-shirt. Underneath the school's logo it said, PHILOSOPHY, IT'S SO MUCH MORE THAN A MAJOR. The kids had gotten me the shirt as a joke gift for my birthday since that had been my major in college. I loved it. The joke was on them. Philosophy *was* a lot more than just a major.

As we slipped out the front door, Mary Catherine called over her shoulder, "Ricky, finish up dinner. Your great-grandfather will be here in a few minutes. He can get everyone organized. We'll be back in thirty to forty minutes. Less if I have to call an ambulance for your father."

Mary Catherine's lilting Irish accent didn't make these sound like a series of orders she expected to be carried out precisely.

But both the kids and I knew that when she used that tone of voice, she was on a mission. In this case, it was our newest hobby: riding mountain bikes.

You might ask, *Who buys mountain bikes when they live in Manhattan?* The answer is, anyone who wants to work up a sweat without going forty miles an hour on a racing bike.

We collected our bikes from the basement and took off. Within twenty seconds of riding behind Mary Catherine, I knew we were headed to her favorite bike trail, which runs along the river next to the Henry Hudson Greenway. It was an easy trail to get to from our building, and if she wanted to work out hard—which she obviously did—this was the spot. When Mary Catherine got like this, it was all I could do to keep up as she pedaled with wild abandon. And God help any poor tourist who happened to step in front of her.

I was huffing and puffing a little bit as I pushed my Fuji off-road mountain bike to catch up to Mary Catherine. Between gasps for air, I managed to eke out, "Something you need to talk about? This isn't just blowing off steam on the bike path. This is running your engine so hard you could blow a rod."

That made her smile and slow her pace considerably. There really weren't many people around. This was also where she liked to talk about sensitive subjects. It was about the only way we could be sure the kids weren't listening in somehow.

Mary Catherine said, "Everything just seems to be happening at once. The wedding, the kids getting all sorts of new interests and making new friends, and Brian's readjustment to life after prison. It's a lot to take on."

"No doubt. And you've done a phenomenal job."

"I didn't drag you out here for compliments. We both need

the exercise. I'm going to fit into that wedding dress if I have to have my spleen removed." Mary Catherine paused, then said in a serious tone, "I'd really like to talk about Brian."

Even a smart-ass like me knew not to joke. "What's up?"

Mary Catherine said, "He disappears during most of the day. Just slips out sometime in the morning and sort of reappears in the afternoon."

I said, "I've been careful not to question him too closely. It's important we show that we trust him."

"Yes, but I feel like we've been walking on eggshells, maybe giving him too much leeway. He's got to understand the rules we laid down when we allowed him to return home, the rules about making good use of his time. And I worry that he's *not* making good use of his time. I worry that he's breaking our trust."

"I get it. But he hasn't been out that long. He's still readjusting. Let's give it just a little time. At least a few more days. Then we'll sit down with Brian and see what's going on. How's that sound?"

She looked over her shoulder and said, "Like we're going to have to ride really hard for that to be okay with me." She started pumping the pedals faster than I thought possible. If nothing else, this new hobby was going to shore up my aerobic ability. Not that I was planning to engage in any foot chases.

CHAPTER 6

WE RODE FOR about half an hour more, then returned home. It didn't take long for us to store the bikes in the basement. We chained them in the storage area and gazed in amazement at the ten other bikes of various sizes locked up next to them.

I'd read that New York was in the top ten of US cities for biking. Certainly the dozen members of my immediate family helped contribute to that statistic.

I planned to stay in my sweaty clothes for dinner until Mary Catherine gave me a look.

"Oh, c'mon," I said. "It won't kill the kids to smell their dad once in a while."

"I wouldn't have a problem with it usually," she replied, "but we're having a guest for dinner."

"If you start calling Seamus a guest, we're never going to have a comfortable dinner again."

"It's not your grandfather. Jane has a friend coming over."

"That's nice. What's her name?"

"It's a boy." She hesitated, then added, "A boyfriend."

"You mean a friend who happens to be a boy, right?"

"You wish."

I thought about it for a moment. "I'm not sure I'm ready for Jane to have a boyfriend."

"Fathers never are. Yet the fact remains. We both need to clean up because the boy will be here shortly."

"Is he from Holy Name?"

Mary Catherine nodded. "Allan Martin III."

"Is his dad the hedge fund guy?"

"He is."

I wasn't sure how to respond. This was a lot for me to take in. Jane was my third-oldest child, after Juliana and Brian. I'd come to terms with Juliana dating, and I thought I was prepared to deal with the other girls doing so too. Apparently I was wrong. I still had four even younger daughters. I hated to think what my future held.

Mary Catherine got cleaned up first, then I took a quick shower. When I wandered back into the kitchen, I was impressed to see how efficiently Ricky, my second-oldest son, had managed to pull together a spectacular spaghetti dinner and get everyone involved. I saw the table was already set, and my grandfather, Seamus, sat at the far end, sipping a glass of red wine, looking well dressed in his clerical collar.

"Comfortable, Seamus?" I asked as I strolled into the dining room.

"Aside from the sarcastic questioning, everything is great. How about you, my boy?"

"Peachy."

Then the doorbell rang and I heard my normally reserved, incredibly smart daughter Jane squeal. An honest-to-God squeal. *What is happening?*

Young Allan Martin III turned out to be a nice-looking man who showed good manners as well. He shook my hand and looked me in the eye. He looked a little like his father. Tall, with blond hair and brown eyes.

Jane stood next to him like they were attached by some invisible, and extremely short, cord.

I noticed, though, that when Brian walked past Allan, he bumped the young man. It looked a little like an accident, but I wondered if there was more to it.

Then Mary Catherine and Ricky called out in unison, "Dinner is on the table!"

CHAPTER 7

EVEN IF YOU'RE used to dinner at our apartment, the sight of all thirteen of us could be overwhelming, though Allan seemed to take it in stride. And, of course, he sat right next to Jane.

I watched Brian, who quietly observed everything around him without showing much interest or emotion. He sat three spots from the end, hunched over his plate of pasta. It was a habit he'd gotten into during his months in prison, and correcting it wasn't on my list of priorities at the moment.

My youngest, Chrissy, had taken to sitting right next to Brian at dinner, as well as at any other time. It was as if she was afraid her big brother might be taken away again. For his part, Brian seemed to appreciate the attention. Never said a word when she scooted her chair a little too close. He always took her hand when she slipped it into his. But tonight he seemed focused on Jane's new boyfriend.

Mary Catherine broke the tension by asking Allan how he liked going to Holy Name.

Allan smiled and said, "My mother thought about sending me to Regis for the superior academics, but my dad wanted me to have a real-world experience. He says attending Holy Name helped him mix with all kinds of people as he was building his career."

I mumbled, "You don't get much better at 'all kinds of people' than this family."

Seamus laughed at that.

Then Brian focused his laser-beam eyes on the young man. "Who do you hang out with at Holy Name?"

Allan hesitated, as if he wasn't sure he was supposed to answer questions from the gallery. He threw out a few names, then shrugged and added, "I also hang out with John Chad and Tim and Terry Jones."

Brian didn't hesitate to say, "The Jones brothers are bad news. I'd recommend you stay away from them, especially if you're going out with Jane."

Jane gave her brother a look. "Chill out, Brian. Those boys are in all of our classes," she explained.

Mary Catherine was about to follow up, but I placed a subtle hand on her leg under the table. I wanted to see where this was going. I also, selfishly, wondered if Brian would ask questions I might shy away from.

Trent, my youngest son, said, "You're on the basketball team at Holy Name, right?"

"Yes, I'm a guard on the varsity team."

"That's not saying a whole lot. I was the captain of a basketball team once. It didn't mean I could play," Brian retorted.

As Jane's sisters Bridget and Fiona erupted in nervous laughter, I realized Brian was talking about the team he played on in prison. I looked over at my grandfather, who was eating quietly but keeping an eye on Brian. The two of them had always had a special connection. I wondered why he was staying so silent.

Brian said, "I heard you play lacrosse too. Holy Name's got a pretty good lacrosse team. How do you think they'll do in the city tournament?"

Allan brightened at the question. "I think we'll take home the trophy this year."

"What makes you so sure?" I asked.

He smiled and said, "Because I'm captain of the team."

Brian subtly rolled his eyes, but I liked Allan's confidence.

Mary Catherine started to engage the young man in a much friendlier and warmer tone. "Have you given any thought to where you might go to college?"

"My parents are insisting on an Ivy League school."

Mary Catherine beamed and said, "You could even stay in the New York area. Columbia is a great school. Even Cornell is at least in the state."

Allan winced and said, "My dad calls Cornell the community college of the Ivy League. He's been pushing me toward Harvard, but I'm worried they're a little stale. From what I know of the place, they're mired in too much tradition. It's a new century, and I want to be on the cutting edge."

I revised my opinion—Allan wasn't confident; he was a cocky little shit. I silently began to hope that Jane would quickly get tired of this entitled ass.

But the way she was looking at him didn't give me much hope.

CHAPTER 8

IT WAS LATE in the evening and I thought everyone was asleep in my little hostel on the Upper West Side. Lying in bed, I used a penlight to read reports from a dozen different detectives about persons of interest who'd been interviewed regarding the recent homicides. I reread a couple of Brett Hollis's reports. One of them had a few speckles of blood on it. Like tears on a sad letter. I didn't know if this made him a tough guy or a biohazard.

I needed some sleep. All the sentences were starting to run together, and it was becoming difficult for me to pick out the useful information in the interviews.

Detectives Terri Hernandez from the Bronx and Javier Tunez from Brooklyn were both leads on homicides similar to my Chloe Tumber case. I knew I could rely on the accuracy of their reports. They were both too sharp to make careless mistakes.

I was startled when Mary Catherine turned in bed and squinted at my weak light.

"I'm sorry. Am I keeping you awake?"

"Are you kidding? I have so many thoughts swirling in my head I'm surprised I even lay down."

"Need more help with the wedding planning?"

"Nah, I've got a handle on the wedding plans. Seamus has been great. He has a good sense of what's important, and he's really come through on a couple of details at the church I needed him to handle. It's like having me mam's help, without all the criticism."

"Don't worry, the criticism will come. Just give it time."

We both giggled. I waited a moment, then said, "Are you getting cold feet? I'd understand. I wouldn't like it, but I get it."

"It's nothing to do with that. Though it is just a bit…overwhelming to think I'll be stepmother to ten children. I love them all to pieces, but it's loads of responsibility, isn't it?"

I marveled at my incredible luck. I had found not only a beautiful woman but one who loved me *and* my kids too.

"I worry about them all," Mary Catherine continued. "I already told you my concerns about Brian, and now I'm a little bothered by Jane's new boyfriend. Does it ever end?"

"Not really, no," I told her truthfully.

Mary Catherine gave me a smile, which reassured me. Then she kissed me and I felt even better. She brushed the papers off my stomach and took the penlight out of my hand. Her soft lips caressed my neck and she nibbled at my ear.

Then Mary Catherine wrapped her delicate hands around my face and pulled me toward her as she stretched out on the bed.

I mumbled, "What's going on?"

"Really? The city's best detective can't figure it out? I worry for the fate of our citizens."

The more she kissed me, the less I worried about anything else. It was exactly what I needed.

CHAPTER 9

I WAS ON edge the next afternoon as I stepped through the front door of One Police Plaza. My lieutenant, NYPD veteran Harry Grissom, and I had been called in for a meeting, and I'd brought Brett Hollis along as comic relief. The swath of white bandages across his face would distract anyone. To his credit, Hollis had not complained once about breaking his own nose while chasing Van Fleet through Harlem.

The conference rooms in this public face of headquarters, where the NYPD often hosted other agencies, journalists, or politicians, tended to be more plush and technologically up-to-date than the cheap furniture and threadbare carpet in the precincts. These rooms looked like government offices are supposed to.

As soon as we stepped into the second-floor conference room, which overlooked the parking area for the highest-ranking

NYPD administrators, I froze. I turned to Harry and said in a very low voice, "I didn't know the FBI would be here."

"Neither did I," he said, stroking his long gunslinger mustache.

In the room were four FBI agents, all of whom seemed to be in a staring contest with us lowly NYPD detectives.

That was the real problem: law-enforcement agencies working together. Even though the national rate of unsolved murders was just under 60 percent, no one really thought the solution was to trust people from other agencies. Not only because they were worried other agencies might steal their cases but, even worse, other agencies might screw up any cases they were brought in on. It was petty and stupid, and I was as guilty as anyone.

It was pretty clear what this meeting was about, even before I saw detectives Terri Hernandez from the Bronx and Javier Tunez from Brooklyn already at the table.

Hernandez smiled and said, "This must be important if they're bringing in big guns like you."

"Nah, can't be that important. The FBI is here."

That comment made Tunez bark out a laugh. Ever since an overzealous FBI agent had tried to charge him with workers' compensation fraud, accusing him of overstating his injury claims from a car accident, Tunez had no use for the federal agency. He'd won his case easily, but he still suffered from the stress, as well as speculation in the press—the media never seemed to believe the FBI could be fallible and screw things up more often than local police.

NYPD inspector Lisa Udell was running the meeting. With her professional demeanor and terrifying reputation, I knew she'd make sure things didn't get out of hand. She was known for chopping your nuts off if you did something stupid. I could get behind that kind of administrator. If you act stupid, you should face the consequences. The flip side of the equation was that if you were in the right, Udell always backed you up. Every time.

Inspector Udell said, "We all know why we're here. We have three murder cases in Manhattan, the Bronx, and Brooklyn. The FBI has graciously offered their help to investigate the similarities in the crime scenes. I thought it would be best if we all sat down and talked about where we are in our investigations."

The door to the conference room opened and two more FBI agents rushed in. One of them looked at me and smiled. I couldn't help but smile back. Emily Parker had helped me out a dozen times over my career. And we'd once come within a moment of having a romantic relationship. That was before Mary Catherine and I had gotten serious. Now I just counted Emily as a good friend who happened to be a damn good cop. No matter who she worked for.

The other FBI agent who'd entered along with Emily was a sharply dressed, forty-something black man. He cleared his throat and said, "My name is Robert Lincoln. I'm the assistant special agent in charge of our New York office. The FBI is prepared to bring in resources and personnel to move this case along."

Every veteran detective in every big city in the US has heard this song and dance before. And in my experience, the assistance flowed only one way: away from us. The FBI seemed to count the NYPD as a resource only to inflate their numbers. They rarely added to a case.

ASAC Lincoln said, "Let's not waste any more time. If you tell us what you've got, maybe we can help."

Harry Grissom said, "We've got three murders and a ton of work to do. What we don't have is time to waste on pointless meetings. I'm sure you've seen our reports. All three known victims were young, white females. They all died from wounds from a sharp implement. But not the same one. Additionally, they each sustained a wound to the left eye. Assuming we're dealing with the same killer in all three circumstances, I think we can safely note that as his signature. Also, each of the crime scenes was excessively, intentionally bloody. The killer's clearly doing that on purpose. And his mutilation of their left eyes is a detail so distinctive that it must be kept from the media. You got some magical database that can point us in the right direction, that's great. But if you're just looking to make sure you're at the podium during a press conference, we need to get back to work."

I couldn't keep my eyes from shifting over to Inspector Udell. I respected an administrator who would remain silent while someone expressed themselves so clearly and disrespectfully to the FBI.

Lincoln didn't seem flustered by the pushback. He calmly straightened his tie and looked directly at Harry Grissom. "Look, Lieutenant, we know you're overworked and understaffed. We think we can help. All we need to do is set up what we're calling Task Force Halo. My people can report to me, and your people can report to you. It's as simple as that."

It hadn't gone unobserved that the sharp ASAC had somehow used *Lieutenant* as if it was some kind of insult.

Grissom took a moment to gather his thoughts, then said, "I appreciate your interest in assisting the NYPD to be more efficient. But in my long experience, task forces tend to slow things down. We're still running and gunning on this case. None of us has time for the extra administration and politics a task force would create. That doesn't mean we can't work together. But it *does* mean that this will be the last official meeting that takes time away from our actual investigations." Harry stroked his mustache once, then looked at everyone around the table. "Am I clearly understood?"

Sometimes I just wanted to kiss my boss.

CHAPTER 10

LIKE ANY MEETING attended by too many law-enforcement officials, this one didn't end as quickly as I would've liked. I still didn't mind taking a moment to chat with Emily.

"Are you in New York permanently?"

She nodded and said, "As permanently as any assignment with the federal government. I like working here and in Virginia. I don't mind if they ship me between the two."

"Tough on the social life."

"It can be a challenge, sure. But we can't all fall in love with someone we pay to watch our kids." Before I could rise to my own defense, Emily said, "That came out a lot cattier than I meant. I'm probably just a little jealous of a beautiful girl with an Irish accent."

"Well, to show you it wasn't a fluke, Mary Catherine and I are getting married in a few weeks."

"The kids must be over the moon." She cut her eyes to the ASAC, who was now talking animatedly with Grissom. "Mike, don't be too tough on Lincoln. In a way, he's a throwback FBI agent. It's not that he believes we're smarter than everyone else. He just doesn't like to be left out of the mix." She looked at me and her face softened. "He's a political animal. You and Harry wouldn't last ten minutes with him."

"I try not to get involved in anyone's politics. But I appreciate the warning." I made my good-byes and grabbed Hollis to head out the door. We had to wait another few minutes for Harry to break free.

I took one look at Hollis's face and said, "Pop into the bathroom, take a look at your bandage."

"Is it leaking?"

"Like the *Titanic*." In just the couple of seconds we'd been talking, a red stain had spread across the entire front of the white gauze and tape covering his nose.

Hollis hurried off. A few minutes later, Harry Grissom stepped out of the meeting. The way the FBI agents turned sharply away from him and left as a unit told me the most recent discussions had not gone any better than the one during the meeting.

I didn't even ask Harry about it. He'd tell me any information I needed to know.

He said, "Get together with Hernandez and Tunez and figure out if you have any common leads. I'll get you any help you need. How's Hollis handling himself?"

"He's smart and not lazy. That usually works out."

"Most guys would milk an injury like his and sit at home for a few weeks. I appreciate that he's not whining about it. I'll put him on background for now and then managing the crazy leads that'll come in as we get more media coverage. We'll have a couple of plainclothes help out as well."

"Sounds good, boss. Anything else?"

"Watch what you share with your FBI buddy."

"She's okay. I trust her."

"She's an FBI agent. If she's doing her job right, you *shouldn't* be able to trust her with any information. I don't care if you use her; I just don't want them screwing up our case. At this point, I don't even care if they try to steal credit. We gotta stop this guy. He's a sick and twisted bastard."

Hollis wandered back with fresh bandages around his nose. His eyes were watering, but he tried to look attentive.

Harry looked at me and said, "I need you to do your best work on this case. And that means a solve."

Hollis managed to say, "What about me?" He sounded like Rudolph the Red-Nosed Reindeer after his father covered his nose with mud.

Harry said, "Bennett's on legwork. You're on research."

My mind was already skipping ahead in the investigation. It's a double-edged sword when your boss has that much faith in you. You can do things your way, but you absolutely have to get results. And quick.

CHAPTER 11

DANIEL OTT WAS a little concerned that he was being rash. He'd finished the job at the insurance company only yesterday and was already seriously intending to make the snotty intern his next victim.

Waiting longer between victims—and distancing himself from any particular office—was meant to give the cops less to go on. But frankly, he was starting not to care. After all, no one ever remembered him. His superpower was being invisible in plain sight. He was completely and utterly unremarkable.

As a young man, that had bothered him. Now he embraced it. He was indistinctive. Even his workouts reflected that attitude. He didn't exercise to get bigger, only to get stronger and faster while maintaining his trim frame.

Now he was standing in Greeley Square Park, about forty feet from the intern, Elaine Anastas, watching her without any fear of being noticed, just as he had watched her two roommates come and go from the apartment since yesterday. Elaine's comment about how glad she was that she'd never have to do a job as lonely as his burned in Ott's brain. *The arrogance. The audacity.* He'd show her.

Elaine sat on a concrete bench in the fading light, reading a paperback of *Where the Crawdads Sing,* her dark hair draped across her pretty face as she concentrated on the book.

He'd made a study of women's clothing trends. Hers was student chic—a knockoff Kate Spade purse and an H&M jacket she wore over an AmazonBasics white T-shirt, and the Target Cherokee cross-trainers she'd clearly decorated herself with a few rhinestones and colorful laces. *Just another pretentious bitch trying to look more sophisticated than she actually is.*

Ott had already seen Elaine's tiny apartment on 30th Street, which she shared with two other girls whose work schedules he had quickly figured out. He had taped the lock on the building's rear door so it would not automatically close. He could slip in and out at any time. Now was his chance to savor and enjoy what was to come.

He turned his attention to speculating about one of the most important decisions he made for each victim: what kind of tools would he use this time?

He reached into the left pocket of his plain blue windbreaker. Would it be the twelve-inch, extra-fine, Phillips-head screwdriver? On the other hand, in his right pocket, the weight and shape of a Milwaukee brand combination wire cutter and stripper made him grin. He'd used that tool only once before, but he loved the way it made a pattern on flesh. Like someone had gnawed on it. One news report from that kill had even mentioned the police thought there might be evidence of bite marks on the corpse. It made him almost giddy thinking about it.

CHAPTER 12

IT TOOK ELAINE ANASTAS a few minutes to get moving once she put her book away in her purse. Daniel Ott barely breathed as she glanced around the park and gathered her stuff. He knew it wouldn't be much of a walk down Sixth Avenue to 30th. No lights on in the apartment. Her roommates were at work, as scheduled.

Ott watched Elaine slip into her building and, a few minutes later, the light come on in her apartment. He cut down the alley behind her building and opened the door he knew would be unlocked. He took the tape off the lock so no one would realize that's how he'd gotten into the building.

He slipped past a maintenance area crammed with broken lamps and microwaves, items the super had probably promised to fix. That was the easiest way to keep tenants quiet. Promise to do your best, but never give an exact date. It was a lot like Ott's job.

He paused at the third-floor door in the stairwell. Again, he questioned himself: Was he moving too quickly? Was it a bad sign that he was unable to control his urges? Sometimes Ott wondered if this was what a drug addict felt, though he knew his affliction was more like a mental illness. When he actually had a victim within his reach, wave after wave of a perfect balance of excitement and calmness would wash over him. He knew his mind would be clear after it was done. That's all he really needed. A clear head.

In a way, he had no choice. He'd be leaving New York City soon—well, in another few weeks. He had one more company scheduled for a complete office software installation. But if he didn't act now, he could end up lying in bed back home in Omaha thinking about nothing but this snarky intern.

No, he had to do it tonight. This girl, she'd made him too agitated. He needed to calm himself. Feel the relief. In a way, Ott was the victim. He had to kill to get mental peace.

Daniel Ott slipped on the heavy rubber surgical gloves he always wore during his murders. He also took a moment to slide fabric booties over his shoes. He felt like a surgeon. Or a medical examiner.

Then he froze, relishing the sensation that washed over him. *There it is.* The first tingling of the first wave of elation.

He found Elaine's door and gave a quick, cheerful double knock. It would sound like someone she knew. He stood there with the sharpened Phillips-head screwdriver in his hand. At the last minute he'd decided against the wire cutter.

He heard the lock turn, and the door opened wide. Elaine really didn't have any clue about living in New York.

Ott said, "Hey, Elaine, remember me?" He threw her a cheerful smile. Why not? He was in a great mood.

He enjoyed the confused look on her face. Even though she'd seen him around her office, she couldn't place his face. It was both satisfying and infuriating at the same time.

She started to say something. Before she could complete a single word, he acted. He swung the screwdriver in his right hand in a wide arc just inside the door. It pierced her throat smoothly. He let go of the handle and just gazed at his fantastic work. The black handle of the screwdriver stuck out of one side of her neck and the bloody end poked out the other side.

Elaine stood straight, just staring at him, still trying to speak. All that came out was a gurgling sound. And blood.

Ott casually stepped inside, shut and locked the door.

It took longer than he'd expected, but the shock from the deeply bleeding wound finally caught up to Elaine. The snobby intern took one step back before her legs gave out. First she dropped to her knees. Then she reached out as if she expected help from him. She didn't look quite so arrogant now.

When he didn't take her hand, Elaine tumbled forward.

This was going to be a night of confusion. At least for the cops.

Using his gloved hands, he smeared Elaine's blood in every room on almost every surface he could find.

Then he began his signature ritual. He took out a vial of blood he had been saving from a previous victim.

There were a dozen or so baseball bobblehead figurines sitting on a shelf next to the kitchen. He separated four of them and dribbled the blood from the vial over their heads. He couldn't keep from chuckling. *What will the cops make of this?* Taunting the police was part of the fun. It was a habit he'd developed over time. It made life a little more interesting. The added thrill made the taunts worth the risk.

Ott was always simple and subtle with his messages. Maybe one day someone would figure it out, though he didn't think it would do them any good. He doubted he'd ever be caught.

Now it was time for his final task. He always left this for last. Ott kneeled next to Elaine's body, now carefully positioned in the middle of a round throw rug. He pulled out his Gerber folding knife and held it in his right hand. It hadn't been terribly expensive, but he was impressed with the quality.

He studied her pretty face and admired her full lips. She'd lost so much blood that her complexion had turned sallow.

Her eyes were open, staring up at him. He plunged his blade into the left one.

CHAPTER 13

IN BED THAT night, after another long day of not-so-promising leads, I again reviewed reports and Mary Catherine tossed and turned. Finally, she sighed and said, "Maybe if I watch TV it will make me sleepy. Do you mind?" Without waiting for my answer, she took the remote.

As soon as I heard the theme music to local news, I wished Mary Catherine had never turned on the TV. The anchor led with a simple line: "With three bloody murders in less than three weeks, the city is on watch."

Well, it was clear the media had already decided our cases were linked. I tried to tune out the news segment, during which a reporter interviewed people about how they planned to protect themselves. Comments ranged from practical to blasé, and one young woman even seemed enthusiastic about the chance to defend herself: "It's kind of cool." And of course one knucklehead lodged the predictable complaint that the cops weren't doing their jobs. I wondered what he would think if he saw me covered with interview transcripts in my bed.

Mary Catherine rolled over and draped an arm across my chest. "One of those murders is your case, isn't it? You need to be careful. It won't be any fun to walk down the aisle if I have to do it alone."

Mary Catherine always had a quip to make me smile. Thankfully the news eventually moved on to other stories, and I drifted off into a deep, exhausted sleep. When my cell phone rang, I was sleeping so soundly—dreaming about my evening with Mary Catherine—I incorporated the ringtone into my dream. It took Mary Catherine's knee in the small of my back to wake me up.

She mumbled an apology as I grabbed the phone.

I heard a male voice. "Mike, sorry for the middle-of-the-night call. It's Dan Jackson down at Manhattan South."

I mumbled the standard answer: "It's okay, Dan. I was just getting up." This is old hat for any cop. Holidays, birthdays, it doesn't matter. You've got to respond.

"Sure you were. Anyway, it looks like we have a homicide down here that's similar to the ones I hear you've been looking at. Two roommates found a female victim with a distinctive facial injury. It's a very messy scene. There's so much blood, forensics isn't a hundred percent sure we're dealing with only one victim. They've just started processing the scene, but they're theorizing that the killer may have taken a second victim away from the scene."

He gave me a little more info and an address just south of Herald Square. I said, "Be there quick as I can."

I rolled over in my incredibly warm and comfortable bed,

then gave Mary Catherine a quick hug. She murmured something. I kissed her on the cheek and said I'd call her later, to which she responded with more murmuring that sounded like "Be careful."

I could get dressed in the dark as quickly and quietly as any human alive. But as I hustled out of the apartment a few minutes later, I caught the flicker of the TV from the living room.

I saw Brian on the couch, concentrating on the TV. I stepped through the dining room toward him, but his attention never wavered from the screen. As soon as he noticed me, he shut it off and slipped something under the pillow next to him on the couch. I didn't have to be a cop to notice that furtive movement. Every parent's experienced it at one point or another.

"Whatcha doin'?" I asked in a friendly tone.

Brian shrugged. "Couldn't sleep. It's so quiet around here at night. I'm not used to it anymore."

"What were you watching?"

"Nothing, really. Just flipping around the channels."

I decided the crime scene I was headed to wasn't going anywhere. I sat on the end of the couch.

Brian said, "You heading out to work?"

I nodded.

"I used to think I wanted to be a cop just like you. I guess that won't ever happen now." His voice had trailed off. With his prison record, he would never be able to get a police job. Another part of the high price he'd paid for his bad choice of working for a drug dealer.

I could sense his depression. I slid a little closer to him. "You know you can talk to me about anything."

"Thanks. I know."

"You want to tell me what's going on?"

"Nothing. Nothing other than I ruined my life and now I'm trying to fix it."

"I've got news for you, Brian, that's all any of us are trying to do, all the time. Some of our mistakes might not be as obvious as yours, but we're all out here trying to fix things."

"Even you?"

"Especially me. Don't think you're going through anything alone."

Then my son surprised me: he leaned over and gave me a hug. But for a moment, I felt like I was holding the old Brian. The cheerful kid who cared more about sports than anything else.

I left the apartment feeling remarkably good. At least as good as I could be, considering I was heading to a murder scene on only a few hours' sleep.

CHAPTER 14

WITH NO TRAFFIC, I was at the address on 30th Street in less than twenty minutes.

Brett Hollis met me at the front of the apartment building wearing a new bandage on his nose, not nearly as big and unwieldy as the previous one.

I couldn't keep from pointing and saying, "It looks better."

"I had to change it because I was having dinner with my mother. There was no way I would've survived her questioning if she'd seen a huge bloody mass on my face."

"What did you tell her happened? Not the truth, I bet. You lied to make it sound less serious, didn't you?"

Hollis shrugged. "I never lie to my mother. I told her I wasn't paying attention while running. That's accurate."

Detective Dan Jackson from Manhattan South poked his

head out of the front door. "You guys ready to come up? We're trying to limit access."

Jackson was known throughout the department for having once chased down and tackled a New York Jets running back who'd punched a woman. Jackson didn't advertise that he had played college football and was a linebacker at Notre Dame—but that Jets running back would never forget. After he spent the night in the hospital with three broken ribs, the guy had had the nerve to claim he'd been hit by a car. Witnesses contradicted him—they all said Jackson ran him down and hit him *like* a car.

I got a feel for the victim's apartment building as we climbed three flights of stairs to the crime scene. It wasn't luxurious, but it wasn't run-down either. Thin but new carpet, decent paint, and lights in the halls. Unremarkable, but better than a lot of Manhattan apartment buildings.

When we slipped out of the third-floor stairwell, I noticed two sets of crime-scene barriers. I expected the one at the door to the apartment. The other cut the hallway in half about ten feet from the door. I looked at Jackson.

The big man said, "You'll understand when you see the scene itself. There'll be a lot of looky-loos coming up here today once word gets around. I want to be able to stop them before they even get close to the apartment."

It made sense. More than one crime scene has been contaminated by inexperienced officers wandering through it.

We paused by the apartment's open front door as a crime-scene tech finished a video walk-through of the apartment. I asked Jackson the obvious questions. "Husband or boyfriend?"

"Roommates said she broke up with her last boyfriend about

five months ago. No one serious since. Coworkers and neighbors all liked her but didn't know her well."

"I guess it's too much to hope for any information from video surveillance cameras."

"No cameras in the immediate area. We're going to canvass the neighborhood in the morning when the businesses are open."

It was time for us to go inside. I elected to go in and leave Hollis behind the second barrier. Jackson had a disposable hooded biohazard suit for me to slip over my regular clothes. I'd done it enough times that it didn't take too long. The suit would keep me from contaminating the crime scene as well as protect me from any pathogens that might be present.

It's no exaggeration to say the scene took my breath away, even with Jackson's warning and my recent experience at Chloe Tumber's apartment. At first, I thought the apartment was just poorly lit. Then I realized there was so much blood smeared on the walls that it made the whole apartment appear dark. With this much blood, I understood the concern that there could be more unaccounted-for victims.

It didn't get any better as I stepped into the living room, where several crime-scene techs were photographing the space from a dozen different angles. In the middle, on a round carpet, lay the body of the young woman. She had a horrendous wound in her neck as well as a stab wound in her left eye. Blood and other fluids had pooled on the floor.

I tried to keep my composure as Jackson led me around the apartment. The victim looked so young. She must've been close in age to my oldest daughter, Juliana. All I could think about was who would notify her parents. To lose a child was horrendous. To lose one like this was unimaginable. I quickly said a prayer for her departed soul.

When we stepped back into the living room, an assortment of baseball bobbleheads caught my eye. The figurines were lined up on a shelf near the kitchen, but there was a gap between four on the right side and ten on the left side. It looked strangely deliberate. Were there some missing? I noticed blood dribbled over the heads of the bobbleheads—but only the four on the right. The application was different from the blood spread on the walls.

What did that mean? I made a note to check the crime-scene photos from Chloe Tumber's apartment, confer with Terri and Javier about any blood at their crime scenes that seemed intentionally placed.

It wasn't obvious to me yet, but the blood on the walls and tabletops and bed told a story. The message I got most strongly was that the killer wasn't finished. No way someone did a killing this methodical, this deliberately bloody, then just quit and never do it again.

This one had me worried.

CHAPTER 15

I STEPPED BACK into the hallway and lowered the hood of my biohazard suit to get some fresh air. Just like Dan Jackson had predicted, there were several uniformed officers out there already, who seemed to have stopped by just to gawk at the bloody scene. Jackson wasn't having any of it.

He barked at patrol officers, a sergeant, and even the local precinct lieutenant to get lost. None of them gave him any shit either. The lieutenant mumbled something about being the local commander on duty but still walked away as he was ordered.

I walked to the other end of the hallway, where Hollis and a couple of other detectives had set up a little command post with computers and evidence boxes.

Hollis sat on the floor at the very end of the hallway, working on a laptop. I was pleased to see he interacted well with the other detectives, gathering information we would need for a summary to our own bosses.

One of the detectives looked up from his computer screen and asked, "Is the FBI here? Someone from the mayor's office is asking."

Another detective said, "They said someone would swing by in the morning. Tell the mayor's office the FBI is in the loop. That should shut them up."

When Hollis saw me, I motioned him toward the apartment. I let him pass the first barrier and then stopped him at the door. He hadn't been issued a biohazard suit because Harry Grissom had him on data collection, but I thought he ought to take a look at this truly bizarre and horrible crime scene.

It was even worse than what we'd seen at Chloe Tumber's place.

I thought I might have to catch Hollis as he looked into the apartment. His legs got shaky and he took a big gulp of air, but he seemed stronger than he had at Chloe's apartment.

"I'm gonna say we're dealing with a true nut in this case," I said.

"That's not an official NYPD term." He tried to smile.

"It's not a term used by any professionals. But I dare someone to look in that apartment and not say whoever did it is bat-shit crazy."

I'll admit, I was creeped out. This guy was a new level of nasty.

CHAPTER 16

I HIT THE streets, and Hollis hit the books.

The next day, after spending all day interviewing techs and comparing photos of the New York crime scenes we were trying to connect, I made a beeline for the Manhattan North Homicide office, one floor of an office building owned by Columbia University but nowhere near campus.

It wasn't particularly flashy, convenient, or blessed with decent views, but I still loved my office. Its best quality was its location—nowhere near One Police Plaza. It was pure homicide investigation, no precinct built around it.

I walked in to find Hollis asleep at his desk, surrounded by stacks of notebooks and color-coded folders. After a few minutes, he popped awake and went right back to reading like he'd never been asleep. That was the mark of a smart cop.

"You ever read about serial killers?" he asked once he realized I was there. He held out a sheaf of printouts.

I shook my head. "I learn by experience."

"Never? I'd think the topic would interest you."

Now I turned to my partner. "I already have interests. Maybe you forgot that I have ten kids? I also have a full caseload. I even have hobbies. Reading about serial killers would be like a lifeguard going to the beach on his day off. Besides, I'm on legwork, you're the one on research. Remember?"

He surprised me by then saying, "Not today. I need a second pair of eyes."

Hollis explained that he had started a series of searches in newspaper databases, thinking maybe he could find a connection there that the police databases had overlooked.

I had to agree he made a good point. For the next hour we aggressively searched published records, from the *New York Times* to local papers to websites dedicated to identifying and tracking serial killers.

"I never knew all these disturbing details about serial killers, like how so many of them favor strangling and stabbing," Hollis said. "This shit is horrible."

I had to agree. The gory photographs bothered me the most. Followed closely by the knowledge that some people *liked* looking at crime-scene photographs. There were dozens of websites dedicated to serial killers that showed almost nothing but gruesome photos of their victims.

Then Hollis had the bright idea to widen the search beyond New York. We came across a news article from San Francisco dated almost a year earlier. There had been two murders there in the span of two weeks; both of the victims were women in their thirties who'd lived alone, and both had been stabbed by sharp implements with their faces "brutally mutilated," according to the article. One of the women had been slashed around the neck, but the other one was what caught my attention. She had been killed by some sort of implement driven directly through her throat—just like Elaine Anastas.

The article noted that while the murders weren't officially linked, the cops suspected it had been the same killer. Now they were both cold cases.

There's that unsolved murder rate again, I thought.

A little while later, Hollis looked up from a search of the Southeast region and said, "There could be something in Atlanta too. Looks like about eight months ago there was a series of murders there—two in apartment buildings, one in an office, and two more in nearby suburbs. All the crime scenes were noted as being especially bloody. Then the killings stopped. Nothing since."

Hollis picked up his sheaf of printouts. I could tell he was working up to a big reveal.

"I read the FBI's report on serial murder. It says the concept of the traveling serial killer is a myth."

"Is that so?" I said. I never would have consulted a report from the FBI. Not that I needed to tell Hollis that.

Hollis continued. "But there are a few notable exceptions. Such as individuals whose work involves interstate travel." He proceeded to quote from the report. "'The nature of their traveling lifestyle provides them with many zones of comfort in which to operate.'"

"I'm listening," I said.

"Ted Bundy is the obvious American example," Hollis said.

"He started in the Pacific Northwest and ended up in Florida. In Russia, a killer called the Red Ripper—named Chiclet or something like that—evaded the Russian cops for more than a decade because he traveled for his job. Killed, like, fifty people."

I thought about it. Hollis raised an interesting idea. "So you're saying we may have one of them?"

I picked up the phone.

Hollis said, "Who're you calling?"

"The FBI."

CHAPTER 17

DANIEL OTT SAT in a trucking office in Queens. This was his new assignment. He could not have been in higher spirits. It was a common state after completing one of his *rituals*. He was confident he wasn't on any police agency's radar. The fact that he never got too cocky kept him grounded in reality. Taunting the police by mixing a trail of fresh blood with cold-case evidence had become an increasingly important part of his urge.

Police officers weren't stupid. They had resources. But Ott had nothing to fear here in New York City, where the police were shackled by a mountain of rules when dealing with citizens.

He still reveled in the last waves of pleasure over what he'd done to Elaine, the intern. He'd never forget the look on her face when the screwdriver annihilated her nervous system. It had been as satisfying as anything he'd ever experienced. *Maybe* the births of his daughters had felt slightly better. But it was close.

He chuckled when he thought about the blood he'd sprinkled across the bobbleheads at Elaine's apartment. If the police believed there was more than one victim, but only one body present at the scene, they would be running in circles. At least for a while.

Ott wished he was home. He was usually more clearheaded and more focused on his family after he found a release for his fantasies. For now, he'd have to focus on work.

The new assignment looked interesting. The trucking company used radios as well as cell phones, and he would integrate them with one computer system. It was exactly the kind of issue Computelex's software was designed to handle. So far, management was no-nonsense. He'd worked a lot of places, and this company actually *did* something. It shipped goods locally and throughout the Northeast. Got results. Not like the insurance companies or medical billing agencies that provided soft services. Electronic paperwork. It seemed like this would be an easy two-week assignment.

The software finished loading, and Ott took out a sticker. Computelex required him to slap the company logo onto any computer he worked on. The two-and-a-half-inch circle showed the company name in blue beneath a smiling, anthropomorphic computer screen with two arms, one holding a telephone, the other a radio.

Ott's phone rang. It must be noon. When he looked at the phone, he saw the daily call from home was indeed right on time, as usual. He answered it with a cheerful, "Hello!"

"Hello, Papa!" His little girls' voices in unison sounded like music.

"How are my dumplings today?"

"Good," his older daughter, Lilly, said. The three-year-old, Tatyana, was probably nodding. The girls told him about a game they had made up. Every time they missed a spelling word, they had to run out the front door and completely around the house. Getting exercise while learning simple words made a good game. He approved.

Then Lilly said, "Mama is making me work on math for an extra hour today. I don't like math. I don't think Mama explains it very well."

Ott had talked to his older daughter about her homeschool classes before. In as even a tone as he could keep, Ott said, "Listen to me. Math is important in life. You're going to learn it no matter what kind of teacher your mother is. If you can't do your times tables and division by the time I get home, you'll be sorry to see me. You understand?"

Lilly said, "Yes, Papa."

Good. She was learning respect.

CHAPTER 18

OTT WAS STILL in a good mood after talking to his daughters when the manager of the trucking company introduced him to some of the employees, mostly large, unfriendly men and a few women.

One of the women caught his attention when she reprimanded two younger employees about time sheets. He wasn't looking for a victim at the moment. It was too soon after Elaine. But this woman was attractive and a little older than him, maybe thirty-eight or forty. Her reddish hair and pretty face reminded him of his first victim. He smiled at the memory.

It was not long after he had moved to Omaha. Even then, he already had started to evolve, using a few tricks of stealth and surveillance, evading detection, even planting an electronic bug or two over the years. Although he didn't like to admit how much he remained in their debt, he had his earliest employer to thank for those skills and the lessons they had taught him, many of which he still used.

Sometimes he thought about the people he used to work with. They were one of the reasons he'd moved to Omaha. In the Midwest, he was less likely to run into any of them.

All he really wanted to do was forget about that experience. He'd rather remember his first murder.

He could recall every detail. It had been a Wednesday afternoon, and he'd been looking for an office in a large building. He had his tools and software to install. He'd inadvertently walked into the wrong office—it turned out to be some kind of staffing group that handled the admin for several companies—and a redheaded woman standing at the front desk had berated him. "You're in the wrong office. They're on the fifth floor. What kind of an idiot computer guy are you?"

She clearly had more to say. But he never heard it. His hand had slipped into his tool pouch and found the handle of his box cutter. Just as the woman screwed up her face to let out another burst of insults, he'd pulled out the box cutter and swiped it across her exposed throat.

It was a natural movement and he performed it quickly. She didn't even seem to realize exactly what had happened, just that she suddenly couldn't get any air. She quickly raised both of her hands to clasp her throat. Then she staggered back, bumped into her desk, and tumbled onto the carpeted floor.

She made a few gurgling sounds and looked like a fish that had been pulled from the water. Ott stared at her throughout the whole event, still not quite realizing what he had done. That's when he felt it. The first wave of excitement and joy. The first urge. It washed over him completely as he stared at the woman on the floor with a huge dark puddle of blood spreading across the carpet.

He didn't understand at the time. It had been an impulse, completely beyond his control. He went about his day and, aside from a few news reports, never heard a word about it. Another cold case that would never be linked to him.

Fortunately, his work assignments kept him moving. He had never killed anyone in the Midwest again.

The only thing he knew for sure was that he would continue doing this forever.

CHAPTER 19

I MET EMILY PARKER for lunch at a place called Empanada Mama on Ninth Avenue just south of 52nd Street. It was the kind of place Mary Catherine would like, if we could ever take the time for a night out in Hell's Kitchen. Boldly colorful art adorned the brick walls and fans rotated along the ceiling.

Emily sat by herself in a booth near the rear of the restaurant. She wore a bright blue skirt and matching blouse. Looking at her, I could see Emily still had a sparkle in her eyes. Working for the FBI hadn't worn her down at all. Her purse, as always, sat on the bench next to her right hand. That way her gun was never far from her reach. It was good tactical sense, which I appreciated.

Emily really was the total package: smart, funny, and pretty. A deadly combination. And her easy smile was infectious. I was well aware of how close we once came to being a couple. I'm not a robot. I'd had romantic feelings for her. If it wasn't for Mary Catherine, maybe I'd still have those feelings. But this meeting was strictly business.

As for Emily's professionalism, she was tops at the Bureau. I always got the impression she was a shark swimming with minnows. And like every shark in the ocean, she was relentless, going all night, night after night, if that's what it took to break the case.

She smiled as I approached and said, "It's funny how the NYPD has no use for the FBI, until they need us."

"Hey, I'm trying to *include* you. If you're uncomfortable with the arrangement, I can find another way to get the information I need."

Emily held up her hands as I took a seat opposite her. She wore a delicate gold ring with a small emerald stone nestled in the heart-shaped center. "Wow, you're getting sensitive in your old age," she said.

"And you're getting sentimental," I shot back. "Still wearing your childhood ring." Then I softened, adding, "I know it means a lot to you."

She nodded her thanks, then leapt back into the fray. "I'm just busting your balls after the way you treated my ASAC at the meeting the other day. I should tell you he's got someone in the mayor's office listening to him."

"We didn't treat him badly. We just shot down his idea. There's a difference, whether Robert Lincoln can see it or not. And the truth is, no one in the mayor's office really listens. He might be telling them things, but they won't do anything about it unless it helps them."

"Cynical."

"Only about government bureaucracy. You have no idea what goes on with the New York mayor's office. It doesn't matter who's the mayor." I sighed, then leaned forward. "Look, we have some theories about our killer. You might be able to help us."

"Me personally? Or the FBI as an agency?"

"I was hoping to deal with you personally. At least until we figure a few things out. That a problem?"

Emily smiled, and I knew she was about to lay some kind of trap.

She said, "Let me make sure I understand. You want the benefits of FBI resources without actually dealing with the FBI?"

"I wouldn't say it quite like that."

"How would you say it?"

"I'd like to ask you, as my friend, to use FBI resources to help me. Because I'm *your* friend." I was pleased to see that my rogue diplomacy made her laugh.

When she regained her composure, Emily said, "So what can I do to help the great Michael Bennett? According to the newspapers over the years, you already have all the answers."

"If I had all the answers, I probably wouldn't still be a cop."

"Yeah, yeah. So what's your theory? I'll help you if I can."

I told her how Hollis and I had found what we thought could be similar cases in San Francisco and Atlanta. Then I said, "It'd be nice to know if the FBI was involved in those cases. It'd be great to have those reports. And most importantly, what do you think of Hollis's theory that this could be the same killer, that he travels around?"

The FBI agent took a few moments to consider everything I'd said. "Let me run it past someone I know at Quantico. The behavioral science people are in a better position to talk about theories like that. I'll keep it quiet. Nothing official."

I said, "What about the FBI's Violent Criminal Apprehension Program or the Radford Serial Killer Database?"

"Databases are only as good as the information entered," she warned. "ViCAP has been around since the 1980s. People relied on ViCAP for a long time until they realized its limitations. Also, whatever I run through the databases will track back to me. If anyone starts asking questions, an electronic trail might make it official."

"If it helps us stop this killer, I could live with that."

CHAPTER 20

BY MIDAFTERNOON, DANIEL OTT decided it was time to take steps toward making life more interesting. For everyone.

He wasn't an hourly employee, so he was free to slip out of the office early. Besides, as usual, no one noticed him leave. He headed back into Manhattan. He'd been working hard on his plan. He needed to use a computer that couldn't be traced back to him. Which was why he ended up at the main branch of the New York Public Library on Fifth Avenue.

He even took a few extra minutes to explore the iconic building before getting down to business. The woodwork on the walls and high ceilings gave it such a solemn and scholarly feel that the idea of coming here to use a public computer seemed tacky. At the same time, however, he resented the amount of money spent on a building like this. Not just the marble walls and wood carved in dramatic shapes on the ceilings and shelving and tables but also the cost of maintaining it. The money could feed half the Midwest, he assumed. He hated the obvious opulence serving pretentious New Yorkers' egos.

He pushed those thoughts out of his mind for the moment. It was time to ratchet up the stress on the cops investigating his killings. This was a wrinkle he had been considering for a long while.

He'd begun leaving messages behind, starting with the third woman he had ever killed. He liked numbers and wanted the police to know he was counting his kills. Since then, almost ten years ago, he'd found he couldn't stop. In fact, he often fought the urge to make the markers he left more and more obvious.

Ott didn't know if anyone had ever figured out any of his taunts—mixing the blood of past and present victims, stabbing them in the eye. He liked the control of puncturing the eye, the splash of the aqueous and vitreous fluids as they released from the anterior and posterior chambers. He liked the definitive proof of that final stab wound—the proof that his was the last face they'd ever see. He still hadn't noticed any mention in the media. Which was why he needed to take this extra step. Get his message heard.

He'd already prepared everything he needed. Technically, patrons were supposed to use library cards to access the computers, but Ott had noticed that if he came there in the afternoon, he could get on to a library computer without anyone caring.

He stepped into the dark paneled room and glanced around quickly. There was one librarian presiding over a computer table with five open machines. He slipped into the seat farthest away from the librarian and immediately created a new Gmail account in the name of Bobby Fisher. He'd used the name Boris Spassky once before and liked the symmetry of his choices.

It took him only a moment to find the email address he needed and another thirty seconds to upload the document from a thumb drive. If the police were too dim to notice his messages, he'd alert the media. Soon everyone would be paying attention to him, the most dangerous killer ever to hit New York. And the only one with a lesson plan.

While he was online, he couldn't help but look up a few articles and video clips featuring pundits speculating about who was behind the recent murders in New York. Ott smiled, knowing that as soon as his message was received, there was going to be a lot more of them.

He loved seeing the so-called experts talk about what the killer might do next. It was like everything else in life: no one knew anything, but they still had to talk. And people were willing to listen. The story was always the same.

Ott clicked on one article from the *New York Post*. It named a Michael Bennett as one of the detectives looking into the crimes. According to the *Post*, Bennett was "New York's top cop," and having him on the case was great news for the city. Ott smiled again. Top cop or not, this Michael Bennett was no threat to him.

More people started to file into the computer room, and Ott decided it was a good time to leave. He closed out the links he had opened on the computer, cleared his search history, and, out of habit, ran an antistatic cloth he kept in his work pouch over the keyboard. In the unlikely circumstance that someone figured out he'd used this terminal to send his message, the wipe down would be enough to eliminate his fingerprints.

As he slipped past a bookshelf, Ott found his way blocked by a pretty young woman carrying a stack of journals in her arms. She had very dark skin and long, straight black hair. She looked exotic and very un-midwestern to him.

He nodded to her just to be polite.

She smiled, revealing perfect dimples, and said, "Next time it would be better if you signed in to use the computer. It doesn't only reserve the computer; it also helps show the city how many people are using the library."

Ott was dazzled by her smile, but his anger rose quickly. How dare she confront him over a minor break in the rules.

He nodded as he slipped past her.

Then he froze.

He realized in an instant that not only had this young woman disrespected him; she also had specifically noticed him. She could remember his face. She was a loose end he would not tolerate.

Ott had a small set of tools in his pouch. Mostly screwdrivers and small wrenches. But he also had the sharp Gerber knife, the same one he'd used on Elaine, the one that came in handy for stripping wires and opening boxes.

Ott was gripped by the impulse to stick the knife into this girl's heart. He glanced around the computer room. There were a dozen people in it, but everyone was focused on their own books or screens. He wondered if they'd have enough privacy if he backed her up into the row of journals she was organizing. It would take only ten seconds. The wild card would be keeping her quiet.

He thought about slashing her throat, like he'd done to the midwestern receptionist. But if he did that, she would definitely make some noise. And there would be a lot of blood in a much-too-public space.

Ott managed to get hold of himself. This was not the time or the place. But there would be a time.

Soon.

CHAPTER 21

HOLLIS DROVE ME home that evening in a city-issued Crown Victoria. I was grateful for the ride. Driving when you're as tired as I was is as bad as driving drunk. People are killed by dozing drivers every day.

As Hollis drove, I prepped him for our morning assignment: a visit to Elaine Anastas's parents. Police procedure dictated an in-person interview with a victim's next of kin. It was going to be a rough one.

I went through the door to my apartment and gave Chrissy her daily swing in the air. Said hello to the kids who were at home. Seeing their smiling faces revived me…for about three minutes. Then I sat down to watch the news, and the next thing I knew, Mary Catherine was sitting next to me.

I started, looked at my fiancée, and said, "What are you, a ninja?"

She laughed. "A sumo wrestler could have waddled up next to you and you wouldn't have noticed."

"How long was I out?"

"About forty minutes. Dinner is in another ten. I can see by the look on your face that it's best I don't even ask you about your day."

"Thanks. Nothing worth discussing. How about you? How was your day?"

Mary Catherine frowned. The downcast expression didn't suit her. Maybe it's because I was used to her normally cheerful demeanor, which was arguably as classically and stereotypically Irish as her face.

I said, "Cut through the chitchat and tell me what's wrong." I wasn't sure I had the stamina to sit through a long story anyway.

Mary Catherine said, "Aside from Jane and her constant babbling about her boyfriend, I'm still worried about Brian. He disappeared again today. Just got home a few minutes ago."

"You can't expect someone recently released from prison to sit in the apartment all day. I'm sure he's just excited for the freedom to move around." I knew there was more to the story. I could tell by the way she hesitated.

"Trent was looking for a library book in their room, and he found Brian's savings account statement. He's withdrawn a total of fifteen hundred dollars since he's been home. I think we should talk to him about it."

This was a lot to come at me out of the daze of a short nap. I tried not to sigh as I considered potential outcomes. "I'd like to let it wait," I said. "It's important Brian knows we trust him. He's not going to like the idea that his brother was snooping on him either."

Mary Catherine didn't particularly agree with my decision. That was another aspect of her Irishness. She could not hide her emotions. Ever. From virtually anyone, and especially me.

I decided to fill her in on a little bit of my day. I jumped right in by saying, "I saw Emily Parker today. She's trying to help me with the homicide case." As I waited for a response, I felt myself tense a little bit. The beauty of the Irish soul can never be underestimated. Unfortunately, it also encompasses an Irish temper. The problem was never knowing what would set it off.

But Mary Catherine looked calm. She took a moment, brushed some hair out of her face, and said, "Emily seems like a good FBI agent. I like to see you getting help. I know you two have history, but what's the point of marrying you if I can't trust you?"

This beautiful Irish girl never failed to surprise me.

CHAPTER 22

AT ABOUT SEVEN thirty the next morning, I stumbled into the kitchen, foggy from not nearly enough sleep. I mumbled "Good morning" to some of my family, grabbed my notebook, and slipped out the door.

And there was Brett Hollis sitting in the Crown Vic, right where he'd said he would be. I was impressed.

The second surprise was that he had stopped by Dunkin' Donuts, and had a cup of coffee and a donut stick for me.

Even so, I'll admit feeling a flash of annoyance that the young detective, who had been keeping the same schedule as me, looked so fresh and ready to go. Even the bandage on his nose looked neater and more secure than before.

I slipped into the passenger seat and nodded a greeting. "On time, ready to go, and not complaining? This already feels like it's going to be a good day."

Hollis said, "Woodstock is about a hundred miles north of the city. I have a route mapped out, and I talked to one of my buddies with the state police. I know where they're patrolling today. We'll make it in record time."

I said to Hollis, "I'd like to get there and back alive. I appreciate your interest in efficiency, but I'll make good use of the time in the car." To his credit, Hollis didn't try to make chitchat. He focused on the road and, even though it made me a little nervous, turned I-87 into some kind of speed trial.

By the time we turned west off the interstate near Hurley and I looked up from my notebook, I was rewarded with a wide-angle view of upstate New York greenery. Pastures and woods were not what I grew up seeing every day, and they were lovely to look at. I gazed out the window and said, "Not much has happened in Woodstock since the music festival."

"What music festival?"

I flinched. Surely my young partner couldn't be so cut off from the cultural past as to have never heard of Woodstock. I gave him a sideways glance, then said, "Are you messing with me?"

He smiled. "A little."

"So you *have* heard of Woodstock, right? Jimi Hendrix, the Grateful Dead, Janis Joplin?"

Hollis shrugged and said, "My grandma told me all about it."

I had to laugh at that and mumbled, "You little shit."

The home belonging to Elaine Anastas's parents sat on the edge of a wide field about fifteen miles south of Woodstock. We passed the mailbox, which leaned to the southeast like the Tower of Pisa, and bumped over the dirt road toward the house. I stopped counting abandoned refrigerators after the first seven.

The patch of grass in the front yard was covered with broken plastic toys, old tires, and a stake with a chain attached to it that I hoped was used for a dog.

Hollis mumbled, "Elaine did well to get out of here."

A woman of about forty-five answered the door. She had the blotchy complexion and red eyes of a grieving mom.

"I'm sorry for your loss," I said to Mrs. Anastas as she let us inside.

Her husband, wearing the same lost expression, answered for both of them as he wandered into the main room from the kitchen. "It was too soon."

Talking to the parents of murder victims is probably my least favorite part of my job. Having to talk to strangers about a child recently lost to a violent crime seems unusually cruel.

I sat with Elaine's parents on the couch in the front room and gave them an update on the case. The couch looked like it might have been salvaged from the woods when they dropped off a refrigerator. Two dogs barked and howled from another room, but that didn't seem to bother the Anastases.

During the conversation, Elaine's mother said, "We weren't crazy about Laney moving to the city, but all she talked about was how great living there was and how she couldn't wait to get out of school and get a job in communications."

I listened intently, then asked, "Mrs. Anastas, did Elaine know a lot of people in the city?"

"She had two roommates, and she had made a lot of friends at her internship," she said.

"How did she meet her roommates?"

"They were friends from college. Nice girls. One of them is in grad school, the other one interns for the Yankees."

The mention of the Yankees made me think of the bobble-heads I'd seen. I wondered if those had belonged to the other girl rather than Elaine.

I nodded, then followed with the crucial question. "Did she mention anyone she *didn't* get along with? A coworker, or maybe a man she met on a bad date?"

"No, nothing like that. She would have told me."

I didn't believe her. I doubted that she and Elaine discussed difficult subjects.

I looked at the weary, grieving woman and realized that she had treated her daughter almost exactly the same way our family was treating Brian. We didn't broach any problems with him for fear of scaring him away.

Maybe I needed to rethink how I was dealing with my oldest son.

CHAPTER 23

EVEN WITH BRETT HOLLIS doing his best impersonation of a NASCAR driver on our return, we weren't back in the office until the afternoon, and I felt the loss of every working hour. We were at a point in the investigation where we were eliminating possibilities rather than chasing leads. That was never a great position to be in.

I still hadn't gotten any FBI information from Emily Parker about potentially similar cases around the country, though I did request and receive crime-scene photos and police reports on the two murders in San Francisco. It was a reach to think we might link these, but I was game to try.

I looked up when I heard the booming voice of Victor Kuehne, a precinct detective who'd been in and out of our office for the last couple of weeks, working with one of our homicide detectives on a case unrelated to ours. Kuehne was known for his gregarious personality and off-color jokes. He was both loved and hated throughout the department.

He was also known for picking on detectives. And enjoying it. I thought he was a bully. Now he turned on Hollis.

"Hollis, man, are you hiding a nose job from us? That bandage seems like it's been on your face a long time."

I opened my mouth to explain that it had been only a couple of days but decided to let Hollis speak for himself.

He didn't, just smiled and shook his head.

Kuehne wasn't deterred. "Didn't you graduate from NYU before you hit the Police Academy? What are you doing, bucking to make chief before you've even gotten your hands dirty?"

Hollis still didn't take the bait.

"Lay off, Kuehne," I said. "He's working on a real case. If you're not careful, we'll get you assigned to it and stick you with a thousand crank leads."

Bullies are rarely interested in dealing with someone who stands up to them. Kuehne was no exception. He didn't say another word as he turned toward the desk he'd been using.

A moment later, Hollis stepped over to my desk and sat in an empty chair. He said, "I appreciate your concern, but I can handle myself. You stepping to my defense just convinces that moron he was right about me. He already thinks I'm not tough enough to be a cop. Now he thinks I'm not even tough enough to defend myself."

He wasn't wrong. All I could do was nod my head and say, "Understood."

What I should have said was that I'd never seen a detective make a tougher run at a fleeing suspect than Hollis had with Billy Van Fleet, but the moment had passed.

A few minutes later, Kuehne strolled by our desks. He considered Hollis for a moment, then finally said, "So tell me, is the nose job just to cover the fact that you got a small pecker?"

Hollis didn't bother looking up from his report. He said in an easy tone, "Your mom didn't mind it last night."

I didn't even try to hide my grin.

Hollis was right. Kuehne walked away, satisfied with Hollis's proper burn.

I glanced again at the San Francisco crime-scene photos I'd gotten in. The photos showed two messy scenes that looked eerily similar to the ones I'd been at recently here in New York. The savagely murdered victims, both slashed around the neck, face, and eyes—and the excessive amount of blood deliberately splashed around the rooms.

I reviewed the case file of one of the victims, a thirty-year-old tech worker who had lived alone in an apartment not far from Fisherman's Wharf. I flipped to a photo of her living room and noticed that lined up on her mantel were tiny figurines of ballerinas and musicians. Several were pushed to one side, then a gap, and then two more figurines. *Interesting.*

The separation between the two groups of figurines reminded me of the similar detail at Elaine Anastas's apartment—those bloody bobbleheads.

Was there a connection?

CHAPTER 24

DANIEL OTT REALIZED the potential risk in stalking the young librarian who'd spoken to him in the computer room in the New York Public Library.

He had only recently killed Elaine, the intern. Normally he'd pause between victims. But he felt pressed to eliminate a witness who might be able to identify him in the future.

He decided achieving that goal outweighed the risk.

Ott was surprised not to have had an instant response to the email he'd sent. It was the most daring action he'd ever taken in relation to his hobby. Although he recognized the hypocrisy between creating a meticulous crime scene and then taunting the police in private and public ways, Ott couldn't explain why he had done it. Maybe it was because they were too stupid to understand how clever he was.

He had already decided the librarian needed to go, so it was easy to forget the fact that he had rarely killed like this before, without preparing his crime-scene rituals and messages.

It hadn't been difficult to figure out which door the library staff used to exit their shifts. He got lucky in spotting the young woman after only about twenty minutes of waiting near the door.

He followed her from the library. She seemed to be a cheerful, friendly young woman. Either that or she knew an inordinate number of people. She waved and nodded hello to dozens of people in the space of three blocks. She was wearing jeans and a plain blouse, nothing remarkable, so he had to keep her long, straight black hair constantly in sight.

Ott found that the longer he followed the girl, the more she intrigued him. He appreciated how she stopped to help an elderly man struggling to get his walker over a curb. She stayed with the man until he entered a McDonald's halfway down the block.

Ott glanced around the street and didn't see many pedestrians. A taxi whizzed by, none of the passengers paying any attention.

All he needed was a quiet moment when no one was around. Just a quick blade through the throat or the chest and then he could walk away.

He thought he'd found that opportunity when she stopped to make a phone call almost twenty minutes after he'd started following her from the library. From half a block away, Ott watched her pace back and forth across an alley. He felt his pulse quicken. He slipped a surgical glove over his right hand as he made his way along the sidewalk, reaching into his tool pouch to pull out the Gerber folding knife.

He'd already decided to step up behind her and slice her throat horizontally. She would make noise and her blood would spill onto the street, but he didn't care what kind of mess he made if they were alone. *The messier the better* was his usual attitude anyway. He imagined she would just crawl into the alley and thrash around until she was dead. With luck, no one would even notice her body for a while.

He came close enough to hear her voice as she talked on the phone. The same voice she had used to reprimand him. He was almost sorry there wouldn't be time for one of his dedicated rituals.

He zeroed in on her. The librarian was facing away from him, chatting away and not paying any attention to her surroundings. Perfect.

Just as he stepped into the alley, he heard more voices. Three men dressed in white were sitting on folding chairs behind a restaurant's back exit. They were cooks, laughing and talking on a break.

All three men glanced up at him. He closed the knife and slipped it back into his pouch. Ott tried to alter his course and casually stepped back onto the sidewalk. He walked quickly out of their sight before he paused for a moment and took a breath.

About thirty seconds later, the young librarian strolled past him without paying any attention at all.

He had missed his best opportunity.

CHAPTER 25

DANIEL OTT FOLLOWED the young librarian another block until she turned and stepped into a Subway sandwich shop. The chain was the gold standard for people in a hurry or students without much money. Basic nutrition without a lot of flavor. It wasn't the flashiest business plan, but they seemed to be doing okay.

Ott was a little confused about what to do next. After feeling his excitement rise when he thought he could reach the librarian in the alley, he had calmed down.

He stopped at the door and held it open for an elderly Indian woman. The hunched woman walked in a shuffling gait. She looked up and smiled a thank-you. He nodded and helped her inside.

Ott merged into the line, putting a couple of people between him and the librarian. He glanced up at a TV bolted to the wall, where his murders led a quick newsbreak.

He wasn't the only one paying attention to the screen. Virtually everyone in line, including the hunched-over Indian woman, looked up at the newscaster. Ott waited to hear if his latest taunt had been discovered. There was coverage of Elaine Anastas's recent murder but nothing about his messages—neither the ones he'd left at the scenes nor the one he'd sent via email.

The snobby intern was garnering more attention dead than she had in her entire life. That made Ott smile. He wasn't sure what emotion it was he now felt bubbling up inside him. Then he realized: it was a sense of power. Every woman who saw that newscast was afraid of him.

As the report ended and the news moved on to the weather, Ott found himself a foot away from the librarian—only a waist-high metal rail between them.

She turned and looked directly at him.

Daniel Ott was caught between excitement and fear. This was the moment of truth. He decided to meet her gaze.

She looked directly at him, then turned back to the menu plastered high on the wall behind the cashier.

Ott stood there for a moment. She'd shown no recognition whatsoever. He had been invisible to her.

That has to stop.

CHAPTER 26

THE FOLLOWING MORNING, I stepped out of my bedroom dressed for work. Even though I'd slept a little during the night, I could feel the stress and pace of the investigation catching up to me. At least the sight of my children getting ready for school gave me some energy and made me smile.

Eddie was scribbling some sort of notes about a computer program he was working on. Fiona was reading a book about a kid in middle school. Brian was already dressed, but Jane and Juliana, the two older girls, were still getting ready. Everyone else was chatting as they ate breakfast around the long table.

I grabbed a bagel breakfast sandwich. No one made these as well as Mary Catherine. She mixed garlic and a splash of hot sauce into the eggs, which struck me as more Latin than Irish, but regardless, it was the best way to start the morning.

I slid into the chair between Mary Catherine and Brian.

Brian had a small duffel bag at his side, another habit I knew he'd picked up from prison: always keeping the things you need most with you at all times.

I asked casually, "What's in the bag, Brian?"

Brian slid his chair to the side and reached for the duffel to open it.

I said, "You don't have to show it to me. I was just curious."

Brian shrugged and set the duffel bag back down. "Just a change of clothes."

A few minutes later, everyone was in the final stages of getting ready for their day. Brian and Juliana had already left. Mary Catherine and I had a quiet moment alone at the breakfast table.

She gave me one of her classic looks for a beat, then said, "I'd have opened the bag and looked in it."

I nodded and said, "Yes, I know."

About thirty minutes later, as I was pulling into a parking spot outside my office, I got a call that there'd been a homicide on Staten Island. When the dispatcher told me the detective at the scene thought I should come, I knew exactly why—and it gave me a knot in my stomach.

I turned the car around and headed for Staten Island.

Staten Island has a special status among the five boroughs of New York. Some joke it's actually part of New Jersey. City workers are well represented in the borough's population, especially NYPD and FDNY. Many cops and firefighters rejoice if they're assigned to Staten Island.

The crime scene was in an apartment building in Emerson Hill, just off Interstate 278. Almost as soon as I stepped out of my car, I saw a familiar face and knew she must be the lead detective who'd called me in. I waited while she directed a couple of patrol officers to push the media back. I couldn't believe the number of TV trucks, until I remembered this murderer was starting to attract a lot of attention.

Detective Raina Rayesh turned to me and smiled. She was a little older than me and preferred lifting weights to running. Her dark hair had streaks of gray in it now, and I noticed more laugh lines on her face. She'd probably say the same about me. But she was the same funny, smart Rayesh, among the sharpest minds in the NYPD.

She gave me a giant hug and said, "I really hope I can find a reason to dump this on you."

I laughed and held up my hands. "I have two homicide cases of my own."

"That's why I want you to take a look at this one." Rayesh reviewed some notes. "Marilyn Shaw, twenty-six. Worked at a hedge fund in Midtown. No known current boyfriend. No one can think of anyone she ever upset."

"Elaine Anastas's mom said the same about her daughter. A young woman enjoying life in the city. No enemies. No boyfriend."

Other than Billy Van Fleet, we hadn't heard about anyone with even a whisper of motive for wanting to hurt Chloe Tumber either.

Rayesh pressed on. "This one looks similar. Like your guy."

I groaned. "First of all, please don't call this sicko my guy. Second, we don't know if he selects his victims at random. I have no third point, but it always sounds better if there are three things to bring up."

Rayesh laughed at my tired old joke. She said, "I'd still like you to take a look at this crime scene and give me your thoughts."

"Is it bad?"

Rayesh shrugged. "There's a dead girl inside. That's always bad. But I've seen worse."

That surprised me. The murder cases we were investigating all had shocking crime scenes, all the same kind of blood-soaked mess, which was part of why they all pointed to being the work of a single killer. But after I followed Rayesh through the checkpoints to Marilyn Shaw's second-floor apartment, I agreed that this one could have been worse. Yet she was also right about the similarities.

The body of a young woman with blond hair lay on the floor near the front door. She'd been stabbed in the chest. The entire front of her white blouse was stained a rust color.

"Looking at the body, it appears the killer stabbed her as soon as she opened the door. Then he stabbed her again in the eye," Rayesh said, pointing to the woman's right eye. "It has to be the same guy." A small pool of blood and fluid had dried on the hardwood floor where the victim's disfigured face rested.

I looked around the apartment. The murderer's MO ticked the same boxes, but the scene seemed…off. It was too clean, too undisturbed. It was clear that the killer had spent a lot of time at all the other scenes—this one felt more perfunctory. Had he been interrupted?

It would take time and forensics to compare all of the evidence, but my gut was telling me something was wrong here. "I don't know, Raina. Something about the scene as a whole feels different," I told her. "I'm not sensing the method behind the murder. There's no blood spread on the walls. I don't see anything else disturbed. This killer I'm tracking, he's deliberately messy. He's into grotesque displays, throwing around a lot of blood, the dramatic way he always stabs all his victims in the left eye, and so on. This seems almost tidy by comparison," I said, shaking my head.

"Back up a second," Rayesh said. "Which eye?"

"The left one. Always the left eye."

"Well, Marilyn Shaw's *right* eye is the one he stabbed this time."

Why had the killer made a change? Was he trying to taunt us?

What was it about the Staten Island case that made me so uneasy?

CHAPTER 27

IT WAS AFTER lunch by the time I got back to the office. The Staten Island crime scene still bothered me. Not the way Elaine Anastas's had, with the blood and gore, but because of the subtle changes in the killer's procedure.

The blotter on my desk was bloodstained. For a moment, I thought I was hallucinating. All the bloody crime scenes I had visited were finally messing with my head.

I used the end of a pen to touch a droplet of blood. It was fresh. I looked at the floor and saw another drop a few feet away. I followed the drops like an old tracker and was not the least bit surprised when they led me to Brett Hollis.

I stood next to my young partner's desk, staring at his bandaged nose. It looked a little worse today, even though it was healing, since now he had two black eyes to go with it.

I said, "What were you doing at my desk?"

"What makes you think I was at your desk?"

I gave him a look and pointed at his own desk, which was speckled with a design of tiny red drops that looked like the solar system.

Hollis quickly touched his nose, then looked down at the blood on the end of his finger. He mumbled, "Shit." Then he looked at me and said, "I was reading some of the reports that came in to you from San Francisco. I've also been searching the internet for similar cases, like the ones we found in Atlanta."

"Did you find anything?"

"Just that there may have been an uptick in unsolved, brutal homicides in major cities. The kind of homicides that aren't obviously related to the drug business or classified as crimes of passion. It doesn't take a whole lot of murders like that to raise the average in the whole country. That's why I think it's significant. But I can't say for sure the homicides are related to our cases."

I nodded. This kid was showing some real signs of creativity and intelligence. I could work with that.

Before I could even make it back to my desk, I noticed Dr. Jill St. Pierre barreling through the office at the only speed she knew: fast. The Haitian-born forensic scientist had been profiled by *New York* magazine for her brilliance in the lab. I'd worked with her—I didn't need to read an article to know how smart she was.

She smiled as she approached and said, "Being engaged agrees with you, Bennett."

"That's nice of you to say, but any benefit I've gotten from being engaged has been negated by these homicides. Please tell me you have something for us, that you didn't come all the way uptown to compliment me."

"Eh, I wasn't really complimenting you. It just seemed like the socially acceptable thing to say." St. Pierre let out her signature laugh. Her acerbic wit rivaled that of any detective I'd ever met.

She plopped down in the wooden chair next to my desk.

I leaned in close and said, "What's up? The look on your face tells me it's not good news."

"I deal with death and sorrow every day. I never have good news. Only news that can help an investigation or slow it down. Which some detectives view as bad."

I nodded. "So which kind of news are you bringing me?"

"I can almost guarantee this will be…confusing news."

"Let me have it."

First, she gave me a physical profile of our killer. "Forensics says he's probably a male about five foot ten, right-handed, and fairly strong based on the wounds on each of the victims. Statistics would indicate we can assume he's probably Caucasian if we're dealing with a serial killer."

I could see her hesitate, as if there was no way I was going to like what she was about to say next.

"An initial analysis of the blood found at the Elaine Anastas crime scene on 30th Street has come back."

I had to break the suspense routine. "C'mon, Jill, you're killing me. What did you find?"

"There are two different sources of blood in the apartment."

"So you agree with theories that there was a second victim?"

St. Pierre shook her head. "Not necessarily. We didn't find much blood from the second sample." She paused. "I also think that blood may have been deliberately placed rather than spilled."

Another bizarre piece of the puzzle? "What makes you say that?" I asked.

"Because of where that blood was located—we only found the second sample on some baseball figurines."

I remembered the bobbleheads that had caught my attention at the scene, and she confirmed that was what she was talking about. *Could the killer have cut himself? Was he marking his crime scene in some way?*

"Were there multiple blood sources found at any of the other crime scenes?"

"Not that we've located so far, but now that we know there might be, we'll be going back over the evidence we've collected to see if anything was missed."

"Any chance you can figure out where the blood from this scene came from?" I asked the forensic scientist.

"Once we have the full DNA profile, I assure you we'll run it through every database we can. If there's an existing profile related to our sample, we'll find it."

Even as I thanked her, my mind was starting to drift off to the endless possibilities. None of them were good.

CHAPTER 28

I WAS STILL processing the information about there being two sources of blood at Elaine Anastas's apartment.

I must've been staring off into space as I considered what this new forensic discovery meant for my case when I heard "Nice to see NYPD so hard at work."

I turned to see a man about my age, dressed in a sharp Armani suit, standing next to my desk. He had Ray-Ban Wayfarer sunglasses perched on an otherwise shiny, bald head. Just another guy trying to project that he was younger than he looked. It wasn't working.

He stuck out his hand and said, "John Macy, advisor to the mayor."

I took his hand and mumbled, "Michael Bennett."

"Yes, I know. That's why I just drove all the way uptown and waded through your maze of security."

"What can I do for you, Mr. Macy? I'm a little busy at the moment."

He sat down, uninvited. "Yes, I could see you were tearing it up as I walked through the office. You looked more like a poet dreaming about the beauty of a waterfall than a detective hunting for a serial killer."

I bristled at his tone. If he was laughing or joking, I didn't mind the comment. But this guy seemed pretty serious.

I had to say, "Looks can be deceiving. I would've guessed you were a model. Maybe the *before* picture in a Rogaine ad."

He let out a forced laugh. "I love cop humor. You know I was with the NYPD."

"Sure. Remind me in what capacity?"

"I was a beat cop." He paused and smiled. "For about five minutes. Then I got smart and went to law school."

I didn't say anything.

"I don't mean any disrespect to law enforcement," Macy continued. "On the bright side, no one's trying to kill me these days."

"It's still early." This guy wasn't taking the hint. I cleared my throat and said, "Look, despite whatever impression you got, I really am swamped. Just tell me what it is you're hoping I can do for you."

Macy pulled a Moleskine notebook and a blue Montblanc pen from a leather satchel and brushed aside some papers from the corner of my desk to create a writing area. Then he looked up at me and said, "All I need is for you to bring me up to speed on the case."

"You mean our active homicide investigation?"

"You know exactly which case I'm talking about. Now give me the details."

I assessed the man. He was in pretty good shape, with only a little bit of a belly. I idly wondered if he'd be a handful if I punched him in the face. Instead, I tried to be mature. I simply said, "I'm sorry. I'm afraid I don't have that kind of time. I have more important things on my plate."

The mayor's aide straightened in his chair. "Nothing is more important than keeping the mayor informed. This newest murder on Staten Island marks a turn in the case."

I almost wanted to share my doubts about the scene on Staten Island. How I didn't think it *was* connected to the other homicides. But I decided to keep my mouth shut.

Macy was undaunted. He said, "Jesus Christ, we can't let this go on much longer. There was a shooting in Brooklyn. A woman was spooked by the murders, accidentally shot her brother coming in late. She said she thought he was the killer coming to attack her. Things are spinning out of control."

I said, "Will the young man live?"

"Probably. You know how these Brooklyn Italians are. Through evolution they're virtually immune to gunfire."

Prick.

He had the nerve to open his mouth again. "That's why you need to wrap up this case and put cuffs on this mope."

I knew he was intentionally using police slang to remind me he had once been a cop, even if it was only for *five minutes*. I said, "We're on it. That's the best I can tell you."

Macy said, "Maybe you're the wrong cop to be leading this investigation."

"Maybe the mayor has the wrong lackey asking questions." That one got a good flash of red across Macy's face.

Instead, he quickly stood up from my desk, glared at me, and said, "I'll be back." Then he turned on his heel and started to march out of the office.

I called after him, "Bring pizza. I'm starving."

CHAPTER 29

DANIEL OTT HAD followed the young librarian home from the Subway sandwich shop to her apartment in a run-down, five-story walk-up in the diverse neighborhood of East Harlem.

Overnight, he had made a simple plan.

Now he sat on the steps across the street from the librarian's building. He was dressed in a gray shirt with the name tag MITCH over the left side of his chest. He'd snagged the uniform from an unattended delivery van in Midtown. No one paid any attention to him at all.

It was early evening. From his vantage point, the street was fairly quiet. The local foot traffic seemed to have rerouted to a block party about two blocks away.

Ott was happy to sit quietly and watch the street, planning his first-ever elimination of a witness. He would forgo the rituals he loved so much. This would not be a big spectacle.

As soon as Ott saw the librarian, his loose end, walking by herself on the other side of the street, he stood up slowly and stretched. He slipped a surgical glove over each hand. He forced himself to casually walk across the empty street.

Once he reached the sidewalk, he turned and headed for the librarian. She was walking slowly, looking in her bag. Probably trying to find her keys. The opportunity was lining up nicely for Ott.

He quickly glanced around in every direction. There were kids playing on some steps a few buildings down. A woman facing away from where he was walking pushed a stroller across the street. This looked like a good window for him to act.

He reached into his pouch and pulled out his Gerber folding knife. He flicked it open with his thumb and looked up at the librarian.

Ott timed his strike perfectly. Just as he passed her, he raised his right hand and made a single, simple slash across the young woman's throat. Smooth and fast. In that instant, he caught her expression of total shock as the blade cut through the flesh and sinew of her lovely throat. She didn't make a sound.

The librarian just tumbled to the sidewalk next to the building's stairs.

Ott took a moment to make sure no one had noticed the flurry of violent action. Then he arranged the woman's body so that in the evening light it looked like she was sitting on the stoop, resting. The ruse might buy him a few more minutes to get out of the area.

Just as he straightened up, taking a moment to admire his handiwork, the door to the apartment building opened. Ott snapped his head in that direction and found himself staring at a young man with a nose stud and long black hair that hung across his face.

The man looked at the librarian and said, "Yara, what's going on?"

Ott watched as the man noticed the librarian's blood dripping down her chest onto the steps. He saw the man's face register his understanding that the librarian had been violently attacked, and that her assailant—Ott—was still standing there, facing him. The young man took a sudden leap over the railing onto the ground, about seven feet below.

Ott was on him in a flash. As the young man started to run, Ott grabbed the back of his T-shirt, swinging the knife wildly and slashing him in the arm and back.

Then the man's shirt ripped. He shot forward but lost his balance and slid onto the sidewalk.

This time, Ott didn't risk another wild slash with his knife. He aimed the point as he swung his arm and caught the man in the side. He felt the blade slip between ribs. He pulled it out with his right hand and spun the man with his left. Just as they were face-to-face, Ott plunged the knife into the man's solar plexus.

Ott left it there for a moment, then twisted and pushed the man at the same time, dropping him next to the apartment steps.

Gasping for air after the heavy physical activity, he sucked in a lungful and scanned the area. No one was raising any alarms.

He started walking quickly away from the scene in the opposite direction of the block party. He slipped the surgical gloves off his hands and into a plastic bag that he tucked into the pocket of his uniform.

As Ott picked up his pace, he couldn't get a handle on the

wild swing of his emotions. He felt vulnerable as he continued walking, but after about ten minutes, he began to feel safe. Most of all, he felt relief that a loose end was now tied up, but not the thrill he usually experienced when he had time to spend with his victims.

As he waited to catch a subway train downtown, he reviewed the events of the evening. Circumstances had forced him into eliminating one loose end, and then another one—his first male victim. There had been no time to perform his rituals. The young man and the librarian were the only two victims whose eyes he had not stabbed, and whose blood largely remained in their dead bodies. But he couldn't stop to think about this significant break from his patterns—and what response it might evoke in Detective Michael Bennett and the NYPD.

He had never planned for any of this. And now he might have to pay.

CHAPTER 30

I WAS AT home, a place where I rarely brought up work issues. But Mary Catherine is very perceptive. She badgered me until I finally told her what was wrong, the whole story about the irritating mayor's aide who'd plagued me in the late afternoon.

She smiled and said, "You'll deal with him. It's not easy, but you know how to handle people. People are like snowflakes."

I said, "Cold and annoying?"

"No, smart guy. Unique. People are unique. Having a way with them is a gift. You know how to use your gift."

"I'd like to return my gift for something else. Maybe cash. Or x-ray vision." I waggled my eyebrows.

Mary Catherine burst out laughing. "If you think that leer is sexy, you're way off. *Creepy* is a much better description for what you just did."

We laughed together and she reached out to take my hand. I leaned forward and we kissed. At first, it was just a quick peck. Then Mary Catherine lingered and I felt her tongue trace the outline of my lips. We started to make out like teenagers left alone at home. Except we were not teenagers. And we were definitely not home alone.

We were reminded of that when two of the boys, Trent and Ricky, came barreling into the living room.

"Can we go to the basketball courts at the end of the street and play with Brian?" Ricky asked.

I felt guilty, because my immediate reaction was that I wasn't sure I wanted the younger boys hanging out with their big brother. Which would mean I had to acknowledge that Brian had made some bad decisions and I was concerned he'd influence the other kids to do the same. Which went against everything I preached in telling Brian that I trusted him.

Luckily, Mary Catherine was the one who started in with the third degree. "All your homework done?"

Both boys answered in unison. "Yes."

"Room clean?"

"Yes."

"Kitchen clean?"

Both the boys stared at her, then at each other.

Mary Catherine let out a laugh. "That was just a test to see if you're paying attention. Although, if you ever want to get on my good side, cleaning the kitchen would be one way to do it."

Trent nodded and said, "Gotcha. I think we can get away without doing it tonight, though. That is, if I'm reading you correctly." He kept such a straight and serious face that it made both Mary Catherine and me burst out laughing.

Then I started thinking about the other boys who sometimes hung out at the basketball court.

Almost without thought I said, "I'll go too."

Ricky said, "Really?"

When I nodded, I was relieved to see that both boys were thrilled at the idea. It reminded me that the kids *wanted* to spend time with their parents. At least some of the time. No matter what they said or how they complained, the kids enjoyed having their parents around. Especially a supercool and athletic one like me. Or, to put it another way, they liked playing against someone they knew they could beat.

Twenty minutes later, we were on the set of four courts down the block. The courts looked like chaos to an outsider, but the kids and a volunteer from the YMCA had devised a pretty good system to make sure everyone had a chance. Two courts held three-on-three games, and the other two courts were open for general shooting and practice. People just shot around one another while they waited to get in on a three-on-three game. I made a mental note to send in my yearly donation to the YMCA.

I wasn't needed to make up numbers, so I made myself comfortable watching from the sidelines. Brian, Ricky, and Trent formed one threesome, and the team got on the game court pretty quickly. I appreciated seeing how Brian encouraged his brothers. He never got upset if they missed a shot. Which was especially good in Ricky's case. At the moment, he was shooting 0 for 6.

One of the older boys on the other team ran past Trent and threw a quick elbow. It knocked the slim teenager for a loop but wasn't anything too blatant.

A second later, Brian was in the kid's face, and I noticed my son's right hand was balled into a fist. He was taking a minor basketball disagreement to another level awfully fast. I knew, and it scared me, that prison had taught him to strike fast and first. I hustled over.

Before I got there, though, Brian had stepped away from the kid. Breathing hard. Almost panting. Actually, I realized, he was breathing *deeply*. There's a difference. I recognized it as part of the anger-management therapy he had started in prison and had continued once he was released.

I patted Brian on the shoulder and mumbled, "Good job, Son."

God bless him. He was doing his best to adjust to the outside world.

We just had to be patient.

CHAPTER 31

EARLY THE NEXT morning, I found myself at a Dunkin'
Donuts on Beekman Street, a few blocks from the Brooklyn
Bridge, chatting with Detective Raina Rayesh. It was nice to
catch up with an old friend, even if gruesome murder was a key
topic of conversation.

It was a long trip from Staten Island for Rayesh just to have a cup
of coffee with an old friend. Unfortunately, a command performance
at One Police Plaza was the real reason she was in Manhattan.

Rayesh said, "Pretty sure I'm getting summoned to headquarters because I wasn't particularly patient or tactful when
the mayor's aide visited."

"Was his name John Macy?"

"Yeah. Said he'd been a cop and understood what we went
through, yada yada yada. So I said, 'Then you'll understand how
I'm too busy to talk to you.'"

"How'd he respond?"

"Don't know. I stepped into the secure investigations office and shut the door. I ignored the receptionist when she kept calling."

I laughed loudly. "You're better than me. I tried to get rid of him and instead just made things worse. And I never did get the pizza I sent him out to pick up."

"We'll see who did a better job brushing off this jack-off after I have my meeting at One Police Plaza. How come you don't have to go?"

I smiled. "Because I have a secret weapon most detectives don't."

"What's that?"

"Harry Grissom. He's much better at these kinds of meetings than I'll ever be. Unlike me, he's smart enough to know which battles to fight. I'll just wait till he calls me after his talk with the chief of detectives."

Rayesh said, "I should've recognized the 'Bennett effect' on Macy when he came to talk to me. He was already annoyed and flustered. A sure sign someone has spoken to you first."

We both laughed.

Rayesh said, "Remember Captain Ramirez, when he was a lieutenant in the Bronx? He was quizzing us about an arrest we made and said, 'That guy was dangerous as shit. Why didn't you call SWAT?' And you said it was because we didn't have their number."

I didn't remember the exact, smart-ass comment, but I remembered Ramirez, an officious prick who used to run our shift.

Rayesh said, "He wanted to transfer you. Instead, we both got medals. I gotta tell you, Mike, you're tough on the dull and lazy."

I said, "What did Mr. Macy have to say when you spoke for that very brief time?"

Rayesh shrugged her shoulders. "Usual. Asked about the homicide. Said the mayor needed the newest information. The usual BS."

"What'd you tell him?"

"Active investigation. Yada, yada, yada." She paused for a moment, then added, "I did tell him it was too early to connect my homicide to the others. And he said he heard the killer stabbed the victim's eye. I had to tell him I didn't know why the killer did that, beyond a thirst for control."

I mumbled, "The world is full of crazy, scary people, Raina. The public usually doesn't see it. Maybe an occasional story about someone who went wild. Never the day-to-day nasty things that go on around us everywhere."

Rayesh said, "Macy's just looking to tell the mayor we've caught someone. He wants something to quiet the news media. An arrest would be just what they need. It's like in the movie *Jaws*. The administrators at City Hall just want the problem to go away before tourist season gets screwed up." She sighed, then perked up. "In all this confusion, I forgot that you're getting married really soon," she said.

"A week from Saturday. If Mary Catherine doesn't leave me before then."

"That's a possibility, because she's really smart. But I've seen the way she looks at you. You tricked her into believing all the press clippings. She's in for the long haul." Then she shook her head. "I don't know, Mike. Maybe we've been on the job too long."

"How do you figure that, Raina?"

She said, "Because all I want to do is move to Boca Raton and tell people how brave I was for the last twenty years in New York City."

"Good plan."

We both started laughing, knowing neither of us actually had any intention of leaving the job any time soon.

CHAPTER 32

I'D TOLD RAINA RAYESH the truth—that while I'd avoided an invitation to One Police Plaza for my rude behavior to the mayor's aide, my boss, Harry Grissom, had been issued his own invitation. That's why I was in the lobby outside the chief of detectives' office, waiting for Harry at about ten o'clock in the morning, a few hours after I'd compared notes with Rayesh.

When he came through the double glass doors that led from the conference room and other administrative offices, Harry shook his head at the sight of me. "I thought you understood it would be better if you were nowhere near here this morning."

"I came to support you."

Harry said, "Mr. Macy will be visiting our office this afternoon."

"What for?"

"To see how Task Force Halo is operating."

"Hollis and I, we're not really a task force. But we're happy to let the FBI call us one if we can get access to their resources as we work the case."

"It's a subtle difference we're not going to explain to the mayor's office." Harry smiled as we stopped and waited for the elevator. "We're going to convince Macy that our task force is fully staffed. We're going to grab a couple of plainclothes and pull some patrol officers to help Hollis run down all the leads we're getting from the tip line." He slapped me on the back. "You're going to make the operation look convincing, and Macy's going to buy it. Got it?"

All I could do was grin. Harry knew more about dealing with administrators and politicians than I could ever hope to understand. He also understood how investigations worked and what motivated detectives. When I thought about it, I realized what a rare combination that was. I hadn't been exaggerating when I'd told Rayesh I had a secret weapon in Harry Grissom.

Harry turned serious as he looked at me. "I will make this clear, Mike. Do not provoke this asshole when he comes to our offices this afternoon. I know he's a pompous jerk, but he's doing his job. He works for the mayor. Understand?"

I nodded. Harry was right. He's also about the only person besides Mary Catherine who can talk to me like that. Well, that's not exactly true. A lot of people can, and do, talk to me like that. Harry and Mary Catherine are the only ones I'll listen to.

Then Harry said, "Give me a rundown on the status of the case."

This was unlike Harry. He tried to keep up with investigations as they were proceeding. It worried me that he wanted to be ready for this mayor's aide. I finally asked him, "What's the real problem here, Harry?"

He looked down at the dirty linoleum floor. Then he said, "That asshole Macy's been trying to have you replaced as lead detective. I don't want to give him any reason to push for that again."

"Does he think he'd be hurting me by taking me off a case that's distracting me from my family and my wedding? A wedding that's happening in less than two weeks?"

"You and I both know it would kill you to be removed from a case. Especially this one."

I thought about it for a moment, then admitted Harry was right. As usual. So I decided to show him I was on board. I gave him a full rundown of the case. Most of it he knew already. But I wanted to underscore some important points.

I said, "There doesn't seem to be any connection between any of our victims. That doesn't mean they were selected at random, but they don't seem to have known one another. Hollis has an interesting theory that our mope travels, maybe for work. We're looking seriously at homicides in other cities that may match ours. Which also reminds me," I said, "can we give Hollis a chance to supervise the task force for real, not just for show? All he'll really do is farm out the leads. He's been running down a lot of them himself. I'm sure he'll appreciate the help."

Harry nodded. "What about the Staten Island homicide? I hear you don't think that case is related to the others. Why not?"

"The scene just feels different from the ones we're already investigating. It was orderly. There was no blood spread over the walls, and the body wasn't really mutilated. A single puncture in the chest, and a stab to her eye. But it was the right eye, when all the others have been the left."

"Any other insights on our killer?"

"Aside from the fact that he typically seems to spend hours at crime scenes? If our theory's correct, he's killed in other cities too. We're thinking it could be close to a dozen victims altogether. Maybe even more. That makes him smart enough not to have been caught already. And dangerous."

Harry nodded, then said, "About this afternoon. Answer any direct questions Macy puts to you, but don't volunteer any information, and don't expand on any points you do make." He patted me on the back. "I need you. We're making progress, even if the mayor's office doesn't believe it."

CHAPTER 33

DANIEL OTT DIDN'T mind working at a desk in the corner of the loading dock. He liked all the sound and activity at this job in Queens. He had an affinity for the workingman. Yet another lesson he'd learned from his first employer.

The men at work on this loading dock and the ones who drove the trucks were definitely hardworking men. Yet as much as he admired them, he also didn't mind lying low for a few days. He needed a chance to rest, gather his thoughts, and plan his future.

He wondered if the plan he had set in motion at the library would produce results. So far, he hadn't seen any reports about his message. Or news of the librarian's death. The police seemed to be spending all their time working a murder on Staten Island. He'd never even been there. Still, the killer seemed to have adopted a pale imitation of Ott's techniques. He was pleased at the flattery yet puzzled. If the media didn't know about the eye stabbing, how did this other killer learn his signature?

When his phone rang, Ott answered it immediately. It was noon. "Hello, my lovely girls."

On speakerphone, with the noise of the workers buzzing around him, his wife and both of his daughters giggled and chatted with him about their days. His wife caught him up on their homeschooling progress, and his daughters regaled him with a story about their cat getting stuck in a tree. The conversation kept him smiling for over an hour.

Then the red-haired woman he'd noticed the other day walked past and yelled about the computer bag lying on the floor of the loading dock, citing a safety hazard. She tried to soften the comment when she realized the bag was his, but she had already made a poor impression.

"Sorry," the redhead apologized. "When you work around messy men all day, you tend to jump the gun on little things. I forgot you were even back here. So quiet I didn't even notice you."

She stepped around the desk and stood just a little too close to Ott as she added, "It'll be nice to be able to talk to everyone over the computer. The drivers prefer radios and the office people like cell phones. You seem to be the answer to all of our problems." She gave him a big smile.

Ott nodded but didn't hold eye contact for very long. But he watched her as she walked away. She had something, some way about her, that was alluring without being wildly attractive. Maybe it was experience? Whatever it was, the image of her smiling face stuck in his head.

A shout caught his attention. Two men were standing on the

loading dock arguing about how to load tires into a long truck that couldn't make the turn to back up to the dock.

Ott stood and stretched, then walked over to where the tires were stacked and looked at the pedestrian walkway down to the street, where the truck was stopped. As much as he liked to remain invisible, sometimes it was irresistible to show off what he could do.

He turned to the loading dock manager and said, "I've got an idea."

The burly manager turned and said, "Anything's gotta be better than taking the tires by hand one at a time."

Daniel grabbed two tires and walked down the pedestrian ramp to the street. He had the driver back up a few feet, then open the side door to his truck. He set both of the tires down, one on the ground and the other propped on top of it and leaning against the truck.

When he hurried back up the ramp, the entire loading dock crew watched with anticipation. Ott thought he had it right. But what if his idea failed? He would feel like an idiot.

The loading dock crew watched silently as he ran back and grabbed two more tires. He looked up at the group staring at him. "If it doesn't work, I'll help you load the tires by hand."

He released one of the tires and watched it roll in a straight line down the ramp. By the time it hit the tire lying on the ground, it was really moving. It bounced up and off the tire that was upright against the side of the truck. It landed exactly where it needed to.

The entire loading dock erupted in applause. The manager moved his massive body toward Ott and said, "How in the hell did you figure that out?"

Ott smiled. "Simple physics. It dictates everything in our lives. I just know how to use it to my advantage."

CHAPTER 34

WHEN I GOT back to my office, Dr. Jill St. Pierre, the forensic scientist, was sitting at my desk, reading my copy of *Men's Health*. As I walked through the squad bay, her dark eyes rose from the pages of the magazine. The fact that she didn't smile when she saw me told me her new information wasn't good.

Since St. Pierre was sitting in my leather office chair, I took the hard wooden chair next to my desk. I purposely didn't say anything as I prepared for the bad news. Whatever it might be.

She said, "I heard you had to make a trip to One Police Plaza. I decided it was better to wait here in case they were sending you back to clean out your desk." Her sly smile made me laugh.

"Technically, I didn't *have* to make the trip. Only Harry Grissom did. I met him down there for support."

"Anything change on the investigation?"

I shook my head. "We have to keep the mayor's office better informed."

"Isn't that the same rule they give every time?"

"Seems like it." I glanced around to make sure no one was close by. "C'mon, Jill, you didn't come all the way up here to chat with me about my morning. Whatcha got?"

She started slowly. "I have a preliminary profile of the second blood sample from the Elaine Anastas scene."

"Could you match it to anything?"

"Yes."

I sat up straight and almost clapped. "You think it's the killer's blood?"

"Nope," she said, dashing my hopes. "But there is a connection. The second sample? It matches a homicide victim killed in Atlanta eight months ago. Hollis tipped us off to the connection and we've been working with Atlanta PD."

I was baffled by what she'd just revealed. Finally I said, "How is that possible?"

St. Pierre shrugged. "I provide the scientific data. Detectives usually do the interpretation." She handed me a manila envelope.

"What's this?"

"Atlanta PD gave us all the reports from the case. They are scanning photographs to email us. They even offered to send a detective up here. And just like here, they think this homicide could be related to several others in the Atlanta area. Apparently these cases have been bugging them for the last eight months."

I leaned back in the chair, thinking about what she'd just told me. When I looked up, the forensic scientist was glancing over one of the reports from Atlanta.

"What do you think this means?" I asked her.

"That's your area, not mine," St. Pierre said. "But I'd theorize that if your killer is getting cute like this, it's probably a sign he's bored. He has to make things more interesting. And that could be extremely dangerous."

CHAPTER 35

IT WAS LATE afternoon by the time John Macy, the mayor's aide, showed up again at Manhattan North. He wore a Brooks Brothers charcoal suit, a red power tie, and an extraordinarily smug expression.

Macy said, "I told you the mayor needs to be informed."

I wanted to reply, *And I told you I was busy trying to catch a killer. I hope you haven't endangered someone else's life by distracting me.* But in deference to Harry Grissom, I just smiled and nodded. I had promised Harry that I wouldn't make any waves.

Macy didn't help with my plan. He said, "I can't believe I had to go through that much trouble just to get a detective with the NYPD to fill me in on a case. I'm busy too. You have any idea how many people work in the mayor's office?"

I said, "About half of them."

Macy gave me a disgusted look but didn't say anything.

Then he shook his head and started marching toward Harry Grissom's office.

Brett Hollis stepped up next to me. "You just *had* to say something, huh."

"Did you hear how he set me up? If this were a criminal case, that would've been considered entrapment."

Hollis and a couple of nearby detectives started to laugh.

Harry trudged out of his office and gave me and Hollis a curt hand signal. We followed him and Macy to the conference room Hollis had turned into his tip-line headquarters.

At a nod from Harry, Hollis explained the operation to Macy. "We're getting three to five thousand leads a day over the tip line. Eighty percent of them can be discounted immediately."

"It seems a little arrogant to discount so many leads so quickly," Macy interrupted.

"Think of it this way, Mr. Macy," Hollis said. "How many calls a week does the mayor's office get about problems?"

The sharply dressed man shrugged. "I don't know. Maybe five hundred?"

"And each of those calls is equally important?"

Macy pursed his lips. "I take your point, Detective Hollis."

Hollis continued with his explanation. "About half the calls to the tip line are either encouragement—like someone saying, 'You guys are doing a great job'—or insults. A lot of those are really nasty. Let's say that leaves us with two thousand concerned citizens offering what they think is relevant information. More than half of those tips are something along the lines of 'The guy who lives next door to me is creepy.' Of the thousand or so tips remaining, about ten percent are new information. But that's still a hundred leads a day for someone to follow up on, with either a direct interview or a phone call. So far, not one lead has been useful. But we still are doing everything we can."

"Does this include leads on all the open homicides? Including the one on Staten Island?"

I stepped in on that one. "We have our doubts about whether the Staten Island murder is connected."

Macy looked outraged. "How can that be? It's clearly the same killer."

I couldn't stand it anymore. "What is that assessment based on, Mr. Macy? You don't have any experience in homicide, even if you were a cop for, as you put it, about five minutes. If we homicide detectives don't use our experience and instincts, nothing would ever get done. We'd waste our time following leads that clearly mean nothing. But we appreciate you coming from the mayor's office and telling us which homicides are related and which aren't."

Macy scowled at me for a few seconds, then looked at Harry Grissom. "Is this what you call controlling your people, Lieutenant? When we met with the chief of detectives, you assured him I'd get full cooperation. I don't think insulting me should be considered cooperation."

Harry glanced at me, then at Macy. I knew the look on his face. He was choosing his words carefully. Finally, he straightened his tie and said, in the steady, calm voice of an FM radio host, "We're trying to cooperate, Mr. Macy. You're not making it very easy."

"Task Force Halo is supposed to be a *joint* task force. Maybe you can tell me why the FBI is not involved in the case," Macy countered.

I kept my mouth shut. I wasn't about to touch this, especially given the evidence we'd been pursuing that indicated the murders might be tied to similar crimes in Atlanta and San Francisco, and that we continued to work through media and police sources—not federal channels. Which reminded me once again that Emily had yet to come through with the information she'd offered to track down.

Harry said, "That's an issue we'll discuss. We'll make a decision based on our discussions. We will apprise you of the decision once we've made it." Then he turned and walked back to his office.

I tried to hide my smile.

Damn, my boss was good at handling assholes.

Macy looked at me and said, "You don't seem to understand I speak to the mayor."

I said, "And the coroner speaks for the dead. The difference is, I listen to the coroner."

The moment I landed my zinger, John Macy stormed back into Grissom's office.

I'd launched a grenade. This meeting could have gone better.

CHAPTER 36

I SAT AT my desk like a kid in middle-school detention. I tried not to focus on Harry Grissom's closed office door, but it was tough to concentrate on anything else.

I could only imagine what the mayor's aide, John Macy, was ranting about inside my lieutenant's office. I assumed that by now he had called someone at One Police Plaza and told them how I was acting like a bratty child. I didn't have much defense for that charge.

I was kicking myself for failing to reel in the worst of my smart-ass tendencies. If one of my kids behaved like this, I'd definitely punish them for it. I didn't deserve anything less.

I noticed some members of the squad had found reasons to be elsewhere. Except for me and Brett Hollis, the office looked like a ghost town.

To help fill the time and ease my anxiety, I turned to Hollis and asked, "What are you working on?"

Hollis barely looked up. "My application to take your spot on the squad permanently."

I sat in silence for a moment until a smile crept across the young detective's face. He really was getting the hang of surviving as a cop: laugh at everything. I said, "Funny. Although it's probably not a bad idea."

"It's a waste of time."

"You don't think I'll get transferred to some precinct in the Bronx?"

"Nope. Because Lieutenant Grissom already told me I could have your spot."

That made me laugh out loud. "Seriously, are you working on anything I can help with? I wouldn't mind being distracted about now."

"I'm doing more research on serial killers. There's gotta be something in all the information and evidence gathered from the multiple crime scenes and calls to the tip line that fits some sort of pattern."

"Isn't that what the FBI's Behavioral Analysis Unit at Quantico is for?"

"From everything I've heard, the FBI doesn't always play fair. We could give them all the information we have and never hear back from them. Or we could give them all our information and then they swoop in and take over the case. I wouldn't care if it meant they caught the killer. But if you haven't noticed, their track record is mediocre at best."

"You're learning," I said to my young partner. And I meant it. I asked Hollis about his research on serial killers. Whether it was official or unofficial, his knowledge of the subject might come in handy.

Hollis lit up at the opportunity to share his research, now that he knew I was truly interested.

"Okay," he began, "so first I was looking at debunking a bunch of stuff. Like, you know how everyone assumes most serial killers are Caucasian?"

I nodded, remembering how Dr. Jill St. Pierre had said just that to me in our earlier conversation.

"Well, the truth is that as more information becomes available, it turns out that the serial killer population mirrors the diverse racial makeup of the US population as a whole. In fact, there's a black guy in his late seventies named Samuel Little who could be the country's most prolific serial killer."

"I'm almost afraid to ask—how many people do they think he's killed?"

"He's confessed to nearly a hundred murders, but they don't have enough credible details to charge him with all of them. Even so, he's still being charged with murders going back to the eighties and nineties. He is very specific in his obsession. He strangled his victims and selected them according to the shape of their neck. He also worked in gritty neighborhoods in multiple states and picked on homeless women and prostitutes, folks he believed would not be missed. Something about his theory must've held water, because it took decades to corral this asshole."

Hollis looked over at me. "It's hard to get a good sense of how many people are actually murdered by serial killers. As I'm sure you know, there are so many unsolved homicides across the country—plus deaths misattributed to overdose, accident, or undetermined causes—that no one can really say whether a serial killer is responsible for them or not."

"I don't think that's our issue here," I said dryly. "In our particular case, we have no reason *not* to believe our suspect is white and male. The forensics team says that based on the application of force, the suspect is probably about five foot ten and fairly strong. And we know he mutilates his victims, stabs their left eyes. I think he likes the feeling of power and control that comes from creating bloody, wild crime scenes. But I also think his technique hinges on how much time he has at each scene. How do you see it?"

Hollis said, "I agree with your assumptions about the time needed to create such nasty crime scenes. I think he's smart. Really smart. And clearly he travels. Probably for work, which would make him a white-collar professional. That combination is what makes him so hard to catch."

I was impressed by the young detective's curiosity. It was the sign of a good cop. "Those are some good theories. I'm proud of you." It was part joke and part serious. Regardless, I noticed it made my junior partner beam. I made a mental note to be a little more generous with the praise.

Then Harry's door opened. I was so deep into my own paranoia about the future of my NYPD career that I tried to figure out if the door had opened in an angry way or a professional way. I listened to the tone of the two men's voices as they exchanged good-byes. Not pleasant.

Macy had only a menacing glance for me as he fumed back across the squad bay floor, this time heading for the exit.

As Harry watched him leave, he ran a hand over his face, looked at me, and shook his head.

I had stepped over the line and I knew it. I also knew I needed to apologize. First to Harry, then, as much as it bugged me, to John Macy.

At the moment, though, I couldn't get a clear read on Harry. Not that it's ever easy. I slid out of my seat and started walking toward him. When I was still twenty feet away, I said, "Harry, I'm sorry. I let him get under my skin."

Harry let out a sigh. That was almost always a really bad sign that he was about to say something no one wanted to hear. I waited for the words *Go home* or, worse, *You're off the case.* I just hoped none of this problem I had created would bleed over onto Hollis. He didn't deserve to be punished for my stupidity.

I said, "What happened? What did Macy demand?"

"At first I tried to reason with the turd. Then he tried to reason with me." Harry chuckled. "Like that ever works." He looked at me in silence for a moment. "Macy came up here to see the operations of our task force, and all he saw was a junior detective pounding the books and a lead detective acting like a child. Basically, he doesn't think you're the right man for this case."

Harry looked at me. He said in a calm and quiet voice, "Get out of here. Go find some perspective. Go talk to your kids, to your beautiful fiancée, or even to your grandfather. Figure out what's more important to you: stopping a killer or annoying a minor city official."

"Should I come back tomorrow?" I wasn't being dramatic. I was dead serious.

"Yes. Unless I call you tonight and tell you not to bother. Which is a possibility." He stared at the door that Macy had raced out of. Then Harry said, "There's something about that guy I don't like. He acts a little like my first wife. He seems pleasant enough until you look a little closer." Harry looked back at me. "You remember when my wife ran off with our mechanic?"

I nodded. It's not unusual to help a fellow cop get through a divorce.

"It was tough. He was a really good mechanic."

CHAPTER 37

IT HAD BEEN months since I'd left the office this early. It was odd to see the sun still shining as I got into my city-issued Chevy Impala. I wasn't ready to explain my early arrival to Mary Catherine. Which was one of the reasons why I took a detour to Holy Name, swung by to visit my grandfather.

I was in need of counseling, or at least a little verbal abuse. Seamus was always good for both. Especially the abuse.

It took a while to get to him, though, as I first had to say hello to several different nuns I had known since I was a child. Basically, every conversation I'd had at Holy Name in the last six months had been about the wedding. And the nuns all said the same thing: "I can't believe little Michael Bennett is getting married!"

I had no trouble *not* being a smart-ass with the nuns. I didn't feel the need to remind them that *little Michael Bennett* had actually been married before, or that ever since I'd lost my first wife, Maeve, I'd been a widower with ten children—all of whom these self-same nuns had personally educated. But since happy talk of the wedding made them smile and laugh, I went along with it. I know that's what Mary Catherine (and Maeve) would have wanted.

I found my grandfather in his office, looking over the shoulder of a twenty-something African American in an Avengers T-shirt working on Seamus's computer. I knew the young man's name was Elgin Brown, and he had a degree from Stony Brook in computer technology. Elgin was by all accounts a great kid (I've noticed as I get older that anyone under thirty is a *kid*).

I said, "What's going on here? Elgin trying to erase all your gambling websites before they're subject to some kind of audit by the Catholic Church?"

My grandfather looked up at me. "Don't be ridiculous. I keep all those websites on my phone only. Elgin is showing me how we could create a website to help kids in the neighborhood who need access to tutors and after-school care."

I smiled. Not only because my grandfather was always trying to do something for the community but also because even in his eighties he wanted to learn new things. He could have just asked Elgin to summarize the information for him. Instead, he wanted to master the skills himself.

Joining the priesthood really hadn't changed Seamus at all. *Gone straight from hell to heaven,* he took to saying when he sold his Hell's Kitchen gin mill and became a man of the cloth. The first thing he learned back then was how to hide his mischievous streak in public.

I waited for a couple of minutes while they finished up their work. I had to admit, my grandfather looked pretty good for his age. At least for now. He'd had a few health scares in the last couple of years. Losing him was one of the scariest concepts I could fathom. The very idea of life without the man who raised me, encouraged me, and always kept me grounded was terrifying. For now, there was nothing I liked more than surprising him at his office.

Seamus again looked up at me. "Shouldn't you be at work rather than bothering an old man?"

Elgin stood up. My grandfather patted him on the back and thanked him. The kid slipped out of the room like a ghost.

I said, "He never makes eye contact with me."

"You intimidate him."

"How?"

"Just being a cop."

"He's never been in trouble. Why's he afraid of the police?"

Seamus shrugged. "It's just how he feels. I think the cops need better PR."

"So I've heard."

Seamus sat on the edge of his desk and said, "So what brings you over here this afternoon?"

I told him all about my struggles with John Macy. Took about five full minutes. I let my anger roll out while telling the story. When I was finished, my grandfather looked at me and said, "Ask God for strength to deal with morons."

"That's it?"

"And if that doesn't work, plant cocaine on him." Seamus waited for a response. When he didn't get one, he said, "What? Isn't that what cops do in movies to get someone in trouble?"

I kept a straight face and said, "In real life we'd plant child pornography on his computer."

"Ah, the new millennium."

"Seriously, any ideas?"

"Jerks like him almost always ruin themselves. Leave him be. Do your duty and it'll all work out. Of that, I have no doubt. Think about your wonderful family and your impending wedding. Tell me you're not just whining to your grandfather about a bully you ran into today."

I couldn't believe it, but I felt better. No one had a handle on humanity like my grandfather.

CHAPTER 38

ANOTHER RESTLESS NIGHT'S sleep did little to improve my perspective as I trudged into the office early the next morning. I was determined to go about my job as best I could. My grandfather was right. I just needed to do my duty. Forget the power play by some political hack.

Harry Grissom stood by the door reading some notice from the building manager. He looked up at me and said, in a way only he could, "Have you pulled your head out of your ass yet?"

"Hope so."

"Good. Because your new partner is on a roll and the two of us have to keep pace." Without another word, Harry led me through the office to the rear conference room, where Hollis had established his tip-line headquarters.

Hollis stood outside the room. He now wore only a simple strip of surgical tape across his nose. The circles around his eyes had turned yellow, a move up from the black eyes the broken nose had given him. He was smiling and looked like a kid bursting to show off for his parents.

He pushed open the door to the conference room, raised his arm like a model from *The Price Is Right*, and said, "Behold, Task Force Halo."

When we stuck our heads in the door, we saw a couple of patrol officers in civilian clothes and two detectives One Police Plaza had sent over. Hollis explained that he had all of them now working on the leads taken from the tip lines.

I could tell Harry was impressed, though all he said was "Halo?"

Hollis was still grinning. "The name may have come from FBI ASAC Robert Lincoln, but we've made it our own. Halo has two meanings: our task force members are angels trying to stop the devil, *and* we're going to pound that devil like in the video game Halo."

Harry nodded, though I'd put money on him never having heard of the video game.

It can be tough being honest with yourself first thing in the morning, but I had to wonder if I had resisted the idea of a task force only because someone else—specifically the FBI— had suggested it.

At least having Hollis and the task force handling all the out-there leads left me free to pursue the one from Jill St. Pierre, about the blood from an Atlanta victim somehow ending up at a Manhattan crime scene.

I connected with Detective Alvin Carter, the lead detective from Atlanta, and spent an hour on the phone talking to him about his homicides.

Carter said, "We had two similar murders in the city of Atlanta proper, but then there were another three that happened in different suburbs—and out of my jurisdiction. I couldn't get those three suburban PDs to coordinate with me. You ever try to deal with competing agencies? It's no fun."

I let out a laugh at the recognition of a kindred spirit. "I have a hard time negotiating with competing precincts, let alone agencies."

"The chief of one of the wealthier suburbs told me he didn't want city crime tarnishing the reputation of his town. He said they would handle their own homicides and basically kept me out of their investigation. The other two suburbs got in line with that stance."

I shared with him Hollis's theory that the killer may have left Atlanta for New York.

"Sorry to say it, but I agree," Carter said. "Sounds like our killer moved to New York. I hope you have better luck catching him than I did."

"It's going to take some kind of luck to figure out how he took blood from a crime scene, stored it, transported it hundreds of miles, and reintroduced it at a second scene. Even if he took the sample in a sterile vial, he'd have to have maintained it under perfect conditions for the blood to be analyzable." I then asked, "Did you get any impressions or ideas from the crime scenes? I don't mean stuff you might put in a report; I'm talking about opinions." There was a long silence on the phone and I was afraid I had lost the detective. Then I realized he was taking the time to consider every angle.

Finally, Carter said, "They were…disturbing scenes. A lot of blood, and the killer seemed to have deliberately spread it around each of the scenes. All five victims were stabbed in the neck or chest, and in their left eyes."

I was taking notes, and I triple underlined that last detail. It was all too familiar.

"Of course we kept that detail from the media," Carter said. "A signature that distinctive risks inviting copycats."

I made another note. New York was following the same plan of keeping the eye stabbing confidential. But I needed more information to be sure.

"Were there any similarities between victims?"

"They were all young women, one black and four white. The black woman was killed in her office—the only one who was— and that scene was the least bloody, as if the killer was pressed for time. The other four victims were found dead in their own homes. I suspect the killer did some surveillance before he struck."

"How long between the first homicide and the final one?"

Carter didn't hesitate. "Almost two months. Fifty-four days to be exact."

I knew what it was like to live through a case like this. It didn't surprise me at all that he knew the exact number of days it had lasted.

"Then the killings stopped as abruptly as they began. We started to wonder if maybe something had happened to the killer, if maybe he'd died. Now it looks like he moved on to New York City."

I said, "Regrettably, he seems to be alive."

Carter said, "The NYPD has serious bragging rights when it comes to the size of their force and resources, and they're not shy about letting smaller PDs know who's the biggest and the best. I hope it's true."

"I hope so too."

CHAPTER 39

DETECTIVE ALVIN CARTER from Atlanta had given me some ideas, and I was becoming convinced that these blood-soaked homicides were all related. I again compared the reports from New York, Atlanta, and San Francisco. I gathered all the files and laid them out on my desk. The crime-scene photos were horrific. I kept studying them, looking for the meaning of the killer's distinctive signatures. The blood. The stabbing of the eyes. The arrangement of knickknacks at the scene. And now the introduction of the blood of a previous victim.

I made a list of follow-up questions for Carter. I wondered if there had been more than one blood sample found at any of the Atlanta crime scenes, and if so, if we could find out whether that blood had come from either of the San Francisco victims.

Hollis approached my desk. I looked over my shoulder at

the conference room where Task Force Halo was operating and asked him, "Any new leads coming in?"

"There are new leads, but a lot of wacky leads, and the hardest thing is trying to organize them all," Hollis said.

That's the way it always happened. Someone above you in the chain of command had the idea to open up phone lines for some tips, and the next thing you knew, all you were doing was listening to crazy people jabbering about their weird neighbors or how they were "psychic" and wanted to help the case.

I didn't miss the irony that we were actually using a task force that had been designed to fake out and shut up the mayor's office. Hollis showed me that the tips weren't only coming in via the phone lines—some helpful citizens were even sending in pages of Cutco and L.L.Bean catalogs with circles around pictures of knives that might be the murder weapons.

"One caller said he has a strange, secretive neighbor in Red Hook who gave him a weird vibe, and who had girls coming and going all the time," Hollis continued. "It turns out that the neighbor is a photographer of high-end nude models. The local precinct detective followed another lead, up in the Bronx, and uncovered a counterfeiting operation. Turned out to be pretty big-time. The detective is going to be recognized by the commissioner."

I could see that the young detective had done a good job managing the onslaught.

"That's always the way—poke around places we normally don't and find all kinds of shit. Opening cases NYPD doesn't even know they have. And then we end up clearing everyone else's cases but not our own."

I was starting to get back in my groove when I noticed someone skulking through the office.

It was the mayor's aide, John Macy.

CHAPTER 40

AS SOON AS I saw John Macy, my mind raced. How to handle him? Should I simply pretend yesterday's encounter never happened? Ignore him and hope he did the same with me? Then I started thinking reasonably, like an adult human being.

He seemed to be walking directly to my desk. Before he reached me, I said, "Hello, John. I'm sorry about yesterday. My jokes got a little out of hand. I was wrong, and I apologize."

Macy was dressed in another stunning designer suit and carried a leather satchel. I wasn't sure what his reply would be. Would he apologize in return? Strike back savagely and inform me I'd been removed from the case?

But Macy's choice was essentially to ignore me. He nodded in acknowledgment that he'd heard me but said nothing. He walked right past my desk and took a seat in front of Brett Hollis.

Hollis looked as surprised as I was.

Macy didn't waste any time. "As I understand it, Detective Hollis, you are now my contact on this case and, for all intents and purposes, the lead detective. At least as far as the mayor's office is concerned."

Hollis started to answer, but Macy cut him off.

"First, I'd like to have an overview of the case. Second, I'd like you to show me exactly how the task force is working. This afternoon I will have a photographer from the mayor's office with me to take pictures, which we will make available to the media."

Hollis fumbled for a reply. I had to bite my tongue. Literally. What kind of moron exposed an active investigation and its tactics while a killer was still out there targeting victims? Politicians and the news media didn't care about the consequences when there was a chance to make a splash or grab a headline.

Macy kept the freight train rolling. "I'm going to check in with you at 10 a.m. and 6 p.m. every day," he told Hollis. "Before each check-in, I expect to have received from you by email a one-page memo summarizing your investigation during the preceding hours."

"I don't have access to the entire case," Hollis demurred. "I'm just running leads off the tip line."

I was impressed at Hollis's misleading statement. The young detective was learning the ways of bureaucracy. I felt a little like Yoda.

Macy didn't miss a beat. "You will confer with Lieutenant Grissom as needed to fill in the gaps in your knowledge."

Hollis sat there, unsure what to do or where to turn. Every cop has been in this spot: a superior from the police department, or a local political hack, pressuring you for information you're not comfortable disclosing.

Macy's face turned more severe as Hollis hesitated in his response. "Was there anything I said you didn't understand?"

"No."

I was secretly glad Hollis didn't add a *sir.* Macy didn't deserve that kind of respect.

Macy eased up and said, "I'm trying to help you, Son. Right now the police have a serious PR problem in this country. The public doesn't rate them as highly as they used to. I want to fix that."

Hollis gave Macy another confused look. "We may have bad PR right now, but we're still way ahead of politicians and lawyers. So at least the people have *some* common sense."

It was hard not to cheer when I saw the scowl on Macy's face. I was also thrilled to witness that my new partner could handle himself just fine.

Macy said, "It won't take much for this killer to push the city into an all-out panic. We need to calm people down and catch this guy before he takes another victim. And smart-ass comments from the local cops won't help the situation. You have your orders. I expect you to carry them out."

On that subject, at least, I agreed with this pompous ass.

CHAPTER 41

MY ALARM CLOCK went off before sunrise, and I grog-gily faced the new day. Last night I'd gotten home after dark. It had been too late for dinner, and I'd barely had the energy to interact with my kids. I missed them, and I missed Mary Catherine. This was not how I wanted to live.

I jumped out of bed quickly and got dressed. I wanted to spend at least some time with the kids this morning. When I stepped into the living room, though, it took me a few moments to process an astonishing sight: all six of my daughters—Juliana, the oldest, plus Jane and the twins, Bridget and Fiona, even Shawna and Chrissy—were lined up facing Mary Catherine.

They were standing at attention, looking like marine recruits about to be inspected by their drill sergeant. All six wore flowy yellow dresses with white lace around the neck and the sleeves.

Only the two youngest, Chrissy and Shawna, looked happy about the exercise.

I said, "What's this? Am I having a dream where there are nothing but beautiful women in the world?"

The older girls did not appreciate my comment. Shawna and Chrissy giggled.

Mary Catherine said, "It's so much easier to coordinate bridesmaids when your groom can provide the entire wedding party. The girls and I have been getting separate fittings, so this is my first chance to see what they look like as a group."

Juliana said, "Like a cluster of grapefruits waiting to be picked."

Jane said, "Please don't take pictures, and if you must, don't let anyone see them. I'd die if Allan ever saw me in this dress."

The twins were caught between the more sophisticated, grown-up girls and the cute, silly little girls. They wisely decided to skip commentary.

Shawna stepped out of line, turned, and looked at her sisters. "I think we all look soooo beautiful. I am so excited about being in the wedding!"

That was all it took to shut down Juliana and Jane. If their little sister was this excited, they weren't going to complain.

Mary Catherine said, "Is everyone happy with her dress? Do they all fit well?"

The girls all nodded or mumbled that they were satisfied. Mary Catherine clapped her hands and said, "Then go change and off to school, all of you."

As the girls scampered away, Mary Catherine turned to me. "Good morning. You seemed so exhausted, I would've bet you'd sleep right through till noon. At least you look better this morning."

"Is it getting that bad?"

"This is the worst I've ever seen a case drain you. Anything new on it? I knew better than to ask you last night."

"I spoke to a detective in Atlanta yesterday. It seems very likely our killer was there too, though about eight months ago. After committing five murders, he abruptly stopped killing there. Maybe we've heard the last of him here too."

"You really think so?"

"No. No, I don't."

Mary Catherine looked around to make sure none of the kids was close by. "Can we talk about Brian for a minute?"

I felt a sudden flutter of panic. *What has my oldest son done now?* I gave a silent nod, steeling myself for what disturbing news might possibly follow that cold open.

"You know I've been curious about where Brian goes every day."

"*Curious, intrusively paranoid*—they're all just words."

She punched me in the arm playfully. For the record, *playfully* doesn't mean it didn't hurt.

"I followed him yesterday morning."

"You conducted surveillance on Brian?" My tone indicated exactly what I thought of the idea.

"I know, I know. It's shady and shifty and I shouldn't have done it. But I'm worried about him. God knows what he's doing. Or who he's meeting with."

I hated that I had to ask. "So what did you find out?"

"I followed him to the subway. He got on the 1 train headed downtown."

"You didn't follow him to see where he was going?"

"I think he might have spotted me. I'm not sure, but I thought it'd be best if I didn't continue."

I let out a smile and said, "Brian was running countersurveillance. Interesting. You got burned and returned to HQ."

Mary Catherine said, "That's all you have to say? *Interesting?* Aren't you worried about your son?"

"You know I am, but he's not breaking any laws by hopping a train downtown. We've got to have some faith in him. On the basketball court the other day, a boy tried to pick a fight with him, but Brian wouldn't engage. I saw how hard he's trying to stick to his anger management program. I'd like to give him a little more of a chance. Let's have breakfast."

I put my arm around Mary Catherine as we walked from the living room into the kitchen. I saw the New York *Daily News* on the kitchen counter, stepped over and picked it up. It was still rolled with the rubber band the doorman used to make the papers easier to deliver.

Mary Catherine grabbed a cup of coffee and headed into the dining room. She took a seat at the end of the dining room table. I sat down next to her and unrolled the paper.

My eyes locked on the headline blaring in bold type: LETTER FROM A KILLER. At that same moment, my phone started to ring. I knew there had to be a connection.

The entire front page of the New York *Daily News* was a letter from the person claiming to be our killer.

To the Women of New York:

Now that you see what I can do, you are right to be afraid. Respect the fear.

I know how to watch. I know how to kill. I know how to evade the police.

Your arrogance has been your downfall. I am the one in control, not you.

Think of the one who has killed the most. I am better than him.

And I'm about to prove it. Again. And again. And again. And again.

Bobby Fisher

The NYPD hadn't gotten any heads-up about the publication of this letter. My phone kept ringing and ringing. I was getting multiple calls from management.

The only one I answered was from Harry Grissom.

CHAPTER 42

DANIEL OTT WALKED the streets of Manhattan. He had to get to work in Queens, but that could wait.

Now that his letter was finally out there, he sensed people were acting differently, and he wanted to experience how it felt to walk among them. As he walked, he noticed that the crowds still bustled about, bumping and pushing, but their overall energy felt more tentative. He also noticed more people reading actual newspapers. Ott realized he was starting to get quite a kick out of seeing how others reacted to his hobby.

How scared they seemed.

He couldn't suppress his smile. *I did this.*

Ott pulled a copy of the New York *Daily News* out of his bag. He'd already read the article that accompanied his letter to the paper. He'd read it six times. Every time, he'd gotten even more excited. He loved that the reporter called him a "maestro of death" who played "a genius game of cat and mouse with the police."

Ott contemplated sending another letter, maybe to a national newspaper, like *USA Today*. He wondered if he should mention the other cities he'd visited, then he hesitated, concerned that someone might piece together his travel itinerary. It was a long shot but one he'd rather not risk. Maybe he'd just point out how clever he was in arranging his counting messages. He couldn't deny the thrill he got from boldly taunting the police.

His phone rang. It was too early in the morning for his usual call with his wife and daughters, but Lena said she needed to talk to him. After Ott spoke to his two daughters for a few minutes, and listened to their stories about the neighbor's dog and how they were learning to use computers almost as well as their dad, they gave the phone back to his wife.

Lena seemed upset. She told him that this morning an older woman had bullied her at the grocery store.

"I was standing in the meat aisle when she reached over and pulled a package of pork chops right out of my hand. She looked at me, then walked away with the pork chops in her basket."

"What did you do?"

"I let it go. I decided it wasn't worth arguing over pork chops. Plus, she was old."

Ott said, "That's what makes you so special. You're not an arrogant bully like so many American women. You stay exactly the way you are. I hope we can raise our daughters to be just like you."

"Aren't you sweet," Lena said. "Do you know yet when you'll be home?"

"I have a couple more things to do here in New York City. I'll head back probably sometime late next week."

"The girls and I can't wait to see you."

"I can't wait to see all of you."

After he finished the call, Ott contemplated his next move.

Helping his wife through a trying experience made him feel that he was repaying part of the debt he owed her. He owed her at least as much as he did his former employers, and that bothered him a little bit.

But his kind, quiet wife would never bother him the way brash, opinionated women did.

Ott was starting to feel like he was doing the women in this city a favor by instilling a little more civility among them. Maybe his lesson plan was more than just a hobby.

CHAPTER 43

MY MORNING COMMUTE was a crazed montage of phone calls and texts as I reread the killer's letter over and over at every stop in traffic. In the letter, the killer had made it clear he was no phony. And he was not done teaching New Yorkers a lesson in civility and manners.

The letter was short, to the point, and clearly designed to cause panic and confusion. Was he trying to gain attention and notoriety, like the Zodiac Killer, Jack the Ripper, and the Golden State Killer had all done in the past? All of those criminals had reached out to the press. He had also raised a challenge. *Think of the one who has killed the most.* I considered the prolific serial killer Hollis had mentioned, Samuel Little.

Which killer was *Bobby Fisher* trying to top?

I was getting sucked into the puzzle. Exactly as the killer wanted me to do.

I had already been on the phone to the NYPD tech department. They were busy talking to the newspaper's computer staff, trying to figure out the origin of the email.

I decided to make a personal visit to the New York *Daily News* building to see the individual in charge of editorials and letters to the editor. I drove directly to the paper's offices, way down by Battery Park and about a mile from One Police Plaza. The editor didn't seem surprised to see an NYPD detective in his office. He also didn't seem to care.

The editor was in his early thirties and was dressed surprisingly casually, given his title. I looked over the framed diplomas hanging on the wall: an undergrad degree from Northwestern's Medill School of Journalism and an MBA from NYU. There were also several trophies on a low, oak bookshelf—though as I slipped past, I saw one was a soccer trophy with a plate that read FOR PARTICIPATION.

With a murder investigation at stake, this guy was going to have to do better than that.

He had the air of a sharp Wall Street banker working for a fraction of the salary—and, by the look of his degrees, a lot more student debt. His slicked-back dark hair and wire-frame glasses made it seem like he couldn't decide if he wanted to be a hotshot media guy or an intellectual.

I skipped the pleasantries and went straight for the confrontation. "I can't believe you wouldn't at least call us for comment before you printed a letter from what could be our lead suspect. What kind of journalism is that?"

"Welcome to the new millennium's journalism, Detective. In today's media world, speed is everything. Look, we weren't trying to screw up your investigation. Fact is, the email sat in the general folder for days before anyone even looked at it.

When our techs confirmed it was sent from a New York–area IP address, we became convinced that he'd sent the letter to everyone in town, so we decided to run it before we could be scooped. And the proof is in our circulation. It's skyrocketing."

"The NYPD isn't trying to censor you or inhibit any First Amendment rights. We're trying to catch a killer. This is an active investigation."

"Which is going nowhere." The young editor made a face, but truthfully, I couldn't read his expression. "When are you going to start doing something about this freak?"

I realized I was getting tired of this kind of conversation, of answering the only question anyone ever asked. "We're approaching this case from every possible angle," I said. "Doing everything we can."

"I admit, Detective, I might not have your experience, but I have a good education and common sense. What about rounding up some suspects? Doing some quick searches? No one cares about search warrants anymore. This shit has got to stop. The people have a right to know that the killer is taunting everyone in New York, including the police. And now that they do know, it's only a matter of time before they start taking matters into their own hands."

I chuckled.

"What's so funny?"

"Your belief system. That the Constitution matters only when there is no crisis. That's not how the world works. We can't all be hypocrites. We have to follow policies and rules set down for legal investigations."

The editor said, "I'll put this argument down to a draw. But the next time the asshole kills someone, Bennett, this conversation goes on the record. And 'Doing everything we can' is going to sound a lot like 'We're not doing anything.'"

CHAPTER 44

AN HOUR LATER, I met Brett Hollis in front of the main branch of the New York Public Library. His face looked much better today. That single strip of tape across his nose didn't seem so out of place. Maybe I was just getting used to it.

The editor at the New York *Daily News* was right about one thing: circulation. And not of library books. Everywhere I looked I saw people with a newspaper under their arms or reading news stories on their phones. A cab rolled by with its windows down. I could hear one of the local AM radio hosts—a well-known sports commentator—talking about the letter from the killer.

Hollis had been busy. He'd gotten a report from the NYPD's Computer Crimes Squad, who had worked with the *Daily News* IT staff and improved on the staff's initial findings. They'd figured out that the email's IP address had originated from a computer inside this library building. The email address provided to the paper was traced back to a newly opened account in the name of Bobby Fisher, no other identifying information attached.

In short, the letter didn't seem to provide any new information on the killer, other than the challenge he had posed. How was that possible?

"By the way," Hollis told me, "I also heard that a staff member here was the victim of a homicide up in East Harlem, just a few days ago. But her case doesn't seem similar to ours. No mutilation, none of our guy's markers."

I asked Hollis how he was doing, dealing with John Macy.

Hollis sighed and looked up at one of the pair of giant marble lions, Patience and Fortitude, that flanked the building's stairs. "He was the last person I saw last night and the first one to call me this morning. But if I'm working with the great and famous Michael Bennett, I guess I should expect a few rough patches."

"Funny."

Hollis asked me, "How'd the meeting with the editor at the *Daily News* go?"

"About like you'd expect. It's very clear to me that they're only interested in the number of papers they sell or clicks the story gets online, not in helping out our homicide investigation. I swear, sometimes it feels like there are some awfully bloodthirsty people in the media who want more murders so they can have juicier stories that sell more papers."

Hollis shook his head in dismay, then said, "So what're we hoping for from our visit to the library?"

"Ideally, a description of some kind. We have the date and time the email was sent. Maybe a security camera got a useful image of the killer. We should be able to narrow down the hours of footage. Maybe a member of the staff even spoke to him. We can get a forensic artist if we have to make a composite."

"I hope we find something. We got nothing useful so far from the tip line."

I turned and looked at the crowds of people passing the library or congregating in front of it. I was struck by the fact that we were looking for a needle in a haystack. A giant haystack. And a needle that moved from city to city.

Patience and fortitude. That's what it would take to catch this killer.

CHAPTER 45

DANIEL OTT STOPPED in front of the main branch of the New York Public Library, contemplating the new research he needed to do today. As before, he preferred to use someone else's computer when looking up anything...unsavory. If anyone searched his laptop, they'd find only his work-related materials and Google searches having to do with the best homeschool curriculums.

The most important part of today's research was not electronic. He was interested in the reaction of the other librarians to the death of the librarian he had killed, along with whoever that other man was.

That's why he was back here today.

He was already wondering about his next victim. He'd be leaving New York in about a week, and it would be nice to enjoy one last night of rituals and excitement in the big city.

Besides, he'd promised the *Daily News* that he would claim another life. And he didn't want to let his readers down.

He looked in the faces of the women striding past the library and saw half a dozen who might fit his needs. Women who looked like they would ignore him if he spoke to them. Women who thought they were better than him, better than everyone.

As he stood for the moment next to the stairs leading into the main entrance of the library, however, he glanced down and saw a frail-looking woman with a child sitting in her lap. She wore a floral dress that looked vintage 1970s. Next to her sat a wire shopping basket holding a stack of clothes with some chips and a half eaten Clif Bar balanced on top.

The woman spoke with a heavy accent. "Can you help us? We need money to get upstate."

She had big brown eyes and seemed completely defeated. The little girl in her lap was about three. Her curly hair was dirty, and she wore a T-shirt stained with grape juice. She gave him the briefest of smiles.

Ott pulled his wallet from his back pocket. When he opened it, he realized all he had was a single ten-dollar bill. He'd meant to stop at the ATM but had forgotten. Ott looked down at the sad pair and handed the woman his ten dollars.

The woman squeezed his hand and said, "Bless you. May God bless you, sir."

"I'll be happy if you use the money to buy that little girl some food. I believe I'm beyond God's blessing. If there is a God," Ott said. He realized that some of the lessons of his childhood had definitely stuck with him. He had nothing against churches, but that wasn't how he'd been raised. Aside from his wedding, he had never been inside one.

Ott left the woman and went into the library. The first time he had visited, he'd made a quick note of the security. Frankly, he'd expected more cameras. There were a few around, but he also noticed several dummy cameras, fake cameras positioned to make security appear beefier. Ott glanced up to make sure they had not installed video cameras since his last visit. His eyes quickly moved up the walls and around the decorative crown molding. There was nothing. No cameras or sensors of any kind.

He walked directly to the computer room and looked up and around. No new cameras there either. He knew the idea was to make the room as inviting and unintimidating to people as possible.

Two staff members were in the room. One was organizing magazines in the corner, and the other sat at a desk, sorting through books that had recently been returned. She paid no attention to who was at the computers, or whether they had signed in.

Like he belonged there, he settled into his place at the third computer from the door. The same one he'd used to send his letter to the New York *Daily News*. He wanted to see the story online even though he'd already read it so many times in print. Often the online stories were accompanied by photos or embedded videos not available in the print edition.

Ott then moved on to other local media stories about the murders. He was interested in learning more about the detective on the case. There were photos of this Michael Bennett in several different settings. Ott didn't think the man looked like a cop. He looked more like an actor. Then Ott did a search on Bennett.

He couldn't believe the number of articles that had run over the years. The man had been lead detective on several major investigations. There were also several human-interest stories about his personal life. He was a widower with ten adopted children. Ott wondered if he'd adopted the children before or after his wife died.

He glanced up from the computer at the two women working in the room. They both appeared subdued. Ott assumed that was because of him, because he had murdered one of their colleagues. He smiled. They had no idea it was her conduct on the job that had put their friend at risk.

The woman behind the desk had a beautiful face and long, lustrous blond hair that flowed over her shoulders. He wondered how much money and effort it took to keep her hair looking like that. Probably enough to feed a poor family in other parts of the world. Just the thought of it made him a little angry.

Ott stretched his neck to get a better view of the woman. He was hoping to read the name tag she wore on her blouse.

Then he got hold of himself. He returned his focus to the computer and started doing a little more research. He wanted to know more about this Michael Bennett before he did anything else. His idea to stir things up might have to wait.

CHAPTER 46

YOU KNOW, I'VE lived in New York my whole life and I've never been in here before," Brett Hollis said as we entered the library. He looked awestruck by the marble walls and high ceilings of the scholarly locale.

"Impressive, isn't it?" I said. "As a tourist destination, it even makes a little money for the city." And as we walked through the famous library, I felt a familiar pride and appreciation for this monument to learning.

I waited while Hollis phoned a tech agent from the NYPD, gathering a few more pieces of the puzzle. Then we continued on to the admin office, where we identified ourselves and were led to Carolyn Richard, a confident older black woman in charge of public services, such as the computer room. Ms. Richard was imposing and elegant, and as soon as I saw her, I thought, *She could be one of the nuns from Holy Name*—especially the way she had her arms folded across her chest when she told us to come in and sit down.

Ms. Richard said, "I assume you're here about Yara Zunis."

Is that the murder victim I just heard about from Hollis? I thought so but wasn't sure, so I kept quiet, let her talk.

"Yara Zunis, one of our librarians. She and her boyfriend were victims of a terrible crime. They were both stabbed to death outside their home in East Harlem."

That didn't fit our killer's MO—as far as we were aware, he only ever killed young women, not couples, and he never killed out in the open. Still, what were the chances that a serial killer uses a specific library's computer and then one of that library's staff is murdered? Was it just a horrible coincidence? Or could there be some sort of connection?

I gathered my thoughts and said, "My utmost condolences to you and your staff on the tragedy you've all suffered. But we're actually here investigating an email that our cyber forensics team believe was sent from your computer room."

"Oh my—is this related to that awful letter I read in the *Daily News*?" Carolyn Richard asked. She was a smart woman, and I could see her quickly reassessing the situation, even as I demurred, citing confidentiality issues.

During the walk to the computer room from her office, I asked Ms. Richard more about Yara Zunis.

"How long had she worked here at the library?"

"Yara was one of our newest and brightest," she said, "a recent graduate from the prestigious Master of Library and Information Science program at Simmons University in Boston. She was making significant contributions. It's such a terrible shame."

She shook her head and sighed. "Is there anything you can tell me about the investigation into her murder? I know it's not your case, but I assume there's communication between precincts."

"I'll have the detectives handling the case get back to you," I told her. I was pretty curious about it myself, to be honest. "For now, our primary concern is the email."

Ms. Richard nodded, then said, "With all these murders in the city, I've been starting to wonder if our staff needs to commute using some kind of buddy system."

The marble floor of the entrance hall gave way to the high marble walls of the periodical/computer room. The two young women working there immediately looked up when Ms. Richard entered.

I quickly scanned the room to get a sense of the security measures in place. I saw a few cameras, but they were mainly dummies. I wondered about the computer sign-in procedures.

I saw a quick movement to my right. I turned but caught only a glimpse of a man wearing a white, short-sleeved shirt and a tie leaving the room.

Why had he caught my attention? Call it instinct.

I glanced back to Hollis. He hadn't seemed to notice the guy, and Ms. Richard was intent on introducing me to the blond woman behind the desk.

Even though the blonde was the person I needed to talk to about the email, I had to excuse myself. "We need to go talk to someone for a minute."

I grabbed Hollis by the arm and pulled him with me out the door, saying, "I saw a man wearing a white, short-sleeved shirt and a tie. As soon as he saw us, he popped out of the room with his head ducked down."

As Hollis kept pace, I added the kicker: "I have a strong feeling that we gotta find this guy and talk to him right away."

CHAPTER 47

SET PERIMETERS AND *start a methodical grid search.* I knew the routine for searches, honed during my days as a uniformed officer in the Bronx and as a homicide detective, hunting everyone from drug suspects to bank robbers.

But that approach took manpower, at least twenty cops to do right. Right now it was just Hollis and me, and I was hesitant to call in reinforcements based on nothing more than my flimsy hunch and a fleeting image. Besides, it would take too long to get backup here and organized.

Instead, I sent Hollis toward the main entrance as I rushed down a hallway in the opposite direction. My last words to the young detective were "Don't do anything stupid. Just hang back and call me on the cell if you see him." I knew advice like that was difficult for a young hotshot like Brett Hollis to follow. He was wearing the damaged proof on his face.

I loped down the empty hallway with my right arm loose at my side so I could reach my Glock if needed. I should've come to a complete stop and *sliced the pie* by looking around each corner, but there wasn't time. Smart policies are all well and good, but no bad guys would ever get caught if we officers followed every policy to the letter, every time.

Sweat slipped down my forehead as my pulse picked up.

To my right was a marble staircase that headed down, away from the main floor. I took the steps two at a time. Just as I skidded onto the tiled floor of the lower level, a figure moved to my right.

I saw a flash of white shirt and dark tie.

I let out a quick "Freeze!" as I reached for my pistol, and in the same instant, I recognized the uniform shirt of a security guard. The man flinched and scooted away from me.

I flashed my badge. "NYPD. Did anyone else come down here?"

He hesitated, then said, "I thought I heard footsteps, but it might have been yours coming down the stairs."

A door down the hall was cracked open. I indicated it with a lift of my chin. "Where does that go?"

"Lower-level maintenance. Nothing there but conduits and heating units."

I raced to the door without another word. The guard called after me, but I didn't have time to waste words. I was hoping for action. I almost hoped he'd call for more security people. A group following me could be useful if the chase ended in a show of force.

I reached the open door and discovered that it led to a narrow, metal staircase descending into a dark, tunnel-like passageway filled with electrical boxes and abandoned computers stacked haphazardly against whitewashed cinder-block walls. Tracks of wires seemed to guide me in one direction. At the same time, something told me to slow down and make every move deliberate.

A light flickered a dozen feet down the hallway. I flipped my coat away from my right hip and slid my hand onto the butt of my duty weapon.

I pulled my phone from my pocket to check on Hollis. No service.

Could Bobby Fisher be down here, setting up for his next match?

CHAPTER 48

FIFTEEN MINUTES EARLIER, Daniel Ott had looked up from the public computer to see the same man he'd just read about on the internet standing by the door. He had done a double take, stolen several more peeks, then was certain. It was that detective, Michael Bennett.

For a moment, Ott calculated the odds of this being a coincidence. No: the police had to be here because of the dead librarian. But did Bennett know that the librarian and her friend were connected to his handiwork? It hurt his brain to think too much about it. He had to slip away. Fast.

Even if Ott hadn't just been reading about the detective, he would have suspected something. Bennett and the other guy he was with just *looked* like police officers—fit, well-dressed, and alert. They had come into the room with an older black woman. Ott watched as the three of them stepped over to the information desk, and while they seemed distracted, he used his soft cloth to wipe the keyboard of prints, quickly gathered his things, and slipped out the door. Almost involuntarily, he'd picked up his pace to a near run.

Mistake. The detective had noticed him leaving.

At the bottom of the marble staircase, Ott fingered a screwdriver in his pocket. A screwdriver through the neck or in an eye would definitely slow down anyone chasing him.

He considered his next move, zeroing in on another stairwell that didn't look public. No marble or frills. He raced for it.

Ott found himself in the lowest level of the library. The Ghostbusters may have prowled the subbasement stacks, but not the maintenance corridors. The stark layout here meant some part of him would be visible anywhere he crouched or lay down. There was no place he could hide.

Then he saw a junction box built into the wall. One of those big industrial suckers. It had to be four feet tall and two feet wide. It was a screw model with no handle.

He had an idea.

He snapped his head in every direction. His heart beat hard in his chest. His hands shook. He used his cheap tie with the Computelex logo to wipe sweat from his face.

The first screw at the top of the box was hard to reach. He was able to remove a couple more screws, but then they slipped from his hand and scattered on the rough concrete floor.

He wasn't sure what he'd find when he opened the box's door. Would it be a mess of wiring inside? Luckily for him, when he finally yanked the door open, he discovered there were no breakers or other more complex electrical connections. This was just a pass-through that redirected most of the wires up to the main floors of the library.

It would be tight, but he could fit inside it if he contorted his body just so. Ott hopped up, then pulled himself all the way into the box. He kept the screwdriver in his right hand. If someone opened the box while he was inside, he'd take a mighty swing at their eyes, leap into the passageway, then run.

With his left hand, he pulled the door shut behind him. He crouched uncomfortably inside the box, perspiration running down his back, ears straining to hear any noises outside.

CHAPTER 49

I MOVED CAUTIOUSLY. The heat down here couldn't account for all the sweat in my eyes. Some of it was nerves.

I had no cell service. No radio. I had to admit that I'd put myself in a stupid situation. If the guy I'd seen was the killer, and if he was down here and managed to get the drop on me, I wasn't sure anyone would even know to look for me here unless the library guard had sounded the alarm.

This area of the library was creepy. The flickering light down the hallway reminded me of the horror movies my older kids were just about brave enough to watch through half closed eyes.

I thought I heard something. A shift. A slight metallic noise. Now I was studying shadows in the poorly lit corridor. My mind was starting to play tricks on me and I was freaking myself out.

Keeping my right hand on the butt of my pistol, I moved

slowly. Once I passed the flickering light, I paused and listened again. I leaned against the wall next to some kind of giant circuit box. I really thought I heard something moving inside.

Mice? Squirrels? Or worse—rats?

I looked down at the concrete and noticed a single screw sitting in the middle of the corridor. I kneeled down and picked it up. Before I rose again to my feet, I rested in a silent crouch. Listening. Feeling like there was someone close by. I cocked my head like a curious dog. But I couldn't pick up the sound again.

Then I heard a noise. It registered on several levels inside my head. I listened and realized it was footsteps. Not someone trying to hide.

Then a voice called out, "Officer! Are you still down here? Officer?"

I called out, "Over here."

The security guard I had seen on the upper level swung into view. He was winded and overheated. His sweaty hair was plastered to his forehead, and he was panting from exertion.

He had to lean down with his hands on his knees and take a couple of gulps of air before he could stand upright and speak. "The cop with the broken nose? He told me to come find you," he said. "He needs you at the main entrance. He said to hurry."

I kept the screw I found on the floor. For no reason that I can explain, it struck me as a potential piece of evidence. I shoved it into my front pocket as I started to jog ahead of the security guard.

CHAPTER 50

AS I BURST OUT of the main doors to the library, I held up my hand to protect against the glare of the sun; though it wasn't all that bright out, my eyes had quickly grown accustomed to the gloom of the basement. I felt relief to have gotten out of there.

Crowds washed by on the street. The security guard directed me to a bench just past the edge of the stairs to the right, where Brett Hollis stood next to a man of about forty-five wearing a short-sleeved shirt and a gaudy purple tie. His thinning hair hung in a loose comb-over. He was sweating in the midday sun. The fact that he was thirty pounds overweight probably didn't help the situation.

The man was not in custody, I noted, and he and Hollis were talking casually. Hollis saw me coming down the stairs and gave me a quick headshake. This wasn't our suspect. As I walked up, Hollis told me, "This gentleman is a vending machine rep who was meeting with the library staff. I already confirmed it. I sent the security guard to look for you before I checked out his story."

I looked at the pudgy, red-faced, balding man. He looked pissed off.

"Do we need to hold him any longer?"

Hollis shrugged. "That's sort of the problem. He won't leave."

The man looked toward Hollis and said, "I'll have your goddamn badge over this." Then he looked at me, making the assumption that, as an older detective, I was probably in charge, and said, "He arrested me without a warrant! I know my rights. I know how you guys operate."

Arrested? I turned to the man and said, "I'm sorry. I'm not sure what you're talking about."

Hollis said, "Sir, you were never under arrest. All I did was talk to you for a couple of minutes about a matter that needed clearing up, and you didn't argue."

"I was too scared. You intimidated me."

All I could say was "C'mon, sir, you got misidentified. We cleared it up in a couple of minutes. Won't you just go about your business?"

The pudgy man barked again. "Bullshit. I want your names and badge numbers. Why are you bothering me when you should be trying to catch that nut cutting up women all over the city?"

I could sense Hollis losing patience with the man. We needed to de-escalate. I reached into my wallet and pulled out a business card. I wrote Harry's name and phone number on the back. I handed it to the man and said, "That's our lieutenant. If you have any complaints, talk to him."

"I'll go straight to the *Post.* I know you cops all watch each other's backs. I'm a US citizen."

I'd had enough. I gave the man a hard look and said, "You have the right to get on with your life. I would recommend you exercise that right as soon as possible. Frankly, I've heard all the shit I want to out of you."

The man started walking away on the sidewalk, muttering to himself. He stopped twenty feet away and shouted, "Cops suck!"

It wasn't original, but he got his point across.

Hollis looked at me and said, "What now?"

"We work with what we have. I was chasing ghosts beneath the library. At least you got to talk to a real person."

"Enduring that conversation was more painful than breaking my nose," Hollis said, and I laughed.

"Now we need to meet with library IT so that we can check the video surveillance to see if our runner shows up."

CHAPTER 51

HOLLIS AND I turned the corner from the library entrance to find a coffee shop on 41st, just off Fifth Avenue. The place was nearly empty of customers. We headed toward the rear and commandeered two wide tables, where we spread out our papers.

I had a cup of plain black coffee and some kind of cruller. Hollis opted for a healthy and hydrating bottle of water. He never would've made the grade when I was a rookie. Back then, drinking coffee during our shifts and alcohol in the evenings felt mandatory. Frankly, I don't miss the old days.

We'd spent more than an hour talking with the head of library security and his IT guy. We'd searched through the available video feeds. I'd noted the dummy cameras, but I was still surprised at how few active feeds they actually maintained.

The head of security had looked at me and shrugged. "We're a library, not a central bank. We have a decent budget, but it's not spent on security cameras. Our biggest expense is staffing exhibits of our permanent collections. Some of the items—like first-edition books by famous authors, or one-of-a-kind photographs and artwork—are quite valuable. We have to prevent tourists from trying to steal a piece of library history. On the flip side, we also need to patrol the quiet spaces where homeless people sneak in to sleep during the day and overnight. But if the guy you're looking for passed by any of the display areas, we may have captured his image."

Not likely, I thought, but I thanked the security head for his time.

At least we had a little more information to work with.

The outburst from the concerned citizen outside the library underscored my biggest worry. New Yorkers aren't shy about criticizing the police, and that guy had felt free to curse us out. God knows an ass like John Macy would use any public outcry as a reason to screw with me, especially as the unsolved murders kept mounting.

I slapped a legal pad down on the table and started writing. The lists of what we were missing and what we still needed to do were far longer than the list of what we had.

When I wondered out loud if I'd caught a glimpse of the killer at the library, Hollis talked me down, reminding me that there was no reason to assume the killer had even been there today, only a case of mistaken identity with the vending machine rep.

With an audible sigh, I conceded his point and then said, "So what's our next move?"

"Maybe the answer lies in the earlier murders. We need to work those connections until we forge a clear link."

It was as good a plan as any. And one that would take us back to the office.

As we started to gather up our stuff, the manager of the coffee shop, a well-built young black man, approached. He said, "I noticed your badges. I was wondering if you guys might help me out."

I said, "What's the problem?"

"There's a homeless guy who sits for hours right in the doorway of my shop. The guy's killing my afternoon business. I called the local precinct a couple of times, but one of the cops I talked to said that the truth is, they don't consider loitering or harassing my customers for change enough of a crime to warrant an arrest."

The manager blew out a frustrated breath, admitting, "I once made the mistake of paying him off. I gave him five dollars to find another spot. But he was back the next day, and he told me it would take ten if I wanted him to move again. He just sat down now. Is there anything you guys can do?"

I looked past the manager to see a white guy with a scraggly gray beard who'd propped himself right in the coffee shop's doorway. He wore an old olive-drab army-surplus jacket. As I watched, two different customers walked toward the front door. First one, then the other, turned away and left rather than step over the man's legs. I could see the manager's point.

I turned to Hollis and said, "This is a good lesson for us as members of the NYPD. The store's owner has made a legitimate request, and I'd like you to handle it. The faster it's taken care of, the faster we can get back on our case."

I purposely hadn't offered any advice to Hollis, and he didn't say a word. He simply jumped to his feet and headed to the door of the coffee shop.

So far, I'd been impressed at how Hollis handled difficult coworkers and even an ass like John Macy, but I wanted to see more of how he dealt with the public. This was a sensitive, potentially volatile situation. He was on his own. I just hoped his solution wasn't too harsh.

The way he barreled through the front door and spun on the sidewalk to confront the man didn't give me much hope. Then the homeless man stood up and faced Hollis. I wondered if I might need to go defuse the situation. But I waited.

Just as he had done with Van Fleet, Hollis put his hand on the man's shoulder. He spoke to him quietly. I saw the man's head nod, and then he shook Hollis's hand. I also noticed something Hollis probably didn't want me to see: my young partner slipping the man a card for the VA New York Regional Office on Houston Street and some cash as he was walking away.

Hollis had done some practical problem-solving. And shown some compassion. I was impressed.

CHAPTER 52

BACK IN THE office, I looked like a crazed hoarder with towering stacks of paper and crime-scene photographs piled high and spread around my desk, on my guest desk chair, and all over the surrounding floor. Other detectives veered around me and avoided eye contact. I'd have to remember this trick in the future when I didn't want to chat.

I was comparing five case files. The two San Francisco homicides were on the desk directly in front of me. I had three of the five total Atlanta-area homicides on the chair next to my desk—two from Detective Carter and one from his cooperative suburban counterpart. Neither of the agencies investigating the other two murders down there were interested in sharing their files with the NYPD. Fine. I didn't have time to argue.

And I didn't have any more time to spare making certain that the killer who'd likely hit first San Francisco and then Atlanta was probably the same one still at large in New York. The one who in a published letter had threatened the entire city that he would kill again.

The city was in a panic, and John Macy was breathing down our necks.

I had a full range of law-enforcement tools at my disposal. Photographs, forensic reports, interviews, even security footage, though nothing identified the killer. The local agencies had also done video walk-throughs of each crime scene. Some were excellent and gave complete views of every surface and angle. Some were rushed and cursory. Not that the detectives and PD photo techs could have ever imagined that the images they were capturing might prove part of a multistate serial-killing spree.

I stared at a set of novelty shot glasses in the crime-scene photos from one of the San Francisco victims. Souvenirs, I assumed, from the victim's travels, advertising Cancún, Kingston, and Key West. One lone shot glass stood about a foot away from five others. Once again, my mind went back to the strange, asymmetrical arrangement of the bobbleheads in Elaine's apartment here in New York...and the ballerina and musician figurines in the other San Francisco victim's apartment.

Once I started searching, I discovered similar arrangements in the other crime-scene photos, from the Bronx and Brooklyn, and in the three Atlanta-area scenes.

For instance, in one of the Atlanta crime-scene photos, I spotted a shelf where three teacups were lined up on the left, and nine were on the right, with about a foot-wide space between the two groups. In one of the other Atlanta victims' homes, a collection of small vases was divided into clusters of two and seven.

There's always a certain amount of luck and chance involved in any investigation. And this methodology of dividing the victims' collections seemed too deliberate not to be significant.

Looking for more evidence to bolster my theory, I brought up the walk-through videos from the third victim in Atlanta. The footage did a pretty good job of covering her entire apartment, though the detective working the camera had been more focused on getting close-ups of the victim's injuries and body than views of the crime scene. I could understand this victim-centric technique, but for my purposes, it was frustrating not to see more of the house.

I let out a short groan of annoyance that caught Brett Hollis's attention.

He stood up from his desk and stepped over to mine. "What are you looking for? Anything specific?"

I pointed to the crime-scene photos. "See those bobbleheads? And these shot glasses? The vases, the teacups, and the figurines? A number of similarly strange-looking setups at different crime scenes, and I'm wondering if the items might've been separated like that deliberately."

"You think the killer was sending a message?"

I made a face. "That's what I'm starting to think, yeah. But I'm just not sure what."

Hollis looked intrigued. He stood behind me as we watched the Atlanta video again. We divided the screen so he looked at the right side and I looked at the left.

About two minutes into the video, Hollis yelped, "There. There it is. Hit Pause." His finger tapped the screen of my laptop.

On a windowsill in the far background there was a barely

noticeable line of grayish dots. We froze the image and tried to enlarge it. There was one dot to the left, and three to the right, a gap of about five inches between them.

Hollis stared at the screen. "What are those? Buttons?" After a second he said loudly, "Coins! Those are dollar coins."

"Nice catch. Good eye."

Hollis said, "We still have no idea what the killer is trying to tell us."

It was something about staring at the dollar coins that made my swirling thoughts click into place. It was as close to an epiphany as I had ever had, at least in police work.

I said, "He's counting his kills for each location." I quickly grabbed the Atlanta-area crime-scene photos. "See? The video is of the first crime scene in the Atlanta area. Look at the date. Then it's three weeks before the next crime scene, in the actual city of Atlanta. That crime scene shows these two little vases on the left. The next crime scene is in some place called Dunwoody, about six days later. It's the set of teacups with three on the left and nine on the right. His third murder in the Atlanta area. Now it all makes sense. Like the bobbleheads at Elaine Anastas's apartment. She was the fourth murder in New York."

It felt right, like we had solved one important piece of the puzzle.

Now I had to find out if the other cases also fit the pattern.

CHAPTER 53

DANIEL OTT SAT in a McDonald's on 42nd Street, a few blocks from the New York Public Library. About every ten minutes, waves of customers entered and exited, effectively switching places. That's what Ott wanted right now: a lot of people around him. He looked at the crowd. He listened to their conversations.

A TV sat high on the wall, playing the news on channel 1. The anchor was quizzing someone from the mayor's office about the investigation into the murders. *His* murders. The city staffer, a man named John Macy, didn't sound particularly confident that an arrest would be made any time soon.

Ott sipped a Diet Coke and realized the sweat that had soaked his collar and under his arms was now dry. No one seemed to be looking for him. He was safe—at least for the moment. He swiveled his head, trying to work out one of the kinks he'd developed after hiding in that junction box for over twenty minutes. Then he straightened out both legs and heard his knees click with relief.

He smiled at a very cute Asian child whose mother had her strapped in a harness, with a leash attached. An older daughter carried shopping bags from inexpensive chain stores, like Claire's and H&M. The little girl on the leash paused right in front of Ott's table, level with his french fries. Her eyes cut from the fries to Ott, and back again.

All Ott could do was smile and nod his head. The little girl snuck two fries and rewarded him with a beautiful smile.

That happy smile reminded him of his own young daughters, waiting for him at home. He would be there with them soon. Now he was starting to feel normal. He relaxed slightly, allowing himself some perspective on the uncharacteristic stumble he had made back at the library, the moment the police had gotten close.

He was still a little freaked-out to have been reading an article about one of the city's best detectives, Michael Bennett, the one working his cases—only to look up and see the man in person. But even the so-called great detective hadn't been able to find him in the lower level of the library.

Daniel Ott sat at the table, finishing the last of his Diet Coke and fries and thinking about what needed to be done. Maybe he'd been thinking too broadly. He didn't need to send more emails to other newspapers. He could stir things up *and* disrupt the police investigation via more decisive and specific action.

He got out his burner smartphone to do a little research. There was one plan of attack that would surely rock the city. Killing Michael Bennett.

He knew the detective worked out of the Manhattan North Homicide office. Had to look at a few city maps to find the exact location of that office, but he was able to discover that the NYPD operated that department from a rented floor and four extra offices in an office building owned by Columbia University on upper Broadway near 133rd Street. Bennett's home address was unlisted, but Ott was good...and smart enough to know that hunting a target who lived in a city apartment with eleven other people was too risky. And he didn't like the idea of threatening children to incite panic.

He reassessed. Okay, maybe killing Bennett was too complicated.

Briefly, he thought about Bennett's family. Ten kids was a lot of children. Ott didn't care what culture you were raised in or how big a farm you had to work—he didn't see how raising ten kids was viable. Especially for a NYPD detective with a high-profile caseload. But Ott dismissed the idea of harming the kids. Besides, if Bennett were sidetracked by a personal issue, another detective would just take his place. And Bennett would probably still be available to consult.

He just needed to get Bennett off the case for a while. If Ott succeeded in injuring the detective or one of his colleagues, he could really throw a monkey wrench into the investigation. If he could do it without making it look like an intentional act of violence, no one would even connect him to the sneak attack on the NYPD.

He enjoyed having a problem like this to work on. His engineering background helped with almost any decision.

CHAPTER 54

I FELT LIKE a Christian walking the halls of the Roman Colosseum on my way to judgment in the arena. Every pair of eyes that set on me made me feel uncomfortable. For some reason, all FBI offices made me feel this way.

A lot of people don't realize that when it comes to law-enforcement agents and employees, the NYPD is much larger than the FBI. We number almost forty thousand cops, while the FBI has only approximately fifteen thousand agents active at any given time. The NYPD even has offices outside New York City. After the 9/11 terrorist attacks, NYPD and city officials felt the FBI could have done a better job providing them with information prior to the attacks, so now NYPD detectives are in several Middle Eastern cities as well as European cities. There's even a contingent of uniformed officers at the Vatican so visitors from New York City can feel reassured if there's a problem and they need to turn to a trusted element.

I was here at the FBI offices today to meet with Emily Parker. She knew my preference was to meet at a restaurant or coffee shop so I didn't have to venture into federal offices like this, but today she'd forced me to come here. Her "invitation" was making me feel like she was playing a prank on me.

Emily greeted me with a hug as she met me in the hallway and led me back to her cluttered cubicle. Before I could sit on the hard plastic chair next to her desk, I had to move aside a pile of files and notebooks. Though who was I to criticize, given the unruly stacks currently covering my desk and floor? Especially since I understood she probably knew exactly where to locate everything she needed. With a mind like hers, filing systems were a waste of time.

Emily smiled and said, "What's so important that I got Michael Bennett to actually come to the FBI office voluntarily? Honestly, the only thing that surprises me more is that you're not in custody."

"Ha ha," I replied. "All jokes aside, I need a sharp brain like yours to consider something we discovered about the killer."

"I can't wait to hear this one." She scooted her chair away from her desk and closer to me.

I cleared off a space on her desk and carefully laid out copies of the crime-scene photographs from New York, San Francisco, and Atlanta. I explained in great detail exactly what Hollis and I had discovered, not only about the bloody crime scenes but also the deliberate arrangement of the collections of objects found inside the victims' homes in each location. I explained our interpretation of them as the killer's way of tallying up his murders.

Emily was attentive but silent, never interrupting me as I explained our theory. That was a sign of a professional law-enforcement agent. Too bad more FBI agents didn't follow her example.

When I was finally finished, she looked me in the eye and said, "Impressive. I usually only hear about a personality mosaic this elaborate being pieced together by one of our people down at the Behavioral Analysis Unit at Quantico."

"What do you think of our theory?"

"It's pretty convincing," she said. "And I'm even more im-pressed knowing you guys came up with it on no budget, very little time, and using only crime-scene photos and public newspaper databases. But not all of the crime scenes have these messages. Like the one on Staten Island."

"That bugs the shit out of me. I've been over those crime-scene photos and back to that apartment several times. Nothing. I don't know if the killer was interrupted and had to leave or if there's some other explanation. But I still think we're onto something."

Emily said, "Maybe the message at the Staten Island crime scene is tiny. Or just not as obvious as these, like a handful of buttons or some grains of sand. Something someone could have accidentally swept up or knocked over. Based on your theory, this guy clearly needs to taunt us. That's ballsy."

I smiled at her dispassionate evaluation of our killer.

She said, "So what do you want from me?"

The research you promised me, I thought, but before I could answer, I heard a voice.

"Detective…?"

I turned in my seat and recognized FBI ASAC Robert

Lincoln from our previous meeting at One Police Plaza. He wore a gray suit with a red power tie and stood at the entrance to Emily's cubicle, snapping his fingers like he couldn't remember my name.

I recognized it as an old trick meant to put me in my place, but I fell into the trap anyway. I offered, "Bennett."

"Yes, of course. What brings you down here? I was under the impression that the NYPD had no use for the FBI."

Emily saved me. God bless her. She said, "Detective Bennett was just updating me on their multiple-homicide case. He's linked the killer we're investigating here to previous homicides in San Francisco and Atlanta."

That caught the FBI supervisor by surprise. "Really? Do you have all his reports, Emily?"

She nodded.

Lincoln said, "And you've confirmed this?"

Emily nodded again.

"Open an FBI case on it. Get in touch with the other jurisdictions. They may be more interested in our help than the NYPD has been." He looked at me. "We'll keep you up-to-date on our case." He paused and threw in a quick, "As time permits."

I smiled and said, "Of course."

Lincoln asked, "Who will be my contact?"

I didn't hesitate. "Macy, John Macy. Technically, he's with the mayor's office. You two should hit it off." I gave him John Macy's card and Lincoln walked away without another word.

Emily looked at me. "You handled that pretty well. You're full of surprises today." She pulled out a blank notepad and said, "I think I have an idea of what I can do for you. I'll run everything in your reports, and in the forensic reports, through every database. I'll also see about getting police reports from the two Atlanta suburbs who refused to cooperate with the NYPD. I'll even see if I can find some travel patterns."

I said, "Emily, you are absolutely the best." And then, "What took you so long?"

She gave me a perfect smile and said, "First, tell me something I don't know. Second, I think we just made it official. We're both on the same case."

CHAPTER 55

SOMEHOW, EVEN AFTER everything I'd dealt with during the day, I made it home with energy to spare. I felt excited to engage with my children or even go for a bike ride with Mary Catherine, if that's what she wanted. We hadn't been riding quite as much as the three times a week she'd intended when we bought the bikes, though we'd ridden enough that I could tell the difference in my endurance.

As usual, as I walked to my apartment, I looked forward to experiencing one of my great joys in life: a greeting from my beautiful children. I didn't care that as they got older, fewer and fewer of them physically met me at the front door. Tonight I just wanted to be with them. Any of them.

So it was a major disappointment when I opened the front door and found no sweet little ones there to greet me. No one at all. Not even the littlest girls, whom I could usually still count on to be excited to see me.

The apartment felt eerily quiet. Something was different. I called out, "Mary Catherine? Chrissy, Shawna?" But I got no response.

I wandered into the kitchen, expecting to find someone in there, but even that was empty. Then I heard someone shout in the living room. Actually, it sounded like several people shouting. Was it an argument? I hurried out of the kitchen, cut through the dining room, and froze at the edge of the living room.

Three of my boys—Trent, Eddie, and Ricky—were all engaged in some kind of monumental battle on our Nintendo gaming system. I watched over their shoulders for a few moments. I couldn't tell who was represented by which avatar on the screen. There was an ogre, a guy in green tights, and what looked like an elf, all fighting with crazy-looking monsters. I'd issued a partial ban on realistic shooting games when the boys were younger. As they grew older, I used the excuse that I didn't want their little sisters exposed to the violence.

These characters may not have had guns, but there was definitely violence. Still, I withheld any comments. Honestly, I was glad to see the boys all playing so well together. I raised my voice to be heard over the clamor of the battling warriors on the TV. "Hey, guys. Where is everyone?"

Immediately, Trent pressed a button and the action froze. The three boys looked up at me like they had been caught stealing cookies.

I assured them that they weren't in trouble. "I'd prefer a game that taught you something, but at least I'm not seeing any brains being splattered by a sniper here."

Ricky gave me a wide grin. "We *are* learning all kinds of things, Dad."

"Like what?"

"How to fight with swords, what magical spells work best, and most importantly, how much fun it is when the girls all go out for a while."

Trent chimed in. "And Eddie figured out how to hack the game to give us access to more powerful weapons."

Is it wrong to be proud of your son when he uses his incredible ability with computers to hack a stupid game like this? It didn't matter. I'm proud of them all.

I said, "Where are Mary Catherine and the girls?"

They said in unison, almost like they had practiced it, "Wedding stuff."

I chuckled. "What about Brian? Have you seen him?"

"Mary Catherine left some money, so he went to go pick up pizza," Eddie said. "He should be back pretty soon."

My stomach tightened when I heard that Brian had some extra cash and had volunteered to go out. I was more worried about him than I'd let on to Mary Catherine. Before I could start my interrogation about how much cash and where he'd said he was going, the front door opened and Brian walked in holding two large pizza boxes.

He looked at me and simply said, "Hey, Dad." No subterfuge, no hiding anything. He put the boxes down on the dining room table, then joined his brothers in the living room.

All four of my boys together, playing a game and getting along. No scene could have made me happier.

I decided to throw caution to the wind and took a slice of pizza into the living room, breaking one of Mary Catherine's most sacred laws: all food must be eaten at the dining room table.

I felt emboldened, but as soon as I sat at the end of the couch with a slice of mushroom and onion pizza in my hand, I considered my actions and quickly asked, "What time did Mary Catherine say they would be back?"

"The girls said they were going to grab something to eat while they were out," Trent said. "I doubt they'll be back before nine o'clock."

I relaxed and took a big bite out of the slice. I was excited to spend an evening with my boys, playing some kind of stupid video game. It was every father's dream.

"Am I allowed to join the game?" I asked.

The boys were delighted at my request. They immediately stopped the game and restarted it to add me as a player. As I basked in the unanimous acclamation, I felt like a celebrity.

Before I could start my turn, though, my phone rang, and I dug it out of my pocket. It was Detective Dan Jackson. All he said was "Looks like we have another homicide."

"Where?"

"SoHo. I'll text you the exact address."

"I'll be there as quick as I can." A tiny part of me shriveled up when I had to inform the kids I was going back to work. It hurt like hell to leave my boys. Especially with those looks on their faces.

A classic example of a cop leaving his own family to protect someone else's.

CHAPTER 56

I FOUND THE building in SoHo, one with three apartments above an Asian grocery offering certified organic produce. The kind of place young hipsters love.

A small, anxious crowd had gathered behind the yellow crime-scene tape. About a dozen people watched intently as NYPD personnel came and went from an unmarked blue door on the right side of the market. It was a mild evening with a cloudless sky. New Yorkers will do anything to get outside for a few minutes in nice weather, but I wished they would move along to a park or the waterfront instead of worrying about a serial killer.

I immediately spotted Detective Dan Jackson's broad form in the shadows next to the building's door. He looked up from where he was directing some NYPD forensic investigators and held up a hand in greeting as I walked toward him. Jackson was sufficiently imposing to stop a fight with just a look. But he also got the most out of the people he worked with. The talent that came naturally to him was a difficult skill to learn, much less to master.

After we slipped hooded biohazard suits over our street clothes and walked up a straight staircase with thick carpet that muffled our steps, Jackson pulled out his notepad. "Lila Stein, twenty-six, didn't show up for work at the county courthouse on Centre Street. She's reliably held her position as a court clerk for the past four years. One of her coworkers stopped by to check on her and got no answer at the door. The coworker called 911, and first responders entered the apartment and found the body. Seems to be in keeping with our serial killer's MO. Dispatch called patrol. They called me. I called you. And here we are on this fine evening."

"You know, Dan, I had other plans for 'this fine evening,'" I said. "They involved video games, pizza, and my teenage sons."

"I feel ya, brother. I was going to watch *Frozen* with my five-year-old twins."

I slid on my filtering mask and followed Dan Jackson through the door. I immediately saw Lila's body, lying on the linoleum floor at the edge of the kitchen, her long brown hair spread out around her head. She almost looked like she was sleeping.

She wore a bathrobe over a sheer nightgown. Blood stained the front of her garments. The stab wound indicated that a blow from a sharp instrument had struck very close to her heart. There was also a puddle of blood and fluid near the right side of her face.

Jackson said, "This scene isn't nearly as bad as the one on 30th, but like that poor vic, this one's also been stabbed in the eye. That's why I figured it was connected to our serial killer."

I glanced around the apartment, careful not to touch anything. I looked down at the victim again, realizing she had been stabbed in the right eye, like Marilyn Shaw. And this apartment was less of a hellscape than some of the others, more like the scene on Staten Island. Not much seemed to have been disturbed beyond the murder victim.

So now we had four victims who'd been stabbed in the left eye and two stabbed in the right. Was I placing too much emphasis on which side the killer chose?

I continued to walk carefully around the apartment. Jackson followed as I explained the working theory Hollis and I had come up with after our examination of the previous scenes in the other cities. About how the killer arranged objects to keep count of his victims. No matter how hard Jackson and I looked, though, we didn't find any of those markers here.

Are Hollis and I on the wrong track? What the hell does this mean?

CHAPTER 57

DANIEL OTT FOUND an internet café in Midtown Manhattan. The little spot served coffee and stale pastries at high prices in exchange for the privilege of signing on to their lightning-fast Wi-Fi. On a busy day, the place resembled a fancy communal diner, the café's three long tables crowded with as many as fifteen customers, mostly younger people with lots of piercings and tattoos.

Ott used a VPN—a virtual private network—to conceal his identity and location after logging on to the Wi-Fi. It might've been overkill, but given his internet research, Ott didn't want to risk anyone accessing his online history from this café.

He hadn't finished his research on Detective Michael Bennett. At the library, he'd found out that the Bennett children went to a Catholic school called Holy Name on the Upper West Side. Ott hacked into the faculty chat room, where the most popular topic of conversation was *Michael Bennett's getting married!*

Now, this was a pleasant surprise. Finally, a personal commitment guaranteed to take Bennett's mind off the case. Ott took a few handwritten notes rather than risk saving any of the hacked links to his computer. He had no real plan just yet. But he trusted one would come.

Just as Ott reached for his overpriced, bitter coffee, a muscular young man in a black T-shirt and baggy black pants turned to him. Ott tried to decipher the tattoos curling around the man's neck and up his face but couldn't tell what any of them meant.

The tattooed man said, "Yo, dude, nice computer. Why don't you let us use it for a little bit?"

One of the man's tablemates, a scrawny young guy about six feet tall, added, "I promise we'll only keep it for a couple of days." The three girls they were with all laughed at his wit.

Ott didn't think this was funny at all. He hated men like this, almost as much as he hated arrogant American women. He decided the best course of action was to ignore them, and purposely focused his attention back on the screen of his tricked-out Lenovo laptop.

The tattooed man wouldn't leave it alone. He stepped in close to Ott. "I was trying to be nice. Let it seem like you were being generous by giving us your computer. Now I'm just going to take it." He reached for the laptop.

As he did, Ott casually drove the point of his steel tactical pen straight through the middle of the man's hand, pinning it to the wooden table. The tattooed man's eyes popped wide and he gasped.

Ott said in a low voice, "Shout or do anything stupid and this pen goes into your throat. Do you understand?"

The man barely nodded. He was so scared he couldn't even

reach across to pull the pen out of his hand. Ott did it for him with one quick jerk. A tiny spout of blood shot into the air and landed back on the man's hand.

Ott said, "Usually my lessons in manners are more severe and intensive. Did this one do the trick? Are you going to bother people you don't know anymore?"

The tattooed man shook his head.

Ott pulled a wad of napkins off the short stack directly in front of him. He handed it to the man, who wrapped it around his hand. Ott calmly used another napkin to wipe up the blood on the table.

Ott said, "Gather your friends quietly and leave. Right now. If I have to deal with you again, you're going to lose an eye. Understand?"

The man nodded again and did just as he was told. He turned to his friends, cleared his throat, and said, "Let's go."

One of the girls said, "I'm not done yet."

The tattooed man snatched her coffee off the table and they all followed him out the door.

Daniel Ott felt very satisfied with himself.

CHAPTER 58

TO A COP in the middle of a serial killer investigation, sleep is a precious commodity. Which is why I felt frustrated when I sensed a movement near my feet that dragged me out of my dream. I mumbled Mary Catherine's name. Then I heard a man's voice. *What the hell?*

I sprang up, completely disoriented. I wasn't in my bed. I wasn't even in my bedroom. I shook my head, then rubbed my eyes. I felt like a toddler waking up from a nap, unsure of where I was.

Finally, I realized I was lying on the couch in our living room. Remnants of the boys' game night were still evident. Extra chairs were pulled around the Nintendo system, which was still hooked to the TV, and two empty pizza boxes sat neatly stacked on the floor, waiting to be recycled.

I looked to the foot of the couch and realized it was Brian who'd brushed my feet as he gathered up some papers and stuffed them into his backpack.

Brian said in a quiet voice, "It's just me, Dad. My phone was stuck in the couch and I needed some of these papers. Sorry." He stood up and slipped on the backpack. "Why are you sleeping on the couch? Did you have a fight with Mary Catherine?"

I shook my head, actually had to think before I answered, as if I'd been drinking the night before and everything was confused. "I got in late, didn't want to wake her, and the next thing I knew you were here." I looked at the blinds and saw slants of sunshine pushing through the slats. "What time is it?"

"About six thirty in the morning. I think everyone else is still asleep. They've all been really quiet."

That quiet was shattered a few moments later as my other sons all came tumbling out of their rooms. I looked at Brian and said, "Thanks for the gentle wake-up, as opposed to the cymbal clash of our very own Bennett family percussion section."

I stood up and realized I was even still wearing my shoes from the night before. My body was stiff, and I tried to shake out my shoulders. I felt like I was doing a walk of shame when I shambled into the dining room. The girls all smiled. Chrissy jumped up and gave me a hug.

Mary Catherine said in a flat voice, "You need more sleep."

I wanted to say, *No shit.* Instead, I just nodded.

Mary Catherine was serious. "The wedding is sooner than you think. I don't want you making yourself sick from not eating or sleeping right." She walked across the kitchen into the dining room, then kissed me gently on the forehead. "The boys told me you got called out again last night. Did you get a break on the serial killer?"

I shook my head and mumbled, "Just another body."

Mary Catherine spoke up so everyone could hear her. "That's why I instituted a no news policy in this house. There's nothing else on the news these days but the murders. CNN is even starting to cover them." She looked at the bright faces around the dining room table and said, "Does everyone understand?"

There were nods and mumbling as Mary Catherine returned to the kitchen. Not watching the news wasn't a particular hardship on my kids. I plopped into the chair at the end of the table and just listened to the simple chatter between the kids. It was nice to get a sense of what was going on with my family.

Jane looked at her phone and frowned. "Allan didn't text me good night."

Juliana teased her sister. "Give it a rest, Jane. We all know you have a boyfriend."

Fiona added, "And we know he's cute."

Bridget chimed in. "And he plays on the lacrosse team."

Jane knew they were winding her up but couldn't help throwing in "*Captain* of the lacrosse team."

Mary Catherine came back out of the kitchen. "That's enough, girls. Leave your sister alone."

I closed my eyes for a moment and immediately felt myself start to doze off. Instead, I stood up again. "Gotta shower and get back into the office. Lots to do." I clapped my hands together as if I was excited about the prospect.

Mary Catherine gave me a stern look. "You can't sleep for a couple more hours?"

"Afraid not."

"This case won't affect our wedding, will it?"

"No way."

She seemed dubious.

I added, "I promise."

Mary Catherine knew I wouldn't break a promise.

CHAPTER 59

I'D LIKE TO say I was more than ready to face another day when I sat down at my desk in the Manhattan North Homicide office. But that would be a lie. Almost as soon as I sat in my new rolling leather chair—Mary Catherine had ordered it from Office Depot after I complained one too many times about city-issued furniture aggravating my aching back—all I wanted to do was put my head down on the desk and go back to sleep. But a twenty-minute nap would do nothing for me. What I really needed was a two-week nap to get back to normal.

To make matters worse, Brett Hollis seemed to be in a very chipper and pleasant mood. He was wearing an even smaller bandage strip across his nose, humming the theme song to *Game of Thrones* as he reviewed tips that had come in overnight.

I sighed as I looked down at the crime-scene photos from the homicide in SoHo, very impressed that Dan Jackson had already gotten someone to print the images and leave a duplicate set on my desk. It was that kind of cooperative attitude that made the NYPD so effective at solving homicides.

Hollis stepped behind my chair and looked over my shoulder at the photographs. "What did you think of the latest scene?"

"It was most similar to the Staten Island crime scene. Definitely a homicide by a sharp implement of some kind, and the killer stabbed the victim's eye—but her right one, *not* her left. And there was blood around the body, but not spread on the apartment walls. No idea yet if any of the blood came from a second sample either."

"Did you find any rearrangement of the victim's collectibles, any sort of counting message?"

"Nothing at all."

Hollis patted me on the back. "It's all going to work out. You keep saying if we all do our jobs we'll catch this guy. We're all doing our jobs now. I'm going to run down a couple of leads from the tip line in an hour or so. That's *my* job."

I let out a chuckle. He was a good kid. Hollis gave me a wave as he walked toward the conference room.

I looked down at my notes from all the homicides in every city we'd identified and then at the new crime-scene photos from Lila Stein's apartment.

I said a quick prayer for her soul. It was probably the fifth time I had prayed for her since last night.

I craned my neck to glance across the wide squad bay, past a dozen desks with empty chairs. Brett Hollis stood in the conference room, organizing the leads with Task Force Halo. I noticed that Hollis was dressing sharper on the days he worked with the task force. Today he wore a nice Arrow dress shirt with a subtle blue tie. He looked good. I was impressed.

Harry Grissom wanted to recruit the best and brightest into his homicide unit, and as I had already told my boss, Hollis was a keeper. He had that little something extra. He could deal with people. He wrote good reports. And he didn't seem to get overwhelmed by assignments that were outside the box. This was part of what I, like a football scout, was supposed to do in my role as a senior detective: Identify needs and then find the right personnel to fill them. Keep management in the loop.

I couldn't suppress a cringe when I noticed the door to the squad bay open and John Macy stalking through the office. That couldn't be good, though since news of another homicide had broken, I'd expected to see him at some point.

He glanced in my direction but ignored me completely.

He marched past me and into the conference room like a member of command staff. I looked over and saw Hollis, whose expression quickly shifted from pleasant to annoyed and then to angry. He gave me a look I had to interpret through the conference room glass. It was definitely something along the lines of *Please come in here.*

Which was just about the last thing I wanted to do. If I never had to interact with John Macy again, I'd consider the rest of my career a success. But I couldn't leave my partner alone. Especially not when he had made it clear he needed support.

I only hoped not to embarrass Harry again.

CHAPTER 60

I STOOD UP, straightened my shirt, and walked to the conference room with purpose. As soon as I opened the door, I heard Brett Hollis say, "Ask him yourself," as he cut his eyes to me.

I looked at John Macy and said, "What can I do for you?" It was as professional and direct as I could manage.

Macy fumed and did little to hide his annoyance at having to acknowledge I was a living, breathing person. Finally, he stood tall and puffed out his chest a bit. He said, "I need details on the latest homicide in SoHo from our man."

I had to think about how to respond. After a moment, I shrugged and said, "There are certain aspects of the murder that make it appear to be the work of the same killer as in our other cases. However, there are also several details that don't match up. We're going to have to wait for forensic reports to come back before we can say anything definitive. And even then, we're still dealing with a killer who's proven adept at not leaving behind any identifying evidence at crime scenes."

Macy shook his head in disgust. "Typical."

"Typical of what?" My voice was taking on a sharper tone already. "Typical of the cop who doesn't want to be skewered for rushing to judgment? You're not a fellow cop I can discuss theories with. You're a politician. I don't trust you not to run off and tell the mayor about a theory I later discover was mistaken. So all I can do is tell you the facts as I know them."

Macy folded his arms in front of him and cranked his condescending tone up to say, "What if you took a guess? Something no one can hold you responsible for." He deliberately slowed down and over-enunciated each of his next words. "Do you think that this homicide is the work of the same killer?"

I looked at Hollis, took a deep breath, and said, "No. I don't think it's the same killer." There, it was out in the open.

For a moment, Macy just stared at me. Then he argued, "I read the initial memo. The victim was fatally slashed and then stabbed in the eye. It *has* to be our killer."

"Wrong," I shot back. "It doesn't *have* to be anything. Look, you asked for my opinion and I gave it. Overall, that whole crime scene just doesn't feel like the work of our killer."

Macy was incredulous. "Now crime scenes have emotions?"

"Credit me with some experience."

Macy nodded his head reluctantly. Arms still folded across his chest.

I continued. "Crime scenes usually show the underlying personality of the killer, especially when we're dealing with serial killers."

Hollis chimed in. "That's correct. My research has shown that a particular killer's MO is often reflected in the scene he leaves behind. Some killers rush, and others take their time. Some killers have serious OCD and the compulsions are reflected in their murder scenes. Maybe the victim's body has to be laid out in a certain way, or the wounds must be inflicted at exactly the same angle every time."

I picked the thread of the conversation back up. "And in this case, while the crime scenes in SoHo and Staten Island seem similar to each other, they don't really seem like any of the others. The differences are significant enough that we can't discount the possibility that they are the work of a second killer."

Macy said, "Are you shitting me? Now you're saying not only that you don't think this most recent murder is part of the pattern but that you don't even think the Staten Island murder is related?" A vein on his forehead started to throb. "A second-killer theory is not going to fly. Do you have any idea what kind of panic that will cause?"

I didn't know what more to say. "Just giving you my experienced opinion. Obviously you're going to have one of your own."

"This is no time for a standoff, Bennett," Macy said. "We need results. Go get some. Now."

With that statement of the obvious, Macy was out the door.

Hollis was next. He sighed and wiped his face. "That was a serious dick-waving contest," he said. "I gotta get out of here for a few minutes. I'm running down those leads I mentioned. All of them are fairly close by and shouldn't take me too long."

"I'll go with you."

Hollis shook his head. "I got this. I can handle a simple lead or two." He winked and patted me on the shoulder, leaving me in charge of the Task Force Halo headquarters.

Four victims—six, if I was wrong about the second killer— and zero suspects. The numbers didn't look good.

CHAPTER 61

DANIEL OTT FOUND himself in the Manhattanville neighborhood of West Harlem, standing outside the building that housed Michael Bennett's Manhattan North Homicide unit. He stood next to a steel support for the elevated train that ran directly across the street from the building.

There were cars parked under the track for blocks in each direction. Many of them looked like police vehicles. A lot of Ford Crown Victorias and Chevy Impalas. He supposed that was one of the main perks of working this far uptown: parking. Apparently free parking. Something that was pretty much lacking everywhere else on the island of Manhattan.

Ott had handled quite a lot of surveillance over the years. With the exception of his first, spontaneous kill and the librarian's unexpected friend—his loose end's loose end—he always researched his victims' movements and habits. But none of them had ever had the slightest idea that Ott was watching them. None of that was as serious as what he was doing now, surveilling a police officer.

He stared across the street at the entrance to the office building. There was a furniture truck in the midst of a delivery. The crew had set several temporary ramps next to curbs so they could roll all kinds of office equipment into the building. There were three stacks of chairs on specialized dollies, each stack more than six feet tall. On separate dollies rested two desks, turned on their sides so that they too rose almost six feet in the air. Everything on the sidewalk was some sort of obstruction.

Great.

Daniel Ott didn't want to be here, watching the building. He was supposed to be at work in Queens, though really, he was ready to get home. He wanted to see his girls. But Bennett was getting too close to identifying him. And he had to admit he did feel a twinge of excitement as he bounced several plans through his head. What could he do to disrupt the investigation, starting right now?

As he watched, he spotted the young detective he'd seen with Bennett at the library, the one with the broken nose, stroll out the front of the building. Today the man wore a blue shirt and tie, and was walking with a woman in a bright yellow skirt. Ott could tell by their body language that the two young people were attracted to each other.

They stopped on the sidewalk near all the office furniture. They stood right on the curb as a bus whizzed past them, yet they barely noticed. The detective said something and smiled. The young woman laughed and placed her hand on his arm.

Another bus rolled past. Ott lost sight of the couple for a few seconds. Then an idea popped into his head.

He crossed the street quickly. He had to balance patience with speed. He wove through the office furniture deliveries, using them as cover to obscure his approach, though they also blocked his vision. Each time the couple shifted position as they continued their animated conversation, Ott lost sight of them.

Ott pulled from his pocket a pair of rubber surgical gloves and, with his gloved right hand, extracted his Gerber folding knife and opened the blade.

Then he heard the hiss of air brakes and a diesel engine. Another of the fast-moving buses coming this way. Ott couldn't believe the timing. He closed the knife and stepped over one of the small ramps lying on the sidewalk. He took a moment behind one of the chair stacks to calculate how fast the bus was moving. The big diesel unit looked to be gaining speed quickly.

All Ott had to do was knock the detective into the middle of the street, where the bus would have no choice but to make him a headline in tomorrow's paper.

The time was now. Ott stepped quickly from behind the stack of chairs, his head down and his legs driving. But he lost his bearings slightly when sidestepping a ramp, and realized that instead of the detective, he was about to run into the woman in the yellow skirt.

Ott tried to redirect or slow his charge, but it was too late. His shoulder connected with the woman's midsection and she let out a loud gasp as he knocked the wind out of her. The woman staggered from the blow and stepped awkwardly from the curb onto the asphalt.

Ott had screwed up. There was no other way to view it. He just stood there, frozen.

Then, unexpectedly, the young detective darted off the

sidewalk and jumped into the street, pushing the woman out of the path of the bus.

The bus driver stomped on the brakes. The big vehicle skidded sideways.

The detective barely had time to look up as the flat nose of the bus struck him squarely, sending his body flying a good fifteen feet, arms and legs flailing as if taking flight...before hitting the ground with a tumbling thud. The bus managed to stop about five feet from the spot where the young man's body now lay in the middle of the street.

The detective's left leg was bent at a sickening angle. His right arm flopped behind his back.

Ott didn't wait to see anything more. He casually turned and walked away from the bus. He didn't rush—remembering how his mistake in the library had gotten him spotted by Bennett—but he didn't waste time either.

He was more than two blocks away when he heard the first siren rushing to the scene.

CHAPTER 62

IT'S NOT EXACTLY unusual for cops to get hurt—or worse—on the job, so this was hardly my first time at the Columbia University Medical Center. But getting exiled from the emergency room and sent to the waiting room was new.

I had raced downstairs from our offices as soon as I'd heard the sickening sound of the bus hitting something, then skidding to a stop. Not that I'd expected to find my partner, of all people, flat on the ground in the middle of the road, limbs akimbo.

I rode in the ambulance with Brett Hollis and had been raising hell to make sure he got the best care. Though maybe I raised a little too much hell, actually, since an Asian American doctor told me that if I didn't get out of the ER, she'd cut the tendons in the back of my leg. I didn't believe her completely, but then again, I wasn't going to bet my mobility on it.

The waiting room seemed especially crowded. Mainly with

patients, but there was also a large contingent of NYPD people in one corner, including a couple of eyewitnesses to Hollis's injury who were saying the incident was no accident. I would need to interview them later.

I saw Harry Grissom talking to a twenty-something woman in a vibrant yellow skirt, whom I vaguely recognized as someone who worked on one of the lower floors in our building.

I also spotted a woman who appeared to be in her mid fifties sitting on the outskirts of the NYPD crowd. She had dark hair and was using a Kleenex to wipe her eyes. She looked familiar, and I realized I recognized her from the family photographs Hollis kept on his desk.

I stepped over to her and said, "Excuse me. I'm Michael Bennett. Are you related to Brett Hollis?"

The woman looked up at me, nodding, and said, "Ann Hollis, Brett's mom. He's told me all about you." She clearly didn't want to say too much for fear of breaking down.

I sat in the empty chair next to her. "I'm so sorry about Brett. I rode in the ambulance here with him, but he was only conscious enough to hold on to my hand."

"The ER doctor gave me a list of his injuries, but I haven't heard anything more. Have you?"

"She didn't even tell me that much, but I'm only his NYPD partner. You're his next of kin."

A tear ran down her left cheek as she looked at me and said, "It's about what you expect from this kind of accident. Shattered pelvis, broken leg, broken arm, concussion. Plus he cracked a front tooth and broke his nose again."

She seemed on the edge of a meltdown. I understood. I would have already melted if this had happened to one of my kids.

She started to sob, and I put my arm around her. Most veteran cops have done some time in a waiting room, comforting the loved ones of fellow cops who'd been injured on the job.

As I sat there, holding my partner's mother, my mind drifted. First, to Hollis's injuries, and his chances of recovery. Yet with the pressure from the mayor's office mounting, it was hard not to make a mental to-do list of next steps in the investigation. Even as a woman literally cried on my shoulder.

Harry caught my eye, and I excused myself from Mrs. Hollis. The lieutenant led me into the hallway, away from the commotion of the waiting room.

Harry nodded over at the woman he'd been talking to earlier, who was now also dabbing her eyes with a Kleenex. "The young lady in yellow over there, Kelly Konick, tells me that Hollis jumped into the road to save her when she was knocked into the street, and he got hit instead."

I was not surprised to hear that Hollis had been injured in an act of bravery. He had already impressed me, and I'd told Grissom as much, but his actions today were in line with the best of the NYPD.

"Ms. Konick says she thinks someone pushed her. Intentionally. But she didn't get a good look at who it was." Harry paused. "It's all speculation right now. But do you think this might've had anything to do with your case?"

I thought about it for a minute and said, "I have no idea. But if it *was* related to us, why would the guy push her and not Hollis?"

I couldn't help but wonder if it was a simple accident. Were we being paranoid? I thought back to the man I saw rushing from the computer room in the library, the strong feeling I'd had that he might be the killer. He had evaded detection that day, but he may have changed course. Instead of trying to outrun the investigation, maybe he was attempting to derail it. But that was crazy talk.

Wasn't it?

CHAPTER 63

BY THE TIME I left the hospital, I was emotionally spent. I'd stayed with Brett Hollis's mother while her son was in surgery. Mrs. Hollis had told me what a good soccer player and student he'd been in school. She dropped in that the only thing he'd ever wanted to do was be a detective. Even after graduating from NYU and getting job offers in the private sector for more money, her Brett wanted to feel like he was contributing.

By the late afternoon, a surgeon who hadn't bothered to change her bloody blue scrubs found Mrs. Hollis in the waiting room. I stayed with her to hear the news.

The doctor had sharp, clear eyes that focused solely on Mrs. Hollis. She said, "We've done everything we can do for today. We stopped all the internal bleeding and set some of the simple breaks. Tonight, an orthopedic surgeon will set his pelvis and left leg. And his nose is going to need plastic surgery. You can go up and visit him in a few minutes, but don't expect much in the way of conversation."

I appreciated the doctor's direct, comprehensive delivery. Hollis's mother and I walked up to the recovery room together. My partner, prone on his hospital bed, looked wrecked. He'd live, thank God, but he was facing a brutal recovery. I stood with Mrs. Hollis for a few minutes while she navigated the tubes and machines, held her son's hand, and spoke to him quietly.

I said a few silent prayers over him, then eventually slipped out to return home to my own family, where I spent that evening laughing and playing games with Mary Catherine and my children, grateful for every minute of it. But even through my happiness, an unease took hold in the back of my mind, and it only intensified overnight.

I woke up troubled, staring at the white ceiling as Mary Catherine snored peacefully next to me. The familiar sound was calming.

The first rays of sunlight crept through the blinds, and then stark reality flooded in.

We had a copycat killer on our hands.

It was the only explanation. This killer had at least two victims. Maybe more. There could be more bodies that hadn't been discovered yet.

I managed to get up, dressed, and out the door without waking anyone else. Which in my apartment is a real accomplishment, no matter what time you attempt it.

I was at my desk, going over everything I had on the Staten Island and SoHo homicides, when Harry Grissom walked into the office.

He stopped and looked at me. Then he checked his watch. "What the hell are you doing here so early?"

"Me? What about you? I thought elderly people needed as much sleep as they could get."

"Funny. I wonder how hard you'd be laughing if I had you organize all the files according to suspect description and number of reports written."

I patted the wooden chair next to my desk. He took a seat cautiously. Then, without pretext, I explained my copycat killer theory.

I pulled out the photos of the two victims from Staten Island and SoHo, Marilyn Shaw and Lila Stein. I set them on the desktop so Harry could see them clearly. "We have to be sure."

Harry shook his head. "I never have to worry about much. You take on enough for both of us."

CHAPTER 64

I DIDN'T WASTE much more time around the office. I was in my car, headed to Staten Island, just as the morning rush hour was picking up.

Detective Raina Rayesh was on the scene of a shooting in the Elm Park area and couldn't meet me at Marilyn Shaw's apartment, but she gave me her blessing to do a follow-up. I appreciated it. In police work, you never want to do anything that gives the appearance of trying to steal someone else's case. So if a colleague gives permission for a follow-up, it signals complete trust.

I was standing outside the apartment, trying to get a feel for what the killer might have seen when looking at the building. As I stood there, a tall Hispanic man stepped out of the main door and walked right up to me. "Can I help you, Detective?" he said with a light accent.

I gave the man a bemused look. "How'd you know I was NYPD?"

"Since that poor girl was killed, most all of the people coming around here are detectives or media types, or rubbernecker creeps. Besides, you look like a cop. And you're driving an Impala."

I laughed. The friendly man turned out to be the building super, and he gave me a tour of the building before we went to Marilyn's apartment.

We stepped around the crime-scene tape, and as the super opened the door, he said, "Nothing's been touched. Once the investigation wraps, I don't know how I'll ever rent this apartment again. Landlords are supposed to tell potential tenants if a violent crime happened in an apartment. It's a tough sales pitch."

"Can't argue that," I said.

"I get it, of course. And God knows I'm not the only one struggling with that these days," the super said ruefully, raising his eyebrows in acknowledgment of the recent murders all across the city.

He told me to pull the door shut when I was done, and I thanked him, then suddenly found myself alone in the apartment. Once again, I noticed the relative tidiness of the scene, especially compared to Chloe's and Elaine's apartments—no blood smeared on the walls, nothing really excessive aside from a significantly sized rusty-brown stain on the hardwood, about six feet from the door.

Such death markers always saddened me—the loss they represented, the people who would miss out on the rest of their lives. If I ever stopped feeling that way, I'd retire. The desire to obtain justice for these victims is what gets homicide detectives like me out of bed in the morning. Unfortunately, it's also what keeps homicide detectives like me awake at night.

I checked the apartment thoroughly but didn't see anything that looked like it could be one of the *counting messages* Hollis and I were sure our killer had left at the other scenes. Marilyn Shaw would have been the fifth victim in New York, after Elaine. The super said nothing in the apartment had been touched, and I believed him, so I couldn't attribute it to anything having been accidentally disturbed either.

I wandered over to inspect a huge array of framed photographs sitting on a shelf along one wall of the living room, all in artistically jumbled rows, with no obvious gaps visible. Marilyn Shaw appeared to have been a very pretty brunette who was present in most of the pictures, along with people I guessed were her parents, her friends, her siblings, and presumably a bunch of nephews. She looked like someone with no worries. These are the kinds of photos that make a homicide detective even more determined.

One photo in the back caught my attention. It was of Marilyn wearing a New York Giants jersey, standing in a sports bar with a TV playing a baseball game directly behind her. A light-haired man was standing next to her, his arms wrapped around her and his smiling face half hidden by her shoulder.

I was surprised to recognize the bar—a place far from Staten Island, much closer to my place on the Upper West Side. It was a spot near Morningside Park on Manhattan Avenue. I used to take my kids there. They had decent food, but the real draw was their collection of old-fashioned games like Skee-Ball and pinball, which the kids loved.

I pulled out my smartphone and took a picture of Marilyn's photo for my records. Who was the man with her in the picture? Why had this photo meant enough for her to print and frame it?

Something told me this could be important.

CHAPTER 65

I DROVE DIRECTLY from the crime scene on Staten Island to Lila Stein's apartment in SoHo. I'd called ahead, and Detective Dan Jackson was waiting in front of the Asian grocery store as I pulled up. The big detective was chatting amiably with a shorter man, the store owner.

Jackson introduced us. The man's name was Tom, and he was a second-generation Chinese American with a little bit of a New Jersey accent he joked he'd picked up while in college at Rutgers. Tom was also the apartment manager, so he gave us a key. As on Staten Island, this apartment was still an active crime scene so had not been touched.

"You really think there's a copycat?" Jackson asked me as we climbed the stairs.

"I wouldn't be here talking to you if I didn't."

We ducked the crime-scene tape and entered the apartment.

I went straight to the long library table in the main space that held Lila Stein's personal mementos: a glass plaque she'd received for being court clerk of the year; a ceramic dog that looked like a niece or nephew had made it; and half a dozen framed photographs.

As at Marilyn's apartment, I could find no evidence that any of Lila's possessions had been grouped in any sort of deliberate way by her killer. I looked over the photographs on the table. I saw Lila and her parents, the older couple standing proudly on either side of their pretty daughter. Lila and her sorority sisters, all cheering for something together. Lila and the Eiffel Tower, the Grand Canyon, at the beach—all trips she'd taken. But when I spotted another photo in the back, I thought I was suffering déjà vu. I reached back and picked it up, immediately recognizing the background—*and* the man standing beside Lila, again with his arms around her, but turned in profile.

Jackson said, "Of all the photos, what's so special about that one?"

I pointed at the photo, running my finger along the upper edge. "See all the NFL logos around the mirror? I know this place," I said, explaining that it was a restaurant/sports bar uptown where I took my kids to play games. I took a photo of Lila's picture, just as I had the one on Staten Island, then set the frame back down.

Jackson said, "You think it means something?"

"I'm working on a theory." I didn't fill Jackson in just yet, or tell him about the other photo I'd found at Marilyn's place. I told him I might call him later.

Jackson slapped me on the back and said, "There's nothing I would rather do on my twins' birthday than follow you around on interviews. I'll leave my phone on."

CHAPTER 66

I WASTED NO time speeding uptown. Neither photograph seemed to have been taken very long ago. Maybe someone at the bar would remember seeing the same man there with two different women. You never knew until you asked.

I parked on the street. It was a little before noon, so when I went through the open door, the place was so empty I thought they might still be closed. Then the portly manager, whom I used to see all the time, wobbled into view from the kitchen.

He looked at me for a moment, then recognition dawned on him. A broad smile swept across his face. "Here by yourself? Where are all those beautiful kids of yours? I'm lucky I didn't go bankrupt when you stopped coming by." He let out a good cackle.

I approached him and stuck out my hand. As we shook, I said, "We'd still be coming, but you know how it goes—as they get older, there are more and more school and sports events we've got to go to."

The manager grinned. "Maybe I can lure you back with a good hamburger for lunch."

I started to shake my head.

The manager said, "Some homemade lemon chicken salad?"

"I'm actually not here to eat. You remember I'm with the NYPD, right?"

He nodded carefully. The kind of nod cops get from people who think they might be suspects and start doing a mental rewind of their recent past. That kind of self-censoring slows down investigations.

I eased his mind. "I'm looking into a pair of homicides. The one thing they had in common was a photograph taken at this bar." I showed him both photos on my phone. "The same man appears in both of them, though it's hard to get a good look at his face."

The chubby man studied the photos carefully, then looked over his shoulder to confirm exactly where in the bar they'd been taken. He wasted no time in leading me over to a hallway that featured a couple of Pop-A-Shot games. "Here's where one photo was taken. I can tell by the TV in the back. The other was obviously taken near the bar. You can see the mirror and all of our NFL gear."

"Do you think we could figure out *when* these photos were taken?"

"I dunno…maybe you can figure out the date of the game going on behind the girl? I can see it's the Yankees and the Red Sox."

I sat at the bar, checked a few websites, and made a few calls.

I was able to figure out the six dates when the Yankees and Red Sox had played recently. All of the games had broadcast on the same channel here, and all had started at 7 p.m. And all the dates were within the last two months. I was onto something.

Lunchtime business in the bar picked up while I was busy on the phone. To his credit, the manager kept himself free to help me if I needed it. We searched through the security videos he had on hand. Of the six dates, he still had security videos from four of the nights.

He set me up in his rear office with a computer. He even brought me a Coke and a sandwich. We both figured I was going to be here awhile.

I started watching the first security video, and fast-forwarded to 7 p.m. I couldn't believe my luck—I struck pay dirt within two minutes. I was easily able to identify Marilyn Shaw from her photograph, and barely another minute of searching turned up the man who appeared in both Lila's and Marilyn's photos. He was a tall white man with sandy hair and an athletic build, and looked to be in his mid to late thirties.

I tried to get a feel for their relationship. They held hands and laughed together, and while the video wasn't perfect, I was at least able to pull some full-face stills of the mystery man off of it and run them through the state photo-ID database.

Then fate stepped in.

CHAPTER 67

AS A PHILOSOPHY major, I've read dozens of quotes about fate. How it favors one person over another. Some sayings assert that fate favors the prepared. Or the determined. Or the virtuous. But often it simply favors the lucky. There's no other way to explain it. And every homicide detective in the world will admit to having a number of cases solved by lucky breaks.

I'd just gotten back to my car when my phone rang. The number was an NYPD exchange, and it turned out to be main dispatch sending through a call from a uniformed patrol officer named Janelle Gibbs.

Officer Gibbs said, "Detective Bennett, I'm sorry to bother you, but I just heard something odd at a domestic and I thought I should pass it along to you."

"It's no bother. Whatcha got?"

"I'm in Brooklyn, in Cobble Hill, at a nice brownstone. Like I said, I got called to this domestic. The husband left and the wife is really, really pissed off."

"I'm listening."

"She confronted her husband about some burner phones she found in the house. He threatened her and stormed out. But the wife's no dummy. She knew they were phones he used for girlfriends." Officer Gibbs sounded sharp. "Anyway, she found out one of the girlfriends' names, and when she told it to me, I recognized it as being the same as one of the victims murdered by that serial killer you're investigating."

"What was the victim's name?"

"Marilyn Shaw."

I felt a rush of excitement. *Can this be the mystery man from Marilyn's—and Lila's—photo?*

"I'll be right there. Don't leave and don't give any info to the wife."

"No problem. I told her I'd be writing reports in my car for a little bit. She's busy with a toddler anyway."

Officer Gibbs gave me the address and I was on my way, yet another trek from one end of the city to the other. I was starting to feel like an Uber driver. In this case, I caught a lucky break and found the FDR open all the way down to the Brooklyn Bridge.

Officer Gibbs was a tall, attractive black woman who seemed way too young to be a cop. Or maybe I was just getting older. I could tell by the look on her face that Gibbs was shocked I'd gotten to the brownstone in Cobble Hill so quickly after her call.

But she had her shit together. She had the info all ready and laid out for me as I walked up.

"The wife is inside with the kid. I haven't reached out to the husband," Officer Gibbs said as she concluded her report.

"You've done a tremendous job. Do you mind coming up to the house with me? Sounds like you and the wife already have a rapport. I don't want to intimidate her."

As we climbed the stairs to the top of the stoop, a woman with messy brown hair stepped out of the open front door with a little boy in her arms.

"Mrs. Cedar, this is Detective Bennett," Officer Gibbs said.

"Please, call me Lauren," the woman said. She hefted the toddler on her hip. "And this is Tyler."

Tyler had blond hair and big, beautiful brown eyes. He smiled, then giggled when I tickled his bare feet.

"Come on inside," Lauren told us.

As soon as I stepped into the living room and looked at the photos lined up on the small fireplace mantel, I had the confirmation I needed, that Lauren Cedar's husband was definitely the same man from the sports bar.

I talked to her for a minute more but didn't want to give out too much information. She was still shaken.

Lauren sniffled, recounting for me the outburst from her husband that had prompted the call to the police. It had started when she found a couple of burner cell phones and confronted him with them, accusing him of cheating on her. Instead of denying it, he'd gone on the offensive, yelling and throwing things around.

She said, "I told him he was being too loud and that he was scaring Tyler. That he was even scaring *me*. You know what he said?"

I shook my head.

"He said that Tyler and I *should* be terrified of him. Then he grabbed my arm and jerked me back into the kitchen." She pulled up the sleeve of her blouse and showed me her right arm, where a perfect imprint of a large hand was already turning into a bluish bruise.

I asked a few more questions and wrote down the information she gave me.

Her husband, Jeffrey Cedar, was an attorney in lower Manhattan, and according to his wife, he was a lying piece of shit.

Which certainly seemed true.

But I was growing more and more convinced that this lying piece of shit might actually be a killer.

My only real question was whether he'd killed them all.

CHAPTER 68

JEFFREY CEDAR SAT in his law office not far from the criminal courthouse in lower Manhattan. He was finding it difficult to concentrate on the client sitting across from him. He'd had an argument with his wife that morning after she questioned where he went at night when he said he was working. Then she accused him of cheating on her. She'd found a couple of the burner phones he often used to stay in touch with the different women he met. He always took care to bring these women to places far from Cobble Hill or lower Manhattan—anywhere, really, as long as it wasn't the kind of spot his wife would ever have any interest in going.

But this morning, no matter what he said or how loud he said it, his wife just wasn't buying it. She seemed to be spinning off the rails, she was so upset. He even had to grab her arms and hold her still just to get her to listen to him. That, added to the sound of his son wailing, had started his day off on a sour note. And it didn't feel like it was getting any better.

Once, about three years ago, Jeffrey had smacked Lauren in the face after she refused to stop nagging him. The blow had left a mark on her cheek for over a week, and he'd had to keep her at home for fear of getting arrested for domestic abuse. Even worse, she'd been pregnant with Tyler at the time. But he'd learned from his mistake. Now he was always careful. Subtle. Never did anything that would show up on his wife's face.

Jeffrey returned his focus to the client sitting at his desk. He twirled his pen in his left hand as he listened to the young man across from him explain that he wasn't actually "dealing" drugs so much as he was "redistributing" them for someone else.

Jeffrey felt like his degree from Syracuse put him a notch above a lot of the other bottom-feeders in the criminal justice system. He did admit to some jealousy at the NYU and Columbia grads working at the big firms. But he'd found his niche and was doing fine on his own. He usually wouldn't even take on a low-end dealer client like this kid, except that said kid's parents had plenty of cash and had thrown a big chunk of it at Jeffrey to clear their son of the drug charges against him.

He tuned in to hear some of what his client was droning on and on about. "The damn cops took my entire stash. All of it. I couldn't believe what dicks they were."

"It sounds like we're going to have to cut a deal, Jason," Jeffrey told him. "It's too hard to explain why you were holding so much heroin and four thousand dollars in cash."

"All I was doing was helping someone out. They needed this stuff delivered. I didn't negotiate with no one. I didn't force no one. All I did was deliver."

"And now, unfortunately, that solid work ethic is going to have to be put on hold for one to five years."

Jeffrey wrapped up that meeting with his disgruntled client and, a few hours later, found himself listening to another douchebag talk about how he had been railroaded. He felt like he'd been listening to this particular pitiful client all day, though they'd been meeting for only about forty minutes.

The client insisted on sticking to the story that his eight-year-old niece was making a wild and unsubstantiated accusation against him. He was outraged that the police had arrested him on the word of a child. He never brought up the fact that forensics had found semen on one of the girl's dresses and that two different psychological assessments had determined the niece was rational and telling the truth.

Jeffrey put on a show for the client, who was already paying an exorbitant rate for his services. "I think we can work this out. It's going to take some extra time on my part. And I'm afraid I can't make any absolute promises. I will, however, need a much larger retainer to pursue the case the way I think it should be pursued."

Without a word, the douchebag client reached into the front pocket of his baggy pants and pulled out a checkbook. Jeffrey had already run the guy's credit score and talked to him about what assets could be open to a civil judgment if his wife's sister's family sued him. Using that as a cover story, he'd learned the guy had more than three hundred thousand dollars in a 401(k) plan and another thirty-five thousand dollars in liquid investments. The only real calculation Jeffrey made was how much he could ask for without scaring the client off. It was almost like betting on a hand in Texas hold 'em poker. If you raised too much, the suckers at the table tended to fold.

When he saw the hesitation on his client's face, Jeffrey said, "I can almost guarantee, no matter what happens, you won't do any jail time. I can point out your record of employment, no previous convictions, and I assume you will be able to get character witnesses to speak on your behalf."

The client nodded solemnly, his long brown hair flopping in front of his face.

Damn, Jeffrey Cedar thought, *this bluff is almost too easy.*

CHAPTER 69

ONCE AGAIN, I was back in my car, returning to Manhattan. Between using my phone, speeding, and no doubt driving recklessly, I was violating a few traffic laws.

I wanted to wait to call in backup until I verified a little more information. I contacted the analyst in our squad and had her run the name Jeffrey Cedar in every database she could access. I had to learn everything I could about this guy before I pulled up to his office.

What I got back was the information that Cedar was thirty-seven years old, had worked as a prosecutor for one year, and then had moved to private practice in the same office for almost nine years. He had been disciplined twice by the state bar, once for misrepresenting his relationship with a witness and once for trying to keep money the government had seized when they agreed to return it to his client. But as was the case with most bar complaints, not much had been done about either ethical lapse. Both times he'd just been put on probation for three months.

He'd also received a number of traffic violations and a bushel of parking tickets, but nothing outstanding.

None of this painted a picture of a homicidal maniac to me. But I did recall the fear in Lauren Cedar's eyes when she talked about her husband. To me, any kind of domestic violence is an indicator of a much more serious problem.

Cedar's office was a few blocks west of the criminal courthouse. Although the twelve-story building looked well-maintained, it had an older fire escape that wrapped around the sides of it like an awkward, rusty snake. To update it would cost a fortune, but it might be worth it. I wouldn't have called it a luxury or high-end building, but it was clearly occupied by professionals.

I lingered in the lobby for a moment and looked at the tenant listing, which was displayed in a glass-paneled case by the elevator. There were at least a dozen attorneys, a couple of architects, an accounting firm that looked like it took up an entire floor, and a couple of administrative offices. I found a listing that had several names on it, including Cedar's. He was on the fifth floor, so I took the elevator up there and found another door with the same names on it when I exited the elevator. As soon as I opened the door, however, I figured out it wasn't a firm—it was just three attorneys sharing a receptionist.

The receptionist looked up and smiled, giving me a very professional "May I help you?"

I smiled back. I wanted to keep this friendly—at least for now. "I need to speak with Jeffrey Cedar."

Her eyes darted to her appointment book, then to the closed door on my left. "Do you have an appointment?"

"I do not." I pulled out my badge. "I just need to ask him a couple of quick questions."

She made no pretense of hiding her phone as she texted someone and received a message in return. She then smoothly informed me, "Mr. Cedar is with a client at the moment."

"I'll wait." I suppressed a smile at the receptionist's uncomfortable squirm in her desk chair.

The receptionist texted some more. I was only mildly worried about Cedar trying to avoid me. My bet was that he would definitely consider himself more than capable of talking his way out of the domestic dispute he probably assumed I was here regarding.

A few minutes later, the door opened and I saw a middle-aged man with long brown hair walk out. He turned in the doorway and said, "Thanks, Jeff. I feel a lot better now."

I popped up before the lawyer could close his door. I could hear the receptionist calling out to me as I pushed Cedar's door open.

I found myself inside a large, comfortable office, staring right at the man I'd seen on the video from the sports bar, in photographs at Lila Stein's and Marilyn Shaw's apartments, as well as at the home he shared with his wife and son.

I still had my badge in my hand. I held it up and said, "Are you Jeffrey Cedar?"

He tried to smile as he stood up. "Officer, is this about my argument this morning?"

"With your wife?"

I could see the relief in his face. What criminal defense attorney couldn't talk his way out of a domestic dispute? I let him relax. His confidence would be his undoing.

I waited a moment before I burst his bubble, then said, "No, this is not about your wife. It's about Marilyn Shaw."

For starters, I thought. This man had a lot to explain, or he'd be pinned for multiple homicides. He was an attorney who'd thought he could walk a tightrope. He had just fallen off, and there was no safety net.

Cedar said, "Who?"

I held up one of the still photos I'd gotten from the sports bar security system. It clearly showed Cedar and Marilyn holding hands.

He tried to act casual. "Oh, you mean Mary. I'd be happy to talk about anything you want. I'm just a little busy right now." He casually picked up his mug of coffee from his desk. "Maybe we can schedule a meeting later."

"Nope."

"Excuse me?"

I spoke slowly. "I want to talk to you right now."

That frustrated Cedar. He sighed and looked away. Then he said, "Not without my attorney."

"Okay, who's your attorney?"

That's when Cedar surprised me. I mean, big-time. By committing the fresh offense of assaulting an officer.

With his left hand, he flung his warm coffee in my face in a smooth motion, then used the heavy mug to swat me across the temple. It felt like a bomb going off right next to me. I saw streaks of light and heard the heavy ringing of a head injury.

Yet even as I felt myself falling, I knew to block Cedar's exit. I felt for the door and shoved it closed as I hit the thick carpet. With what energy and clarity I had left, I rolled toward the door so Cedar couldn't open it.

I kept my right eye open as I reached for my Glock. I couldn't risk him coming at me again. If he managed to kick me in the throat, I'd be done.

Once again, I was surprised by the guy.

Cedar saw my movement as I reached for my weapon, and he panicked. He raced across the room, opened a tall window, kicked out the screen, and jumped.

CHAPTER 70

JUST AS I managed to get to my feet, the receptionist burst through the door.

"Jeffrey!" she called, rushing to the open window. Her voice was filled with emotion—not shock, but something deeper. Her boss's bizarre exit meant something more to her than just a disappearing paycheck.

I was right behind her. I still couldn't believe that the low-rent attorney had jumped. Not far, though, it turned out. The fire escape was less than three feet below the windowsill.

Craning my head—still dizzy from the blow Cedar had dealt—out the window, I saw my assailant making his way down the old fire escape. He was already two floors below us and moving fast.

I didn't like the look of the drop from the fire escape. But I had no choice. I couldn't risk him escaping arrest. Not if he was our killer.

I got on my phone and called dispatch directly. As soon as someone came on the line, I said quickly, "This is Detective Michael Bennett of Manhattan North Homicide. I have a suspect on the run. His name is Jeffrey Cedar, thirty-seven years old. White male, over six feet, sandy hair." I gave my location and told the dispatcher to get some patrol cars headed my way. Immediately. And to have the office building locked down. The receptionist could not be allowed to leave the premises.

My forehead was throbbing. I'd definitely have a bump where Cedar had hit me. I crawled out of the office window and onto the fire escape. I immediately regretted it. My acrophobia kicked in big-time. I'm not fond of heights. As soon as I took a few steps down the fire escape toward the fleeing man, I realized I could have taken the internal stairs. But on the other hand, if I didn't keep Cedar in sight, who knows what direction he'd run—and then I'd have no chance of finding him.

I focused on making sure my feet connected with each metal step as I carefully but quickly climbed down the fire escape. I had a little spin in my vision, the world swirling as I took in the distance to the ground. The sounds of the city faded to a soft white noise. My determination to get justice for Cedar's victims pushed through any fears I had.

I'd just about reached the third floor when Cedar managed to make the jump down to the narrow road below.

He never once looked back, although he must have heard the clattering sound of my footsteps in pursuit. I guess he thought he'd hit me hard enough to slow me down. Like I said, his confidence would be his undoing.

CHAPTER 71

MY LEGS WEREN'T quite as shaky by the time I made it to the fire escape's second floor. I had just seen Jeffrey Cedar running through the street and around the corner of a building. I knew he was headed west.

Once I landed on solid ground, I felt my stomach rumble like I'd just gotten off the Cyclone in Coney Island. I was panting. I swallowed the feeling and kept going.

My rubber-soled work shoes are not dedicated running shoes, but I made it to the street and turned the corner in an all-out sprint. I didn't shout or draw attention to myself. Cedar wasn't going to stop at the command *Stop! Police!* Instead, I relied on my running ability to close the distance.

My plan went into the toilet once Cedar looked behind him and saw me gaining ground. Then he shoved aside a couple of people next to him and picked up the pace from a fast lope to a mad dash.

I looked around, hoping one of the patrol cars I had called for would come roaring up and save the day. That didn't appear likely at this moment. I had to keep running. I could feel the sweat bead on my forehead and my lungs start to burn as I pushed my own pace.

Cedar was almost a block ahead of me now. All I could do was look for his white shirt. Then he came to a sudden stop. I thought he might be surrendering. Or maybe he pulled a muscle. Instead, he turned to his right and grabbed a messenger just getting on a bicycle.

Cedar threw the guy to the ground, then jumped on the bike awkwardly. The seat was set to the messenger's much shorter height, not Cedar's large frame, but he still got moving pretty fast. There was no way I could catch him.

Just as I came to this conclusion, I reached a stand marked CITI BIKE. A woman was sliding one of the blue unisex bikes popular with commuters and tourists into one of the slots. Before the locking mechanism could click into place, I shouted, "Excuse me! I'm sorry!" as I grabbed her bike and hopped onto it. It was a little low for me as well. But I stood on the pedals and started pumping for everything I was worth. I called over my shoulder to the woman, "I'll return it, I promise!"

I had to dodge two men who tried to gallantly stop me. I didn't even bother yelling *Police* or *NYPD*. I just threaded the needle between the men trying to grab me, and found myself about a block behind Jeffrey Cedar.

I fell into a rhythm on the bike and realized once again how much riding with Mary Catherine had helped my stamina as well as my leg strength. I started to close in on Cedar. Now we were almost to the Hudson and it looked like he was turning south.

He cut across West Street without even looking for oncoming traffic. The man was desperate. And I had no idea where this idiot was headed.

I put my head down and pumped the pedals hard.

CHAPTER 72

THERE WERE A lot more pedestrians here. Mostly tour-ists looking at the waterfront. That didn't help me in any way. Now I could only see Jeffrey Cedar every time his head bobbed up from a pedal stroke. But he was definitely riding south as hard as he could.

Eventually he slowed his pace, and again I closed the distance between us. Once I had to slam on the brakes and throw the bike into a slide to avoid hitting a woman with a double baby stroller. For all my effort and a scrape on my ankle, all I got was a dirty look from her.

Now the crowd had thinned, but I don't think Jeffrey Cedar had any idea I was behind him. He had definitely slowed down and was sitting comfortably on his bike seat instead of pumping the pedals from a standing position.

We weren't too far from Rockefeller Park. I couldn't think

of any place near there that would be of use to Cedar. If he really wanted to escape, he needed to be headed to the Staten Island Ferry or finding some other way off Manhattan. The Holland Tunnel was north of us, but he'd need a vehicle to get through that.

My heart and legs were burning. I had no idea where this asshole was going, or if he even had a plan. Billy Van Fleet had run, even though he wasn't guilty. I couldn't let those circumstances repeat with Cedar.

I was surprised how quickly I'd caught up to him, and I was beginning to contemplate a wild leap from my bike to his when he must've sensed me closing in. He dared a quick peek over his left shoulder, then he swerved right. Hard. Now we found ourselves in the grassy picnic area of Rockefeller Park.

It wasn't that busy on a weekday, though I still heard squeals and shouts as Cedar cut between people lounging on the lawn.

He risked another look over his shoulder, but it was poor timing. He struck a giant man wearing a red Nebraska Cornhuskers shirt. They both went down onto the thick grass. The man in the red shirt snarled as he tried to rise to his feet. He was older than Cedar but looked like he could rip the attorney in half. Cedar popped up onto his feet, though, and abandoned the bike, setting off toward the water. But the Cornhusker reached out and somehow managed to grab Cedar's foot as he was fleeing.

I successfully turned my bike sideways and skidded to a halt just in front of them.

Cedar kicked the man with his other foot and freed himself. He bolted toward the seawall.

I started running after him. The sun was bright in the cloudless sky, and no breeze came off the water. I realized right then that the heat was going to get to me quickly. I still had my phone but hoped one of the patrol cars I'd asked for earlier would show up. There really isn't a cop around when you need one.

Cedar was running along the low seawall and had a good stride. I saw one of the smaller tour boats, about forty feet, cruising parallel with the wall. I couldn't imagine what they were looking at around here, but I could hear the guide's voice over a tinny loudspeaker.

Cedar took one more look at me over his shoulder. He must've realized at that point that I wasn't going to give up. I sure hoped *he* would. But, of course, he didn't.

Instead, he sprinted hard and leapt off the seawall. I slowed my run and watched as he timed his jump perfectly. He landed on the rear section of the tour boat. He was on the deck behind a gaggle of elderly women, who all shrieked when he landed.

I watched as Cedar wobbled for a moment with his arms outstretched. He scrambled for a handhold at the stern of the boat but, when he didn't find one, started to lose his balance.

I stood at the seawall along with a couple of other pedestrians who had stopped to watch the show, feeling helpless as we watched in horror as Cedar bobbed and slid on the rear deck…then tumbled over the stern.

I already had my phone out, ready to call a rescue boat, when I saw the position of his landing—almost directly behind the stern. The anguished sound of his screams will be etched in my memory forever as I, and everyone nearby, witnessed Jeffrey Cedar get dragged underwater and chopped to bits by the boat's propellers.

Ten seconds later, it was all over. The captain of the boat had raced to cut the engines when he realized what was happening, but it was already too late. A red film spread across the surface of the water like something out of a horror movie.

I was frozen, staring at the gruesome scene. So was everyone else. Aside from a couple of people crying on the boat, no one nearby made a sound.

I had to sit on the low seawall for a moment. Everything caught up to me at once. The stress of the last weeks. The exhaustion of chasing a murder suspect. The grisly murders of at least six young women here in New York. The concern over whether Hollis would improve. And now the macabre scene in front of me.

There was nothing more anyone could do except wait for the cavalry, the first responders activated by dozens of eyewitness calls to 911. And try to keep from vomiting, and embarrassing myself and the NYPD.

CHAPTER 73

WHILE I HAD been chasing down Jeffrey Cedar, his receptionist had been brought by patrol car to Manhattan North Homicide. Her name was Olivia Green, and I paid her a visit in the interview room where she'd been waiting with her attorney—conveniently, one of Cedar's former colleagues.

Judging by the look of shock on her face, she was struggling to absorb the disturbing events of the day. Not only had her former boss struck and then fled from a detective, but she herself was being held in custody.

"Ms. Green," I said, "do you know why you're here?"

She shook her head.

I remembered the emotional look on her face when Cedar jumped out his office window. I needed to determine the nature of their relationship.

"Ms. Green, you worked for Mr. Cedar. Did you date him too?"

She looked genuinely stunned by the accusation, and so did her attorney.

"Never," she said. "I'm an old friend of Lauren's. I babysit Tyler all the time."

"Did you know that earlier today Lauren called the police?"

"No," she said. "Is she all right? Is Tyler hurt?"

"Tyler is fine," I said. "But Lauren showed me a bruise on her arm in the shape of her husband's hand. She said he hurt her when she confronted him with evidence he'd been cheating on her. Both of the women he'd been seeing are dead. And he may have had other victims."

"Jeffrey may have a temper, and I believe he may have cheated, but he's not a killer," the receptionist protested.

Olivia Green was quite insistent. She was also wrong.

"A killer is exactly what he *was*," I said. "And note my use of the past tense. I'm sorry to inform you that Jeffrey Cedar is dead. He died trying to escape arrest for the crimes he committed. And in order to avoid your own arrest, I need you to corroborate Mr. Cedar's whereabouts on the dates of multiple homicides currently under investigation by the NYPD."

She opened her mouth to speak, until her lawyer cut in.

"My client has nothing to say at this time."

A uniformed officer brought in boxes containing the contents of the receptionist's desk and placed them on the table.

"You're a meticulous record keeper, Ms. Green," I said. "We've collected paper calendars going back years. Show us the current one. And the mileage logs on the car Mr. Cedar claimed as a business expense."

With a trembling hand, she opened the boxes, looking

through the contents until she found the requested documents and set them on the table.

"Did Mr. Cedar travel much?" I asked.

"Before Tyler was born, yes," she said. "Not so much recently. But he did drive his car all over the city."

And there, in Olivia Green's perfect handwriting, was all the proof I needed. Cedar had almost certainly murdered Marilyn Shaw and Lila Stein—but on the evening Chloe Tumber was killed, he'd been in court, awaiting the decision of a deliberating jury. And the records showed equally airtight alibis for the murders of Elaine Anastas and the other two victims in Brooklyn and the Bronx.

Now I was positive. Jeffrey Cedar was a copycat. We still had the real killer to catch.

CHAPTER 74

AS I CAME out of the interview room, I ran into Harry Grissom. He had been observing my questioning of Olivia Green.

"Great work, Mike," my lieutenant said. "Now I need you to go home and get some rest. You're no good to me or the investigation if you're exhausted and distracted."

"I've been exhausted and distracted for over a month."

"Well, I don't want it to go any further. Take tomorrow off if you need it. Spend some time with that beautiful family of yours."

I took his word as command.

I came in the front door just before dinnertime, about the same time as Brian. He was carrying his small duffel bag and nodded hello. He shrugged when I asked how it was going. Was this the new normal in communication with my oldest boy?

Before I could get into any further questions with him, we

both heard crying. When you have ten kids, the sound of crying isn't immediately concerning, since it's not all that uncommon—it's likely that someone's just annoyed with someone else.

Brian followed me into the dining room, where we located the source of the crying: Jane, at the end of the table, sobbing hysterically into a very wet paper towel. Mary Catherine sat on one side of Jane, stroking her hair. Juliana sat on the other, holding a roll of paper towels. There was a pile of crumpled towels in the middle of the table.

In between sobs, Jane said, "I-I-I just can't believe he would do this!"

I'd been around long enough to guess almost exactly what had happened.

Brian was still new to this game. He said, "What who did?"

Juliana looked up at her brother and explained, "Allan broke up with Jane. No notice, nothing. When she tried to talk to him, he just told her it was over."

That set off a new round of wailing from Jane. "And-and we were supposed to go to the school dance this weekend!"

Brian muttered, "That asshole."

Instinctively, I placed a hand on his shoulder to calm him down.

Brian jerked away from my touch and stormed out of the room.

I stepped to the dining room table and gave Jane a kiss on the top of her head. I wished I were better at this kind of thing. I knew I'd have to deal with it a lot more as the girls got older. But I was at a loss. I did my best to teach the boys to always respect women, and at least, from the little bit I heard through gasps and crying, I didn't get the impression Allan had been disrespectful. Just thoughtless. But I still wanted Jane to feel better.

The front door slammed. Hard. I looked at Mary Catherine. She said, "Has to be Brian."

I rushed out the front door, but he had already caught the elevator down to the lobby. An angry Brian roaming the streets and hunting a clueless Allan Martin III made me very nervous.

CHAPTER 75

I TOLD THE girls I was going out to catch Brian. I grabbed my keys and raced downstairs. The doorman said Brian had turned left after he'd burst through the doors onto the street.

Sure, Jane was upset, but that was part of life. She'd get over her first breakup. I hoped Brian realized the same thing.

I couldn't see him in either direction. I jogged toward the left. Now my imagination started to kick in. I felt my stomach begin to burn as I considered all the terrible things Brian could do to an unsuspecting high schooler.

Before I knew it, I was three blocks away from the apartment. I thought of the basketball courts a few blocks from here where Brian liked to hang out. I broke into an all-out run. This was not the family time I had envisioned.

A quick overview of the courts did not produce Brian. I was

at a loss. Then I spotted one of the young men who coordinated the leagues.

"Have you seen Brian?" I asked.

"Not in a couple of days."

I groaned in frustration.

"Have you checked Holy Name? I know he likes their courts. Don't you guys have some relative who works there?"

I thanked him and burst into a sprint I didn't realize I was capable of after my draining chase of Cedar. Clearly the bike riding with Mary Catherine had had more effect on me than I'd thought.

I slowed as I approached the church and called my grandfather. He didn't answer. Seamus wasn't big on cell phones. He thought they caused cancer. On several occasions he had claimed he would start using his cell phone around his ninetieth birthday. He figured by then it wouldn't matter.

When I got to campus, I threaded my way through the courtyards that led to the basketball gym. A couple of the nuns tried to engage me in conversation. They were still full of questions about the wedding. I was as polite as possible without ever stopping, not even for a moment.

Brian was taking anger management classes, but he also had strong protective instincts. And right now, the two might be about to combust. If someone had wronged his sister, no training could keep that primal rage in check.

The image of a bloody Allan Martin III, beaten, or with a shiv stuck in his stomach, popped into my head. I could also imagine Allan's father in court, disparaging my son as a bad influence and a danger to the Martin family. The final part of that equation was Brian being locked away like a rabid dog. I was panicked. It made me run faster. Much faster.

I burst through the doors on the upper deck of the gymnasium and heard the sounds of a pickup basketball game in progress. There were voices and a few hoots and hollers.

I froze at the sight of Brian playing one-on-one with Allan Martin. My other boys, Trent, Eddie, and Ricky, sat in the front row, cheering their brother on.

No one was dead. There wasn't even any blood. I eased onto the very top bleacher. I realized my legs were shaky. I wasn't sure if it was from the sprint or the fear I'd had about what Brian could've done.

I watched silently. Both of the boys were better than I'd thought. Allan sunk a three pointer. Brian hit three fifteen-foot jumpers. On the last one, after the ball had slipped through the hoop and bounced on the hardwood floor, the boys stood face-to-face.

Brian called out, "Game." He stared down the younger boy and said, "Do it. Do it right now."

I was intrigued, but also ready to intervene if Brian was ordering Allan to do something out of line. I watched as they both stepped over to the bleachers. Allan retrieved his phone, and the other boys gathered around him.

I made my way down the bleachers until I was in the lower level, not too far from the boys. None of them noticed—they were all too focused on Allan's phone.

Ricky said, "Put it on speaker."

Allan said, "Don't you trust me?"

"Not even a little. Now put your phone on speaker so we can all hear it."

Allan pushed a few buttons.

"Hello?" said a voice I immediately recognized as Jane's.

Allan didn't waste any time. "I'm sorry for breaking up with you, Jane. It was a mistake. Is there any chance you would still go to the dance with me?"

There was almost no hesitation on the line as Jane answered. "No." Then she hung up.

I couldn't keep a wide smile from spreading across my face.

My three younger boys all started to hoot and chide Allan.

Trent said, "She's already over you, loser."

Eddie said, "Can't play basketball, don't know women. Good luck in the future."

All four of my boys walked out and left the entitled little shit standing in the gym by himself.

CHAPTER 76

THE NEXT MORNING, I lingered long enough to eat breakfast with the family. Jane looked much better. Being able to turn Allan down had meant a lot to her.

Mary Catherine lingered over our kiss good-bye at the front door. It'd been so long that I'd forgotten what a good mood felt like. She made me promise to call her soon with an update on Brett Hollis. I hopped into my city-issued Chevy Impala and made the short drive to the Columbia University Medical Center.

Outside Hollis's room, I took a moment to compose myself. As I opened the door, I heard a voice behind me. I turned to find a tall nurse with reddish hair.

"What are you doing?" she demanded.

I closed the door. "I was going to visit my partner, Brett Hollis. Isn't this his room?"

"He's resting right now. They set his pelvis last night. Come back sometime after lunch and he'll be ready for visitors."

I knew not to argue with the nurse. Nurses are right up there with nuns, judges, and teachers.

It took almost no time for me to make it back to my car. I had a number of assignments I wanted to cover today.

Mainly, I was checking with employers of the victims from our homicides, my own follow-up to the initial Task Force Halo outreach.

It took me less than an hour to visit the workplaces of the victims in Brooklyn and the Bronx, as well as Columbia Law School, where Chloe Tumber had been enrolled. No one had any new information. I would hit the rest after I saw Brett Hollis this afternoon. I might even get home before dark again.

Almost as soon as I settled at my desk, I saw John Macy trudging through the office, straight toward me. "I heard Hollis is out of action," he said. "I guess we're stuck with each other."

I thought about that for a moment. I looked up at the well-dressed mayor's aide and said, "Let me just wash up. Have a seat and make yourself comfortable."

Macy seemed to appreciate my new attitude. He smiled and pulled a notebook out of the leather satchel he always carried. He settled in at Hollis's desk, not thinking twice about reorganizing Hollis's papers.

I went to the bathroom and washed my hands. I didn't want to lie.

Then I left the office. I decided it would probably be a good idea to finish my visits with the other businesses before I went back to the hospital.

I smiled as I drove away, wondering how long Macy would sit quietly at the desk before he started asking about me.

CHAPTER 77

THE PEOPLE AT Manhattan Family Insurance, where victim Elaine Anastas had interned, were pleasant and tried to be helpful. They all spoke highly of her.

Not that I'd expected anything else—most people only seem to recall a homicide victim's positive qualities, although someone's bad traits are more likely to have led to their death. Not that that necessarily applied when we were talking about a serial killer. Still, I tried to hide my impatience when I heard on endless loop: "Elaine was so bright." "Elaine was so driven." "Elaine came from someplace upstate but managed to make it in the city." High praise from fellow New Yorkers.

About the fifth person I spoke to was a man named Luis Munoz. Munoz was dressed in a black suit with a yellow tie and acted more like he owned the place than managed it. He also made sure to tell me that he'd gotten his MBA at Columbia.

We sat at adjoining empty desks. After Munoz went on and on about what a good intern Elaine had been, I said a little harshly, "C'mon. It's just us. I'm not going to make any notes. And I promise I won't remember who tells me what. But this bland information about Elaine won't help me capture her killer. I need to understand who she really was. Can you help me?"

Munoz considered my position and finally said, "Okay. Truth is, I knew Laney reasonably well. I even met one of her two roommates at an office happy hour. I can't remember the girl's name, but she interned with the Yankees. She loved baseball."

I had spoken to that roommate. It had been her bobbleheads I'd first noticed.

Munoz continued. "Laney was highly social. Almost had, like, a phobia of loners or of being alone."

I asked a few more questions and was impressed by how forthright Munoz was being. He even admitted that Elaine had once turned him down for a date. *Not that, as her supervisor, he should have been asking,* I thought, keeping the future working lives of my daughters in mind.

As I started to wrap things up, I noticed a sticker, then saw that duplicates had been applied to the frame of every computer monitor and landline phone in the office. The stickers showed a cartoon computer, its long arms holding a radio in one hand and a telephone in the other. Underneath it was a company name: Computelex.

The branding struck me as unusual so I took a picture of it with my phone.

I thanked Munoz and decided it was time to head over to the hospital.

CHAPTER 78

THE NURSE CARING for Brett Hollis recognized me from this morning, nodded, and waved her hand toward his room.

I opened the door quietly. Mrs. Hollis looked up at me from where she sat by her son, holding his hand.

As I stepped farther into the room, I saw Hollis was awake. He even managed a smile. His face didn't look too bad, though he was back to bandages across his nose. I guess I was used to it. He also had one arm in a cast, and one leg as well. He didn't look very comfortable lying in the bed.

Hollis managed a weak, "Hey."

"Hey," I said back.

Mrs. Hollis stood up. She said, "Brett's been through a lot. They set his pelvis late last night. The doctor seems happy with his progress."

"I'm just here to say hello," I assured her.

She gave me a stern look. "Three minutes. That's it. When I come back from the bathroom, you've got to go."

I nodded my agreement. I liked her. I could see where Hollis got his smarts.

I sat down in the same chair his mother had been in. I wanted to chat with Hollis. Cheer him up. But the truth was, I had an agenda.

I leaned in close and asked, "Remember anything?"

Hollis smiled. "All business. I respect that." His voice faded out. I handed him the cup from his nightstand and helped him sip some water. Then he started again. "A guy tumbled into Kelly and I just reacted."

I remembered Harry Grissom telling me that Kelly Konick was the pretty girl in the yellow skirt who'd been there with Hollis. "Can you remember anything about the guy?"

"I never got a good look at him. From what I saw, he looked average. Exactly average. I wouldn't be able to identify the guy if he walked in with a sign that said, 'I pushed your colleague in front of that bus.'"

I laughed dutifully. But the idea of a man being invisible because he was so unremarkable—that stuck in my head.

"Any thoughts on why he might've pushed Kelly? We have a couple of witnesses who said it looked deliberate from a distance."

Hollis shook his head. "I was kinda distracted, and a little nervous because I'm really into Kelly. I wasn't paying attention to anything except her."

The door opened and Mrs. Hollis walked in. I stood up and told Hollis, "I'll be back tomorrow. Rest and do what your mom says."

Hollis gave another weak smile as he said, "I always do."

CHAPTER 79

AN UNEXPECTED CALL diverted me from following up with Ms. Richard at the New York Public Library. Instead, I met FBI agent Emily Parker at a Starbucks not too far from the hospital.

Emily had requested the meeting but hadn't explained the reason behind her invitation.

She was already seated and pushed a plain black coffee toward me. "Hail the New York hero. You single-handedly prevented Jeffrey Cedar from killing again."

As I slid onto the opposite chair, I said, "I appreciate you not making me visit the FBI offices again, especially to congratulate me on a case that seems to be only partially solved."

She couldn't hide her own smile. "As much fun as that was, I'd rather Robert Lincoln not see me with you." She took a quick sip of her own coffee. "I'm sure you get that a lot. People saying they'd rather not be associated with you. People avoiding you. The usual."

I had to smile as I replied, "Actually, I get it more than I care to admit. Though hopefully all that will stop once I'm happily married."

We both let out a good laugh at that.

Emily plopped down two thick case files on the table between us. "Time to talk shop," she said, turning serious. "Tell me what you've found on the killer remaining at large."

I told her about my unorthodox briefing with Hollis from his hospital bed.

"Hollis gave me the idea that he could be someone so un-remarkable he's virtually invisible," I said. "That's not to say it was our killer who pushed Kelly Konick in front of the bus, but I'm open to the possibility. If he blends in everywhere, there's a likelihood he's quite ordinary-looking."

"Interesting," Emily said. "Maybe that's why we've got no reports of anyone noticing anything strange near any of the crimes. Not in any of the businesses where the victims worked or around where they lived."

I had to admit it was gratifying to hear the nation's "premier" law-enforcement agency agree with me.

Emily leaned in close. "The people at Quantico believe our killer targets women he feels have disrespected him."

I related my interview with Luis Munoz, Elaine Anastas's manager at Manhattan Family Insurance, that he had mentioned she'd had a phobia of loners. Maybe she had encountered one and somehow insulted him.

"Could a loner also be a ghost?" I wondered aloud. "Or a killer?"

CHAPTER 80

I DROVE HOME after my meeting with Emily Parker. Traffic was slow, and I was grateful. With ten kids and a busy office, sometimes it's hard to find a quiet place to think. Like a lot of cops, the best place for me to mull things over is in my car.

For once in the progress of this case, I felt pretty good about my day. Brett Hollis seemed stronger than I'd expected, and I'd gained some valuable information that had been validated by the FBI.

Stopped at a light on Amsterdam Avenue, I tried to put all the pieces together. I believed our killer was a traveler. I didn't think he was from New York. But how to find out more? There were no databases for *jobs with travel*. No businesses were going to come forward and suggest one of their employees was a killer.

I had two more employer interviews scheduled for the next morning. I thought I knew all the right questions to ask.

It felt like things were back to normal when I walked through my front door. Chrissy and Shawna gave me a hug. The other kids were doing their homework at the dining room table. There was very little drama.

Jane looked reserved, but not melancholy. I didn't want to make a big fuss over her. Juliana had told me that the boys had circulated it at school that Jane had been the one to dump Allan. The story of her saying no to him over the phone was true enough. I guess it's all in how you spin it. And, apparently, in how many brothers and sisters you have to tell the story.

The front door opened and I smiled at the sight of my grandfather, Seamus. A moment later, his IT guy, Elgin, followed. Seamus introduced Elgin, then let the kids introduce themselves to him. It was no small feat.

Seamus pulled me into the kitchen and said, "I hope you and Mary Catherine don't mind that I brought Elgin over for dinner without checking first."

I said, "You know I don't mind. I also know you don't care whether I mind or not."

Seamus chuckled. "Just trying to follow social convention, my boy."

My grandfather, Mary Catherine, and I stood in the kitchen for a moment. Elgin seemed amazed at the number of people at the table. I smiled at the gangly young man as he took in the group.

I called from the kitchen, "Yes, Elgin, this is normal."

He managed a shy smile as he looked up and said to all of us, "Usually, it's just me and my mom at home."

Having Elgin at the dinner table helped take the focus off Jane and her funk. For a quiet computer nerd, Elgin didn't seem to mind the attention.

Of course, he and Eddie bonded over computers, losing everyone else at the table as they dove deep into the details of networks and hacking. Elgin reached into his backpack and pulled out a magazine called *2600*. He handed it over to Eddie.

Eddie's eyes lit up. "Wow, the latest issue. Thanks!"

Mary Catherine inquired, "What kind of magazine is that?"

"It's a magazine for hackers. Really cutting-edge stuff," Eddie blurted out.

Elgin looked down at the table but added, "There's nothing in it Eddie hasn't already seen. I just thought he'd get a kick out of reading it."

Mary Catherine nodded, trying to avoid openly endorsing hacking.

After dinner, Seamus took me aside. In a low voice he said, "I wanted Elgin to see you as a real person, with the family. He's been following the investigation, and he mentioned that it's difficult for him to think of cops as regular people."

There were two sides to every story, and I took the NYPD's. "The news always avoids any talk of a cop's family or the kids left behind when a cop is murdered. I'm glad you brought him. He seems like a good kid." I smiled. "He's smart and gets along with the others."

Seamus clapped his hands together and rubbed them. "Great. Now for the next order of business: your wedding. Specifically, you need to write your vows."

"I'm working on it."

My grandfather winced and said, "That's a tired excuse. How hard can it be for you to write four or five lines?"

"Can it be a limerick? Mary Catherine *is* Irish, after all."

"So are we. If you do a limerick, she'll slug you. After I get the first crack at you."

I tried to hide my smile as I said, "There once was a girl from Tipperary. Her body was not terribly hairy. She—"

My grandfather punched me in the arm and walked away.

CHAPTER 81

THE NEXT MORNING, my first stop was the bustling medical supply office near Columbia where Chloe Tumber, the third New York homicide victim, had worked part-time while she was in school.

The manager, a pleasant woman, was clearly busy but didn't rush me or my questions, though she didn't have much information either. No one in the office did. There was no one as forthcoming as Luis Munoz here. Even when I made the offer to go off the record, no one had any information to give me about Chloe other than that she was twenty-six years old and a whiz with data entry. But apparently she'd kept to herself and also kept unusual hours due to her class schedule.

I thanked the manager but mentally wrote this place off as another dead end. Before I gathered my things and stood up to go, I took a moment to check my phone and messages.

Then I saw it: the same sticker I'd seen at the insurance company yesterday. Stuck on the front edge of a computer monitor. The cartoon of a computer with rubbery arms holding a radio and a phone. Computelex.

It took a moment for it to register, then a thousand new questions rushed into my brain. I reached up and stopped the first person walking past me.

"Excuse me," I said, putting my finger on the sticker in the corner of the computer monitor. "Do you know what that is?"

"Oh, yeah, it's from the company that installed computer software to coordinate our phones and radios and some of our vans. There's a sticker on every piece of equipment that was updated."

"When were they here?"

"Maybe three weeks ago?"

I did a quick calculation and realized that was shortly before Chloe Tumber had been murdered. "How many people from the company were here to install the software?"

"I think it was just one dude. Honestly, I don't remember much about him. He was only here for about a week."

He was a ghost, I thought.

CHAPTER 82

DANIEL OTT WAS essentially finished with the software and hardware upgrades at the trucking company in Queens but was enjoying hanging out with the men on the loading dock. They'd come to him for a couple of other engineering issues after he'd impressed them with his system of loading tires so quickly. They'd even invited him out for a beer one evening after work. He'd never experienced this kind of friendliness before.

Now he was just wrapping up the last few issues before heading home to Omaha. Ott wasn't quite sure he was ready to leave New York. He was reveling in the media attention, and he doubted he'd get the same amount of news coverage anywhere else. Reading the articles and hearing the TV stations relentlessly covering his crimes tickled him.

Ott wanted one more notch in his belt before leaving New York. That would be his last word to Detective Michael Bennett.

Since he had not seen any news stories about the bus hitting the younger detective, he assumed the investigation was ongoing. If the detective had died, there would've been a report about it. Perhaps injuring him was just as good. Maybe even better. It would distract other people in his unit. They would visit him in the hospital, wasting time.

He had heard a couple of the truck drivers talk about the excellent hamburgers at a sports bar on Greenpoint Avenue called The Queen's Castle, and he decided to go for an early lunch. The place looked a little hokey on the outside with fake towers and turrets, but Ott felt his stomach rumble, looked at the menu posted outside, and then stepped through the door.

He glanced around the dimly lit sports bar and noticed that the half dozen flat-screen TVs hanging on the walls were all dark and silent. The door next to the bar led to the kitchen. He didn't see anyone back there.

Then he heard a woman's thick Long Island accent. "What the hell? It's not even eleven. We're not open yet."

Ott looked up to see a tall, athletic-looking woman with frizzy black hair behind the bar, dressed all in black.

Ott stated, "Sorry, I was hungry."

"Jesus Christ, eat around noon like everyone else," she muttered.

Ott didn't like the verbal abuse. Especially when he had done nothing to deserve it. He calculated the odds of other workers showing up if he took action right now against the woman yelling at him to leave.

He felt for the knife in his front pocket. He pictured what he would do to her given enough time. It made him feel excited instead of annoyed. *Why wait?*

The woman continued to work behind the bar. She didn't look up again.

He slipped on his rubber surgical gloves and circled the area, measuring his angle of attack. He inched closer, blade extended. The bartender still had her head down, slicing a small mountain of lemons and limes. She'd never see him strike.

Suddenly Ott heard the noise of the front door opening, and a man's voice called out to the bartender. "Boss told me to come in early, help you prep. Tell me you're glad to see me!"

Ott wasn't glad. He quickly folded and stowed the Gerber knife, ducked his head, turned, and walked out the way he'd come in.

Ott decided he would follow her home later and make her his grand statement before he left New York. He wouldn't even bother with reconnaissance. If she lived with anyone else, they could be part of his farewell masterpiece too. He was already picturing it in his mind. Walls smeared with blood. Her body laid out in the middle of the living room.

New York really was going to be a hard place to leave.

CHAPTER 83

MY HEART WAS thumping as I jumped into my car and raced back up Broadway. Despite state and local ordinances, I had my cell phone in hand. Out of habit, I almost dialed Brett Hollis. Instead, I tried Harry Grissom. There was no answer. For all I knew, he was down at One Police Plaza, explaining how I'd left John Macy alone in the office. Then I tried Emily Parker. I got her voicemail.

As soon as I got to my desk, my next call was to Alvin Carter in the Atlanta Police Department.

As soon as he answered, I blurted, "This is Michael Bennett with the NYPD. I think I might be onto something. Have you ever heard of a company called Computelex?"

"Nope. Not that I recall."

"Can you check with the employers of the victims down there to see if anyone from that company ever visited their offices?"

"What do you got?"

"Two victims, each worked at different businesses in separate industries. Both businesses had someone from this company Computelex on-site, working on their computers."

There was a moment's pause. "Your theory is that the killer works for this computer company?"

"I know it's a long shot, but the timelines match up. I'm following up on whether the fact that a Computelex employee visited the office of both victims is statistically unlikely. If it was a big company like Microsoft, maybe. But I've never heard of this Computelex."

"I'm on it."

I then made the same call to San Francisco PD.

I had checked further with Manhattan Family Insurance, where Elaine Anastas had interned, and the medical supply company that had employed Chloe Tumber. The best they could tell me about the Computelex representative was that he was a white male. Neither company was even sure of his name. Someone from the insurance company thought it might be David. No one at either company saw him interact with the victims.

I heard a voice and glanced up from my computer screen to see John Macy standing at my desk with another man I didn't recognize.

Macy said, "I guess you thought it was pretty funny to leave me here in the office."

I went back to my computer. "Not now, Macy. I'm busy." I tuned him out.

"I don't think you're that busy. In fact, I know you're not. This is Detective William Funcher."

I kept my head directly in front of the monitor as I said, "Nice to meet you, Detective Funcher."

Macy said, "He's your replacement. You're no longer on the serial killer case." Finally I looked up at the men. Funcher looked uncomfortable. Macy was beaming. This was what he'd been waiting for. And he wanted to add a little drama to it. I hated to disappoint him.

"Where do you work now, Funcher?"

"The One-Eleven."

"Where's that, Queens?"

"Yeah, 215th Street."

"You work in homicide?"

"General assignment."

"And how do you know Mr. Macy?"

The fact that I didn't get an answer right away told me this wasn't a case of a competent detective rising to the top. Funcher was just the first guy Macy could find who'd agreed to come up here.

I wrote down the information from my computer screen about Computelex. They were based in Omaha, Nebraska, but claimed to cover the whole country. This might be the right lead.

I looked up again at the two men standing in front of my desk. "Fortunately, I don't work for you, Macy. I work for a guy named Harry Grissom. And if he walks in here and tells me I'm replaced, I will give everything I have to Detective Funcher. Until then, like I said, I am really busy."

That's when Macy made a major error. He touched me without permission.

CHAPTER 84

AS SOON AS I felt John Macy's hands on my shoulders, something in me snapped. It may seem minor, but what he did is technically an assault. That's what I kept in my head as I reacted. I could picture it in a report. *I was in fear for my safety after he assaulted me.* That sounded good. I was going to go with that.

I really don't know if it was instinct or machismo that made me spring out of the chair and turn to face Macy. I could've told him to cut it out and kept working. Instead, I was now face-to-face with the mayor's aide.

I snarled, "Keep your damn hands off me."

Macy wasn't about to back down either. "You know what I can do to your career? You're nothing but a minor cog in city government."

"For a minor cog, you seem to spend a lot of time keeping me from turning with all the other cogs."

"I don't like your attitude one bit. You have no respect for your superiors."

That caught me by surprise. I'll admit I'm a smart-ass. I'll admit I can't control my mouth. But I have a great deal of respect for my superiors. Any man or woman who worked their way up the ladder at the NYPD deserved respect.

I said, "I respect my lieutenant. I respect our captain. I respect the commissioner of the NYPD."

Macy said, "But not me?"

"You're not my superior."

"I'm the commissioner's superior." Macy looked like he was losing it. His voice was becoming a little shrill. His eyes were twice as big as normal. And he was sputtering. Any time a politician is at a loss for words, watch out.

That's why it didn't surprise me too much when he grabbed my shirt with both hands. He pulled me close to him like a school-yard bully and raised his voice. "You hear me, Bennett? I—"

That's when I decided to react. Maybe *retaliate* is the better word. But I knew I had to do it subtly.

I'm not saying I set up the mayor's aide. I will say that as a cop, I'm aware of my surroundings at all times. At least I try to be. I had the chair that was right next to me hooked with my right foot. It was pretty close to Macy. All I did was nudge it. Okay, a little more than a nudge. It hit him directly in the groin. That's why he stopped mid-sentence.

Macy released his grip on my shirt and stumbled back a few feet until he bumped into the leather office chair and flopped into it like a bag of old potatoes. Clearly his main concern was the excruciating pain radiating from his testicles. Every man knows the feeling.

I casually turned my attention to the cop, Funcher. "How'd you really end up in this embarrassing and awkward position?"

He slowly backed away from me and raised his hands so I could see he wanted nothing to do with me or this situation.

Funcher said, "I know Macy socially, through my wife. In my circles, he has a reputation for being loose-lipped, but he was all business this time. He told my sergeant the mayor's office needed me, so I agreed to meet him here this morning."

"So you're not looking to snake this case?"

"No way."

"Then we're good." I completely ignored both men and went back to work.

After about thirty seconds, Funcher turned to leave.

I called after him. "Wait." When he turned to look at me, I said, "Take your date with you." I tilted my head at Macy.

Funcher said, "No can do. I'm going back to the One-Eleven. He's not authorized to ride in an NYPD vehicle." The detective turned and walked away without another word.

I liked Funcher. To the point. No fuss. And smart enough to realize when he was in over his head.

Harry walked into the office, passing Funcher on his way out. My lieutenant strolled over to my desk and asked, "Who was that?"

"He dropped Macy off here."

He and I both looked over at Macy, who appeared to be recovering from the blow to the testicles. Harry dropped his voice, "Jesus, what's that ass want now?"

I shrugged and said, "I guess he just wanted to hang out."

We both gave the motionless mayor's aide another glance, then I said to Harry, "Let's talk."

As soon as we were out of Macy's earshot, I said, "I need to fill you in on a computer company that may be important to the case."

CHAPTER 85

I HAD NEVER done so much investigative work from my desk. By the afternoon, I had compiled all the information on Computelex I could find from the internet. I even had the phone number of the head of human resources, one Lynn McKague. The photo on the company website showed an attractive, friendly-looking woman with a broad smile.

I dialed, and as the phone rang, I said a silent prayer that she'd answer. I needed to actually talk to her. I didn't want to risk leaving a message. For all I knew, the man in question could be Computelex's employee of the year, or she could even be his girlfriend.

A bright, friendly voice answered the phone with "HR, this is Lynn."

"Lynn McKague?"

"That's right. Who's this?"

I gave her my full, formal title.

"Hello, *Detective*," she said cautiously.

"Ms. McKague, I need a few minutes of your time."

"Before I answer any questions," she said, "you're calling about company business, not about me personally, correct?"

"That's correct."

"I'm sorry, but unless you've got a subpoena, company policy forbids me from continuing this conversation. The privacy of our clients is important to our business model."

"This isn't about one of your clients. It's about an employee."

"I wish I could help, but I'm afraid the same rule applies."

I had to take a moment to consider my next course of action. I said, "Can you confirm an individual's employment status?"

"If you have a name, I can verify that employee's work history. That I can do."

"Is there a white male Computelex employee currently working in the New York area?" I rolled the dice, hoping I wouldn't spook her—or the man I was looking for. "It's important that I speak to this person about a lead on a string of homicides."

"Is he a witness? I can send him a message to contact you."

"No, I would ask you please *not* to say anything to him."

"So he's *not* a witness. This sounds more serious." It was half statement, half question.

I didn't respond.

There was a long silence on her end.

I finally said, "Ms. McKague? Did I lose you?"

"No, you didn't lose me. I was reviewing some records." The HR manager hesitated again. Then she stammered, "What ki-kind of questions do you need answered?"

I almost leapt up from my chair and cheered. Instead, I focused and said, "We understand that a man in your employ travels on contract work. I'm going to give you some dates and locations. A name would help a great deal. Barring that, a yes or no on whether at those times this employee was working in those cities."

Lynn McKague spoke slowly. "Yes, I am able to merely confirm information you have already."

I gave her the dates of the Atlanta and San Francisco homicides. I could hear her fingers tapping at her keyboard. I waited while she checked the information.

When she came back on the line, there was a slight tremor in her voice. "Yes, one employee was also in Atlanta and San Francisco during the dates you gave me. He has worked for us for a number of years." After an awkward pause, she asked, "What's this about?"

I could've given her some snarky reply like *I'm not allowed to tell you without a subpoena.* But this case was too important to screw around.

"And when did he arrive in New York City?"

"He's been there for slightly over six weeks." Well within the range of the homicides here. I could almost hear Lynn McKague mentally debating her next admission. "His name is Daniel Ott."

Daniel Ott. This was our man. I was sure of it. "One last question, Ms. McKague. Would you be willing to share with me the name of the hotel where Mr. Ott is staying in New York City?"

After only a brief pause, she gave me the name and address of a chain hotel in the Flatiron District.

She also gave me Daniel Ott's cell phone number.

"Ms. McKague," I said, "thank you for your help."

I meant it.

CHAPTER 86

THE INSTANT I ended the call to Omaha, my phone rang. Pam Lundsford from San Francisco PD was on the line.

She started right off with "These cases weren't mine. The original detective, Sean Lynch, has retired since then. This case aged him. He left the force, but he's never given up on it. His theory was that the killer left town. Maybe he was right."

I agreed. It's what he did while he was *in* town that I needed to pin down.

Detective Lundsford said, "I saw your homicides on CNN. Bad break that the killer you caught was a copycat. I hope this doesn't kill your lead on the main suspect."

"I have some new information there," I assured her.

"Good, because I contacted the victims' employers like you asked. No link to Computelex. I checked it four different ways and made sure the representative from the employer knew exactly what I was asking."

Not the answer I was expecting. I explained that Computelex had just confirmed our killer's presence in San Francisco at the time of both murders.

"I have an idea," Detective Lundsford said. "Can I bring Lynch in? He might have another angle."

"Sure. Either it's going to be over soon or this lead won't mean anything."

After I hung up the phone, it rang again. Detective Alvin Carter from Atlanta calling. I answered it immediately. "You got good news for me, Alvin? I got confirmation from Computelex that a Daniel Ott was working in Atlanta on the dates of all five homicides, but I need more."

Carter said, "Well…"

He was about to drop something on me. Most detectives can't pass up a chance for a little dramatic pause.

Carter continued, "The victim who was murdered at a real-tor's office, Holly Jones? This was my case."

I said, "I sense you're about to impress me with some spectacular police work."

"You have no idea."

"Go ahead. Hit me with it."

Alvin Carter said, "I canvassed the area after the homicide. Went a couple of blocks in each direction. One of the companies about a block away delivered wholesale flowers to florists and grocery stores all over Georgia. A really big operation."

"And?"

"I called them. They *did* contract Computelex to combine their delivery van radios, telephone, and computer activity. It turns out the Computelex tech was there at the same time the killing spree was going on in this area."

There was a long silence between us on the telephone as I let that information sink in.

I said, "Did you get a description of the tech?"

"Average-looking white guy. That was the best they could come up with. His name was Daniel Ott. He had to sign in every day for insurance reasons. No one at the company has given him a single thought since he left. He made almost no impact on them."

I said, "I owe you a beer."

"Catch this asshole and I'll buy *you* a keg."

"You're on," I said.

Now, this was how detectives were supposed to operate.

As soon as I hung up, I called out, "Harry!"

CHAPTER 87

DANIEL OTT GOT lucky and saw the grumpy barmaid leaving The Queen's Castle not long after lunch. It was days like this, when he found someone truly deserving of his attention, that he was glad he was so careful. As long as he could maintain his cool, he knew he could do this indefinitely.

He followed her for a few blocks, then saw her go into an apartment building. A few minutes later, someone opened the blinds in the corner apartment on the third floor. Ott smiled. He calculated how much time he wanted to spend with this barmaid. He'd already decided that if anyone else was home, he'd take them down with her.

He reached down and touched the work pouch on his belt. It had a knife, some zip ties, and a pair of gloves. He also had a seven-inch steel rod. He had wondered what it would be like to drive the rod through someone's temple. Or maybe hold it over her chest and let her contemplate what was about to happen. Power surged through him when he was deciding how someone might die.

He pictured this woman on the floor of her apartment, duct tape wrapped around her mouth. Ott could sit on top of her as long as he wanted before he attacked her eye. Before he taunted the police by mixing her blood with the blood from a previous victim. He couldn't remember anyone he'd looked forward to dealing with more than this barmaid. It was as much for her behavior and attitude as it was about his leaving a legacy here in New York.

If that happened with the help of a foolish copycat, so be it. CNN was already talking about him. He couldn't imagine the coverage when yet another body landed in the morgue. By then he would be back in Omaha, recharging before he went out into the world again.

His phone rang in his pocket. He casually picked it up without taking his eyes off the apartment. Even as he heard his younger daughter's voice say, "Hello, Daddy!" he never stopped staring at the apartment.

He said, "Hello, my angel."

"When are you coming home, Daddy?"

He could hear his wife prompting his daughter. He said, "Soon, my angel, soon."

"Are you almost done in York City?"

Ott heard his wife correct her.

The little girl repeated, "Are you almost done in New York City?"

"Yes, little angel. I only have one more job to complete." He smiled.

CHAPTER 88

IT DIDN'T TAKE me long to schedule a team meeting in the Gramercy Park area at the Thirteenth Precinct, the closest precinct to the hotel where Daniel Ott was staying.

All the homicide detectives with cases related to this killer were here: Terri Hernandez, looking like an athletic college student even with her heavy ballistic vest; Javier Tunez, reviewing case details on his phone; Dan Jackson, a mountain in his tactical gear; Raina Rayesh, focused and going through notes.

And all of us were wearing our blue NYPD raid jackets. We detectives were going by the book today.

We also had a uniformed sergeant and five uniformed patrol officers. This was a newer tactic we'd used in the last few years. People got so concerned about the chance of someone impersonating a detective, having a uniformed officer with us often helped. Harry Grissom had arranged for that. The big sergeant was named Mike Sadecki. He looked like he shaved with a machete. I was glad to have him with us.

"We're not here to do anything fancy. Some of us will stay outside in case he runs. We'll all stay on channel 3 on our radios," Harry explained. "We got no warrant. We just want to get eyes on this guy. Talk to him for a few minutes without worrying about dealing with the district attorney or anything like that. If we got a warrant, we couldn't talk to him, because it's assumed he's represented. That's just stupid local DA policy."

Raina Rayesh asked, "How sure are you about this guy?"

I answered that. "If he's not our suspect, there are a lot of coincidences. His work schedule puts him in three different cities during three corresponding murder sprees." I distributed printouts of his driver's license. "He's about five foot ten, very average-looking. No one ever seems to notice him."

Twenty minutes later, we had developed a simple but effective plan: Harry, Raina, and I would walk into the hotel lobby with Sergeant Sadecki.

The hotel was six stories tall and tucked between two fifteen-story buildings, its exterior so bright and cheerful that it looked out of place in the city. This wasn't a Ritz-Carlton or even a Marriott. This was the kind of place a family traveling on a budget stayed— or where a company put up a worker on extended assignment.

There were two clerks behind the counter but no one else in the plain, practical lobby. I walked toward a middle-aged woman with neatly tied-back brown hair who looked to be the senior clerk, but she turned away and disappeared into a room behind the front desk. That left a young, hipster-looking dude with mismatched earrings and hair that looked like it hadn't been combed in a couple of days.

The young man looked up at the uniformed sergeant and me. We stepped all the way to the counter so we could look over into the space behind it.

The clerk was clearly surprised. And not terribly happy to see us police officers inside the hotel. "What do you guys need?"

I smiled and stayed polite. "Do you have a Daniel Ott registered here?"

"Can't tell you. Can't tell the cops anything without a warrant."

The sergeant used a fatherly tone when he said, "Son, this is really important. We're just asking if he's here."

"And I'm just telling you, I can't say anything without a warrant."

"Can't or won't?"

"Both."

I asked, "Is your supervisor here?"

"Nope. I'm the assistant manager. And I'm telling you to get a warrant. I'm also about to tell you to leave the hotel unless you have one." He worked hard at leveling an intimidating stare at Sadecki.

I put a hand on the sergeant's shoulder. Sadecki was used to dealing with this attitude toward the police. But he clearly had no patience for it.

I said with a smile, "We'll call your corporate office and wait in the lobby here."

"You can't wait in the lobby."

As we turned, Sergeant Sadecki said, "Go ahead, call the cops on us."

CHAPTER 89

I STOOD WITH Sergeant Sadecki and Detective Raina Rayesh in the corner of the empty lobby farthest from the desk clerk.

I had an idea.

I called Terri Hernandez on the radio. "We're having a problem with the clerk. Can you turn your raid coat inside out, then come through the lobby and go up the stairs? Just wait there for me to call you. Don't take any action or do anything."

All she said was "Give me thirty seconds."

That's why I like working with my friends. They never give me excuses.

A minute later, I had the big sergeant block the clerk's view of me while I pulled out my cell phone and called the hotel. The clerk picked up on the first ring. As soon as he said his standard welcome, I kept my voice very low and raspy.

I said, "Dude, I'm glad you answered. This is Daniel Ott. Cops might be looking for me." I glanced over my shoulder.

The clerk was working hard to keep a neutral face. All he said was "Okay."

I continued on as Daniel Ott. "Can you get to my room right now?"

"Not this second."

"I got a thousand bucks if you can come up and help me for less than a minute."

"Yes, sir, I'll be right up."

I smiled at the way the clerk tried to keep his tone professional and efficient.

Just then, Terri walked past us. She turned and took the stairway like she'd been staying at the hotel for weeks. No one gave her a second look.

The clerk called for the woman from the back room and asked her to watch the front desk. He made a point of saying loudly, so we all could hear him, "And don't tell the cops anything. They don't have a warrant."

I watched the clerk get into the elevator. When it stopped on the third floor, I called Terri quickly to tell her what floor to check.

"I'll swing by," she said. "Call you back in a minute."

Less than a minute later, my phone rang. Terri said, "Ott's there, in room 319, on the west side of the building. The clerk was talking to him as I walked past. All I saw was a white male in a short-sleeved white shirt and blue pants. Almost like uniform pants. Very average-looking."

Concise yet thorough. As good a report as I had ever heard. Sounded like our guy.

Today was the day we'd finally meet. I was sure of it.

CHAPTER 90

THROUGH RUNNING WATER, Daniel Ott heard the knock on his door. He was at the sink, sanitizing the tool he had used to kill the barmaid. His last New York City kill.

Ott looked through the peephole and immediately recognized the scraggly hotel clerk. He twisted his head and could see there was no one standing next to the man. He opened the door slowly.

Ott stared at the young man but got no response. Finally, he said, "Yes?"

The clerk said, "You just called the front desk and said the cops were looking for you. I couldn't answer you because they were standing nearby. I played them like fools."

Ott assessed the clerk's bad posture and dirty fingernails. He doubted the young man had played anyone for a fool.

Just then an attractive woman with dark hair walked past in

the hallway. Her eyes cut into the room for just a moment. Ott immediately pegged her for a cop. Detective Michael Bennett couldn't be far behind.

Ott stepped over to the table where his work pouch sat. He pulled on a fresh pair of rubber gloves, replaced the freshly washed tool, picked up the kit, and clipped it onto his belt.

"The cops are downstairs in the lobby right now?" he asked.

The clerk looked confused. "Yes. Isn't that why you called me?"

Ott could put the pieces of this puzzle together. He knew they had tricked this dull-witted clerk, and he knew he had to get moving right now.

The clerk said, "You said there'd be a thousand bucks in it for me if I helped you."

"You haven't figured out that wasn't me on the phone? They were just trying to trick you into giving away my room number." Ott almost felt bad for the clerk. The young man's look of confusion turned to disappointment.

Ott pulled out his wallet. He had withdrawn some extra cash in preparation for his trip home. He handed a fistful of twenties and tens to the clerk. "I don't know how much is there, but I'll try to get you some more. I need you to do something that will help me out and piss off the cops at the same time."

The clerk smiled. "All right!"

"Is the woman who passed us still in the hallway?"

The clerk looked in each direction. "I don't see anyone."

Ott stepped into the hallway and shut the door silently. He whispered as they walked to the stairwell, "Run down the stairs and shout, *He's out on the fire escape, climbing to the roof!* Make sure the cops hear you," Ott stressed to the clerk.

"Then what do I do?"

"Run out the front door. Don't stop for anything."

"How will I get the rest of the money from you?"

Ott was surprised the clerk had thought that far ahead. "I'll leave it in an envelope at the front desk later."

The clerk said, "What do the cops want you for?"

Ott paused, then said, "I burned down an ICE building."

"Cool."

"Do what I said and we'll both be heroes."

Ott sent the clerk scurrying down the main stairs. He looked in every direction and saw no sign of the woman from earlier.

Ott headed for the rear stairway. The door was locked, but it took only a couple of twists with the screwdriver to pop it open.

He hoped his hasty plan would work.

CHAPTER 91

I WAS STARTLED by a shout. I looked up at the wide staircase and saw the hipster clerk rushing down. It took a moment to realize what he was saying.

The scrawny clerk yelled, "He's on the fire escape! He's climbing to the roof!"

Sergeant Sadecki said, "What?"

When the clerk reached the bottom of the stairs, he turned and ran right out the front door of the hotel.

Instantly, I called Terri on her cell phone. "The clerk just ran out of here shouting that Ott is on the fire escape climbing to the roof."

Terri said, "Stand by one sec." She came back on the phone and said, "The door to 319 is closed and locked."

"Can you see the fire escape from anywhere?"

Another few seconds later and Terri said, "I can see most of it from a window at the end of the corridor. I don't see anyone on it from this vantage point."

I said, "Stay on the door in case it's a trick. Listen on the radio." I wasted no time in turning to the sergeant. "Alert your guys outside. Call in some more help. And while you're at it, call Grissom. Ott might be anywhere by now."

I raced up the stairs as the others started to fan out and search for our suspect.

I found Terri Hernandez in front of 319. I pulled my gun, and she did the same. Without a word, I turned and kicked the door to 319. With a loud crack, it snapped open and slammed into the wall.

We entered the two-room suite with our guns pointed in front of us. I swung to my left to make sure the bathroom was empty. Terri kept moving forward into the small living room. She waited for me to catch up as we moved into the bedroom.

Terri cleared the second bathroom.

I did a quick sweep under the bed and in the closet. Nothing. The windows were all closed and locked from the inside.

I tried to think where Ott might have gone.

I got on the radio. "The room's empty. It doesn't look like he got on the fire escape. There are at least two levels underground. Mostly for maintenance and storage. Has anyone seen anything there?"

The uniformed sergeant came on and said they had covered the entire outside and he had someone searching the roof.

Detective Raina Rayesh came on the radio and said, "The other clerk tells me Ott checked in six weeks and three days ago. She gave me a set of passkeys so we don't have to kick in any doors."

Terri Hernandez mumbled, "Too late."

Terri and I met the cops from the roof and we searched each floor, stairwell, and elevator carefully. We found nothing.

More cops arrived, including my lieutenant, but we still had no idea where Daniel Ott had disappeared to. Harry Grissom put his arm around my shoulders, knowing how I must feel.

He said, "This is a win. We know who this guy is now. What he looks like. For once we can use the media to our advantage."

CHAPTER 92

I SAT WITH Harry Grissom in the hotel lobby as for the second time in days we crafted a news release revealing the identifying details of a serial killer.

By the time we'd announced Jeffrey Cedar's crimes, he was already dead.

This was a far more sensitive situation. We would be getting a murderous fugitive's name and picture out into the public in the midst of an active hunt for him. Plus, there was an incoming report of a fresh homicide, done at an apartment in Queens, that fit Ott's profile. The public needed to understand that anyone who got in his way could be in danger. Or, for different reasons, anyone who had helped him.

Raina Rayesh had questioned the male clerk when he returned to the hotel. Under a little pressure, he confessed that he'd helped Ott escape. He said he did it for money and admitted that he'd come back to look for the balance of his payout.

When Raina told him his actions amounted to aiding and abetting a fugitive, which made him an accessory to Ott's crimes, the clerk tried to walk it all back, saying he thought Ott was only involved in some kind of antifa bullshit, not the murders that had been all over the news.

As she cuffed him, Raina had said, "Tell it to your lawyer."

We never did need to call on the retired Detective Lynch from SFPD, but Harry and I did have to prepare for a talk with the bigwigs at One Police Plaza. But first, while Harry finished the details on the press release, I wanted to take another look around the hotel.

Raina gave me the ring of passkeys, and I went down a level to a dark storage area. The same key opened all the locked maintenance doors. Behind one of the doors was the maintenance stairwell. It went down another level.

I couldn't be sure if someone had searched here, so I took the stairs down. It was about as I'd expected: dark and musty, with an unused workbench covered with tools sitting in the corner. Seemed like the kind of place a killer on the run might hide out. Especially one who used tools only as weapons.

I thought about calling Terri Hernandez to come down and give me a hand, but I realized I could see the entire level. Especially now that it was becoming clear that Ott had somehow given us the slip, I didn't need any help. I took a few minutes to look in the corners and under a couple of cabinets, but there was nowhere to hide here, and no street exit. The only way in or out of this room was via the maintenance stairwell or the elevator.

As I turned back to the stairwell, I noticed a familiar structure. One of those big, wall-mounted circuit boxes. Maybe they
were called junction boxes.

Where had I seen one of these before?

I hesitated, looking at the box.

CHAPTER 93

OTT COULDN'T SEE his watch, but by counting his breaths, he knew he'd spent at least thirty minutes crammed inside a junction box on the bottom floor of his extended-stay hotel. This one hadn't been nearly as hard to get into as the one at the library. But between the conduit and wires streaming through the box, it was just as uncomfortable.

The question was, how long would the cops search? His escape plan hinged on the cops thinking he had left the area. Enough time had probably passed to make them believe it.

Noises buzzed through the junction box. He heard a couple of air conditioners cycling. He also heard the distant sound of a toilet flushing. And then, for the past few minutes, silence.

He was preparing to open the door and slide out of the box when he heard a noise so close that it could only have been made by someone looking for him. But it couldn't be.

The quick glimpse he'd gotten of the room had told him it was rarely used.

He thought about what he had on him. Tools, his wallet, his burner phone, and his personal phone. Not that he could use the personal phone again. Ever. Or his credit cards. He hadn't even thought about never seeing his daughters or wife again. But those were the facts laid out in front of him.

Once he escaped from this hotel, he'd have to leave his whole life as Daniel Ott behind.

Ott shifted his weight. He stayed in place for a moment, listening. Then he raised his left arm enough to move the sliding lock and open the door to the junction box.

He let it swing wide. In the glow from the single light on in the corner, the room appeared to be empty. He sat there for a moment, listening. Then he stretched his legs out and let them drop over the side of the box, giving himself a moment to let the blood return to his limbs. Finally, Ott slid out of the box and landed quietly on the rough concrete floor.

He had to smile. The cops may have figured out who he was and where he was staying, but they had not caught him. He was still smarter than them.

Ott turned to close the door to the junction box. He didn't want anyone getting any ideas about how he had escaped. He might use a similar hiding place again.

As he turned from the box, Ott was startled to see a tall man casually leaning against the door to the stairwell. It took a moment, but he recognized him as Detective Michael Bennett.

"Nice try, Ott," Bennett said, "but you already used the same trick at the library. I'm slow, but I still pick up on patterns given enough chances."

Ott's eyes darted around the room, and he reached for a tool from his pouch.

Bennett didn't change his tone. "Don't even think about it." He moved his right hand and showed Ott he was holding a pistol. "And I already sounded the alarm. You're not getting away from NYPD this time."

Ott raised his hands slowly.

CHAPTER 94

I ARRESTED DANIEL OTT without incident.

Arrested without incident. That's always the best line in a report.

With Harry Grissom's help, we soon had Ott ensconced in an interview room at the Thirteenth Precinct. It might've been the fastest I ever got a murder suspect from the field to a full-blown interview.

The room was wired for sound and video, but I wasn't going to take any chances. He was a tech guy, probably studied engineering. That meant he would be working the room, looking for an escape hatch. Not this time.

I sat behind a cheap wood-veneer table on an uncomfortable plastic chair facing Daniel Ott, who was struggling to get used to the constraint of having his hands cuffed behind his back. He kept knocking the metal against the back of his plastic chair.

I pulled out my notebook and my tape recorder.

There was also an old-style two-way mirror. We couldn't see anything in the outer room, but I could imagine how many people were crammed in there to hear this interview of a killer who had bested law enforcement for nearly a year, though his streak could've been even longer.

I had already gotten a few calls, with increasing frequency, from Emily Parker at the FBI. She probably wanted to tip me off that the FBI was about to horn in. Typical. She'd been too busy to access FBI resources when I needed them, and now that I'd found our suspect without her help, I was too busy to talk.

It's unusual to interview a suspect solo. Partners practice the substance and order of their questions, who will do the asking and who will take notes. This was not a usual situation. Thank God I had a boss who had faith in me. He realized I'd be better off on my own.

I read Ott his rights and made sure he understood each of them. I asked him the usual questions, like name, age, and marital status. He didn't seem to hold back any information. He told me about his wife and two daughters in Omaha. Then he surprised me by saying, "I read that you have ten kids. How does that work?"

This guy was a level beyond most criminals. He was the first suspect ever to confess that he'd researched me, and I was completely thrown when he started questioning *me* in the middle of a police interview. Usually the person whose hands aren't cuffed is the one asking the questions.

I decided to answer him, thought it was a step in the right direction for building rapport. "It usually works pretty well," I said, "but organizing ten kids can be a challenge."

There was nothing threatening about his physical appearance.

He was a pleasant-looking, clean, reasonably well-dressed man. Most people wouldn't have a problem talking to him.

I did. I was the father of six daughters, and he'd killed more women than I had in my entire family.

He seemed so normal, or *The man I knew could never murder people,* I could already imagine Ott's neighbors saying when the media descended upon them.

I asked, "You need anything? Something to eat? A drink?" Suspects were quick to claim mistreatment, and I wasn't about to lose this crucial statement on that account.

Ott looked me right in the eye and said, "I'm not hungry. And your process is inefficient. I can save us all some time."

"How's that? From the moment you committed your first murder you were on stolen time. You stole years of your victims' lives that they and their loved ones will never get back."

"That's one way of looking at my actions, Detective Bennett," Ott said. "I see them differently."

We were approaching a stalemate, so I changed tack.

"How do you choose your victims?" I asked.

"American women with their attitudes and smart mouths set me off," he said. "I heard an intern at an insurance office brag that she was studying communications in college so she'd never have to be a lonely telephone tech. Can you believe that? I am a grown man who provides for his family and that little bitch was looking down her nose at me."

He was talking about Elaine Anastas.

"That's why you killed her, and then wrote that threatening letter, 'To the Women of New York'?"

"I was teaching them a lesson. I wrote that I would kill the ones who didn't respect me, and I always do exactly what I say,"

Ott sneered. "I've been killing women for ten years, Detective Bennett, longer than that partner of yours has been on the force. A significant portion of your own career."

I can sit quietly through the most horrifying stories, nodding along with what feels like perverse encouragement. Lots of *I see* or *Wow* as a suspect continues detailing incriminating actions, when all along I really want to scream *You sick asshole.*

But in all my years interviewing suspects, this was the first time I had ever been left absolutely speechless.

I forced myself to continue the interview.

"Do I understand you correctly?" I said. "Are you making a confession?"

"I confess to committing the capital offense of first-degree murder. *Many* times over."

"Mr. Ott, I've advised you of your rights," I said. "Are you sure you want to continue?"

"Oh, I'm just getting started," Ott said. "You have no idea what I've done, what I planned to be doing for the rest of my life, until you came along. You, who didn't even understand the messages I left."

I ignored his taunt. "Why don't you start by telling me about the homicides here in New York. Then we'll review Atlanta and San Francisco, where your presence was verified during all of the related murders in those cities."

"That's how you found me, isn't it?" Ott asked. "Timed the murders to the schedule of my contract work?"

I knew better than to confirm any information. "There were a lot of factors that went into your arrest."

Ott ignored my non-answer to his question and continued. "And then you saw me at the library. That was my big mistake.

I got so used to most people looking right through me that at a crucial time I forgot a detective might be watching. You got my attention that day as a worthy opponent," Ott said. "I tried and failed to derail your investigation. You won. And now I won't hold anything back. I promise."

I sat there, astonished, as Daniel Ott began listing the murders he'd committed in New York City.

"When I first arrived in New York," he said, "I went exploring, looking for interesting neighborhoods and people I wanted to spend time with."

"That's your way of saying you wanted to kill them, isn't it?" I asked.

He nodded, then said, "I found a woman in the Bronx, and one in Brooklyn. I don't even know their names, only that they had loud American mouths on them."

Ott made no effort to hide his obsession with forcing women to obey rules and show respect. I shuddered to think how he treated his wife and daughters.

"It was easier to get to know the women in Manhattan," Ott said. "I met them on the job. One was a law student moonlighting in a medical supply office. And I told you about that disrespectful intern already."

"She had a name," I said. "Elaine. Her mother and friends called her Laney."

CHAPTER 95

TACTICALLY, IT WASN'T the smartest idea to loosen Daniel Ott's handcuffs and move them to the front, but I had to reward him for being so forthright.

Though Ott, by his own admission, had made some mistakes, I knew he was skilled and he was smart. Scary smart. He'd evaded us a number of times. I didn't want to find out he was some kind of martial arts genius or an assassin who could take a straw and cram it up your nose into your brain. Or maybe I'd just watched too many Jason Bourne movies.

"Tell me about the librarian," I said, focusing on one of the recent murders I was not absolutely sure he'd committed. I wanted confirmation one way or the other. "That's where your pattern seems to have suddenly shifted."

"I didn't want to kill the librarian," Ott said, "and I didn't enjoy it the way I did spending time with the others. When she confronted me in the computer room, she saw my face, and I couldn't risk her recognizing me."

"That doesn't explain why you killed the young man," I said.

"He was there." Ott shrugged. "I tried to do a quick job in front of the apartment building since there were people nearby, so I slashed her across her throat and intended to keep walking. Then that guy came out of the building at the wrong time and saw her dead body. I had to kill him too. I had no choice."

There's always a choice, I wanted to say, but someone like Ott would never understand.

"And the bartender from The Queen's Castle?" I asked, referring to the incident report I had been handed as I entered the interview room.

"My latest victim," Ott said with a fearsome smile. "How I did enjoy her, once she stopped talking."

This story was getting sicker and sicker, but I had mostly known the answers to the questions I had been asking Ott. I was about to forge into unknown territory.

"What about the murder on Staten Island?"

"Staten Island?" he said. "I've never even been there."

"You had nothing to do with the stabbing of Marilyn Shaw in her apartment?" I said, showing Ott a picture of the murder victim.

He leaned back like we were old friends having a beer after work. "That must've been the one I read about in the paper. I have enjoyed reading about myself, but you know as well as I do that the media is wrong most of the time. It should have been obvious I wasn't the Staten Island killer."

I took my time writing some notes. I needed to think about this. I wanted him to think about it too.

I asked him about the SoHo homicide, which was another one he hadn't confessed to. "What about Lila Stein in SoHo?" Again, I displayed a photo of the victim.

He shook his head. "Not me."

I looked at Ott, trying to get a feel for him. Here was a guy who had freely admitted to committing half a dozen murders in the city. Plus more across the country that he'd done throughout the past decade. I had to dig deeper.

"In your letter to the New York *Daily News*," I said, "you wrote, 'Think of the one who has killed the most. I am better than him.' Who is that?"

"The person who killed those two women was trying to copy me," Ott said. "Everyone should copy the master, the one who has killed the most. The Butcher of Rostov. The Red Ripper. I learned his ways when I was a young man, working for my first employer."

Ott's confession had been flowing, then suddenly he'd turned cryptic. My mind flashed on the prolific serial killers Ott had been tracking. *Little. Bundy. Chikatilo.*

I took an educated guess. "Andrei Chikatilo."

Ott looked surprised and pleased. "You know the master's name."

But there was more I had to know.

"You took the blood of your victims and mixed it with blood at fresh crime scenes," I said. "You haven't been home for more than six weeks. Where is the blood of your New York victims?"

"The blood vials I collected here are in sealed plastic bags inside a can falsely labeled shaving cream. You can find it in my hotel room. The others are in a safe in my home office. I wouldn't want my girls getting into them."

I couldn't resist asking, "Why do you mutilate the women's left eyes?"

"That's simple. I stand over them, and they're completely in my control. The last sight they see is my face."

Internally, I was reeling with horror, but I couldn't stop the interview.

"Did you push a woman in front of a bus near our office?"

"By the elevated train?"

I nodded, already knowing the response.

"I *meant* to shove the detective with the broken nose. He tried to be a hero and lost."

I had to move off the subject before I got too angry and did something stupid. I simmered for a minute. I was too wound up that Ott had made Hollis his target. That he had known about my kids, about Mary Catherine and our wedding. I couldn't focus.

But there was one more question I had to ask. "Why did you sign your letter 'Bobby Fisher'?"

Before Ott could answer, I heard voices outside the door. Loud voices. Arguing.

CHAPTER 96

THE SOUNDS OUTSIDE the interview room brought even Daniel Ott up short.

Someone bumped against the door. This was more than an argument. This was a scuffle. Then I heard Harry Grissom's voice. He was regaining order.

I stood up and gestured for Ott to stay seated. I walked across the small interview room and popped open the door. I stuck my head out into the hallway with the idea of shouting, *Keep it down!*

Instead, I was shocked into silence at the sight of Harry and a precinct captain named Jefferson squaring off with several extremely well-dressed people, including Robert Lincoln, the assistant special agent in charge of the New York FBI office.

How did they even know we made an arrest? Are they trying to physically steal our suspect?

What I said was "Hey, what's going on?" My voice sounded remarkably calm, especially considering my confusion.

Emily Parker stepped through the pack of people. She looked at Harry as if she was trying to calm down an angry lion. Then she turned to me. "We have a federal warrant for your suspect, Daniel Ott."

I stepped out into the hall and shut the interview room door behind me. "You worked a separate case on him? Without even talking to me?"

"Mike, it's not what you think."

It was Harry Grissom who spoke next. "*I* think it's bullshit. This is just some kind of stupid FBI ploy. They're claiming this mope is a spy."

I twisted my face as I looked at Emily.

She nodded.

A spy? That's why Emily had been stalling the help she'd promised me. She was after a bigger prize.

The world seemed to be spinning too quickly. I'd had my run-ins with the FBI over the years. I'd cracked a lot of jokes about the federal agency. Never in my wildest dreams had I thought they were capable of taking control of a suspect who was in the midst of confessing to multiple homicides. The only real question I had was if they had fabricated an excuse to steal my suspect, or if they'd specifically withheld information and waited for the right time to screw up my case.

It was Robert Lincoln who took advantage of my shock. He stepped forward and slipped into the interrogation room so smoothly, I barely even noticed him sliding past me.

I stepped back into the room as well. Ott didn't acknowledge anything unusual going on.

Lincoln looked at him and said, "You're Daniel Ott, correct?"
He nodded.

"I'm Robert Lincoln with the FBI. You're in the custody of the NYPD, but I have a federal warrant. It has nothing to do with the homicides Detective Bennett has been questioning you about."

Ott said quietly, "I've been expecting you. My previous employer must have sent you."

"And who would that be?"

"The Russian government."

I stepped between him and the FBI ASAC. I turned to the FBI ASAC and said, "What the hell are you talking about? What's your warrant for?"

The athletic, well-dressed man smiled. "Espionage. He came to the US about twelve years ago working for the Russian government. They lost track of him almost a decade ago. And so did we. But now we finally have him."

"You mean, *I* have him."

"Not any longer."

CHAPTER 97

THE LITTLE INTERVIEW room was crowded with NYPD brass and FBI agents. Ott continued to sit quietly on the plastic chair with his handcuffed hands folded in his lap. Two FBI agents stood on either side of Ott like someone from the NYPD might try to grab him and run.

Ott wasn't Jason Bourne. And he wasn't Andrei Chikatilo. But he *was* dangerous.

I was smart enough to let Harry Grissom do most of the talking. The way he snatched the warrant out of Robert Lincoln's hands told me just how pissed off he really was.

Harry turned to the FBI ASAC and said, "Where's the affidavit for the warrant?"

"It's sealed. National security. You don't need to see it anyway. All you need to know is that it's a legitimate warrant that says the FBI is taking custody of Daniel Ott. Are you disputing that?" Lincoln was sharp and not about to wilt under the searing glare of my lieutenant.

Emily Parker quietly tugged on my elbow and moved me out into the slightly less crowded hallway. She said, "This is no joke, Mike. The case is legit. Daniel Ott came here as a spy under the assigned American identity David Hastings. He was told to marry and raise an American family, but about ten years ago he met a Polish woman and used her contacts to change his identity. Then he disappeared."

"Is serial killing part of his assignment?"

"He is a trained assassin, but we've learned that as a young man, he developed an interest in the Russian serial killer Andrei Chikatilo that escalated into an obsession when Chikatilo was executed in 1994. He was never known to have acted on it. We now know that was false information."

"How'd you pick up on the fact that Daniel Ott used to be David Hastings?"

"We suspected it from a DNA hit from a cold case in Omaha. Then we heard from a source in the NYPD that you'd made an arrest, and the source also sent us a copy of Ott's fingerprints from here at the precinct. All we had to do was fill in the last part of the affidavit and here we are."

"So this isn't just some cheap ploy by your asshole boss?"

"He's been circling for days, waiting for you to make the solve. Several of us wanted him to wait until after you finished your interviews and Ott was booked into Rikers Island. Lincoln did want you to get credit for that."

I wanted to believe my old friend, but Lincoln never wanted to share credit, especially with me. I stepped back into the room. An agent I didn't recognize spoke to Ott in what sounded like Russian. Ott answered him. Also in what I assumed was Russian.

As two FBI agents helped Ott to his feet, Harry Grissom leaned in close to me and said, "At least he's not getting back on the street. It hurts to lose a suspect this way, but we did everything we could."

"I know, Harry. All I wanted to do was stop the killings. I'm getting used to the FBI taking credit for shit." Then I smiled.

Harry gave me a concerned look and said, "You're not having some kind of seizure, are you?"

"No, Harry. Ott is going to prison, and I'm getting married. Moving on."

Ott turned to me as he was led to the door. "I'm glad you'll get to see your daughters grow up, Detective Bennett. That's what I'll miss the most."

CHAPTER 98

I **MANAGED TO** time my homecoming to the news of the arrest hitting the airwaves. It was a sweet moment. Mary Catherine greeted me with a big hug and a kiss on the lips. The kids joined in with cheers and high fives all around.

Stopping these murders was an important accomplishment, but I was having a seriously hard time wrapping my head around the shadow case—in which Daniel Ott was not only a killer but a killer spy.

It was an unbelievable story. My wife-to-be was the second person I told. First honors belonged to my NYPD partner.

I had stopped in to visit Hollis on my way home. Even from his hospital bed, with half his body in a cast, he'd still managed a pretty good string of obscenities describing his outrage over the FBI stealing our case.

Our professional bonding ended the moment Brett Hollis's

mother entered the room, however, and motioned me out into the hallway with her.

Mrs. Hollis said, "Are you trying to stir him up? I'm running out for a sandwich. Don't be here when I get back."

I had to ask. "Have I done something to offend you?"

She clearly had an answer at the ready, but paused, almost as if for dramatic effect. "You allowed him to believe that he could be like you, and that delusion nearly got him killed. I have no use for the NYPD. Or for you."

"Your son is a fine detective, a credit to the force," I said.

"But he will never be 'Michael Bennett.' If he keeps trying for the impossible, it will cost him his life."

She was dead serious. I had to wonder if there was any truth to what she was saying. *Had* I put Hollis in danger? Or was Ott to blame?

As I stepped back into the room, I found Hollis sitting up in bed, reading a book about serial killers. Of course.

"I see you're studying for our next case, but I can say with authority our serial killer case is closed," I said. "You made a lot of the important breakthroughs. You should be proud."

"I just followed your lead," he said. But then his bright smile faded.

Hollis had responded well to praise in the past but now seemed distracted. He hadn't really been listening to what I was saying because he had been waiting to tell me something.

He stopped to gather himself, as if rehearsing his next words in his mind before speaking them. "I wasn't reading that book for our next case. In fact, there won't be another case. Not with us working as partners. Not any case." He stopped short, choked up, and stifled a sob.

What the hell is Hollis talking about?

"What are you saying?" I asked. "What's wrong?"

He raised a hand, and my gaze followed, settling on the stack of papers resting on his night stand.

"What's that? Workers' comp paperwork?"

Hollis shook his head. "That's what I've been trying to tell you," he said, pausing to run a tissue across his face. "I've been examined by two different department doctors. They want me to go out on disability." His voice had trailed off, like that of a beaten man.

It was the first I'd heard of this career-ending medical directive. I stood in silence, shocked.

"What are the doctors' main concerns?" I finally asked.

Hollis said, "It has to do with liability. The injuries I sustained from the impact of the bus were too pervasive, and too damaging to withstand the physical stress of detective work."

He blew his nose, then looked me in the eye. "I'm going to physical therapy starting next week. I'll see how that goes." He tried to sit up straighter. "There's a chance I could come back. They say they'll have to monitor me closely, especially my legs and hips. My mom is all about me leaving the NYPD and trying another line of work."

This young man was truly torn. The pressure from his mom wasn't making it any easier on him. But maybe there was some truth to what she was saying. Maybe, without even realizing it, I'd put pressure on him. By believing in him, I'd emboldened him to do too much too soon. On the other hand, it was because of his courageous actions that Kelly Konick was still alive and a dangerous killer was off the streets.

I studied the bruises around his face. Finally, I said, "What do *you* want to do?"

"I want to be a cop." His voice had some power in it now.

"Why?"

"I want to make a difference. To help people."

I nodded. "Those are the right reasons to be a cop. Most people have never felt the desire to work in our profession, which makes that feeling, that drive, impossible to understand. Police work has been such an important part of my life, but I realized something as I got older."

"What?"

"There are *other* important things in life. There are *other* ways to help people. You need to decide where to dedicate your talents."

"What I want to do is come back to work. Do you think I'd be able to come back to our squad?" He sounded like a kid asking permission to go out on a Saturday night.

I smiled. "I guarantee you'd be welcomed back as a star."

For the first time since I'd arrived, he looked hopeful.

This man had earned the right to be called my partner.

CHAPTER 99

MARY CATHERINE HAD the best idea for working it all out, just as she always did.

My late wife, Maeve, had been the one to introduce us, in a way. Maeve had been the one who'd hired Mary Catherine, sight unseen, from Ireland. Mary Catherine had shown up on my doorstep just when I needed her. I knew this was no coincidence. Maeve had planned out a happy life for me even while she was dying of cancer. Maeve had done it all. That was the way she was. Unselfish.

And so was Mary Catherine. She could read the strain on my face, about Hollis, about Ott, about everything except my family.

"You need a good bike ride," she said, ordering me to change. Shawna and Chrissy spoke up, then Eddie, Trent, and Jane. Five of ten kids wanted to come with us.

Mary Catherine said, "Anyone who can keep up is welcome to come along."

I knew that was the kind of challenge she and I would both regret.

We started out slowly—after I first had to pump up a couple of tires in the basement, and everyone had to find and put on their approved bike helmets—carefully working our way toward the bike paths in Riverside Park.

Once we got in the park, Shawna turned and grinned. She said, "Mary Catherine, you can come with us." She paused for best possible dramatic effect, then added, "If you can keep up."

That's how I remember the massive bike race starting. I pedaled until I thought my legs would drop off. My lungs burned and my vision might have blurred a little bit. And I still could not catch my fiancée. No one could. She had the form and grace of a professional cyclist.

I could say the race lasted for days and people died from exhaustion. But that wouldn't do it justice. The way Mary Catherine rode down those young people and then raced ahead of all of us, she was putting on a show.

She had a competitive streak and had somehow effectively hidden it from us until now. Or maybe we had just refused to see it. The kids would never look at her quite the same way again. Neither would I.

By the time I caught up to her near a water fountain that we used as a meeting point, she was sitting on a park bench with her helmet off like she'd been waiting for us for hours. All I could do was laugh—once I could breathe again, that is.

The kids stared at Mary Catherine like she had jumped off the pages of a Marvel comic book.

I sat down next to her as the kids got water and greeted a couple of their friends who had been playing in the park.

I said, "I like to see you smile after slapping down the kids and me."

"That *was* fun," she agreed. "But it's not why I'm smiling so much."

"Oh, yeah? Why *are* you smiling so much, then?"

"Our wedding is only a few days away. This Saturday, you'll be my husband."

I reached over and took her beautiful face in my hands and kissed her. She kissed me back. It almost made me forget we were in public. That is, until the kids crowded around us.

Trent said, "Why don't you guys get a room?"

Jane said, "Did I act that way around Allan?"

Trent and Eddie nodded at the same time.

All Jane could say was "Ouch. I'll keep that in mind in the future."

Then we all folded into a laughing, hugging ball of crazy New Yorkers.

CHAPTER 100

ON OUR WAY home, I said a silent prayer, thanking God for the wonderful life I had. And for my bright, healthy kids and my smart, beautiful fiancée. I was in a particularly grateful mood.

Then came Fiona and her seventh-grade math homework. It never got any easier, no matter how many times I helped each of the kids in succession.

Fiona hadn't put out a general call for assistance. Only her dad's help would do, and I couldn't ignore it. But holy cow. I'd been pretty good at math in school. The same school that Fiona went to now. How could I look at this page and not understand a single instruction?

After about fifteen minutes of reading the problems and searching through her book for an example I understood, I had to look at Fiona and say, "We need more help. Ask Eddie."

From my seat at the dining room table, I called to Mary

Catherine in the kitchen. Her reply was short and to the point. "I can't spare Eddie. You're the one with a college degree."

I said, "A degree in philosophy doesn't prepare you for seventh-grade math."

"Does it prepare you for anything?"

"'I am the wisest man alive, for I know one thing, and that is that I know nothing,'" I quoted. "Socrates."

Mary Catherine said, "You were already proving your point. You didn't have to back it up with a quote."

Brian casually strolled over to the dining room table. He looked at the book and checked some information on an earlier page. Then he explained to Fiona how to do the problems. Correctly. Amazing.

When Brian was finished, Fiona looked at me and said, "Thanks, Dad."

"What'd I do?"

Fiona smiled. "You adopted a smart kid like Brian."

I let out a laugh. "I guess that *was* a good move."

Brian's smile compounded my good mood. If things are going well with the kids, nothing else really matters.

Mary Catherine called out a good-bye. She was taking the girls for a dress fitting that would last a few hours. The younger boys were all in their rooms, working on some school project. That left just Brian and me.

He was in the living room, reading a *Men's Health* magazine. I flopped down on the other end of the couch where he was sitting.

"How's it going?" I asked.

He grunted. It wasn't hostile or disrespectful. Just efficient. Then he said, "How's it going with you?"

"Honestly," I told him, "I don't really know. I'm just glad to be home."

I decided I needed an answer to the question that had been bothering Mary Catherine and me for so long. I turned to my oldest son and said, "Where do you go all day?"

Brian closed the magazine and gave me a weak smile.

I said, "You can tell me, off the record if you want." After an uncomfortable silence, I added, "I know about the bank withdrawals. I'm not trying to be nosy. I want the best for you. I'm here to help. Any way I can." I hoped my voice wasn't betraying the fear and desperation I was feeling. I really couldn't imagine what Brian might say right now. And suddenly it occurred to me that it could be worse than anything I could dream of.

Brian sighed. He started slowly. "It was going to be a wedding gift."

"Brian, we don't need—"

He held up his hand. "No, Dad, it's not like that."

Now he had my full attention.

Brian said, "Remember when I said I was looking into air-conditioning repair?"

I didn't. I probably heard him tell me and then put it down to one of those ideas kids talk about but never act on.

Brian said, "I didn't make much of a plan at first, but then I signed up to finish my certification. I'll be done in about three weeks. I've already got a job with a company that services office buildings in Manhattan."

I had a lot of questions, but this was my son's story to tell. I let him talk.

Brian said, "I heard people saying how trade school was better than college, so I looked at a few different trades, and air-conditioning repair seems to make the most sense. And I like it."

If Brian expected me to give him a speech, he was wrong. All I did was turn and hug this young man who'd made me so proud.

As I sat there holding my son, I felt my eyes start to water. Then Brian started to cry. I finally felt like I had my son home again.

CHAPTER 101

THE NEXT DAY, I found myself standing in a crowd outside One Police Plaza. Harry Grissom had called me to tell me about the news conference. He said I didn't have to be there. He also said if I did come, it would last only an hour at most. Though I didn't see how that was likely once I heard the mayor start with "Once again our city is safe."

I tuned him out, sorry I'd wasted my morning coming down here. Then I turned to my right and saw John Macy standing near me, sharply dressed in a dark suit with a red tie.

He faced me and said, "Detective, nice to see you. Too bad you couldn't keep hold of your prisoner."

"Too bad you couldn't keep hold of confidential information," I countered. "Your buddy Funcher dropped a hint that you have a tendency to overshare during happy hour. I asked around, and sure enough, the late Jeffrey Cedar was on the outer edge of your circle.

You were the one who let slip to a copycat serial killer the detail about Ott's signature of stabbing his victims in the eye. The detail we were withholding from the press. But you didn't tell Cedar which eye. Ott is right-handed. And Cedar was left-handed. Which explains why Ott went for the left eye and Cedar for the right."

As I turned away from him in disgust, I added, "How're your balls feeling? The mayor is about to put them in a sling." Harry Grissom had stepped up on the other side of me. Macy had a lot of questions to answer, and he wouldn't be going anywhere until he did.

We listened as the mayor, the NYPD commissioner, and Robert Lincoln, assistant special agent in charge of the FBI in New York, all made comments about the arrest of Daniel Ott. There was no mention of him being a spy.

Harry Grissom leaned toward me and said, "Macy has been reassigned. He now reviews business licensing for anything that doesn't relate to food or beverage."

"Sounds like a slice of heaven."

Harry chuckled. "I've still got friends who don't put up with people screwing with the NYPD. But there is a catch."

"I don't like the sound of that. What sort of catch?"

Harry said, "There was no copycat killer. Receptionist Olivia Green was lying—not about Jeffrey Cedar but in her dealings with the IRS. In exchange for amnesty, she'll say Cedar panicked after having a domestic dispute with his wife and died avoiding arrest. Daniel Ott takes the blame for all the murders. The mayor's office prefers to calm public fears about two different killers loose in the city."

"But none of it's true."

"Neither is Santa Claus, but people still believe," Grissom said. "See you at the wedding."

CHAPTER 102

MY WEDDING DAY arrived. I sat in a small room just off the altar of Holy Name. Mary Catherine and I were putting the kids to good use today. Brian was my best man. Trent, Eddie, and Ricky were the groomsmen and ushers. Juliana was the maid of honor. Jane, Bridget, and Fiona were bridesmaids. Shawna and Chrissy were the flower girl and ring bearer respectively. My grandfather, Seamus, would be the one to marry us.

Following tradition, I had not seen or spoken to Mary Catherine today. She and the girls had spent the night in a hotel. It was as close to a bachelorette party as Mary Catherine wanted.

The boys and I had had a pretty good bachelor party too. We'd continued the video game marathon that had been interrupted in the line of duty, and we also managed to eat six pizzas, drink eight liters of soda, and destroy a pile of chicken wings.

At the moment, Brian sat with me, and the other boys rotated to my side as their ushering duties allowed. They all looked extremely sharp in their tuxedos.

Sister Sheilah popped her head into the little room where we waited. She was in full habit but looked different somehow. Then I realized she was wearing makeup. Not a ton, but enough to change her look dramatically.

Sister Sheilah said, "It's showtime. Your boys have seated all the guests, and your grandfather told me to get you moving."

Brian and I stood together. He took a moment to straighten my tie and brush a microscopic piece of lint off my shoulder.

Then Sister Sheilah stepped forward. As a child, I'd been her student, and she'd also taught all ten of my children. In her eyes, I'd never grown up. Sheilah looked at me, giggled, and pinched me on the cheek, repeating the words she'd been saying for months: "I can't believe our little Michael Bennett is getting married."

Today, it was finally true.

She kissed me on the forehead, and I received her blessing.

Brian and I took our positions at the front of the church. It was all I could do not to cry at the sight of my sons escorting their sisters down the aisle to take their places near the altar.

Chrissy followed, holding our rings, and Shawna dropped rose petals on the way to join us at the front of the church. This was a family event. Only Maeve was absent. I felt her looking down on me and smiling at the happiness she'd brought me and the kids by sending Mary Catherine.

The crowd was a sea of familiar faces. Harry Grissom sat next to Terri Hernandez. All the priests and nuns from the church intermingled with dozens of friends.

A movement flashed in the back corner of the church, and I craned my neck to see. It was Brett Hollis, sitting in a wheelchair, raising his arm in something between a wave and a salute. I was honored by his presence, even more so that he was accompanied by detectives from our squad—not his mother.

It was tough to keep the stupid grin off my face. Everything was great.

Then it got better. Almost to the point of fantasy.

The organist played the opening chords to the "Bridal Chorus"—"Here Comes the Bride." Mary Catherine, dressed all in white, took her cue, appearing to float along the rose petals Shawna had tossed onto the carpeted aisle.

The veil covered her face, but I could tell she was beaming with joy. She touched hands with several people in the pews as she continued her graceful glide toward me.

She was so gorgeous, I barely noticed my grandfather walking her down the aisle. He looked sharp too. Dressed in his best vestments, he stood tall and walked with a determined pace, planting each foot carefully.

I felt the lump in my throat grow as a few tears started to leak out of my eyes and my hands trembled.

Then Mary Catherine stopped, joining me at the altar, and taking hold of both of my hands. The effect was instantaneous, as calming as a shot of a tranquilizer.

Things rolled quickly from there. I know my grandfather conducted the service, but I cannot recall a word of it. I don't even remember reading the vows I had written and that Juliana and Jane had approved.

All that I remember—all that I will remember until I'm an old man—is lifting Mary Catherine's veil and melting when I saw her beautiful porcelain face, yet with a pale spray of freckles, like any good Irish girl should have.

We kissed. Our first kiss as husband and wife. And then we were enveloped by a sea of children and an elderly priest. We stood in front of all of our friends, hugging like we'd never let go.

It was probably the best moment of my entire life.

Have You Read Them All?

STEP ON A CRACK
(with Michael Ledwidge)

The most powerful people in the world have gathered for a funeral in New York City. They don't know it's a trap devised by a ruthless mastermind, and it's up to Michael Bennett to save every last hostage.

RUN FOR YOUR LIFE
(with Michael Ledwidge)

The Teacher is giving New York a lesson it will never forget, slaughtering the powerful and the arrogant. Michael Bennett discovers a vital pattern, but has only a few hours to save the city.

WORST CASE
(with Michael Ledwidge)

Children from wealthy families are being abducted. But the captor isn't demanding money. He's quizzing his hostages on the price others pay for their luxurious lives, and one wrong answer is fatal.

TICK TOCK
(with Michael Ledwidge)

New York is in chaos as a rash of horrifying copycat crimes tears through the city. Michael Bennett investigates, but not even he could predict the earth-shattering enormity of this killer's plan.

I, MICHAEL BENNETT
(with Michael Ledwidge)

Bennett arrests infamous South American crime lord Manuel
Perrine. From jail, Perrine vows to rain terror down upon
New York City – and to get revenge on Michael Bennett.

GONE
(with Michael Ledwidge)

Perrine is back and deadlier than ever. Bennett must make an
impossible decision: stay and protect his family, or hunt down
the man who is their biggest threat.

BURN
(with Michael Ledwidge)

A group of well-dressed men enter a condemned building.
Later, a charred body is found. Michael Bennett is about to
enter a secret underground world of terrifying depravity.

ALERT
(with Michael Ledwidge)

Two devastating catastrophes hit New York in quick
succession, putting everyone on edge. Bennett is given the
near impossible task of hunting down the shadowy terror
group responsible.

BULLSEYE
(with Michael Ledwidge)

As the most powerful men on earth gather for a meeting of
the UN, Bennett receives shocking intelligence that there
will be an assassination attempt on the US president.
Are the Russian government behind the plot?

HAUNTED
(with James O. Born)

Michael Bennett is ready for a vacation after a series of crises push him, and his family, to the brink. But when he gets pulled into a shocking case, Bennett is fighting to protect a town, the law, and the family that he loves.

AMBUSH
(with James O. Born)

When an anonymous tip proves to be a trap, Michael Bennett believes he personally is being targetted. And not just him, but his family too.

BLINDSIDE
(with James O. Born)

The mayor of New York has a daughter who's missing. Detective Michael Bennett has a son who's in prison. Can one father help the other?

ABOUT THE AUTHORS

JAMES PATTERSON is one of the best-known and biggest-selling writers of all time. His books have sold in excess of 385 million copies worldwide. He is the author of some of the most popular series of the past two decades – the Alex Cross, Women's Murder Club, Detective Michael Bennett and Private novels – and he has written many other number one bestsellers including non-fiction and stand-alone thrillers.

James is passionate about encouraging children to read. Inspired by his own son who was a reluctant reader, he also writes a range of books for young readers including the Middle School, Treasure Hunters, Dog Diaries and Max Einstein series. James has donated millions in grants to independent bookshops and has been the most borrowed author in UK libraries for the past thirteen years in a row. He lives in Florida with his family.

JAMES O. BORN is an award-winning crime and science-fiction novelist as well as a career law-enforcement agent. A native Floridian, he still lives in the Sunshine State.

THE PRESIDENT'S DAUGHTER

BY

BILL CLINTON

—— AND ——

JAMES PATTERSON

COMING IN JUNE 2021

Lake Marie, New Hampshire

AN HOUR OR SO after my daughter, Mel, leaves, I've showered, had my second cup of coffee, and read the newspapers—just skimming them, really, for it's a sad state of affairs when you eventually realize just how wrong journalists can be in covering stories. With a handsaw and a set of pruning shears, I head off to the south side of our property.

It's a special place, even though my wife, Samantha, has spent less than a month here in all her visits. Most of the land in the area is conservation land, never to be built upon, and of the people who do live here, almost all follow the old New Hampshire tradition of never bothering their neighbors or gossiping about them to visitors or news reporters.

Out on the lake is a white Boston Whaler with two men supposedly fishing, although they are Secret Service. Last year the *Union Leader* newspaper did a little piece about the agents stationed aboard the boat—calling them the unluckiest fishermen in the state—but since then, they've been pretty much left alone.

3

As I'm chopping, cutting, and piling brush, I think back to two famed fellow POTUS brush cutters—Ronald Reagan and George W. Bush—and how their exertions never quite made sense to a lot of people. They thought, *Hey, you've been at the pinnacle of fame and power, why go out and get your hands dirty?*

I saw at a stubborn pine sapling that's near an old stone wall on the property, and think, *Because it helps. It keeps your mind occupied, your thoughts busy, so you don't continually flash back to memories of your presidential term.*

The long and fruitless meetings with congressional leaders from both sides of the aisle, talking with them, arguing with them, and sometimes pleading with them, at one point saying, "Damn it, we're all Americans here—isn't there anything we can work on to move our country forward?"

And constantly getting the same smug, superior answers. "Don't blame us, Mr. President. Blame *them*."

The late nights in the Oval Office, signing letters of condolence to the families of the best of us, men and women who had died for the idea of America, not the squabbling and revenge-minded nation we have become. And three times running across the names of men I knew and fought with, back when I was younger, fitter, and with the teams.

And other late nights as well, reviewing what was called—in typical innocuous, bureaucratic fashion—the Disposition Matrix database, prepared by the National Counterterrorism Center, but was really known as the "kill list." Months of work, research, surveillance, and intelligence intercepts resulting in a list of known terrorists who were a clear and present danger to the United States. And there I was, sitting by myself, and like a Roman emperor of old, I put a check mark next to those I decided were going to be killed in the next few days.

The sapling finally comes down.

Mission accomplished.

I look up and see something odd flying in the distance.

I stop, shade my eyes. Since moving here, I've gotten used to the different kinds of birds moving in and around Lake Marie, including the loons, whose night calls sound like someone's being throttled, but I don't recognize what's flying over there now.

I watch for a few seconds, and then it disappears behind the far tree line.

And I get back to work, something suddenly bothering me, something I can't quite figure out.

BASE OF THE HUNTSMEN TRAIL

Mount Rollins, New Hampshire

IN THE FRONT SEAT of a black Cadillac Escalade, the older man rubs at his clean-shaven chin and looks at the video display from the laptop set up on top of the center console. Sitting next to him in the passenger seat, the younger man has a rectangular control system in his hand, with two small joysticks and other switches. He is controlling a drone with a video system, and they've just watched the home of former president Matthew Keating disappear from view.

It pleases the older man to see the West's famed drone technology turned against them. For years he's done the same thing with their wireless networks and cell phones, triggering devices and creating the bombs that shattered so many bodies and sowed so much terror.

And the Internet—which promised so much when it came out to bind the world as one—ended up turning into a well-used and safe communications network for him and his warriors.

6

The Cadillac they're sitting in was stolen this morning from a young couple and their infant in northern Vermont, after the two men abandoned their stolen pickup truck. There's still a bit of blood spatter and brain matter on the dashboard in front of them. An empty baby's seat is in the rear, along with a flowered cloth bag stuffed with toys and other childish things.

"Next?" the older man asks.

"We find the girl," he says. "It shouldn't take long."

"Do it," the older man says, watching with quiet envy and fascination as the younger man manipulates the controls of the complex machine while the drone's camera-made images appear on the computer screen.

"There. There she is."

From a bird's-eye view, he thinks, staring at the screen. A red sedan moves along the narrow paved roads.

He says, "And you are sure that the Americans, that they are not tracking you?"

"Impossible," the younger man next to him says in confidence. "There are thousands of such drones at play across this country right now. The officials who control the airspace, they have rules about where drones can go, and how high and low they can go, but most people ignore the rules."

"But their Secret Service—"

"Once President Matthew Keating left office, his daughter was no longer due the Secret Service protection. It's the law, if you can believe it. Under special circumstances, it can be requested, but no, not with her. The daughter wants to be on her own, going to school, without armed guards near her."

He murmurs, "A brave girl, then."

"And foolish," comes the reply.

And a stupid father, he thinks, to let his daughter roam at will like this, with no guards, no security.

The camera in the air follows the vehicle with no difficulty, and the older man shakes his head, again looking around him at the rich land and forests. Such an impossibly plentiful and gifted country, but why in Allah's name do they persist in meddling and interfering and being colonialists around the world?

A flash of anger sears through him.

If only they would stay home, how many innocents would still be alive?

"There," his companion says. "As I earlier learned…they are stopping here. At the beginning of the trail called Sherman's Path."

The vehicle on screen pulls into a dirt lot still visible from the air. Again, the older man is stunned at how easy it was to find the girl's schedule by looking at websites and bulletin boards from her college, from something called the Dartmouth Outing Club. Less than an hour's work and research has brought him here, looking down at her, like some blessed, all-seeing spirit.

He stares at the screen once more. Other vehicles are parked in the lot, and the girl and the boy get out. Both retrieve knapsacks from the rear of the vehicle. There's an embrace, a kiss, and then they walk away from the vehicles and disappear into the woods.

"Satisfied?" his companion asks.

For years, he thinks in satisfaction, the West has used these drones to rain down hellfire upon his friends, his fighters, and, yes, his family and other families. Fat and comfortable men (and women!) sipping their sugary drinks in comfortable chairs in safety, killing from thousands of kilometers away, seeing the silent explosions but not once hearing them, or hearing the shrieking and crying of the wounded and dying, and then driving home without a care in the world.

Now, it's his turn.

His turn to look from the sky.

Like a falcon on the hunt, he thinks.

Patiently and quietly waiting to strike.

SHERMAN'S PATH

Mount Rollins, New Hampshire

IT'S A CLEAR, cool, and gorgeous day on Sherman's Path, and Mel Keating is enjoying this climb up to Mount Rollins, where she and her boyfriend, Nick Kenyon, will spend the night with other members of the Dartmouth Outing Club at a small hut the club owns near the summit. She stops for a moment on a granite outcropping and puts her thumbs through her knapsack's straps.

Nick emerges from the trail and surrounding scrub brush, smiling, face a bit sweaty, bright blue knapsack on his back, and he takes her extended hand as he reaches her. "Damn nice view, Mel," he says.

She kisses him. "I've got a better view ahead."

"Where?"

"Just you wait."

She lets go of his hand and gazes at the rolling peaks of the White Mountains and the deep green of the forests, and notices the way some of the trees look a darker shade of green from the overhead clouds gently scudding by. Out beyond the trees is the Connecticut River and the mountains of Vermont.

Mel takes a deep, cleansing breath.

Just her and Nick and nobody else.

She lowers her glasses, and everything instantly turns to muddled shapes of green and blue. Nothing to see, nothing to spot. She remembers the boring times at state dinners back at the White House, when she'd be sitting with Mom and Dad, and she'd lower her glasses so all she could see were colored blobs. That made the time pass, when she really didn't want to be there, didn't really want to see all those well-dressed men and women pretending to like Dad and be his friend so they could get something in return.

Mel slides the glasses back up, and everything comes into view.

That's what she likes.

Being ignored and seeing only what she wants to see.

Nick reaches between the knapsack and rubs her neck. "What are you looking at?"

"Nothing."

"Oh, that doesn't sound good."

Mel laughs. "Silly man, it's the best! No staff, no news reporters, no cameras, no television correspondents, no Secret Service agents standing like dark-suited statues in the corner. Nobody! Just you and me."

"Sounds lonely," Nick says.

She slaps his butt. "Don't you get it? There's nobody keeping an eye on me, and I'm loving every second of it. Come along, let's get moving."

Some minutes later, Nick is sitting at the edge of a small mountain-side pool, ringed with boulders and saplings and shrubs, letting his feet soak, enjoying the sun on his back, thinking of how damn lucky he is.

He had been shy at first when meeting Mel last semester in an African history seminar—everyone on the Dartmouth campus knew who she was, so that was no secret—and he had no interest in trying to even talk to her until Mel started getting crap thrown at her one day in class. She had said something about the importance of microloans in Africa, and a few loudmouths started hammering her about being ignorant of the real world, being privileged, and not having an authentic life.

When the loudmouths took a moment to catch their respective breaths, Nick surprised himself by saying, "I grew up in a third-floor apartment in Southie. My Dad was a lineman for the electric company, my Mom worked cleaning other people's homes and clipped coupons to go grocery shopping, and man, I'd trade that authentic life for privilege any day of the week."

A bunch of the students laughed. Mel caught his eye with a smile and he asked her after class to get a coffee or something at Lou's Bakery, and that's how it started.

Him, a scholarship student, dating the daughter of President Matt Keating.

What a world.

What a life.

Sitting on a moss-colored boulder, Mel nudges him and says, "How's your feet?"

"Feeling cold and fine."

"Then let's do the whole thing," she says, standing up, tugging off her gray Dartmouth sweatshirt. "Feel like a swim?"

He smiles. "Mel…someone could see us!"

She smiles right back, wearing just a tan sports bra under

the sweatshirt, as she starts lowering her shorts. "Here? In the middle of a national forest? Lighten up, sweetie. Nobody's around for miles."

After she strips, Mel yelps out as she jumps into the pool, keeping her head and glasses above water. The water is cold and sharp. Poor Nick takes his time, wading in, shifting his weight as he tries to keep his footing on the slippery rocks, and he yowls like a hurt puppy when the cold mountain water reaches just below his waist.

The pond is small, and Mel reaches the other side with three strong strokes, and she swims back, the cold water now bracing, making her heart race, everything tingling. She tilts her head back, looking up past the tall pines and seeing the bright, bare blue patch of sky. Nothing. Nobody watching her, following her, recording her.

Bliss.

Another yelp from Nick, and she turns her head to him. Nick had wanted to go Navy ROTC, but a bad set of lungs prevented him from doing so, and even though she knows Dad wishes he'd get a haircut, his Southie background and interest in the Navy scored Nick in the plus side of the boyfriend column with Dad.

Nick lowers himself farther into the water, until it reaches his strong shoulders. "Did you see the sign-up list for the overnight at the cabin?" he asks. "Sorry to say, Cam Carlucci is coming."

"I know," she says, treading water, leaning back, letting her hair soak, looking up at the sharp blue and empty sky.

"You know he's going to want you to—"

Mel looks back at Nick. "Yeah. He and his buds want to go to the Seabrook nuclear plant this Labor Day weekend, occupy it, and shut it down."

Poor Nick's lips seem to be turning blue. "They sure want you there."

In a mocking tone, Mel imitates Cam and says, "'Oh, Mel, you can make such an impact if you get arrested. Think of the headlines. Think of your influence.' To hell with him. They don't want me there as me. They want a puppet they can prop up to get coverage."

Nick laughs. "You going to tell him that tonight?"

"Nah," she says. "He's not worth it. I'll tell him I have plans for Labor Day weekend instead."

Her boyfriend looks puzzled. "You do?"

She swims to him and gives him a kiss, hands on his shoulders. "Dopey boy, yes, with you."

His hands move through the water to her waist, and she's enjoying the touch—just as she hears voices and looks up.

For the first time in a long time she's frightened.

LAKE MARIE

New Hampshire

AFTER GETTING OUT of the shower for the second time today (the first after taking a spectacular tumble in a muddy patch of dirt) and drying off, I idly play the which-body-scar-goes-to-which-op when my iPhone rings. I wrap a towel around me, picking up the phone, knowing only about twenty people in the world have this number. Occasionally, though, a call comes in from "John" in Mumbai pretending to be a Microsoft employee in Redmond, Washington. I've been tempted to tell John who he's really talking to, but I've resisted the urge.

This time, however, the number is blocked, and puzzled, I answer the phone.

"Keating," I say.

A strong woman's voice comes through. "Mr. President? This is Sarah Palumbo, calling from the NSC."

The name quickly pops up in my mind. Sarah's been the deputy national security advisor for the National Security

Council since my term, and she should have gotten the director's position when Melissa Powell retired to go back to academia. But someone to whom President Barnes owed a favor got the position. A former Army brigadier general and deputy director at the CIA, Sarah knows her stuff, from the annual output of Russian oilfields to the status of Colombian cartel smuggling submarines.

"Sarah, good to hear from you," I say, still dripping some water onto the bathroom's tile floor. "How're your mom and dad doing? Enjoying the snowbird life in Florida?"

Sarah and her family grew up in Buffalo, where lake effect winter storms can dump up to four feet of snow in an afternoon. She chuckles and says, "They're loving every warm second of it. Sir, do you have a moment?"

"My day is full of moments," I reply. "What's going on?"

"Sir...," and the tone of her voice instantly changes, worrying me. "Sir, this is unofficial, but I wanted to let you know what I learned this morning. Sometimes the bureaucracy takes too long to respond to emerging developments, and I don't want that to happen here. It's too important."

I say, "Go on."

She says, "I was sitting in for the director at today's threat-assessment meeting, going over the President's Daily Brief and other interagency reports."

With those words of jargon, I'm instantly transported back to being POTUS, and I'm not sure I like it.

"What's going on, Sarah?"

The briefest of pauses. "Sir, we've noticed an uptick in chatter from various terrorist cells in the Mideast, Europe, and Canada. Nothing we can specifically attach a name or a date to, but something is on the horizon, something bad, something that will generate a lot of attention."

Shit, I think. "All right," I say. "Terrorists are keying themselves up to strike. Why are you calling me? Who are they after?"

"Mr. President," she says, "they're coming after you."

'CLINTON'S INSIDER SECRETS AND PATTERSON'S STORYTELLING GENIUS MAKE THIS THE POLITICAL THRILLER OF THE DECADE'

LEE CHILD

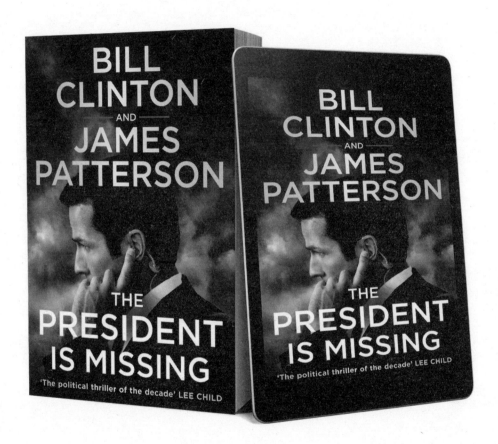

'Difficult to put down'
Daily Express

'Satisfying and surprising'
Guardian

'A quick, slick, gripping read'
The Times

'A high-octane collaboration . . . addictive'
Daily Telegraph

'An unmissable, breakneck ride into Moscow's dark underworld'
JAMES SWALLOW

'Great action sequences ... breathtaking twists and turns'
ANTHONY HOROWITZ

'Exhilarating, high-stakes action'
LESLEY KARA

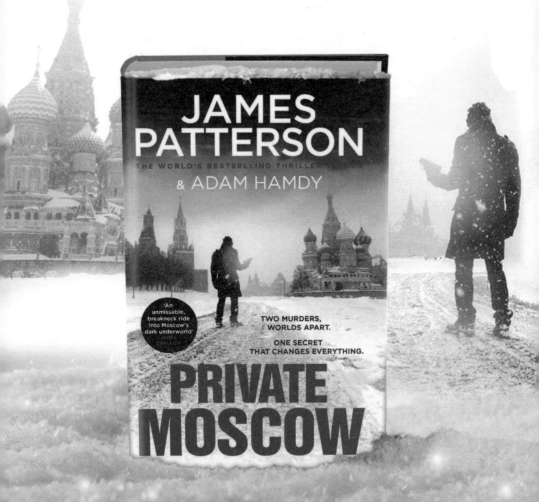

A STAND-ALONE THRILLER

THE COAST-TO-COAST MURDERS

James Patterson
& J. D. Barker

Michael and Megan Fitzgerald are siblings who share a troubling past. Both adopted, and now grown, they trust each other before anyone else. They've had to.

When a young woman is found murdered in Michael's LA apartment, he is the chief suspect and quickly arrested. But then there's another killing that is strikingly similar. And another. And not just in LA – as the spree spreads across the country, the FBI become involved in a nationwide manhunt.

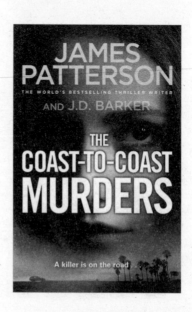

THE KENNEDY CURSE

James Patterson & Cynthia Fagen

Across decades and generations, the Kennedys have been a family of charismatic adventurers, raised to take risks and excel. Their name is synonymous with American royalty. Their commitment to public service is legendary. But, for all the successes, the family has been blighted by assassinations, fatal accidents, drug and alcohol abuse and sex scandals.

To this day, the Kennedys occupy a unique, contradictory place in the world's imagination: at once familiar and unknowable; charmed and cursed. *The Kennedy Curse* is a revealing, fascinating account of America's most famous family, as told by the world's most trusted storyteller.

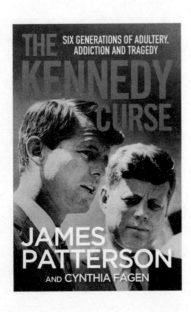

Also by James Patterson

ALEX CROSS NOVELS

Along Came a Spider • Kiss the Girls • Jack and Jill • Cat and Mouse • Pop Goes the Weasel • Roses are Red • Violets are Blue • Four Blind Mice • The Big Bad Wolf • London Bridges • Mary, Mary • Cross • Double Cross • Cross Country • Alex Cross's Trial (*with Richard DiLallo*) • I, Alex Cross • Cross Fire • Kill Alex Cross • Merry Christmas, Alex Cross • Alex Cross, Run • Cross My Heart • Hope to Die • Cross Justice • Cross the Line • The People vs. Alex Cross • Target: Alex Cross • Criss Cross • Deadly Cross

THE WOMEN'S MURDER CLUB SERIES

1st to Die • 2nd Chance (*with Andrew Gross*) • 3rd Degree (*with Andrew Gross*) • 4th of July (*with Maxine Paetro*) • The 5th Horseman (*with Maxine Paetro*) • The 6th Target (*with Maxine Paetro*) • 7th Heaven (*with Maxine Paetro*) • 8th Confession (*with Maxine Paetro*) • 9th Judgement (*with Maxine Paetro*) • 10th Anniversary (*with Maxine Paetro*) • 11th Hour (*with Maxine Paetro*) • 12th of Never (*with Maxine Paetro*) • Unlucky 13 (*with Maxine Paetro*) • 14th Deadly Sin (*with Maxine Paetro*) • 15th Affair (*with Maxine Paetro*) • 16th Seduction (*with Maxine Paetro*) • 17th Suspect (*with Maxine Paetro*) • 18th Abduction (*with Maxine Paetro*) • 19th Christmas (*with Maxine Paetro*) • 20th Victim (*with Maxine Paetro*)

PRIVATE NOVELS

Private (*with Maxine Paetro*) • Private London (*with Mark Pearson*) • Private Games (*with Mark Sullivan*) • Private: No. 1 Suspect (*with Maxine Paetro*) • Private Berlin (*with Mark Sullivan*) • Private Down Under (*with Michael White*) • Private L.A. (*with Mark Sullivan*) • Private India (*with Ashwin Sanghi*) • Private Vegas (*with Maxine Paetro*) • Private Sydney (*with Kathryn Fox*) • Private Paris (*with Mark Sullivan*) • The Games (*with Mark Sullivan*) • Private Delhi (*with Ashwin Sanghi*) • Private Princess (*with Rees Jones*) • Private Moscow (*with Adam Hamdy*)

NYPD RED SERIES

NYPD Red (*with Marshall Karp*) • NYPD Red 2 (*with Marshall Karp*) • NYPD Red 3 (*with Marshall Karp*) • NYPD Red 4 (*with Marshall Karp*) • NYPD Red 5 (*with Marshall Karp*) • NYPD Red 6 (*with Marshall Karp*)

DETECTIVE HARRIET BLUE SERIES

Never Never (*with Candice Fox*) • Fifty Fifty (*with Candice Fox*) • Liar Liar (*with Candice Fox*) • Hush Hush (*with Candice Fox*)

INSTINCT SERIES

Instinct (*with Howard Roughan, previously published as* Murder Games) • Killer Instinct (*with Howard Roughan*)

STAND-ALONE THRILLERS

The Thomas Berryman Number • Hide and Seek • Black Market • The Midnight Club • Sail (*with Howard Roughan*) • Swimsuit (*with Maxine Paetro*) • Don't Blink (*with Howard Roughan*) • Postcard Killers (*with Liza Marklund*) • Toys (*with Neil McMahon*) • Now You See Her (*with Michael Ledwidge*) • Kill Me If You Can (*with Marshall Karp*) • Guilty Wives (*with David Ellis*) • Zoo (*with Michael Ledwidge*) • Second Honeymoon (*with Howard Roughan*) • Mistress (*with David Ellis*) • Invisible (*with David Ellis*) • Truth or Die (*with Howard Roughan*) • Murder House (*with David Ellis*) • The Black Book (*with David Ellis*) • The Store (*with Richard DiLallo*) • Texas Ranger (*with Andrew Bourelle*) • The President is Missing (*with Bill Clinton*) • Revenge (*with Andrew Holmes*) • Juror No. 3 (*with Nancy Allen*) • The First Lady (*with Brendan DuBois*) • The Chef (*with Max DiLallo*) • Out of Sight (*with Brendan DuBois*) • Unsolved (*with David Ellis*) • The Inn (*with Candice Fox*) • Lost (*with James O. Born*) • Texas Outlaw (*with Andrew Bourelle*) • The Summer House (*with Brendan DuBois*) • 1st Case (*with Chris Tebbetts*) • Cajun Justice (*with Tucker Axum*) • The Midwife Murders (*with Richard DiLallo*) • The Coast-to-Coast Murders (*with J. D. Barker*) • Three Women Disappear (*with Shan Serafin*)

NON-FICTION

Torn Apart (*with Hal and Cory Friedman*) • The Murder of King Tut (*with Martin Dugard*) • All-American Murder (*with Alex Abramovich and Mike Harvkey*) • The Kennedy Curse (*with Cynthia Fagen*) • The Last Days of John Lennon (*with Casey Sherman and Dave Wedge*)

MURDER IS FOREVER TRUE CRIME

Murder, Interrupted (*with Alex Abramovich and Christopher Charles*) • Home Sweet Murder (*with Andrew Bourelle and Scott Slaven*) • Murder Beyond the Grave (*with Andrew Bourelle and Christopher Charles*) • Murder Thy Neighbour (*with Andrew Bourelle and Max DiLallo*) • Murder of Innocence (*with Max DiLallo and Andrew Bourelle*) • Till Murder Do Us Part (*with Andrew Bourelle and Max DiLallo*)

COLLECTIONS

Triple Threat (*with Max DiLallo and Andrew Bourelle*) • Kill or Be Killed (*with Maxine Paetro, Rees Jones, Shan Serafin and Emily Raymond*) • The Moores are Missing (*with Loren D. Estleman, Sam Hawken and Ed Chatterton*) • The Family Lawyer (*with Robert Rotstein, Christopher Charles and Rachel Howzell Hall*) • Murder in Paradise (*with Doug Allyn, Connor Hyde and Duane Swierczynski*) • The House Next Door (*with Susan DiLallo, Max DiLallo and Brendan DuBois*) • 13-Minute Murder (*with Shan Serafin, Christopher Farnsworth and Scott Slaven*) • The River Murders (*with James O. Born*)

For more information about James Patterson's novels, visit www.penguin.co.uk